Jones. M

# A RADICAL LIFE

# A RADICAL LIFE

## *The Biography of Megan Lloyd George, 1902–66*

## MERVYN JONES

9/361405

HUTCHINSON

LONDON   SYDNEY   AUCKLAND   JOHANNESBURG

Copyright © Mervyn Jones 1991

The right of Mervyn Jones to be identified as
Author of this work has been asserted by
Mervyn Jones in accordance with the Copyright,
Designs and Patents Act, 1988

*All right reserved*

This edition first published in 1991 by
Hutchinson

**Random Century Group Ltd**
20 Vauxhall Bridge Road, London SW1V 2SA

**Random Century Australia (Pty) Ltd**
20 Alfred Street, Milsons Point, Sydney, NSW 2061, Australia

**Random Century New Zealand Ltd**
PO Box 40–086, Glenfield, Auckland 10, New Zealand

**Random Century South Africa (Pty) Ltd**
PO Box 337, Bergvlei, 2012, South Africa

British Library Cataloguing in Publication Data
Jones, Mervyn 1922–
   A radical life : the biography of Megan Lloyd George,
   1902–66.
   1. Great Britain. Politics. Lloyd George, Megan
   I. Title
   941.082092

ISBN 0–09–174829–1

Set in Sabon by Speedset Ltd, Ellesmere Port

Printed and bound in Great Britain by
Clays Ltd, St Ives PLC

# Contents

# List of Illustrations

FRONTISPIECE PHOTOGRAPH
Megan Lloyd George (*D.L. Carey Evans*)

PLATE SECTION
No

ILLUSTRATIONS
*Page*

# Preface

This book has a life-story of its own. The original choice for an author was John Morgan, and there could have been no better choice; he was intuitively attuned to everything that speaks of Wales and Welshness, and had been personally acquainted with Megan Lloyd George. He had written only a synopsis, however, when he was attacked by a cancer that proved fatal. John and I had been friends. We had both reported Lady Megan's triumphant by-election campaign in Carmarthen in 1957, he for the *New Statesman* and I for *Tribune*. Shocked and saddened by the news of his death, I went to Swansea for the funeral. At the graveside, I shook hands with another friend, Gloria Ferris, the literary agent who had laid the foundations of the project. A couple of weeks later, she proposed that I should take up the task. I was furnished with a box of letters, introductions to members of the Lloyd George family, and the notes of the preliminary research carried out by Mary Morgan, John's wife. My first acknowledgement is to Mary for generously placing this material at my disposal. The letters are quoted exactly as Noel-Baker wrote them. His stylistic peculiarities (for example, he never inserted an apostrophe in the contraction 'its' for 'it is') have been preserved.

I was surprised to learn that, although everybody with an interest in political history had heard of Megan Lloyd George, no biography had yet been written. A fifty-page booklet by Emyr Price, sponsored by the Gwynedd County Council, provides a useful summary of her career, but is naturally limited in scope. Perhaps she has been overshadowed, even in memory, by her celebrated father. Perhaps her importance has been diminished because the Liberal Party, to which she belonged through twenty-two years in Parliament, was inexorably dwindling throughout that period, and because she never held governmental office. Yet her refusal of office for reasons of principle on the sole occasion when it was offered to her was an episode that did her honour, and was one of many chapters in the story that has never been fully told or explained.

There is much, indeed, that should be known and remembered. Megan Lloyd George was a loyal and intransigent Radical – the word was often on her lips – and battled persistently, though ultimately in vain, to restore the Radical tradition in the Liberal Party. She was equally resolute and intransigent as a feminist and played her part in the campaign for equal pay in the 1940s, which has been largely ignored or minimised by historians of the period. Then, in the 1950s, she was a central figure in the campaign for a Welsh Parliament, which failed to achieve its specific objective but contributed significantly to a revival of Welsh national consciousness. Here are three good reasons to make the writing of this book a justified enterprise.

A life has many facets – public and private, professional and personal, intellectual and emotional. I have not thought it wrong to devote considerable space to Megan's private life and her intimate relationships, particularly the one relationship that dominated this aspect of her life for twenty years, but I have deliberately placed the primary emphasis on her political concerns and activities.

Megan bequeathed her papers to her nephew, David Lloyd ('Benjy' to the family) Carey Evans, and the main item in this bequest consists of the box of letters that I mentioned – a total of 554 letters written to her by Philip Noel-Baker. I am grateful to Mr Carey Evans for giving me access to these letters, and to Mr Francis Noel-Baker for permission to quote from them. The first of the letters was written on 14 March 1940, and the last on 5 October 1957. This is, of course, a considerable collection. Nevertheless it is incomplete, and the reader should be aware of three gaps in the sequence.

Firstly, although it can be stated with certainty that Megan Lloyd George and Philip Noel-Baker became lovers in 1936 or 1937, there are no surviving letters written earlier than 1940.

At the outbreak of war in 1939, Megan entrusted her letters for safe keeping to William Elverston-Trickett, the solicitor to the Lloyd George family. After she died, it was discovered that he had chosen to destroy them. He had himself been one of her admirers in her younger days, and he also destroyed a number of letters which she had written to him. Whether they were letters of affection or of rejection, we shall never know.

Secondly, there are no letters between 18 December 1940 and 2 November 1944. This is because, as the reader will learn, the relationship was broken off during this period.

Thirdly, there are no letters between 24 December 1947 and 30 March 1950. This time, there is no reason to suppose that the relationship was interrupted, and therefore no obvious reason for the gap in the letters. We can only conclude either that Megan failed to keep letters during these two years, or – more probably – that some letters were accidentally lost when her papers were collected after her death.

What we possess is, unfortunately, a onesided correspondence. Megan was a notoriously poor correspondent, and her letters to Philip were undoubtedly much fewer than his to her. She did, however, write some letters, since he occasionally thanks her for a letter or comments on it. But no letters from Megan are to be found in the Noel-Baker archives at Churchill College, Cambridge, and it must be presumed that he destroyed them, very likely just after reading them. The only surviving letter, written on 28 February 1952, is one that Megan forgot to post.

We have fifteen letters written by Megan to her close friend, Thelma Cazalet-Keir. I am grateful to the latter's nephew, Mr Justice Edward Cazalet, for permission to quote from them. We also have a few letters written by Megan to members of her family, to her secretary, and in one case to her constituency agent in Anglesey.

In writing a biography of someone who lived in the recent past, interviews are invaluable, and one must reconcile oneself to the macabre aspects of collecting them while they are still feasible. It was my misfortune that Thelma Cazalet-Keir died a month before I was invited to write this book. It was my good fortune that I was able to interview Megan's sister Olwen (Lady Carey Evans) and the last survivor of David Lloyd George's political staff, A. J. Sylvester. My gratitude, alas, cannot reach them. She died a few weeks before she would have reached her ninety-eighth birthday, and he a few weeks before he would have become a centenarian.

My thanks are due to members of the Lloyd George family who gave me their indispensable co-operation: first and foremost to Benjy Carey Evans and his wife Annwen for their unstinting kindness and hospitality.

Thanks, also, to all those who generously gave me the benefit of their memories and their knowledge: Sir Richard Acland, Lord (Desmond) Banks, Cliff Bere, Robin Carey Evans, Lady (Barbara) Castle, Lord Cledwyn (Cledwyn Hughes), Lady Valerie Daniels,

Helena Dightam, Gwynfor Evans, Michael Foot, Trevor Griffiths, John Grigg, Lord (Jo) Grimond, Glyn Tegai Hughes, Myra Hughes, Lord (Roy) Jenkins, Catherine Johnson, Dr Tudor Jones, Lady (Patricia) Llewellyn-Davies, Earl Lloyd George, Jennifer Longford, Dafydd Miles, Hubert Morgan, Priscilla Morton, Bob Newton, Francis Noel-Baker, Frances Prole, Cliff Prothero, Lord (Gwilym) Prys-Davies, Megan Reeves, Emrys Roberts, Wilfrid Roberts, Lady (Marion) Salmon, Lady (Nancy) Seear, Zosia Starzecka, Lord Tenby, Clement Thomas, Glyn Thomas, Jeremy Thorpe, Ursula Thorpe, and Lady (Eirene) White.

Thanks, no less, to the consistently helpful staff of the National Library of Wales, the London Library, the Fawcett Library, the Marx Memorial Library, Bristol University Library, Churchill College, Cambridge, Lambeth Palace Library and BBC Written Archives.

I have drawn extensively on published diaries and letters, especially on the fascinating diaries of Frances Stevenson and A. J. Sylvester. I have, of course, consulted various historical works and biographies: but, since most of them are tangential to Megan Lloyd George, I have not appended a bibliography.

I have used the anglicised forms of place-names such as Caernarvon, Conway and Merioneth. I realise that this may earn the disapproval of Welsh patriots; but I decided, after much trepidation, to favour the forms which were in general use in Megan's lifetime and which are to be found in letters and newspapers of the period.

Lastly, a note on pronunciation: the name 'Megan' is not pronounced 'Meegan'.

# CHAPTER ONE

# Inheritance

1

Megan Arfon Lloyd George was born in the small town of Criccieth, in North Wales, on 22 April 1902. Her brothers and sisters had been born in Criccieth too: Richard in 1889, Mair Eluned in 1890, Olwen in 1892 and Gwilym in 1894. Their mother, Margaret Lloyd George, took care that they should be true sons and daughters of Wales. Arfon is the name of the district that contains the highest and wildest mountains of Wales, including Wyddfa (Snowdon to the English); it was the stronghold of the princes of Gwynedd, and is associated in Welsh minds with traditions of distinctive identity and defiant independence. Thus, even Megan's middle name cast her for the role of champion of Welsh freedom.

Her father, David Lloyd George, was the Liberal MP for Caernarvon Boroughs, a rather unusual constituency which covered six towns – Caernarvon, Bangor, Conway, Pwllheli, Nevin and Criccieth – but not the rural areas that separated them. Since the House of Commons was sitting, he was in London when Megan was born. He wrote to Margaret next day: 'I cannot put into words the thrill of joy and affection which passed through me on reading the telegram announcing that all had passed off well.'[1] The joy may well have been inspired by the eight-year interval that had followed Gwilym's birth. Often, 'afterthought' children are the most cherished.

The house in which Megan was born was one of a semi-detached pair, built at the expense of Margaret's parents, who occupied the adjoining house. The substantial, three-storey dwellings face the sea and rise by a flight of stone steps from the road to Portmadoc. They were (though they are not now) the last houses on the eastern fringe of Criccieth.

Dashing across the road, the children could be on the beach in a couple of minutes. Swimming was less favoured than it is today, but the Lloyd Georges enjoyed beach games and beach picnics whenever the weather was good enough. When they headed inland, they walked for miles through the fields, the woods and the rocky hillsides. Megan recalled later that her father could never resist leading the family onward if they came to a 'Trespassers will be Prosecuted' sign. Even today – despite the caravan sites and the petrol stations – it is not difficult to see this countryside as Megan saw it in her childhood. Time has not changed the look of the stone-built farmhouses, the irregular pattern of small fields, the herds of sheep, the clumps of old oak trees. This is a well-settled, hard-working countryside, whose people have learned through centuries to make the best use of every acre.

On a longer expedition, the Lloyd Georges could reach the neighbourhood of Blaenau Ffestiniog and contemplate an extra-ordinary spectacle, which can still astonish the visitor. The mountains had been relentlessly slashed and excavated to slice away thousands of tons of slate, which was in constant demand to cover the roofs of houses, churches and chapels (with a useful market in the schoolroom too). Twenty miles to the north, almost three thousand men worked in the Bethesda quarry owned by Lord Penrhyn. It was then, and it is now, the biggest slate quarry in the world. We are accustomed to think of North Wales as the rural half of the country, in contrast to the industrial South, but there were strong similarities between the slate quarries and the coal-mines of the Glamorgan valleys. There was the same desecration of the environment, the same highly profitable exploitation of the labour force, the same neglect of safety, and hence the same bitter antagonism between owners and workers. While Megan was an infant, the Bethesda quarries were halted by a long and determined strike. Dragoons were called in to break it, fighting broke out, and twenty-six men were charged with riot offences. Lloyd George, who was a solicitor as well as an MP, defended them vigorously and secured acquittals for most of them.

In 1989 a young woman in Bethesda said to the author: 'He was a good Socialist, whatever.' She was mistaken: Lloyd George was never a Socialist. Yet she was justified in remembering him as a champion of the propertyless against the privileged; the rhetoric in a typical Lloyd George speech struck the same emotional note as the speeches of

Socialist pioneers, except that he inveighed against landlords rather than against capitalists. Here is a good example:

Landlords consume millions of the wealth of the land of this country without turning a sod to create it. They are the monopolists who spend untold millions of the products of our mines and manufactures without blasting a rock, handling a machine, or even wielding a pen to build up that wealth. . . . These riches, intended by providence for the people, are intercepted before they reach them.[2]

In the most famous speech of his career, the Limehouse speech of 1909, he reverted to this theme:

The landlords are receiving eight millions a year by way of royalties. What for? They never deposited the coal in the earth. . . . Who laid the foundations of the mountains? Was it the landlord?

Megan would have heard these demanding questions as she went with her father on an outing to the ravaged slopes of Ffestiniog. The sense of outraged justice and the voice of protest were at the heart of her inheritance.

She learned, too, that the social structure of North Wales was marked by class distinctions as clearly perceptible as the fault-lines in the rocks. Certainly, there were class distinctions in other parts of Britain; but it was in Wales that the divergences of economic status, language, religion and political allegiance all coincided, and thus reinforced one another.

At the apex of the social pyramid stood a small number of wealthy landowning families. Although most were of Welsh origin, they were heavily anglicised; they sent their sons to public schools in England and employed English governesses for their daughters. Their language was English. They could muster, at best, a limited amount of Welsh to communicate with their employees, just as they would have acquired a little Hindustani if they had been in India. Their religion was that of the Established Church. They voted Conservative and required their inferiors to do the same. In 1868 an infuriated Lord Penrhyn had evicted scores of tenants and sacked eighty men from his quarry for voting against the Tory candidate, who was his son. A few years later a Liberal government introduced the secret ballot to check such acts of victimisation.

The middle class of North Wales consisted of relatively prosperous farmers (some owning and some leasing their land), professionals such as doctors and solicitors, shopkeepers, and craftsmen or builders who generally employed a few wage-workers. As a rule they were fluent in both English and Welsh, with a tendency to use English for business purposes and Welsh in the home. They were Nonconformists in religion – typically Methodists or Presbyterians, occasionally Quakers. The salaried Nonconformist ministers were a component, often influential, of this middle class. Some people in this class voted Tory, out of either conviction or deference, but most of them were Liberals, upholding a political creed which stressed individual rights, free trade, economy in public spending, and strictly limited governmental functions.

The broad base of the pyramid was composed of the humbler ranks of tenant farmers; farm labourers and shepherds; domestic servants employed by the middle and upper classes; and the working class in the strict sense, including quarrymen and railwaymen. The language of the poorer classes was invariably Welsh. Some could speak English, especially if they lived in the towns rather than the countryside, but at the time of Megan's birth most of them could not. They were always Nonconformists and generally Baptists, while some adhered to small sects which made it a principle to have no full-time paid minister. One such sect was the Disciples of Christ, whose preacher in Criccieth was Megan's great-uncle, Richard Lloyd.[3] They were Liberals, but the Liberal leaders whom they trusted were those known as Radicals. What they wanted from a Liberal government was positive action for the relief of poverty; the most deeply felt demand was for an old-age pension. In 1902 political journalists were speaking of 'the new Liberalism', as distinct from the old Gladstonian Liberalism. Its most articulate spokesman was David Lloyd George.

2

Such was the Caernarvonshire of 1902. Beyond and around it was the world of 1902, which young Megan would inherit and gradually comprehend. That world was in various ways unlike our own, but linked to ours by many continuing threads.

Neatly enough, the nineteenth century and the long reign of Queen Victoria had ended together: the Queen died in the first month of the new century. Her funeral was attended by an array of emperors, kings and grand dukes, mostly related to her. Some prescient watchers may have sensed that an era was coming to an end; if so, they were right. Within twenty years, the Emperors of Germany and Austria would be exiles, and the King of England would be declining to give asylum to the last Tsar of Russia.

It was, nevertheless, the Age of Empire, when imperialism was both a power system and a creed. The sharpest analysis of the system, J. A. Hobson's book *Imperialism*, was published in 1902. Since 1885 the British Empire had expanded by the addition (to give these territories their modern names) of Nigeria, Kenya, Uganda, Zimbabwe, Zambia, Malawi, Sarawak, Brunei and Tonga. God seemed to favour the invocation that was set in 1902 to Elgar's music: 'Wider still and wider shall thy bounds be set.' France, Germany, Portugal and Belgium had also acquired vast acreages far from the homeland. The United States, having just annexed the Philippines, was urged by Rudyard Kipling to 'take up the white man's burden'.

At the turn of the century, British imperialism received a severe jolt. The South African war, whose purpose was to subdue the independent Boer republics, began with humiliating defeats, was prolonged by the dogged resistance of Boer commandos, and eventually cost 29,000 British lives. To break that resistance, civilians were caged in enclosures for which some clumsy bureaucrat invented the name 'concentration camps'. The war ended when Megan was less than a month old.

The period of Megan's childhood, when people looked back on it after the trauma of the 1914–18 war, seemed to wear a face of tranquillity and stability. It did not feel like that at the time. The new century brought expectations of innovation, rapid change and excitement. In 1902 the developments that we regard as characteristically twentieth-century – the motor car, the aeroplane, the cinema, the radio – were either already on stage or just in the wings. The mood was one of curiosity, and on the whole of optimism. Catching that mood with his habitual skill, H. G. Wells had come out with a book entitled *Anticipations*. His readers were bidden to look forward to the rise to power of a new elite of scientists and engineers, to a World State that would supersede outworn nationalism, and to franker and easier relationships between men and women. The third of these prophecies proved more accurate than the others.

It was a time when the 'new woman' was hailed, derided and incessantly discussed as much as the 'liberated woman' of the 1970s. She would be thoughtful, resolute, and determined not to tolerate male domination – like Nora in Ibsen's *A Doll's House* (first London production, 1889), Sue Bridehead in Hardy's *Jude the Obscure* (1895) and Ann Whitefield in Shaw's *Man and Superman* (1903). Women were pressing at the closed, or slowly opening, doors of the universities, the medical profession and the law. Their most insistent demand was for the right to vote, which they had won only in Australia, New

Zealand and four thinly populated American states. It was in 1903 that Emmeline Pankhurst, with her daughters Christabel and Sylvia, founded the Women's Social and Political Union to launch a sustained campaign.

Even a scientifically educated person would have been baffled by talk of psychoanalysis, the conditioned reflex or relativity, but all three terms would soon enter the intellectual vocabulary. Freud had published *The Interpretation of Dreams*, selling only a few hundred copies, and in 1902 he began to preside over meetings of the Wednesday Psychological Society, later giving it the more formal name of Vienna Psycho-Analytic Society. Pavlov, researching in St Petersburg on the digestive system of dogs (his work earned him a Nobel Prize in 1904), was observing that they salivated when they heard the dinner-bell. Einstein, while earning his living at the Basle Patent Office, was pondering the ideas that in 1905 enabled him to give the world the fateful formula $E=mc^2$.

The nineteenth century had been the age of the railway, and its decline was nowhere in sight as the twentieth century opened. One could travel by train from New York to San Francisco, from Paris to Constantinople on the opulent Orient Express, or from Calcutta to Peshawar. The world's longest line, the Trans-Siberian from Moscow to Vladivostok, sold its first tickets in 1903.

No one in 1902 could have predicted that the motorway would rival the railway, but cars were at least a status symbol, with 23,000 licensed in Britain. They were produced by numerous small companies, of which the great majority fell victim to intense competition; the 1902 names that survive today are Daimler, Mercedes, Renault and Peugeot. France was regarded as the leading automobile country, but a British motorist, driving a Napier, won the Paris–Vienna road race of 1902.

On sea, liners were crossing the Atlantic in six days or a little less. In 1902 the British government advanced low-interest capital to the Cunard line for building two new ships, the *Lusitania* and the *Mauretania*, which would use the newly developed turbine engines and reach a speed of 25 knots. The *Lusitania* was to be torpedoed in 1915, but the *Mauretania* stayed in service into the 1930s.

Many a dinner-table resounded to arguments about whether it would ever be possible to travel through the air. Some optimists championed the aeroplane, some preferred the autogiro (we now say 'helicopter'), and others put their money on the helium balloon. The Wright brothers settled the question in 1903.

For speedy communication, it was the age of the telegram. People made appointments, broke the news of accident or death and even proposed marriage by sending a wire, delivered in urban areas within an hour. Those who desired yet greater immediacy were getting telephones installed; by 1902 there were over 50,000 subscribers in British cities. The Italian inventor Marconi had begun to send messages by wireless (in Morse code, not audible speech). In 1902 a message tapped out on a hilltop in Cornwall spanned the ocean to be picked up in Newfoundland.

An up-to-the-minute reader in 1902 could have bought Henry James's *The Wings of the Dove*, Joseph Conrad's *Heart of Darkness*, Rudyard Kipling's *Just So Stories*, Arthur Conan Doyle's *The Hound of the Baskervilles* and Arnold Bennett's *Anna of the Five Towns*. Marcel Proust was working on the first version of what became *A la Recherche du Temps Perdu*, but it did not satisfy him and remained unpublished until decades later. Thomas Mann, however, was making a successful début with *Buddenbrooks*. James Joyce, twenty years old, dedicated himself to 'silence, exile and cunning' and went to live in Paris.

In the visual arts, Paris was the unchallenged centre. It had attracted Van Gogh from Holland, Munch from Norway, Sickert and Gwen John from England. Forty years after the birth of impressionism, some of its luminaries – Renoir, Pissarro, Monet, Degas, Cézanne – were still alive and working. Young artists were continuing the tradition; a discerning collector in 1902 might have bought Picasso and Matisse.

The opera was the most popular musical form; Debussy and Delius were among those who had operatic premières in 1902. The smash hit of the period, Puccini's *Madame Butterfly*, followed in 1904. In the concert hall, 1902 saw the first performances of Mahler's Fifth Symphony and Sibelius's Second.

Of the names that became most famous or infamous as the century advanced, the only one that a newspaper reader would have recognised in 1902 was Winston Churchill. This young man had fought as a cavalry officer at the Battle of Omdurman, covered the South African war as *Morning Post* correspondent and made a daring escape from captivity, and then been elected as Conservative MP for Oldham. Franklin D. Roosevelt was still in his second year at Harvard. Joseph Dzugashvili, sentenced for operating an illegal printing press, was in prison at Batum; he did not adopt the name of Stalin until 1913. Adolf Hitler, a thirteen-year-old schoolboy, was hoping for a career as an artist.

3

Elected to Parliament in 1890, David Lloyd George was a back-bencher until 1906. These were difficult years for a man with high ambitions – difficult, too, in a material sense, for MPs were unpaid. Luckily, Lloyd George's partner in his law practice was his brother William, who was content to slog away in the office at Portmadoc and share the earnings. David's other resource was political journalism; he was a fluent writer, and the guineas for articles in the Welsh and sometimes the London press mounted up usefully. Even so, this was a period of struggle and endurance. Megan, the daughter who from childhood knew her father as a senior Cabinet minister, must have listened with awe to his memories of the penny-pinching economies, the comfortless lodgings in South London, the meals of tea and buns.

Right from the start, Lloyd George was building a reputation. He had been an MP for only a couple of months when he spoke at a big Liberal meeting in the Free Trade Hall, Manchester, and received an ovation. The reputation was that of a Radical, admired by the rank and file of the party and coolly regarded by some of its leaders. His strategy, as well as his natural inclination, was to press on with one campaign after another. But careful scrutiny reveals that each campaign was attended by subtleties and ambiguities of which his supporters were not always aware.[4]

Even before he became an MP, Lloyd George had been active in a movement called *Cymru Fydd* – the name could be translated as 'Wales of the Future' – which demanded that the Welsh people should have the right to manage their own affairs. The turmoil over Home Rule for Ireland, then a major political issue, gave him the opportunity to put forward the idea of 'Home Rule all round', by which he meant that there should be Parliaments for Ireland, Wales and Scotland; the Westminster Parliament would be responsible essentially for foreign policy, defence and the British Empire. But, while Lloyd George championed the Welsh national identity, he fully accepted the British identity too. Although his speeches were imbued with the spirit of Welsh patriotism, they were liberally sprinkled with references to 'the British nation', 'the British people' and even 'the British race'. His personal ambitions were certainly British in scope; he had no more desire to be Prime Minister of an independent Wales than Napoleon had to be King of Corsica.

As a Welsh patriot, Lloyd George also upheld the rights of the Free Churches, to which the majority of the Welsh people belonged. The compulsory payment of tithes, which went to the maintenance of the

Established Church and the salaries of the clergy, was a burning grievance for Nonconformists; the reform urged by Lloyd George (and ultimately achieved in 1919) was disestablishment. Another grievance stemmed from the Education Act introduced by the Tory leader, A. J. Balfour, in 1902. Under this Act, the county councils were to finance Church schools, now known as 'voluntary schools', as well as the state-sponsored board schools. In many rural areas the Church school was the only school, and Lloyd George had attended one at Llanystumdwy, the village near Criccieth where he grew up. Often, the Church schools required children to recite the Anglican creed and the teachers had to be communicants of the Established Church. Nonconformists were outraged by the idea of paying rates to support such schools, and Lloyd George was prominent in the campaign of protest against Balfour's proposals. For him, the Free Churches were democratic, popular institutions integral to the life of Wales. In one speech he declared:

On the one side you see the great baronial castle and the stately Elizabethan mansion, and on the other side a little red-brick building with a word on a board, either Methodist or Congregationalist or Baptist. One thing you may be certain about, and that is that the little chapel is the only place in the village that will stand up to that castle. All the men in the village who would decline to cringe, they are there. Those little buildings – unsightly sometimes – they are the sanctuaries and citadels of village independence.[5]

What he did not tell his audiences (this speech was delivered at the Free Church Temple in London) was that he himself had no religious belief. He had been baptised by his uncle, Richard Lloyd, in the icy waters of the river Dwyfor, but – according to the account he gave to a boyhood friend[6] – he lost his faith at the age of twelve. In London, he attended services at the Welsh Baptist chapel quite frequently throughout his life, but this was to demonstrate his Welshness and to enjoy the pleasure of joining in the singing. In the privacy of his family, he said that when he died he would like to be Leader of the Opposition in heaven, taking advantage of the ample material for votes of censure.

Margaret Lloyd George, on the other hand, was a sincere and devout Methodist. The husband and wife reached an agreement that their children would be brought up alternately as Methodists and Baptists; thus the first, third and fifth children – Dick, Olwen and Megan – were Methodists. As a child and as an adult, Megan was a serious religious believer (more so than any of her brothers and sisters), worshipped at the Methodist chapel, and often began the day with a period of private prayer. It was one of the links between Megan and her mother, less often commented on than her affinities with her father, but no less real and significant.

Another Free Church attitude with which Lloyd George identified himself was opposition to the evils of drink. He denounced the brewery owners – 'the beerage' – for making money from a harmful addiction and from the misery of wives and children. He also advanced the theory that drink had caused the downfall of the Egyptian, Assyrian, Babylonian and Roman Empires; only the Persian Empire, where abstinence was the rule, had flourished.[7] Personally, he despised men who yielded to the addiction and was disgusted by the drunkenness which he observed in the bars of the House of Commons and in fashionable West End restaurants. However – although the temperance movement was influential among Radicals and Socialists, notably in Wales and Scotland – Lloyd George was never a total abstainer. He enjoyed a glass of Irish whiskey and, once he was able to afford it, a bottle of vintage wine (perhaps this testifies to his confidence in his ability to keep his drinking within limits). The total abstainer of the family was Margaret. In this sphere, Megan followed her father; in adult life, she liked to drink in moderation, but favoured the tea-room of the House of Commons and was seldom seen in the bar.

In general, Lloyd George's attitudes were never so extreme or so uncompromising as those of more fervent partisans. At the height of the controversy over Church disestablishment, he remarked: 'You have in Wales the best men on either side – Churchmen and Nonconformists – devoting their energies to this deplorable struggle.'[8] Indeed, he almost negotiated a compromise settlement through private meetings with an intelligent cleric, the Bishop of St Asaph. Always, while he threw himself enthusiastically into his campaigns and did his best to hit his opponents hard, he was sensitive to the sterility of endless warfare and was on the lookout for a practicable resolution of the conflict. To charges of hypocrisy, he had his reply: in politics, confrontation is a method, but achievement is the objective.

The issue that placed Lloyd George most visibly on the Radical left of his party, and also brought him into the forefront of the political world, was the South African war. While some Liberals supported the war and others sought to evade a firm stand, he was vehemently against it. This exposed him to patriotic denunciations – a Tory leaflet in the 1900 general election charged that Lloyd George 'has been on the enemy's side throughout the war and has insulted the Generals and Soldiers of the Queen'[9] – and even to physical assaults, including the famous occasion when he had to escape from Birmingham Town Hall disguised in a policeman's uniform.

He had two reasons for opposing the war. He saw the Boers as a small community wishing only to manage their own affairs in their own way; their menaced rights ranked, in his mind, with the rights that he sought for the people of Wales. Secondly, the cost of the war absorbed resources that could have been devoted to social progress and the relief of poverty. 'Not a Lyddite shell exploded', he told an audience dramatically, 'but it carried away an old age pension.'[10] He was ready, indeed, to employ the rhetoric of pacifism. 'What does war mean?' he demanded, and gave the answer: 'It means casting aside reason, thought and intellect and resorting to violence – to murder.'[11] As on other occasions, the rhetoric simplified his real view. In retrospect, he explained to friends: 'People think that because I was a pro-Boer I am anti-war in general. I am not against war a bit.'[12]

The war issue divided and embarrassed the Liberal Party. On one occasion, thirty-one Liberals backed an anti-war motion, forty voted with the Tories and the rest abstained. The party leader, Sir Henry Campbell-Bannerman, managed to hold the party together by direct-ing criticism against the concentration camps. Once the war was over and domestic questions came to the fore, the country began to tire of the long spell of Conservative government and Liberals felt that their time was coming.

4

After David Lloyd George became a major political figure, some contemporaries dismissed his wife as a simple country woman of limited capacities (although those who met her seldom made this error). She was, in reality, a woman of strong character and considerable ability. The false impression gained currency because she did not choose to involve herself in national, let alone international, politics. In Wales, on her home ground, she was a formidable figure. During the First World War she raised millions of pounds for charities and was honoured with the title of Dame; this had nothing to do with her position as the Prime Minister's wife. In 1928, she worked effectively to secure Megan's nomination as Liberal candidate for Anglesey. She was also the first woman JP in Wales.

Rooted in Wales, and establishing herself as the first citizen of Criccieth, Margaret saw no reason to live in London simply because her husband was an MP. She had no London friends, she disliked the smoky air and the fogs, and she was strongly of the opinion that it was better for the children to grow up in Wales. It was an argument that was difficult to resolve. Lloyd George felt he was being reasonable by offering to live in Ealing or Acton – where, he assured her, 'the air is quite as good as anything you can get in Wales' – or even in Brighton, although commuting from that distance had not yet become a normal custom. Making a plea for sympathy, he told her: 'I have scores of times come home in the dead of night to a cold, dark & comfortless flat without a soul to greet me.'[13] There were darker messages, too: 'You can't leave me in town alone. . . . Heaven knows what it might eventually lead me to.'[14]

In 1899 Lloyd George took the step of renting a whole house – 179 Trinity Road, on the borders of Balham and Tooting – instead of a flat. Margaret reconciled herself to living in London for the greater part of the year, and the children attended London schools. But Dick, who was sent to Dulwich, was so badly bullied at the time when his father was 'on the enemy's side' during the Boer War that he had to be taken away and sent to be educated in Wales. Margaret still took advantage of any convincing reason to spend lengthy periods in Criccieth, and one reason was her last pregnancy and the birth of Megan. When Megan was a month old and Margaret had not yet brought the child to London, Lloyd George exploded. 'Why,' he wrote, 'the poor Boer women had often to trek on wagons through sun & rain over open rough country for days when baby was only a fortnight or three weeks old.'[15]

In the first four years of her life, Megan probably spent more time in Criccieth than in London. Even when Margaret was in London, the little girl could safely be left in Criccieth in the care of a nursemaid, and with her grandparents next door. She was a Welsh little girl, playing with other Welsh children, hearing the Welsh language in the High Street shops, speaking it as her natural tongue. She imbibed the idea that Criccieth was her home, and London was an exciting place to which she was taken for varying periods. In this life, her mother was a constant (if not quite invariable) presence, while her father was a figure of drama and wonder whom she saw less often than she wished.

The general election for which the Liberals had waited impatiently came in January 1906, and they scored a landslide victory on a scale never yet seen since Britain had been a parliamentary democracy. They had 397 members in the new House of Commons, and could count on the general support of the 83 Irish Nationalists and the 29 MPs belonging to the newly created Labour Party. The Tories, with a mere 157 seats, were a weak and disheartened opposition. Not a single Tory survived in Wales; except for Merthyr Tydfil, where Keir Hardie was Labour member, the Liberals held all the thirty-six seats. Lloyd

George's majority in Caernarvon Boroughs, a bare eighteen votes when he first won the seat, rose to over a thousand.

He was offered the position of President of the Board of Trade, with a seat in the Cabinet. It was a considerable promotion for a back-bencher, even a backbencher with the parliamentary experience and public reputation that Lloyd George had accumulated. Clearly, Campbell-Bannerman wanted a Radical in the Cabinet to balance the formidable trio of right-wingers – H. H. Asquith, who became Chancellor of the Exchequer, Sir Edward Grey (Foreign Secretary) and R. B. Haldane (Secretary for War).

Everything was going well for the Lloyd George family. But in November 1907 they suffered a catastrophic blow. Mair Eluned, seventeen years old, was suddenly taken ill with appendicitis. An emergency operation was performed, but she did not recover from it and died five days later.

Mair had been her father's favourite. She was beautiful, sweet-natured and affectionate; her teachers at Clapham High School gave her glowing reports, and she had exceptional musical talent. It is a fair guess that she gave Lloyd George the close companionship and the uncritical admiration that he did not receive from her mother. Her death plunged him into agonising grief, perhaps intensified by remorse. It appears that he reproached himself for failing, in the midst of his demanding work at the Board of Trade, to make adequate arrangements for the hazardous operation (which, as usual in those days, was performed at home).

Always fonder of his daughters than of his sons, Lloyd George needed a favourite daughter and, as soon as the immediate grief was past, sought to fill the place left vacant by Mair's death. Olwen was already fifteen and he could not be sure that she would accept the role of her father's companion, admirer and pupil. But Megan was still only five.

Megan was not another Mair. She was a high-spirited and sometimes naughty child. However, Lloyd George expected her to be as close to him as Mair had been. Already she revelled in listening to his stories and laughing at his jokes. Above all, he could see in her a reflection of himself. He saw – and was eager to encourage – the quick intelligence, the independence and the irreverent disrespect for hallowed authority that had made him the man he was. As Megan grew up, observers often remarked on how much she had inherited from him. John Grigg, Lloyd George's biographer, writes that she shared 'his caprice, his feverish vitality, his love of company, his passion for politics'.[16]

Megan's role as favourite was soon recognised in the family, not least by herself. Olwen wrote in recollection:

Megan was a delightful child, pretty, intelligent, lively and full of fun, but thoroughly spoilt by all the family. Father was the worst culprit, and loved taking her out with him and showing her off. . . . Megan loved all that, and got quite conceited over all the attention she was getting. When I came home from school one day she said: 'I am in the papers much more than you are!' I used to tell her that criminals also got their names in the papers.[17]

Lloyd George could not bear to stay in the house where Mair had died; indeed, for the rest of his life he avoided driving through that part of South London. With a higher income than in earlier years – his ministerial salary was £2000 a year – he took a lease of a house in Chelsea. However, the Lloyd Georges lived in this house for only a few months. More changes were on the way.

# CHAPTER TWO

# Growing Up in Downing Street

## 1

Sir Henry Campbell-Bannerman, in failing health and indeed near to death, resigned in April 1908. Asquith became Prime Minister, and Lloyd George succeeded him as Chancellor of the Exchequer. This senior post carried a salary of £5000, worth about £75,000 in today's purchasing power. From this time onward, the Lloyd George family always lived in easy circumstances. It also meant a move to 11 Downing Street. The famous cul-de-sac off Whitehall was the Lloyd Georges' address for the next fourteen years, and in that period they shifted their furniture only once, when they made the short but significant move from Number 11 to Number 10.

The disposable money gave them a new Welsh home. Now a celebrity, Lloyd George complained that holiday visitors were staring in at his front windows from the main road when he spent the summer at Criccieth. He bought an acre of land on the hillside above the town and had a house built there. It was a family home with spacious rooms and a broad staircase, in the style of the period, and it had magnificent views over the sea, and, from the back, toward the mountains. He called it Brynawelon – Hill of Breezes – which had also been the name of his former home, but was much more appropriate for this upland mansion. On sloping ground below the house, there was enough space for Margaret, a skilful and enthusiastic gardener, to plant her favourite trees and flowers. There was even room near the house for the construction of a small cottage, which was put to various uses over the years but was generally occupied by a chauffeur (neither of the Lloyd

Georges ever learned to drive). Megan loved the new Brynawelon from the beginning, and it was to be her home for all her life.

The atmosphere of 11 Downing Street, too, was that of a family home. When Lloyd George wanted to see other ministers, or experts in a subject on which he needed information, he invited them to a meal or a cup of tea, and members of the family were present as a matter of course. Indeed, Lloyd George was the originator of the working breakfast. The family, however, was sometimes a small one. Margaret was at Brynawelon whenever she could manage it, and the three older children were sent to boarding schools. Megan got used to being alone in the house with her father, the housekeeper and the servants. The housekeeper, brought from Criccieth, was a shrewd and capable woman named Sarah Jones – often addressed as Lallie, which may have been Megan's infantile attempt to pronounce 'Sarah' or perhaps 'Sally'. In the chequered history of the Lloyd Georges, Sarah Jones was a fixture; she had joined the household in 1900, and she stayed until she died in 1958.

In a talk on 'Childhood Reminiscences' to Carmarthen Rotary Club in 1962, Megan emphasised that 11 Downing Street was 'a Welsh home' in the sense that the language spoken in it was Welsh. 'Woe betide any member of the family who at home showed the least departure from the mother tongue,' she said. However, 'woe betide' implies that the Welsh speaking had to be enforced and that the children preferred to express themselves in English. The Lloyd George family letters are written in English, with colloquial Welsh phrases interpolated here and there. But Megan always called her father 'Tada', the Welsh equivalent of 'Dad'.

Doubtless Megan spoke Welsh with Sarah, and spoke Sarah's kind of Welsh. Emlyn Williams, who met her in 1927, and who came from a working-class Welsh background, noted that she spoke 'a Welsh as peasant-flavoured as that of any of my four grandparents'.[1] Glyn Tegai Hughes, who shared platforms with her in the 1950s, found her Welsh colloquial and demotic, and guessed that she had learned it from the family servants. 'It was perfect for punchy lines and the emotional appeal, and of course her accent was perfect too, but I doubted whether she could write in Welsh, nor could she handle complicated constitutional or economic issues in Welsh.'[2]

In 1910 Lloyd George invited Balfour, the Tory leader, to dinner with the purpose of resolving a political crisis by discreet negotiation. In a handwritten note he told Balfour: 'The servants are Welsh and could not follow the conversation and the only other person present would be my little daughter of 8 summers.'[3] He could not really have believed that his servants had neglected to learn any English while living in London, but perhaps he expected Balfour to believe it. It was most unusual in 1910 (as it would be today) for a child of eight to sit in on a crucial political discussion, but Megan was not an ordinary child, and was not being given an ordinary upbringing.

Admittedly, a child of this age could not have gained much from listening to discussions of political theory; but Lloyd George was not a theorist (nor, at any time in her life, was Megan). What she was watching was a drama, in which her father was the hero, his opponents were the villains, and other characters – such as Balfour in this instance – were doubtful quantities to be neutralised by her father's persuasive skill. An episode in the political contests of the time, observed from a ringside seat, could well be more exciting than any tale told by Hans Andersen or the Brothers Grimm.

Thus Megan's awareness was developing ahead of her years, and it was stimulated by her natural intelligence. According to a profile written in 1950: 'She was a brilliant child, so brilliant that Lloyd George's entourage were amazed to see the champion sometimes outpointed in family discussions.'[4] Whether or not the adjective 'brilliant' is fully justified, this was evidently an impression that stayed in the minds of those consulted by the profile writer.

In those years, relations between Number 10 and Number 11 were cool and formal. Asquith and Lloyd George respected each other – both were men of outstanding ability – but could not like each other. The Prime Minister's ultra-refined manners and accent grated on Lloyd George; and, to make matters worse, his snobbish, tactless wife, Margot, made no secret of her contempt for the *arriviste* solicitor from the backwoods of Wales. Prime Minister and Chancellor lunched or dined together only about once every two or three weeks. Considering that there were many questions of policy which were worth an informal discussion before being placed on the Cabinet agenda, and considering that they lived next door, this was not much.

Ten years older than Lloyd George, Asquith had been married twice. One of his four children by his first marriage, his daughter Violet, was a young woman of strong character and exceptional intelligence, keenly interested in politics. Like Megan, she ardently admired her father; like Megan, she enjoyed living in Downing Street. But in 1908, when Megan was only six, Violet was twenty-one and a guest at adult dinner-parties. It is unlikely that she took much notice of the little girl next door.

One Asquith and one Lloyd George, however, were on terms of intimacy. Anthony Asquith, the Prime Minister's youngest son –

always known as 'Puffin', both in childhood and in later life when he became a successful film director – was the same age as Megan. She recalled later:

I fell in love with the sweet, pixie-like boy next door. We became inseparable and kept running through the intercommunicating doors from one house to the other, romped rather noisily up and down stairs, and played hide-and-seek in the vast warren of rooms in the two houses.[5]

Once, when the children were ten years old, their escapades gave rise to serious alarm. Number 10 had an ancient, creaking lift, seldom used because it was quicker to walk upstairs. Megan and Puffin got into it and began an ascent, but it stopped and stuck between floors. As there was no alarm system, they had to stay there. When they were missed, it was feared that they had been kidnapped by militant suffragettes, and search parties were sent out to scour Whitehall and St James's Park. The children were found at last when someone wanted to use the lift.

Lloyd George's closest friends in the government came from very different backgrounds. Winston Churchill, who had entered Parliament as a Tory and changed sides, was a nephew of the Duke of Marlborough. Lloyd George, though he joked about it, enjoyed a weekend at Blenheim Palace, and Churchill enjoyed a weekend at Brynawelon. After following Lloyd George to the Board of Trade, Churchill became Home Secretary and then First Lord of the Admiralty. Rufus Isaacs, who became Attorney-General in 1910, was the son of a fruit merchant and had grown up in the narrow streets of Spitalfields, then an almost entirely Jewish neighbourhood. Another friend was Sir George Riddell, the millionaire proprietor of the *News of the World* (Lloyd George was an enemy of the idle rich, but had nothing against the energetic and enterprising rich). He introduced Lloyd George to golf, a game that goes well with intimate and discursive conversation. Then he had a house built at Walton Heath in Surrey, close to the golf course, and put it at Lloyd George's disposal.

2

Megan's early education was distinctly haphazard. We can only guess who taught her to read – perhaps her mother, perhaps a brother or sister, perhaps Sarah Jones. Up to the age of nine, she was acquiring knowledge in a random way by asking questions of all and sundry, and this may well have shaped the unsystematic habits and the dislike of disciplined study for which she was noted in later life.

In the nineteenth century it had been usual for girls in well-to-do families to be taught by a governess in the family schoolroom instead of going to school – often until they were ready for the marriage market, but at least until they were about ten years old. In the Edwardian period this system was beginning to appear old-fashioned and was prevalent among the aristocracy rather than the professional middle-classes, so it is surprising to find Lloyd George adhering to the tradition. What is yet more surprising is that Megan did not even have a governess. Strictly speaking, the Chancellor of the Exchequer was breaking the law. The Education Act of 1870 laid down that every child over the age of five must receive adequate instruction, either in school or from a tutor, governess or professionally qualified parent.

However, in 1911, when Megan was nine, her father (or her mother, or both) realised that the situation was unsatisfactory. They decided to send her to school in the autumn and to prepare her by tutoring in the summer. Lloyd George undertook to find someone who could teach his daughter the French language and the piano, then seen as suitable accomplishments for girls. He consulted Mrs Woodhouse, headmistress of Clapham High School, which Mair had attended until her death. Mrs Woodhouse recommended a former pupil named Frances Stevenson.

Miss Stevenson was admirably qualified for the job. Her grandmother, who lived with the Stevenson family, was French and always spoke French to Frances, and had also given her a thorough musical training. After doing well at school, Frances went to Royal Holloway College and took a degree in classics, an unusual achievement for a girl in those times. Now aged twenty-two, she was teaching at Allenswood School in Wimbledon, but she did not want to spend her life as a teacher and was hoping for an opening in some other kind of work.

She had been friendly with Mair when they were at school together and had gone with her to the Welsh Baptist chapel (for musical rather than religious reasons). There she had been introduced to Mair's father and found him fascinating. When Frances arrived at Brynawelon to start her summer job, Lloyd George was staying with the royal family at Balmoral, but she was welcomed by Margaret. Teaching Megan was a pleasure; years later, in her autobiography, Frances described Megan as 'an enchanting child'. She also enjoyed the exceptional hot weather,[6] the beautiful countryside, and the picnics and rambles with Dick and Olwen who were not much younger than she was.

Megan, although she cannot have liked being kept in for lessons and piano practice, took to Frances happily enough, or so she wrote to her father. He wrote in reply:

My darling little Megan . . .
I am so glad that you like your new companion and that you get on so well together. I knew you would. I want you to learn French and music so that you can talk French like a petite Parisienne and play the piano like Paderewski. I am so looking forward to seeing your bright face.[7]

After staying at Balmoral and then at Andrew Carnegie's mansion in Scotland, Lloyd George had three weeks at Brynawelon. Seeing this famous man in his home environment, Frances found him more fascinating than ever.

In the autumn, Megan began her education at Allenswood School, where Frances was teaching. She boarded there from Monday to Friday and came home at weekends, but her father quite often appeared at the school unexpectedly and whisked her away for a cream tea. Quite often, too, he whisked Miss Stevenson away for an evening concert or a dinner at a quiet restaurant.

Undoubtedly, Frances was far from being the first young woman who had been escorted to a quiet restaurant by Lloyd George, particularly when he was in London and his wife was in Criccieth. 'I was aware from an early age that there were other women in his life,' wrote his daughter Olwen. Nor did she find it surprising: 'He had an enormous fascination for women, and they always went more than half way to meet his advances. Many of his friends felt he should be protected against women; they flocked round him and often threw themselves at him.'[8]

How many 'other women' Lloyd George actually slept with in the years after his arrival in London in 1890, it is impossible to say. None of his affairs had amounted to a serious emotional attachment, but there were constant rumours and there were accusations from Margaret. Always preferring the counter-offensive to the defensive, Lloyd George rebuked her for writing 'foolish letters'. Indeed, Lloyd George was one of those husbands who could neither be faithful to his wife nor contemplate excluding her from his life. He was over sixty years old when he wrote this letter to her:

You talk as if my affection for you came and went. No more than the sea does because the tide ebbs and flows. . . . You say I have my weakness. So has anyone that ever lived & the greater the man the greater the weakness. It is only insipid, wishy washy fellows that have no weaknesses. . . . You must make allowances for the waywardness & wildness of a man of my type. What if I were drunk as well? I can give you two samples you know of both the weaknesses in one man and their wives do their best under those conditions. What about Asquith & Birkenhead? I could tell you stories of both – women & wine. Believe me *hen gariad* [old darling] I am at bottom as fond of you as ever.[9]

At some time in 1912, the Chancellor of the Exchequer – forty-nine years old and nearing the zenith of his political career – told the young teacher that he was in love with her. There is no doubt that he was telling her the truth. For the first time in his career of waywardness and wildness, this was something far more profound and durable than a gust of passion or a flirtation. Frances was already admitting to herself that she was in love with him; what held her back was the conflict with what she called, in her later memoirs, her 'essentially Victorian upbringing'. In a diary entry written in 1914, two years after this period of courtship, she recorded that she and her lover had been talking of 'the autumn, when we used to meet once a week, and I hovered between doubt and longing, dread and desire; and of the time in the House of Commons, when I left him because I would not agree to his proposals, but returned soon after to say that I could not face life without him, and would do what he wished.'[10]

What Lloyd George wished was clear-cut and frankly stated. While he was in love with Frances, he had also observed that she was a highly intelligent and capable person who would make an excellent private secretary. He offered her this job, as she put it, 'on his terms'. It was, in fact, a package offer as secretary and mistress, and it was irresistible. Even if she had not loved him, the opportunity for daily contact with the most remarkable political figure of the time would have been extremely tempting.

The job as secretary gave her a desk at the Treasury and official status in the Civil Service. There was some criticism of an appointment which sidestepped the regular procedure of competitive examination, but this criticism did not arise from suspicions about the other part of the deal. There had been criticism, too, when a journalist named Vaughan Nash was recruited to become secretary to Campbell-Bannerman and then to Asquith.

Playing fair by his own lights, Lloyd George made it clear to Frances that he was determined not to be caught in the glare of a public scandal that might jeopardise his political career. In his first year as an MP, the downfall of Parnell had given him a warning to be remembered. Frances, like most young women of her time, would have liked to be

respectably married, and it is also clear from her diary that she would have liked to be a mother. Lloyd George, while ruling out the idea of a divorce, sympathised with her feelings. A few years later she wrote:

He said he has been thinking. . . of how he wished he could marry me. But we both agreed that we must put that thought out of our minds. . . . However, he has sworn to marry me if he ever finds himself in a position to do so, and I am content with that.[11]

Yet she considered that, in quotation marks at least, they were 'married'; and, with the punctiliousness of a good secretary, she noted the date when this happened. It was 21 January 1913 – three days before his official silver wedding.

3

In a speech in 1928, when she was at the outset of her political career, Megan explained why it came naturally to her: 'I've had politics for breakfast, lunch, tea and dinner all my life.' The years of her childhood were, indeed, as intensely political and as turbulent as any in British history. Only mythology supports the belief that the skies were clear and serene until the unexpected thunderclap of Sarajevo. In reality, there were at least five storm-centres: the struggle for women's suffrage, the conflict between the Liberal government and the Tory House of Lords, an unprecedented wave of strikes, the drift towards civil war in Ireland, and the mounting international tension which brought Europe to the brink of war in 1905 and 1911. We are concerned here only with their impact on an alert little girl living in Downing Street, but we must bear in mind that each of these events was dramatic and disturbing – and that they were all happening at the same time.

On 13 October 1908 a women's suffrage rally was held in Trafalgar Square and leaflets were distributed calling on women to 'rush the House of Commons'. To demonstrate his belief that there was no cause for alarm, Lloyd George decided to walk from Downing Street to the House with his little daughter. There was, in fact, no widespread violence, but the heart of London looked anything but normal. The streets were closed to traffic, knots of angry men stood ready to stop the women, and 6000 police were posted near the House. The Chancellor was cheered by some and reviled by others as he walked along, explaining to his daughter what it was all about and why everyone looked so excited. In the end, there was no rush, but one

woman succeeded in making her way to the floor of the House and interrupting the debate.

Lloyd George was emphatically in favour of votes for women. He assured a deputation in 1907: 'It is such an obviously reasonable thing that I cannot conceive the right of man to deny it.'[12] According to Frances, 'Ibsen's *Doll's House* was the work that converted him to woman suffrage and presented the woman's point of view to him.'[13] Indeed, there was a clear majority in favour among Liberal MPs and also among Liberal ministers. The obstacle was that the Prime Minister was not in favour (although his daughter Violet showed obvious signs of her potential as an MP).

The campaign rapidly mounted in militancy. Women chained themselves to railings, smashed the windows of 10 Downing Street, courted arrest and endured the torment of forcible feeding. Eventually a bill was introduced in the Commons to give women the vote on the same terms as men. This was a deceptive formula, since men had the vote only if they were house-owners or recognised tenants. About 60 per cent of adult males were voters, with a distinct bias toward the middle-class. The bill would enfranchise only women (generally widows or spinsters) who owned houses or tenancies – probably no more than one adult woman in eight. Lloyd George, with other Liberals, quickly grasped that most of the women enfranchised by this scheme would vote Tory. He voted against the bill, and it came to nothing.

This episode divided the suffrage movement, but Christabel Pankhurst's followers took revenge on men such as Lloyd George who could be stigmatised as hypocrites. A bomb planted by a woman called Emily Davison damaged the house being built for him at Walton Heath. Violence was resumed, the Velázquez *Venus* in the National Gallery was slashed, and Emily Davison sacrificed her life by throwing herself under the King's horse in the 1913 Derby. The battle was called off only when war came in 1914.

In his 1908 budget, Lloyd George had provided for old-age pensions for the first time in history. The scheme had been prepared while Asquith was at the Treasury, but Lloyd George had been pressing for it since 1890, so the pensioners did him justice as well as honour when they referred to their weekly five shillings as 'the Lloyd George'. In the 1909 budget, he paved the way for a comprehensive scheme of national insurance, to cover medical treatment for insured workers and their families, unemployment benefit, disability and blindness benefit, and maternity benefit to be paid direct to the mother. To pay for these benefits, he announced heavy increases in taxation, especially on unearned incomes, and brought in a tax on the wealth derived by landowners from development or mineral rights. 'This is a war budget', he told the Commons, 'for raising money to wage implacable warfare against poverty and squalidness.'

For the first time in history, the budget was rejected by the House of Lords. Speaking to a working-class audience in Limehouse, Lloyd George warned the peers:

Let them realise what they are doing. They are forcing a revolution, and they will get it. The Lords may decree a revolution, but the people will direct it. If they begin, issues will be raised that they little dream of. Questions will be asked which are now whispered in humble voices, and answers will be demanded then with authority.

The Tories had long relied on the Upper House, in which they had a huge majority, to maintain the traditional balance of social power, and Liberals had realised that this obstacle to change must sooner or later be challenged. Now the battle was to be fought out. Lloyd George told his constituents:

I cannot pretend to regret this conflict with which we are now confronted. It is well that democracies should now and again engage in these great struggles for a wider freedom and a higher life. They represent stages in the advance of the people from the bondage of the past to the blessings of the future.[14]

Passions ran high. For Radicals, Lloyd George was the People's Champion. For ladies and gentlemen of property, he was a reckless demagogue bent on the destruction of the England they knew. The latter predominated among the parents at fee-paying schools. Allenswood, where Megan was enrolled in 1911, was a classy establishment; Olwen was at Roedean and Gwilym at Eastbourne. Megan recalled later: 'Gradually we became conscious . . . of a certain hostility, particularly when we went to school. . . . We were marked children. We soon found that in our schools we had not made a popular choice for a father.'[15]

A general election was called in January 1910. The Liberals retained their majority but lost a good deal of ground by comparison with 1906. The Lords belatedly passed the budget, but would not renounce their veto power. The government therefore drew up a Parliament Bill which would compel the Lords to accept any bill that had passed the Commons in two successive years. The problem was that this could become effective only if the Lords accepted the Parliament Bill itself. If they refused, Asquith would have to request the King to create enough new peers – about 500 – to make a Liberal majority in the Lords.

At this juncture, Lloyd George the campaigner metamorphosed into Lloyd George the compromiser. He produced a startling solution to the crisis: the formation of a coalition government of Liberals and Tories. This was the plan broached to Balfour, the Tory Leader, at a discreet dinner, with only Megan and the servants to overhear the discussion. Balfour liked the idea, but his colleagues rejected it, and the battle was resumed.

King George V required another election before he would consent to create the Liberal peers. This election, in December 1910, produced almost exactly the same result as in January. By May 1911 it was known that the King would grant the government's request. Even so, many of the Tory peers were determined to resist to the last. But on 10 August, the day set for the crucial vote, the temperature in London was 97 degrees Fahrenheit. Sweltering in their dark suits and stiff collars, the peers yearned for the fishing streams and grouse moors. When the vote was taken, there was a narrow majority for surrender.

The reasons for the disappointing Liberal poll in the 1910 elections were economic. Prices had risen throughout the decade, undermining the working-class standard of living. Two strikes in 1911, first by seamen and then by dockers, brought the ports to a standstill. In Liverpool there were clashes between strikers and blacklegs, troops were sent in, and two men were shot dead. Then came a nation-wide railway strike, curtailed by Lloyd George's skilful mediation after two days without trains. The next year, 1912, saw the biggest strike that had ever occurred in Britain, when the 850,000 miners came out to demand a national minimum wage. Asquith and Lloyd George both took part in negotiations leading to a compromise settlement. In 1913 Irish dockers went on strike and closed the port of Dublin for months. Poor families in the wretched Dublin slums suffered terrible privations in the winter of 1913–14, and the strikers were forced back to work by sheer hunger.

Ireland, indeed, was the government's most intractable problem. The Liberals were committed in principle to Home Rule, and after the elections of 1910 they were dependent on the parliamentary support of the Irish Nationalists. However, they faced the determined opposition of about a million Protestants in Ulster, backed by British Tories ever since the Conservative Party had decided, in the phrase coined by Lord Randolph Churchill (Winston's father), to 'play the Orange card'. It was mainly because of their hostility to Home Rule that the Tories rejected the coalition plan in 1910, and in 1911 they forced Balfour out of the leadership. He was succeeded by Andrew Bonar Law, who had made money as a Glasgow businessman and was expected to be tougher and more combative than the gentlemanly Balfour. Actually, Bonar Law was more moderate and flexible in outlook than his followers thought. But the one subject on which he took an uncompromising line was Home Rule, for his father had been a Presbyterian minister in Ulster. In Ulster itself, a ferocious champion of the Protestant cause emerged: Sir Edward Carson, a formidable lawyer whose greatest triumph in the courts had been his ruthless cross-examination of Oscar Wilde.

In 1913 the government introduced a Home Rule Bill and promised to accompany it by an amending bill which would allow any dissenting Irish county to opt out of Home Rule for six years. Carson and the Tories rejected this compromise, and the bill was defeated in the Lords. The crunch would come when, thanks to the Parliament Act, Home Rule could be put into effect over the Lord's veto. Carson organised an Ulster Volunteer Force of 100,000 men, pledged to resist Home Rule by any means in their power. On the other side, the nationalists organised the Irish Volunteers, joined by 160,000 men, including 50,000 from the Catholic community in Ulster.

In theory, the government's policy could be enforced by British troops. But most of the officers had Tory sympathies, and a good many were Ulstermen; besides, they had taken an oath of loyalty to the King, not to the government. Pointedly, the King wrote to Asquith:

You will, I am sure, bear in mind that ours is a voluntary Army; and Soldiers are none the less Citizens; by birth, religion and environment they may have strong feelings on the Irish question. . . . Will it be wise, will it be fair to the Sovereign as head of the Army, to subject the discipline, and indeed the loyalty of his troops to such a strain?[16]

In March 1914 the commander and sixty officers of the Cavalry Brigade stationed near Dublin declared that they would resign if ordered to implement a policy to which they were opposed. Apparently it would be left to the rival volunteer forces to do the shooting. In April a huge consignment of rifles and ammunition was landed at Larne for the use of the Ulster Volunteer Force. In July a smaller but still useful cargo of weapons was landed at Howth for the Irish Volunteers. Both consignments came from Germany. At Howth the police tried to seize the cargo and several people were killed in subsequent fighting.

Megan was now twelve years old, and well able to understand the issues at stake and the gravity of the situation. When the family went to Brynawelon for the summer holidays, her father stayed in London. In the July days, the Lloyd Georges doubtless gave more thought to the news from Dublin and Belfast than to the Austrian ultimatum to Serbia – but that was true of almost everyone in Britain. They were aware, however, that the Entente Cordiale, a virtual alliance between Britain and France, entitled the French to call for British help in the event of an attack from Germany. They also knew that, if it came to war, Lloyd George would face a painful personal decision. The Britain of that time had strong (and sedulously inculcated) traditions of bellicose patriotism; yet it had other traditions, embodying detestation of the cruelty and inhumanity of war. These traditions were deeply rooted, in particular, in the Nonconformist community and in Wales.

On 2 August 1914 the Cabinet met in the knowledge that Germany and France were at war. In a hasty letter to Margaret, Lloyd George wrote:

I am moving through a nightmare world these days. . . . I am filled with horror at the prospect [of war]. I am even more horrified that I should ever appear to have a share in it but I must bear my share of the ghastly burden though it scorches my flesh to do so.[17]

It was open to him to resign if Britain entered the war – two Liberal ministers did so – and to put himself at the head of a peace party, but there is no evidence that he was ever seriously inclined to follow this course. Frances Stevenson, who was close to him in the critical days, wrote in retrospect: 'My own opinion is that L.G.'s mind was really made up from the first, that he knew we would have to go in.'[18]

By the time that Megan returned to London at the end of the school holidays, both her brothers were in uniform. She saw posters with the stern message 'KITCHENER NEEDS YOU' and queues of young men outside the recruiting stations. If she walked the short distance to Charing Cross Station, she could see wounded men on stretchers being lifted from hospital trains. To be twelve years old in 1914 – and, especially, to be David Lloyd George's daughter – was to grow up fast.

4

The war began disastrously. German forces advanced deep into France and threatened Paris; in the nick of time, French reinforcements were rushed to defence lines on the River Marne in Paris taxis. The British advance-guard was almost annihilated at Mons and had to make a hasty retreat to cover the Channel ports. On the eastern front, the Germans inflicted a severe defeat on the Russians, to the dismay of those who had predicted that the 'Russian steamroller' would trundle on to Berlin.

'War is too important to be left to military men': that often-quoted phrase was spoken in 1916 by Aristide Briand, then Prime Minister of France, in conversation with Lloyd George.[19] It was certainly the first lesson that had to be learned. Once the German advance was checked, the troops on both sides dug themselves into the ground, creating a line of trenches from the Channel to Switzerland. British generals still thought in terms of mobile warfare, decisive one-day battles and heroic charges by infantry and cavalry. Their only strategy was to launch attacks designed to overrun the enemy trenches; this took no account of the formidable development of artillery and machine-guns since the nineteenth century, which gave defenders the edge over attackers and made every offensive a futile massacre.

Field Marshal Kitchener, who had been brought into the government as Secretary for War, complained that the troops were using too much ammunition. In a revealing conversation with Balfour which came to the alert ears of Frances Stevenson, he declared that General French, commander of the British Expeditionary Force, was 'far too extravagant'.

'And consider the casualties,' Balfour sighed. 'There must have been nearly ten thousand men lost in these engagements.'

'It isn't the men I mind,' Kitchener retorted. 'I can replace the men at once, but I can't replace the shells so easily.'[20]

In fact, Britain had not begun to gear up its industries for the needs of war, and the production of shells was pitifully inadequate. Lloyd George knew all about this, and not just from official reports. Gwilym was in the Royal Artillery, and had the painful experience of having nothing to fire from his guns. Dick was also at the front; he had taken an engineering degree at Cambridge before the war and was now serving with the Royal Engineers. He wrote to tell his father that the lack of artillery support was deeply depressing for the infantry soldiers who had to face a well-equipped enemy.

Asquith, patently no war leader, was the target of growing criticism. A *Manchester Guardian* leading article in May 1915 demanded: 'How can any slacker be blamed when the Government itself is slack?'[21] In that month, Asquith reluctantly agreed to bring the Tories into his government and make it a coalition. He also agreed to create a Ministry of Munitions, and offered the job to Lloyd George. This was scarcely a tempting offer; the task was daunting, and in political terms it was a step down for the Chancellor of the Exchequer.

'One day in 1915', Megan recalled in later years, 'seems to mark the end of my childhood.' Her father fetched her from school and took her to a tea-shop in Putney.

> He told me how the German artillery were pounding our troops, and how we were so short of shells that our gunners were down to one round a day, and he said that the Prime Minister had asked him to take on the job of providing munitions. . . . Should he take it on? Could he do the job? . . . We sat in that tea-shop for over an hour talking it over, and then he took me back to my school. Next day I heard that he had become Minister of Munitions, and I felt that I had put away some of my childish things.[22]

Lloyd George at once demanded, and obtained, powers to take over factories needed for war production and cancel existing contracts. He ordered the building of scores of National Factories, publicly owned and managed under his ministry's control. The unions were persuaded to allow skilled work to be done by new employees – even women – who had not served the traditional apprenticeship. Within a year, the output of heavy guns was increased almost a hundredfold. As many shells were being produced in four days as had been produced in a year before Lloyd George took over. Dick Lloyd George wrote: 'The difference at the front was seen within a matter of weeks. . . . I shall never forget the look of delighted surprise on the faces of the men.'[23]

Sadly, the improvement encouraged the generals to launch new offensives, now preceded by massive and prolonged artillery bombardments, whose main effect was to warn the Germans of what was coming. Sir Douglas Haig, who had taken over the command from French, launched a huge offensive on the Somme front on 1 July 1916. A month later, Winston Churchill pronounced a verdict in a memorandum to the Cabinet:

> In personnel the results of the operation have been disastrous; in terrain they have been absolutely barren. . . . The British offensive *per se* has been a great failure.[24]

Undeniable though this was, Haig continued the offensive until 15 November. At no point did the advance exceed seven miles. Casualties reached a total of 498,000, including 124,000 killed or missing. German losses were only two-thirds of the British. The Somme was the graveyard of Kitchener's army of volunteers, and the rest of the war was fought by reluctant, frightened, miserably unhappy conscripts.

Kitchener himself never witnessed this catastrophe. The government had decided to send him, with Lloyd George, on a mission to Russia to stiffen the shaky war effort of the Tsarist Empire. Before they could set off, the Easter Rising erupted in Dublin, and Asquith asked Lloyd George to stay at home and take on political responsibility for Ireland. Kitchener embarked on his journey aboard a battleship, which hit a mine in the North Sea. His body was never found.[25] It was a nasty shock for Megan; but for the Prime Minister's altered decision, she would have been fatherless.

A new Secretary for War was needed. Asquith offered the job to Bonar Law, but he took a modest view of his own capacity as a military strategist and urged Asquith to appoint Lloyd George. Asquith did so, but with reluctance; he had come to believe that Lloyd George was plotting to supplant him in Number 10. Lord Beaverbrook, the most perceptive chronicler of political events at that time, observed: 'It was clear that the decision to appoint Lloyd George to the War Office had been forced on an unwilling Prime Minister.'[26]

Those who were close to Lloyd George knew that he regarded the position of Prime Minister as a poisoned chalice. He told Frances that 'he would simply get blamed for losing the war, and having the negotiating of an unfavourable peace.'[27] Another of his secretaries, Thomas Jones, found that 'a black pessimism was his prevailing mood in these autumn months of 1916.'[28]

Asquith, however, was going downhill at an alarming rate. He knew that he had no effective control of the conduct of the war, and was aware that others knew it. He sustained a severe personal blow when his son Raymond was killed at the front. Another blow came when Venetia Stanley, a woman for whom he cherished a sentimental devotion, married an up-and-coming minister, Edwin Montagu. He was now drinking enough to have earned the nickname of 'Old Squiffy', and on at least one occasion he was visibly tottering as he made his way to the front bench in the Commons. Lord Crawford, a newcomer to the Cabinet, drew an unflattering portrait: 'Asquith somnolent – hands shaky and cheeks pendulous. He exercised little control over debate, seemed rather bored.'[29] Frances duly noted that Lloyd George told her: 'He says it is impossible to get the P.M. to do anything. . . . He just sits there and uses the whole of his crafty brain to squash any plan for action that is put forward.'[30] Her impression was: 'Everyone tells the same tale – that the country is sick of the present government and loathes and despises Asquith.' But 'everyone' was an exaggeration. Asquith still had his friends and supporters, especially among right-wing Liberals who had viewed Lloyd George's radical campaigning without enthusiasm before the war. One of these was Reginald McKenna, who had been given Lloyd George's job as Chancellor and did not want to lose it.

On 25 November 1916 Bonar Law proposed the formation of a

small War Council, to consist of Asquith, himself, Lloyd George and Carson. (With the Ulster problem in mothballs, the last two were now on good terms.) Asquith's reaction was that the plan had been devised by Lloyd George 'with the purpose, not perhaps at the moment, but as soon as a fitting pretext could be found, of his displacing me'.[31] Believing that he had the support of the majority of Cabinet ministers, both Liberal and Tory, he adopted an ingenious strategy: he would resign, no one else would be able to form a government, and he would return in triumph.

The strategy backfired. Backed by Bonar Law, Lloyd George undertook to form a government and succeeded. Balfour, when invited to take the Foreign Office, immediately agreed. Other Tories – Lord Curzon, Lord Robert Cecil, Sir Austen Chamberlain – followed his example. A Labour Party gathering, after hearing Lloyd George speak, authorised Arthur Henderson to join the government. Asquith, McKenna and the Liberal veterans were out in the cold.

Asquith had been Prime Minister for eight and a half years, the longest tenure since Lord Liverpool in the early nineteenth century. Had he accepted a well-deserved rest from his labours, he would have departed in an atmosphere of goodwill (the relief would have been politely muted). But politicians, for the most part, are more apt to hold on to the day of enforced ejection than to choose dignified retirement. The Asquiths left Downing Street in embittered mood. Margot wrote: 'I was shocked and wounded by the meanness, ingratitude and lack of loyalty.'[32] Violet – who was shortly to marry her father's secretary, Sir Maurice Bonham Carter – found it hard to reconcile herself to the fact that she was no longer the Prime Minister's daughter. To the end of her life, she never wavered in her belief that her father had been the victim of a nefarious, treacherous Lloyd George coup.

It was Megan Lloyd George, from now on, who could rejoice in being the Prime Minister's daughter. Allenswood School had closed down, and she was at Garrett Hall School, Banstead – somewhat further from central London, but still within easy reach of home, and also within reach of Walton Heath, where Lloyd George's house had been repaired. Gone were the days when her father's name was a source of hostility; in 1916 it was more likely to inspire respect. The parents of her schoolfellows, whatever their political allegiance, would be relieved that a man of energy and decision had moved into Number 10. Indeed, millions of people were hoping that, through the horrors and sacrifices of the war, Lloyd George would find the path to victory. The man who was most dubious about it was Lloyd George himself.

It would hardly have been surprising if the Prime Minister's young daughter – his favourite since the age of five – had been a spoilt child. Her former teacher was in the best position to take a cool, considered view of her. A few days before Megan's fifteenth birthday, Frances wrote:

She is an amusing little person, but is getting rather artificial. D [David Lloyd George] thinks she is getting selfish, but that is not her fault, for she has not been taught to be unselfish. I think she is wonderfully unspoilt, considering the way she has been brought up.[33]

## 5

The love affair with Frances had become an essential part of Lloyd George's life, and all the more so because of the strains and anxieties of the war. In August 1915, while taking a short holiday at Folkestone, he wrote to her:

My own sweet child,
I received both your darling letters and they were like nectar for lips parched with a great passion. I have been these 2 or 3 days thinking things of unutterable tenderness & love for my little cariad. My affection for her has deepened & sweetened beyond anything words can tell.[34]

It was mostly at Walton Heath that they could be alone together. Over the New Year of 1915, with the family at Brynawelon, the lovers spent a record nineteen days at the house in Surrey. Frances wrote in her diary on 17 January: 'It has been like an idyll, but alas! came to an end yesterday, when the family returned from Criccieth and I returned home.'

Home for Frances, at this time, was her parents' house in Wallington, a South London suburb. But in March 1915 there was a row, when Mr and Mrs Stevenson voiced their disapproval of her love life and tried to persuade her to end the relationship. 'They do not understand. . . . They think I am his plaything, and that he will fling me aside when he has finished with me.'[35] Frances left home and took a flat in Chester Square in Belgravia. She could walk to Whitehall to start the day's work, and Lloyd George could walk to her flat for the evening. In those days, ministers were not shadowed by detectives.

One day in 1916, Margaret entered a room in 11 Downing Street and heard her husband talking on the phone to Frances, doubtless in affectionate terms. There was an angry scene; as he reported later to

Frances, Margaret said: 'I know very well whom you would marry if anything happened to me.'[36] Probably this incident merely provided Margaret with confirmation of what she had guessed years earlier. She never condoned Lloyd George's unfaithfulness, but she decided that making rows was useless, as well as being beneath her dignity. He remarked complacently to Frances: 'She is very tolerant, considering that she knows everything that is going on.'[37]

When in playful mood, Lloyd George called his mistress Pussy, which was not in fact a lovers' name but a childhood nickname. His letters to her were eventually published under the title *My Darling Pussy*, although not many of them begin thus. The other members of Lloyd George's staff called her Miss Stevenson, but the formality gradually broke down and they began to address her as Frances. Lloyd George had recruited a personal staff which included J.T. Davies and Thomas Jones – both Welshmen and both established civil servants – and A. J. Sylvester, whose great merit was his astonishing speed as a shorthand writer. These three were in the secret of the relationship between Lloyd George and Frances, but no one else was admitted to it. A younger man, Philip Kerr, joined the office a little later; and when Lloyd George became Prime Minister he appointed Colonel Maurice Hankey as secretary to the Cabinet, a post which had not hitherto existed. A note from Lloyd George to Frances in 1917 read: 'You might phone from Treasury on Friday if you can come, but don't let Hankey see you.' Another note warned her: 'Kerr opens all letters – so beware.'[38]

Among Lloyd George's friends, Riddell was undoubtedly in the secret, and Beaverbrook and Churchill probably guessed. Frances worried about Lucy Masterman, wife of a Liberal politician: 'Probably she disapproves of our relations, for she most surely knows.'[39] One evening in 1920, she had to keep a cool head when seated at dinner beside the Prince of Wales:

He must know about D and me, because he said: 'Mrs Lloyd George does not spend much time in London, does she?' with a meaning look. I said: 'No, she prefers being in Criccieth' and let him infer what he liked.[40]

But those who guessed were few; and it was Frances's high reputation as a confidential secretary that shielded her from being identified as a mistress. True enough, Lloyd George was credited with strong sexual proclivities and few moral restraints. However, given the customs of the age, he was envisaged as enjoying himself with a chorus-girl or a music-hall artiste – or perhaps the skittish and amusing wife of some pompous politician – not with a woman capable of serious work. All photographs of Frances show her modestly and neatly dressed, with not a hair out of place. As Sylvester said: 'No one would suspect her of a sexual relationship with anybody. You'd take her to be a prim schoolteacher.'[41]

6

Lloyd George's War Cabinet, a small executive body, had five members. The others were Bonar Law as Chancellor of the Exchequer, Lord Curzon, Lord Milner (a militant imperialist, but a man of ideas and ability) and Arthur Henderson to represent the Labour movement. Most of Lloyd George's other appointments were fairly successful, and the one outright failure was that of Neville Chamberlain as Director of National Service. A tactless and opinionated man, he tried to get men into the army wholesale without consideration for war factories which needed skilled labour. After six months, the Prime Minister requested his resignation. His biographer relates that 'his feelings were sore, his private comment acrid'.[42] Twenty years later, he had not forgiven Lloyd George.

The crucial problem for Lloyd George was to impose his will on the generals. Their loyalty was to the King and they made skilful use of their court connections; Field-Marshal Haig's wife was a lady-in-waiting. When Lloyd George criticised Haig's strategy, the King sent him a note cautioning him to think of the Field-marshal's prestige. The Prime Minister replied: 'The most important thing seems to me that the lives of our gallant soldiers should not be squandered as they were last summer'[43] – a retort which had more justice than prudence.

More lives were indeed squandered. Haig wanted an offensive in Flanders; Lloyd George, as Hankey testified, 'was absolutely convinced that the attack in Flanders had not the remotest prospect of success',[44] but he could not overrule the Field-marshal. Like the Somme, the battle of Passchendaele began in July and was prolonged into November. Like the Somme, it was a horror and a failure. By the end of 1917, victory seemed further off than ever. The United States had entered the war, but had so far contributed only a token force. On the other hand, the Bolshevik revolution had taken Russia out of the war. The western front was a scene of disaster. As for the other Allies, Serbia and Romania had been crushed and the Italians were reeling back in disorder from their defeat at Caporetto. In March 1918 the Germans launched a massive onslaught and endangered Paris again. An entire British army, the 5th, was shattered.

Politically, Lloyd George was in peril. Asquith was still the official leader of the Liberal Party. If Lloyd George's direction of the war could be shown to be ineffective, the Asquithians would try to bring him down. If he lost a parliamentary vote of confidence he could be obliged to resign, a proven failure, after little more than a year in power. It was an anxious time for him – and for his family. Dick and Gwilym were still at the front, and the dangers were greater with the enemy thrusting ahead. Olwen had been married in 1917 to a doctor serving with the army, Thomas Carey Evans. She almost lost him when a ship on which he was travelling was torpedoed and sunk.

By August the Allies were beginning to push the Germans back and planning for a 1919 campaign. Few people suspected that Germany and Austria-Hungary were collapsing from within and were on the verge of revolution. On 11 November the German generals accepted defeat and signed an armistice. Victory, coming so unexpectedly, seemed like a miracle.

Yet the cost was grievous. Almost a million young men were buried in huge cemeteries in France, or were lost for ever in the mud churned by the shells. The moral cost, too, was saddening. In important respects, the war had divided rather than united the nation. Those who survived felt pride in the heroism of the fallen, but also shame for men who had secured a 'cushy berth' and evaded the danger, for the callous and incompetent generals, for capitalists and traders who had enriched themselves from their country's needs. In what seems to be a rough draft for an essay, headed 'The Missing Generation', Megan wrote:

No stone had been left unturned by the storm which had mercilessly battered, shattered and torn every limb of civilisation. . . . The world, a sorry place at best, had had a nightmare. . . . Men who had outlived the war and its heroes came home expecting to find their homes as they had left them, but they didn't know that during their absence a new type of Englishman had sprung up – a creature made by opportunity and chance, not high intellect and natural refinement – a product of the war who fed on the carcasses of the heroic! A profiteer![45]

These ideas are unlikely to have been put into Megan's mind by her teachers or schoolfellows, nor indeed by her father and his colleagues. Intent on war production, Lloyd George had not objected to big profits being made by industrialists so long as they delivered the goods. At sixteen, Megan was clearly thinking for herself.

With his leadership vindicated by victory, Lloyd George decided to hold an immediate general election. In June 1918 a Franchise Act had been passed giving the vote to all citizens who had reached the stipulated age. Women as well as men were given the vote without any revival of the pre-war conflicts; only a few MPs voted against this provision. Complete equality, however, had not arrived. Since the population always included more women than men, and almost a million men had been killed in the war, there was a prospect that the electoral registers would show a strong female preponderance. So it was decided that, while men could vote at the age of twenty-one, women would not be allowed to vote until they were thirty.

Lloyd George faced a political dilemma. If he chose, he could declare that the coalition, as a wartime expedient, was at an end, and the parties would oppose each other in the traditional manner. This would demonstrate his faith in democracy and his return to his Liberal – even Radical – stance. But it would mean parting company with men such as Bonar Law with whom he had worked happily and who had no wish to start fighting him. Besides, in an election on party lines there was a strong likelihood of a Tory victory. The Tories had run the Liberals close in 1910, and they stood to benefit by the patriotic or chauvinistic emotions brought to the surface by war. They were a united party, while the Liberals were divided by sharp and recent quarrels. Lloyd George was very popular, but he was not the Liberal Party's leader; the voters would not be keen to send the discredited Asquith back to Downing Street. Lloyd George would not be Prime Minister even if the Liberals won, nor Leader of the Opposition if the Liberals lost. He would be playing second fiddle (if he was in the orchestra at all) to an Asquith who hated him and would seize every chance to humiliate him. It was not an inviting prospect.

The alternative was to keep the coalition going, and ask the voters to opt for candidates who supported it. It could be argued convincingly that there were great tasks ahead, both in reconstruction at home (Lloyd George coined the effective, if often misquoted, phrase 'a fit country for heroes to live in') and in making a peace that would justify the sacrifices of war: and that these aims could best be achieved by a united government endorsed by the great majority of voters. Since the only opposition groups would be the Labour Party and the Asquith section of the Liberals, a coalition victory was practically guaranteed. The drawback was that the Tories would probably outnumber the Liberals in the House; and they might eventually decide that they wanted a Prime Minister of their own and dismiss Lloyd George.

It did not take Lloyd George long to make up his mind. Even before the election campaign opened, Tory and (coalition) Liberal Party managers struck a bargain; 150 Liberal candidates would be unopposed by the Tories. Asquith referred to this arrangement scornfully as 'the coupon', an allusion to the coupons in wartime ration books.

The outcome of the election was of course a sweeping coalition victory, but it was even more of a Tory victory than had been expected. Of the Liberals with the coupon, only 136 won their seats; some were defeated by Labour candidates, or by Tories who refused to honour the deal. Conservative victories reached the huge total of 387. Lloyd George was faced, as Michael Foot has put it, with a 'raucous, bovine, flag-wagging Tory majority'.[46] Frances recalled in her autobiography that he was 'staggered and depressed' by the result.[47]

If it was any consolation, Asquith had even more cause to be depressed. He lost his own seat, and only twenty-six of his followers were elected.

Lloyd George had invited the Labour Party to stay with the coalition and accept coupons, but a party conference resolved to fight independently. Labour won fifty-nine seats, an encouraging score in the circumstances, and became the official opposition for the first time.

The old Irish Nationalist Party, seeking Home Rule and allied with the Liberals, had vanished. Since the suppression of the Easter Rising and the execution of its leaders, Padraic Pearse and James Connolly, the mood in Ireland was 'changed, changed utterly'. Candidates of Sinn Fein, a new movement demanding complete independence, won every Irish seat except in Ulster, refused to take their seats at Westminster and gathered in Dublin as the First Dail of the Irish Republic. One of them was Constance Gore-Booth (Countess Markiewicz), who has her place in history as the first woman elected to the House of Commons – but not, thanks to the boycott, the first woman to sit there.

A few days after New Year 1919, Lloyd George went to Paris to join the French, American and Italian heads of government in shaping a peace treaty. Olwen and her husband proposed to make a short stay in Paris, though they would soon be going to India; Tom Carey Evans was a captain in the Indian Medical Service. Even Dame Margaret was lured into a visit to Paris, distant from Criccieth though it was. Megan pleaded to go too, and her father could not refuse her request.

# CHAPTER THREE

# Family Battles

Megan was surely in a cheerful mood when she arrived in Paris on 11 January 1919. She had crossed the Channel for the first time in her life. She had now left Garrett Hall School and was to spend a year at a finishing school in Paris. A note in the diary she had begun to keep reads: 'Secretarial training during morning hours – diploma if possible.' However, nothing came of this project, nor did the diary last more than a few weeks.[1] Meanwhile she would be close to her father as the peace conference convened. Men whom she had known since childhood would be there, including Winston Churchill and Rufus Isaacs, now ennobled as Lord Reading. Undoubtedly, she would also be well placed to meet interesting young men.

Lloyd George was already in Paris, installed in a rented flat in Rue Nitot. The Hotel Majestic was the headquarters of the British delegation, and was swarming with civil servants, army and navy officers, experts in economic and other spheres, and the more favoured among the many journalists covering the conference. Among the civil servants was Frances Stevenson. Megan had been expected to stay at the flat, but, as Frances wrote:

She soon decided that life there would be dull in comparison with the conditions prevailing at the Hotel Majestic, and obtained permission to share my room there instead. . . . She became a very popular figure at the Majestic, and enjoyed to the full the gaiety and attractions which Paris offered at that time.[2]

To convey both the atmosphere at the Majestic and the flavour of Megan's lively personality, one cannot do better than to quote from her diary:

*Sunday, Jan. 12.* Met Lord Reading on the way to the restaurant. When he saw me he immediately rose and leaving a friend came over to talk to me. 'Well, how are you?' 'Oh, splendid, thanks.' 'With whom are you lunching today?' 'I am sorry, I am lunching with Miss Stevenson & Mr Davies.' 'What a pity. I have been thinking of getting at you this morning. Please remind me, we will arrange something another day. We will go out together.'

Went to restaurant – Botha, Hughes, Smuts, C.I.G.S., Maharajah of Bikaner & son, Sinha among people there.[3] Very jolly lunch. First of all prevented from coming in by waiter but saved by Foreign Office man.

*Monday, Jan. 13.* Went to the Louvre. Went up a quaint 'moving staircase', a very ricketty affair altogether, down which Miss Stev. refused to come. The shops are not so well arranged and managed as in England but their merchandise is so very much more attractive & smart.

*Tuesday, Jan. 14.* Venizelos[4] came to brekker, forgot all about him & overslept myself to 9.20, arriving in the dining-room about 10 o'clock. Breakfast finished. Tada jokingly said: 'No butter for you, only dry toast.' Whereupon Mr V. passed over the butter. . . . Dinner here, Lord Reading, Mr Bonar Law, Mr Kerr, Tada & myself. Very jolly little party. Bed.

*Wednesday, Jan. 15.* Went to tea with Lady Rothermere, thought her very charming, pretty & jolly. C.I.G.S. Miss Cazalet, *not* pretty but most fascinating, niece of Sir Arthur Pearson. . . . Dinner at the Majestic. Lord Reading asked Miss S. what I was going to do. She said: 'Dine with me and Mr Davies.' 'What a pity, she might have dined with us.' Wanted me to, apparently. Danced after dinner. Good fun. . . . F.E.[5] said Tada had heard of this dancing and nothing would keep him away from it. Brought Lord Reading, Mr Balfour with him.

## On Thursday, Megan visited Saint-Germain:

Harmsworth & Kerr took me into the castle. Very dull inside, nothing but Roman remains & how I do hate them.

*Friday, Jan. 17.* Went out to have nails manicured. . . . Remembered that I was lunching with Lady Pearson & Miss Cazalet. Couldn't get a car, all ours had gone. Went to Majestic and a naval officer gave me his car.

## The formal opening session of the conference was the next day:

Father, believing the great conference to commence at 3 o'clock and that President Poincaré who was to open the show would arrive at 3.30, he arrived there at 3.5 or 10 to find the President one-third of the way through his speech. *Quel faut pas!* [Megan's spelling][6]

On Sunday, Megan went to Reims with her father and Frances to see the great cathedral, which had been severely damaged in the war.

Went to the cathedral – smash-up something awful. The old Cardinal met us, in robes & red gloves, very nice woolly-looking old chap. Listened to a band of blackies – extraordinary.

A week later she was beginning to grow bored.

*Sunday, Jan. 26.*   Dinner at the flat. Went to Majestic after dinner. Saw the dancing but was virtuous & did *not* dance myself.

*Monday, Jan. 27.*   After dinner we trotted off to the Majestic but it was so very boring. There were practically *no* men & those who were there were very dull. Returned fairly early in an excessively bad temper.

In Paris, Megan met two girls of her age who became close friends: Thelma Cazalet and Ursula Norton-Griffiths. Thanks to the diary, her first meeting with Thelma can be dated precisely. She was indeed not particularly pretty, but photographs give an unmistakable impression of her alertness and intelligence. Megan and Ursula met a few weeks later; both were at finishing schools, though not at the same one, and they were constant companions as they explored Paris. Back in London, they were débutantes and were presented at court in the same season. Megan was a bridesmaid when Ursula was married in 1922, and was a godmother to her first child. Lloyd George soon became fond of both Thelma and Ursula, and they were regular summer guests at Brynawelon during the 1920s. He had always enjoyed the company of bright, amusing young women; he was no longer an enthusiastic seducer now that Frances was his established mistress, but he took pleasure in charming them and attracting their admiration. Incidentally, Megan, Thelma and Ursula were all accomplished gardeners; Thelma, indeed, ran a successful flower business in her later years. Ursula's garden in Kent still displays a cherry tree and a magnolia which were gifts from Megan.

Both these friends belonged to Tory families and – nominally at least – were themselves Tories. Ursula was the daughter of a Conservative MP. As Ursula Thorpe, she was also the wife of a Conservative MP, but her son Jeremy was to become the leader of the Liberal Party. Thelma's brother Victor was a Tory MP, and she herself entered the House as a Conservative in 1931. But none of the Lloyd Georges – certainly neither Megan nor her father – chose their friends for reasons of political allegiance rather than personal inclination. Besides, Ursula and Thelma were not Tories of a dogmatic or prejudiced kind. Thelma was embarrassed by the wealth that had been amassed by the Cazalet family, and reflected later that this 'was probably the cause of my tendency to seek my closest friends among people belonging to the Left – the Lloyd George family being the outstanding example'.[7] It should be remembered, finally, that when these friendships took root in 1919 Lloyd George was heading a coalition government of which most Tories thoroughly approved. Colonel Norton-Griffiths, Ursula's father, considered himself to be a Coalition Unionist MP with the accent on the former word as much as the latter. If it was improper for a Tory to express admiration for Lloyd George in 1909, it was certainly not in 1919.

While the girls enjoyed the shops and *pâtisseries* of Paris, Lloyd George worked hard at the peace treaty. The map of Europe had to be redrawn in conformity with President Woodrow Wilson's principle of national self-determination, with provision for the new nations of Czechoslovakia and Yugoslavia and for a reborn Poland. According to the tally kept by Sylvester, 674 decisions were made in 206 meetings. Somehow it was all done by the end of May.

The central problem was the treatment of Germany. On the morrow of the Armistice, Lloyd George had proclaimed:

We must not allow any sense of revenge, any spirit of greed, any grasping desire to override the fundamental principles of righteousness. . . . [We must avoid] base, sordid, squalid ideas of vengeance and of avarice.[8]

He soon found that Georges Clemenceau, the French Prime Minister, thought only of keeping Germany permanently weak and making her bear the cost of the war, and that this outlook was shared by the British Tories on whom the coalition government depended. The Treaty of Versailles, which the Germans signed under duress on 28 June 1919, was heavily punitive. The Rhineland, a large and populous slice of western Germany, was to be occupied by Allied troops for fifteen years and closed to German armed forces thereafter. Germany was allowed to have only a small army and no air force. Reparations were fixed at a level beyond the capacity of the Germany economy. Lloyd George knew that the brilliant young economist John Maynard Keynes was right in predicting that Versailles would be damaging for Europe as well as for Germany. He also knew the truth in the cartoon by Will Dyson of the *Daily Herald*, in which Clemenceau was made to say: 'Curious! I seem to hear a child weeping' – the child being labelled, with uncanny prescience, '1940 class'.

However, he hoped that the new League of Nations, the other outcome of the Paris talks, would be a real safeguard against future wars. The League's constitution, or Covenant, provided for the peaceful and equitable settlement of disputes, and it was anticipated that Germany, after a period of probation, would become a member on a footing of equality (in fact, she was admitted in 1925). The Covenant was drafted by Lord Robert Cecil, a Tory member of Lloyd George's government but a devotee of the League idea, with the assistance of a young man named Philip Baker whose father, J. Allen Baker, had been a Liberal MP and a consistent advocate of peace and disarmament.

Whatever Lloyd George's own feelings about Versailles, it was hailed as a triumph. The King and Queen went to Victoria Station to meet their Prime Minister, an honour that no monarch had ever bestowed on a subject. The Welsh wizard had won the war and rounded off the victory with a popular treaty; his prestige stood at an all-time high. F. E. Smith remarked that, if Britain had the same political system as the United States, Lloyd George would be elected President by a landslide, and there was no reason to doubt this judgement.

2

In January 1920, Frances Stevenson noted in her dairy that Megan had promised to return to the Paris finishing school after the Christmas holiday but had failed to do so. Her father was annoyed; 'he will not easily forgive her for this breach of faith,' Frances wrote primly.[9] But Megan was soon forgiven, and came to live at 10 Downing Street again.

In the 1920s it was not altogether easy to know what to do with a clever, independent-minded girl. Megan had done reasonably well at school, but no one imagined that she was the scholarly type.[10] There seems to have been no suggestion of a university education. Both her brothers had been to Cambridge, but it was not usual for girls unless they wanted to qualify for a specific career. In the 1930s, when her niece Valerie (Dick's daughter) wanted to go to Oxford and got no encouragement from her parents, Megan said emphatically that Valerie should go and that she greatly regretted not having gone to a university herself.[11] However, she made no such request at the right time.

Acting was certainly among Megan's talents. She had been a much-praised Cordelia in the school play at Garrett Hall, and was often involved in amateur theatricals. Her niece Margaret (Olwen's daughter) remembers a musical revue staged at Criccieth in which Megan gave an effective performance in the role of a bossy landlady.[12] Throughout her life she was a keen and appreciative playgoer and was also very fond of the ballet. It is easy to connect these tastes with her own gifts and predilections; as well as being a good amateur actress, she loved dancing and cut a good figure on the dance-floor. Her preferences in the theatre were conventional, with an emphasis on Shakespeare. She seldom failed to spend a few nights at Stratford-upon-Avon in the summer season. The only 'fringe' production that she is known to have attended was at the Embassy, Swiss Cottage, in December 1928, when she saw Emlyn Williams's first play, but this was a matter of friendship. In 1927 Williams had taken a summer job in Criccieth teaching French to Megan's cousin William (then ten years old), had got to know the family and had taken on the extra job of teaching Megan Italian. Her French was already fluent, and she picked up Italian quickly.

Although some people thought that she was planning to go on the stage professionally – or that she ought to – Williams makes it clear in his memoirs that she had no such intention.[13] Still, it is reasonable to see an affinity between this non-existent career and the political career which Megan actually pursued. From her first appearance on Liberal Party platforms, she was full of self-confidence and entirely free from 'stage fright', she never fluffed her lines, and her style of speaking was generally described as dramatic.

In our own day, a girl in Megan's position would look for a job – perhaps in journalism or television, perhaps with an organisation such as Oxfam or Amnesty. But in the 1920s girls were not normally asked, 'What are you doing?', with the implication that they ought to be doing something. Megan may well have felt that she was actively employed by being at Number 10, making life easier for Tada and picking up useful information for him. Besides, Thelma and Ursula were in London, a big city generated a constant flow of new friendships and invitations, and Megan can seldom have been at a loss to fill her time.

It is hard to say whether, at this stage, Megan contemplated a political career. Under the terms of the Franchise Act, she could not stand for Parliament until she was thirty – and, at eighteen, that must have seemed a long way off. What is certain is that her fascination with politics never slackened. At home, it was still 'politics for breakfast, lunch, tea and dinner'; Thelma and Ursula were politically minded; and several young men in Megan's circle were aiming to put the letters MP after their names, including her brother Gwilym. We can be sure that she would have rejected the idea that it was a legitimate ambition for a man but not for a woman.

From a social point of view, Megan Lloyd George was hard to classify. She had been presented at court and was on nodding terms with the Prince of Wales, the most eligible bachelor of the time. (Indeed, some gossips suggested that they might make a match – an intriguing historical 'if'.) She was fully at home in the fashionable world of the West End: the world of 'the season', afternoons spent choosing new dresses or watching a fashion parade, evenings at the opera or a charity ball, late hours at a night-club listening to ragtime and dancing the Charleston. 'These late nights are too much for her – night after night of theatres and dances,' her father complained in a letter to her mother.[14] Yet she was equally at home and equally happy at Criccieth, wearing old clothes, working in the garden, helping Sarah in the kitchen, chatting with childhood friends in her 'peasant-flavoured' Welsh, listening to the gramophone and going to bed at nine-thirty. Perceptively, Emlyn Williams noted 'the twofoldness of her personality' – 'a London dazzler at home with cottagers under Snowdon' who was also 'a Welsh girl holding her own in Claridge's with Margot Asquith'.[15] (This was hardly the right name to drop, in view of the enmity between the Asquiths and the Lloyd Georges, but Williams was not well up in politics.)

To complicate matters, it was a time when many people seriously feared – and others hoped – that the world of wealth and privilege would soon be swept away, like the yet more glittering world of St Petersburg a few years before. After he acquired a new country home at Churt, Lloyd George told Thelma, 'When the Communists take over, remember that there will always be a chicken for you at Churt', and she felt it was 'only half in joke'.[16] In 1919 revolutionary regimes had briefly held power in Munich and Budapest. The Red Army, after defeating the Whites in Russia's civil war, advanced menacingly into Poland in 1920. In Britain, within a couple of years, soldiers demanding instant demobilisation mutinied and rioted; the police force, for the only time in history, went on strike; London dockers refused to load a ship with arms for Poland; and a nation-wide coal strike was averted only by subsidies to prevent the threatened wage-cuts. Such was the background to a meeting of coalition Liberal MPs addressed by Lloyd George on 18 March 1920. As leaked to The Times (the meeting was private, so there is no verbatim report), the points made by the Prime Minister were:

The Labour Party doctrine was common ownership, known in France as

Communism, in Germany as Socialism, and in Russia as Bolshevism. . . . Four-fifths of the country was industrial and commercial; this country was more top-heavy than any other, and therefore a crash would be the greater. Civilisation was in jeopardy in every land. Without closer co-operation, the forces of subversion would triumph.

The report was read jubilantly in Moscow. Lenin was putting the finishing touches to his book *Left-Wing Communism*, and he inserted a dedication:

I dedicate this pamphlet to the Right Honourable Mr Lloyd George as a token of my gratitude for his speech of March 18, 1920, which was almost Marxist and, in any case, exceedingly useful for Communists and Bolsheviks throughout the world.

There were other reasons for alarm. Ireland was in revolt; the Irish Republican Army, commanded by the brilliant and ingenious Michael Collins, controlled large parts of the country. In a war of guerrilla fighting, ambushes and individual killings, at least a thousand lives were lost in 1920. India too was in revolt; countless numbers of campaigners for independence were ready to engage in civil disobedience and law-breaking at the behest of the mysteriously charismatic Mahatma Gandhi. Lloyd George sent his old friend Lord Reading to take over as Viceroy, but the task of restoring order was formidable. All these pressures were pushing the Prime Minister to the right of the political stage. It was the Tories who were most alarmed by the Communist menace, most hostile to any concession to the Irish rebels and most insistent that the Raj must be preserved. Besides, Lloyd George had been sitting round the Cabinet table with Tories since May 1915; inevitably, bonds of friendship and trust had been forged. Looking back years later, Frances reflected:

He is instinctively drawn towards Tories for his friendships, and hates the sanctimonious humbug which seems to characterise the majority of successful Liberals. His great friends have been people like Winston, F.E., Horne, Geddes and Riddell. He always says there are no Liberals who would make a jolly dinner-party such as we used to have in the days of the old Coalition.[17]

By 1920 Lloyd George was advocating a virtual merger of the (coalition) Liberal and Conservative parties. The buzz-word of the moment was 'fusion'. Letters to *The Times* were proposing names for a merged party – National Democratic Party or National Reform Party. But the plan foundered at the 18 March meeting, when it received a hostile reception from Liberal ministers as well as back-bench MPs. There was solid, outraged resistance to the notion of ending the historic Liberal tradition. At a dinner at Cherkley, Beaverbrook's country house, Lloyd George recognised that his scheme was dead. According to Beaverbrook, 'He regretted the decision. Dame Margaret, who came with him, rejoiced. She never liked the Tories and never failed to say just so.'[18]

There can be little doubt that Megan shared this attitude. It was one of the occasions on which she found herself closer to her mother than to her father. She too 'never liked the Tories' (other than her personal friends). Jo Grimond, who got to know Megan in the 1950s, commented sharply (in his memoirs) that she spoke of her father as though he had always been a consistent Radical and a root-and-branch foe of Toryism. Episodes such as the secret overture to Balfour in 1910 and, still more, the 'fusion' scheme of 1920 were memories that she preferred not to call to mind.

3

It is safe to assume that when Megan went to Paris in 1919 she had no idea that Frances Stevenson was her father's mistress. Had she even suspected it, she would not have been willing to share a hotel room or even a lunch-table with Frances. Her diary refers respectfully to 'Miss Stevenson' – the tutor of childhood days, and the guide and chaperone in the foreign city.

Some time in 1920 or 1921, Megan became aware of the relationship. Perhaps she made her own observations and put two and two together; perhaps her mother decided that she was old enough to know. Olwen, who was in India at the time, wrote later: 'Probably Megan was the last of the family to become aware of the relationship between Frances and Father, and when it did dawn on her it was a shock, because she liked Frances and had enjoyed her company.'[19] This is putting it very mildly. Megan was a many-sided person: she was a clever, fun-loving girl, but also capable of intense emotional feeling and indeed suffering. Almost certainly, she was devastated by the truth she now had to confront.

She had, in a sense, regarded Frances as an elder sister, to be admired for her calmness, her systematic mind, her competence in practical matters – the qualities that Megan herself lacked. With these qualities, she had taken Frances's integrity for granted. But, if she had liked and admired Frances, she had adored her father. Inevitably, she had heard talk about his 'eye for the ladies' (clearly Olwen had no illusions), but she had not allowed herself to imagine that anything serious was involved. Therefore, she felt in the deepest sense betrayed.

Moreover, her father's unfaithfulness was a betrayal of her mother. Megan knew that her parents sometimes irritated each other and had doubtless heard them exchange angry words, but they were both strong personalities, and her mother was not a subservient 'great man's wife'. A frank, outspoken style was a prominent trait of both David and Margaret Lloyd George, and seemed to show that their marriage rested on a firm basis of mutual trust and truth-telling. Instead of that, her mother had been deceived and humiliated by her father. For Megan, this was unbearable. Sylvester, a shrewd observer, judged: 'She adored her father, but she adored her mother even more.'[20]

Since it was impossible for Megan, even now, to hate her father, she hated Frances. She persuaded herself that, without Frances, the Lloyd George marriage would have been what she had hitherto imagined it to be. As Sylvester put it: 'She blamed Frances for splitting the family.' And that was a crime, for the Lloyd George family was an organism with a bloodstream of mutual loyalty – a league against the world. Whoever injured it must be unforgivable. Megan's hatred for Frances was bitter, furious and implacable; it would last as long as they both lived.

There was another factor. Megan was the child who had since early years been closest to her father, and she was the child who was single. Dick had been married since 1917 to Roberta McAlpine, daughter of the wealthy building contractor. Olwen was married in the same year. In 1921 Gwilym married Edna Jones from Denbigh. By the mid-1920s they all had children. It was only Megan, therefore, who had no intimate attachments except to her father and mother. To varying degrees, Dick, Olwen and Gwilym all deplored their father's conduct and were hostile to Frances, but the intensity of their feelings was mitigated by the fact that they were building families of their own.

Megan's anger was compounded by frustration, for there was little she could do about the situation. It was for Margaret, if she chose, to make dramatic scenes, sever relations with her husband or demand a divorce, but she turned aside from these options. All that Megan could do was to make the lovers aware that they were being tracked and watched, and to make Frances uncomfortable by a campaign of irritations.

Over the Easter weekend of 1921, Lloyd George and Frances (travelling separately from London, as usual, to avoid observation) were guests of the millionaire Sir Philip Sassoon at his house at

Lympne, in Kent. Lord French, the wartime general, was among the house-party; discretion was not among his qualities. In May, Frances wrote in her dairy:

Lord French came to lunch today and I sat by him. Megan on his other side pricked up her ears when he referred to our meeting at Lympne at Easter. . . . She knew her father was there. She is a little too clever, but not clever enough to do her father in, which she is constantly attempting.[21]

This was soon followed by a curious little intrigue. The Crown Prince of Japan, Hirohito, was to spend a weekend at Chequers, the country house which had recently been given to the nation for the use of the Prime Minister. Megan told her mother that her presence was required, although in reality her father had made no such request. Margaret appeared at Chequers in a bad mood, for she hated formal occasions attended by royalty. The purpose of this stratagem was to make it impossible for Frances to be at Chequers, since wife and mistress never met. Frances commented: 'It is the fortunes of war and cannot be helped. D. is frightfully angry with Megan, but of course he hasn't much of a case!'[22]

By July, her patience was wearing thin:

Had a divine weekend at Chequers, though Megan rather troublesome, and turning up just before lunch on Sunday resented things being in my hands & was very cross and rude. Everyone noticed how bad-tempered she was. Her frivolous life is taking away from her charm & looks. No one seems to have any control over her or to be responsible for her comings & goings.[23]

It is a matter of judgement whether Megan's life at this time was really to be condemned as frivolous. Frances, always a serious person even when she herself was young, had high standards. Besides, there had been a change in social customs and ideas of what was acceptable. Noel Coward's plays and Evelyn Waugh's early novels remind us that the 1920s were the age of night-clubs, discordant jazz rhythms, 'boyfriends' and 'girlfriends', short skirts and long cigarette-holders – all repugnant to those who had grown up in a different period. Manners too had become more direct and informal; a mode of speech that was outspoken in 1921 would have been rude in 1911. In any case, if Megan was indeed rude, bad-tempered or frivolous, the reason may well be found in her disturbed reaction to what she now knew about her father and Frances.

A warning from Sir Robert Horne added to Frances's worries:

Horne has been telling him [Lloyd George] that people are talking about us and that we are too reckless. . . . Horne says that Megan also has been talking to people about me, and criticising her father, thinking I suppose that she would put a stop to it in that way, and not realising that all she would succeed in doing is to discredit her father. But I don't think she would stop at anything to obtain her ends. . . . I think Horne is right that we are too reckless and go about too much together, and we shall have to be more careful about that.[24]

Faced with these problems, Lloyd George decided to acquire a house where he and Frances would be safe. Chequers had a somewhat official character, and a resident staff who might be tale-bearers. If he had a house of his own, his wife would in principle have a right to go there, but there was a good chance that she would be elsewhere (presumably at Brynawelon) when he went there with Frances. In any case, Lloyd George was not fond of Chequers. It was in a valley and had no view, something that he considered essential in a country residence.

Churt is a small village between Hindhead and Farnham. The high ground on the border of Surrey and Hampshire is a geographical oddity. In the midst of the chalky soil and lush farmland typical of the south of England, one unexpectedly finds a sandy heath and a landscape of pine trees and heather. Here, in this relatively wild and sparsely populated part of the country, Lloyd George decided to acquire land and build a house.

Frances was sent to select the exact spot, ensuring that it would have a view towards the south. Although the house did not yet exist, Lloyd George had found a name for it – Bron-y-de, meaning 'Breast of the South'. Reliable though Frances was in every other respect, unfortunately she had no sense of direction. Before he could spare the time to visit the site himself, Lloyd George was committed to a property with a view to the north. When Margaret saw the house under construction, she remarked acidly that it should have been called 'Bottom of the South'.

By this time, Lloyd George was beginning to surmount his political problems. After difficult negotiations, a treaty with the Irish Free State – as it was called to avoid the challenging word 'Republic' – was signed on 5 December 1921. Some defiant Republicans refused to accept it, and Michael Collins, after signing it, told a friend that he had signed his death-warrant. He was right, for he was ambushed and killed in the ensuing civil war between Free Staters and Republicans. However, British troops were out of Ireland; no more British lads would risk death at the hands of the IRA – until 1970.

In Europe, the tide of Communism had receded. Lloyd George

decided that the time had come to bring the 'outcast nations' –
defeated Germany and Bolshevik Russia – back into the European
comity. He organised an all-European conference to meet in Genoa in
April 1922, with the aim of revising the harsher clauses of the
Versailles Treaty and inaugurating an era of settled peace.

Margaret decided that she would go to Genoa with her husband and
that Megan would go too. Presumably, this was a repetition of the
Chequers ploy, for it deprived Frances of a trip that she would have
enjoyed. But the conference made no progress: France, with Poincaré
now at the head of the government, refused to relax the crushing
burden of reparations. Writing to Frances, Lloyd George described the
scene: 'The Russians difficult – hesitating – with their judgment
warped in doctrine. The French selfish – the Germans impotent – the
Italians willing but feeble – the little countries scared'.[25] He was
missing her. The conference lasted for six weeks, and they had never
been apart for so long. In another letter he wrote:

Megan is getting very sick of this place. Worrying her mother for permission
to return to London. It won't do for you to come the moment they go. On the
other hand if you come whilst they are here Megan is quite capable of taking
advantage of that to say she insists upon returning because you are here. That
would create a first class scandal as the place is a hotbed of gossip and
rumour.[26]

However, the conference came to an abrupt end. One of its ground-
rules was that any agreements should be discussed in plenary session
and accepted by everyone present. Disregarding this convention, the
German and Russian delegates met quietly at Rapallo and signed a
treaty of friendship. The French were furious. Lloyd George was
dismayed, and had to admit that nothing further could be achieved.
Genoa might have been his last success. The future would bring him no
others.

4

There was a good reason why Megan was chafing in Genoa and
wanted to go home. She was in love, and wanted to marry the man
whom she loved. It was an episode she never spoke of in later years.
Indeed, it is difficult to be completely sure of what happened, since the
only available account derives from Olwen, who told the story to her
son Robin when he was an adult (perhaps in the 1940s), and he
repeated it to the author in 1990. Moreover, Olwen was in India at the

time of the episode and could only have been told of it in letters, or on her return. It appears, however, that Megan had allowed herself to become involved with a man of whom her parents strongly dis-approved.

The man was Stephen McKenna, a nephew of the Liberal politician Reginald McKenna. Fourteen years older than Megan, he had not fought in the war because of his (real or alleged) delicate health, but he had been employed on intelligence duties and had accompanied Balfour, then Foreign Secretary, on a political mission to the United States in 1917. He was known to the public, however, as a successful popular novelist. By 1922 he had published twelve novels, including the bestselling *Sonia* and *Confessions of a Well-Meaning Woman*. Ultimately – he lived to the age of seventy-nine – he wrote fifty novels, as well as several travel books and a biography of his uncle.

McKenna's novels were accomplished, entertaining, easy to read, and cleverly tailored to suit the taste of his readers. They now seem badly dated, but this is partly because of qualities that, at the time, were assets – his accurate observation of upper-class social habits and his ready use of contemporary slang. His plots were artificial, but ingenious and fast-moving. In his wartime novel *Ninety-Six Hours' Leave*, the hero manages within this brief period to impersonate an Italian prince, foil a sinister gang of enemy agents and win the love of a beautiful girl. The novel's opening sentence deserves immortality:

Fully conscious of a slender figure and well-fitting uniform, Lieutenant Chris Markham leaned gracefully against the counter of the telegraph office, negligently giving play to immaturely polygamous instincts.

Another character says breezily, 'I never ask a woman to understand anything' and exclaims: 'And some of them want the vote, my God!' McKenna's men were more inclined to take women than to take them seriously. He was, of course, working within the conventions of the lending-library novel of the period.

Distinctly in the style of the period, too, was McKenna's persona as a man about town. In a compilation called *Twentieth-Century Writers* he is described as 'a genial and continual host' and as a brilliant talker, ranked as the successor to Oscar Wilde.[27] He went to the opera every night in the season and entertained his friends afterwards in his chambers in Lincoln's Inn (he had been called to the Bar, but did not practise). As this portrait noted, 'he bases his stories on the sophisti-cated society that he knows best.' His life and his writings reinforced each other.

In fact, he was well equipped to attract a venturesome girl of twenty

Smyrna and Constantinople (which we now know as Istanbul) to Turkey. But since 'greater Greece' had been Lloyd George's personal cause, the Chanak débâcle was a political disaster for him.

His response to his difficulties was to call a general election for 15 November 1922. It was predictable that the coalition would win again – if it still existed. Many Tories were eager to break it up and fight as an unfettered party, but their nominal leader, Austen Chamberlain, was loyal to Lloyd George. Bonar Law had retired from active politics in 1921 because he felt unwell and was reluctant to resume the leadership. Under heavy pressure, he agreed to take up the burden if given a clean bill of health by his doctor, Sir Thomas Horder. Horder examined him and assured him that he was in good condition. Exactly one year later, he died of cancer.

When the Tory MPs met at the Carlton Club, Bonar Law accepted the leadership, and the decision to break up the coalition was taken by a two-to-one majority. Lloyd George could have stayed on as Prime Minister until after the election, but he resigned at once and Bonar Law moved into Downing Street. Megan wrote to Olwen:

We are very very busy packing to go away. . . . I have never seen such a lot of rubbish collected in all my life. The general election will be a rest after this. . . . Tada had wonderful receptions both at Manchester & Leeds and made wonderful speeches in both places. The people are absolutely with him. . . . Whatever happens Tada will be the power.[32]

Her optimism came from love and from inexperience. The people elected 345 Conservative MPs, a comfortable majority. Labour came second with 142 seats. Only 117 Liberals were elected, of whom roughly half were Lloyd George supporters and half were Asquithians. For the Lloyd George family, there was only one justification for opening the champagne: Gwilym entered the House as member for Pembroke.

Lloyd George would not have been human if he had not felt the jolt when he found himself out of office and on the opposition benches for the first time in seventeen years. No more Cabinet meetings, no more power of decision, no more appointments at his disposal. But he was still under sixty years old, and in unimpaired health and vigour. Political observers and journalists agreed that he would be back in Downing Street sooner or later. He was able to write to Frances:

We'll pull through. We are passing through the worst time – immediately after the fall. But it is nothing to Asquith's. He retired an accepted failure – without a triumph to redeem his fame. . . . Nothing can rob me of what I have accomplished.[33]

6

For Megan, he was still her adored Tada. He would be her model and her inspiration throughout her political career, and her life-story can be understood only in relation to his. Many others, however, gave him their admiring affection. He can be counted among a fairly small number of political leaders – Churchill was another – who commanded the devotion of their families and intimates, of their secretaries and office staff, and of millions who saw them from afar. Thomas Jones remembered his 'amazing courage and good temper' and also 'the genial and human warmth he created, his buoyancy, his playful humour, his driving power in the presence of which no one could work hard enough or fast enough or ably enough'. Jones added that he was 'accessible, sympathetic, cheerful in triumph and adversity alike'; and that 'he was not afflicted with envy or jealousy, the vices of lesser men.'[34]

Those who saw him in action were always impressed by his tremendous capacity for hard work, his fertility in producing fresh ideas or 'wheezes', and his resilience in the face of obstacles – but most of all by his powers of persuasion. Time and again, people who went to see him to protest against a line of policy left his room wondering how they had been bewitched into accepting it. The secret lay in his inexhaustible interest in his fellow humans, coupled with a sharp insight into their strengths or weaknesses. Explaining to Megan's friend Thelma Cazalet why he enjoyed international conferences, he said: 'I love dealing with men. The handling of men is very fascinating indeed – even more so than the handling of women.'[35] (One can imagine the roguish smile that accompanied these words.) As he once told Frances, he liked staying in hotels because of the opportunity to observe strangers and make guesses about them. His biographer, John Grigg, remarks that he had the outlook and the capacities of a novelist.

Indeed, he had many points in common with one particular novelist: Charles Dickens. Both men possessed phenomenal energy and drove themselves to spells of intensive work, sometimes culminating in a sudden collapse. Both were mercurial, revelling in triumphs and infuriated (though not depressed) by setbacks. Both had quick tempers and were capable of rashly giving offence, but had a streak of generosity and were able to shake hands after a quarrel – even to apologise. Both could put on performances that had the quality of good acting, and were excellent mimics. Both detested snobbery and privilege and liked to ridicule the aristocracy, while enjoying the fruits of wealth and the company of self-made rich men. Both were profoundly attached to a native environment (London for Dickens, Wales for Lloyd George) but also had a passion for foreign travel. Finally, each of these remarkable men got bored with his wife and had a clandestine relationship with a mistress young enough to have been a daughter.

'Living with Tada', Megan once said, 'was like living on the edge of a volcano.'[36] Some felt the danger rather than the excitement. Stanley Baldwin called Lloyd George 'a dynamic force', but this was not meant as a tribute, for he added that a dynamic force was 'a very terrible thing'. In fact, Baldwin loathed Lloyd George, and the speech in which he used these words (at the Carlton Club in 1922) was effective in injuring him.

The charge most often levelled against Lloyd George (and it is a charge regularly levelled by the English against the Welsh) was that he was too clever – that is, too clever to be trusted.[37] Even the admiring Thomas Jones, who was Welsh, admitted: 'His mind had few deep grooves and was endlessly adjustable and accommodating.'[38] An Asquithian Liberal, Sir John Simon, put it thus: 'Cleverness, ingenuity, adroitness! There has been nothing like it in human history. But after all, character is more than cleverness.'[39] This, of course, was an authentically English scale of values. Paul Cambon, French ambassador when Lloyd George became Prime Minister, explained in a dispatch to Paris:

He is a Welshman, not an Englishman. In fact, he is the reverse of an Englishman: enthusiastic, bright, quick-witted and unsettled. An Englishman never goes back on what he has once said; Lloyd George is apt to perform evolutions, his words have not always the weight of a Balfour's or a Bonar Law's.[40]

Asquith, when objecting to Lloyd George as a member of the proposed War Council in 1916, said flatly: 'He does not inspire trust.' Neville Chamberlain wrote with ponderous sarcasm: 'It is strange how our beloved Prime Minister inspires all who come near him with complete mistrust of his having any fixed principles.'[41] Sir Francis Acland, a Liberal, exclaimed: 'What a really jumpy unstable un-reliable devil L.G. is!'[42] Megan, not surprisingly, rejected the charge. In 1956, when she was shown the script of a radio portrait of her father, she told the editor at the BBC: 'There is one theme to which I take strong exception.' A contributor to the programme, J. J. Mallon, had suggested that Lloyd George was not trusted in the same way as Asquith or Churchill. Megan pointed out: 'Winston has changed his party twice and has been as distrusted . . . as any man in public life.'[43]

Perhaps the shrewdest comment was made by Thelma Cazalet:

He is extraordinarily many-sided; and that is why the average person who is only two- or three-sided himself finds it hard to understand a man who has at least a dozen different sides to his nature. He is the most sincere and insincere man I have ever met; he is the most honest and dishonest man I have ever met; he is the most grateful and ungrateful man I have ever met.[44]

David Low, 1929.                                                                                        *By courtesy of the 'Evening Standard'*

THE LLOYD GEORGE FAMILY DICTATE THEIR MEMOIRS

# CHAPTER FOUR

# Towards Anglesey

## 1

In September 1923 Megan went with her parents for a tour of the United States and Canada. The party included two secretaries, A.J. Sylvester and William Sutherland, to organise the itinerary and deal with the press, and Sarah Jones to attend to matters of personal comfort.

The USA had dealt a severe blow to Lloyd George's hopes by retreating into isolationism and refusing to join the League of Nations. Despite this repudiation of Europe, or perhaps in unconscious atonement, Americans were ready to extend a lavish welcome to 'the man who won the war'. A Prime Minister ejected from power by his own voters was crossing the Atlantic to be hailed and fêted – an occurrence to be repeated in 1946.

As the ship carrying the Lloyd Georges entered New York harbour, it was escorted by two chartered steamers – one full of Greeks, welcoming the statesman who had championed them against Turkey, and the other full of Jews, expressing their gratitude for the National Home provided for them under the British mandate in Palestine. Landing on Manhattan, the guests listened to familiar songs from a Welsh choir and shook hands with British war veterans (who had mostly emigrated because of unemployment at home). On the route to the civic reception by the mayor, 50,000 Americans lined the downtown streets.

The party went on to Montreal, with Lloyd George making fifteen speeches at stops on the way. Megan did not speak, but Sylvester recorded that, when she bowed and smiled to the crowds, 'I detected in her the same "mass appeal" which her father possessed.'[1] They arrived in Ottawa at the same time as the Prince of Wales, who was visiting the Dominion. At a ceremonial ball, the Prince opened the dancing with Megan as his partner. Then they re-entered the United States for appearances at Chicago, St Louis and eight other cities; made a pilgrimage to the birthplace of Abraham Lincoln, who had been Lloyd George's hero (or, as we might say nowadays, role model) in boyhood; and lunched at the White House with President Harding. It would be almost thirty years before Megan went to America again, as a celebrity in her own right.

Chatting with reporters at Southampton on his return to Britain, Lloyd George told them that he had been able to address a vast crowd in a sports stadium by means of a machine called an amplifier, and added: 'I also had experience of another machine. I don't think you have it here, but it is a machine which I think is going to revolutionise public speaking. It is called the Radio or Broadcasting.'[2]

Bonar Law was dead, and the new Prime Minister was Stanley Baldwin. Quite unexpectedly, he announced in October that he was embarking on a policy of protection, or import tariffs. Since Bonar Law had promised that the Tory government would make no innovations in this sphere, Baldwin was committing himself to another election. It was a blunder of the kind that he never made again; voters do not like unnecessary elections.

Since free trade was part of the traditional Liberal creed, this was a catalyst for the reunification of the Liberal Party. Lloyd George and Asquith met on 13 November, smiled and shook hands for the benefit of the press, and agreed on a statement that all Liberal candidates would be supported 'without regard to any past differences'. Liberals in general, except irreconcilable enemies such as Reginald McKenna, were glad to welcome Lloyd George. Charles Masterman, who had been a Liberal whip in 1910, said: 'When Lloyd George came back to the party, ideas came back to the party.'[3] There were plenty of ideas, clearly bearing the stamp of Lloyd George's mind rather than Asquith's, in the Liberal manifesto, which called for an ambitious programme of public works to improve the environment and provide jobs. It also called for 'political, legal and economic equality' between men and women. This implied votes for women at the age of twenty-one, and might even be taken to imply equal pay – a very bold idea at that time.

The Tories held on to 258 seats: they were still the largest party in Parliament, but had lost their absolute majority. Labour progressed to

191 seats. Working-class constituencies in South Wales, Yorkshire and Tyneside had swung decisively to Labour and would never be Liberal territory again. The Liberals emerged with 158 MPs, an improvement on the 1922 election, but it was observed that they had more than their share of good luck and won a number of 'natural' Tory seats such as Bath and Chichester. The *Guardian* commented: 'It is indeed curious how many Liberal successes there have been in places which have cathedrals, racecourses and esplanades.'

It was an awkward situation. Never before had there been three parties of comparable strength. Baldwin could not carry on because both Labour and the Liberals would oppose any protection measure. Asquith was firmly opposed to another coalition. The only remaining possibility was a Labour government, and on 22 January 1924 James Ramsay MacDonald became Britain's first Labour Prime Minister. The King wrote in his diary: 'Today twenty-three years ago dear Grandmama died. I wonder what she would have thought of a Labour government!'[4]

2

Megan learned of this historic event from a distance of five thousand miles. She had been invited by Lord Reading, the Viceroy of India, to be his guest in his palatial residence in New Delhi, just completed to Sir Edwin Lutyens's design, and she made the journey in December 1923. Reading had succeeded in quelling the civil disobedience campaign by a skilful combination of sticks for the demonstrators in the streets and carrots for Wogs[5] who might be tempted by jobs and honours. As a friend of the Lloyd George family, he had appointed Olwen's husband, Tom Carey Evans, as his personal physician, but in fact Tom was far from pleased at being obliged to accept this honorific post, which sidetracked his career; nor did he attach much value to the knighthood which went with the job. Tom and Olwen came home at the end of 1923, so Megan was taking her sister's place at the viceregal court.

The invitation may have been engineered by her parents. She had fallen in love again, apparently with another unsuitable man. He can be identified only as 'Terry'.[6] Unluckily for Megan's peace of mind, when she reached India she met a man of Terry's type – 'not nearly so good to look at but very charming,' she told Thelma.

It is amazing, darling, that wherever I go, East or West, I should be reminded of him when I am trying so very hard to forget. There seems to be a malicious fate pursuing me. Still I have made up my mind that I *will* forget him – while I am out here![7]

She had scarcely arrived in New Delhi when she was carried off for a Christmas visit to Burma (then governed as part of the Raj) with a round of lavish dinners and garden parties, varied by trips on the Irrawaddy in a state barge built to resemble a pagoda. Whether or not he had a hint from his old friend, Lord Reading was determined to fill Megan's time and offer her an endless sequence of diversions.

The Viceroy's entourage was entirely British, but she was able to meet a few Indians who enjoyed official approval, such as the Maharajah of Alwar. He was, she informed Thelma, 'the most attractive and at the same time the most civil creature you can meet – cultured, and a dreamer'. However, the cultured autocrat's main interest was in meting out death to the fauna of the jungle by methods which Megan did not find very attractive:

He goes in for the unpleasant game of 'sitting up for the panther', which consists of tying up a wretched goat in the jungle with an electric light shining full on to it – the cage, well creepered with greenery, where people of evil disposition lie up! In the course of time the panther, attracted by the bleating of goat, arrives & eats him. While he is engrossed in his supper, the creatures in the cage become active & shoot him. Of course it is the most inhuman game, but Alwar likes it. I sat up for the panther with H.E. & Alwar – you huddle up in the cage, sometimes for three quarters of an hour or more, without moving a muscle, sneezing or coughing – and after that, the panther never came. I can't say I was sorry.

When the hot weather came, Reading persuaded Megan to accompany the court to summer quarters at Simla, high up amid the spectacular beauty of the Himalayas. Lloyd George, who had assumed that she would be coming home by this time, wrote: 'My heart fell when I heard you are not expected back until the autumn. I miss your joyous little presence so much.'[8] But Megan greatly enjoyed herself at Simla, and later told Thelma that she had 'the best six months of my life'. Reading assured Dame Margaret: 'She is having the most wonderful time in Simla and seems to enjoy every minute of it. . . . She has a splendid capacity for enjoyment – it is attractive and refreshing to see her.'[9] Megan took a leading part in a production by the Simla Amateur Dramatic Society, 'which meant a lot of real hard work'. But the highlight of the season was the Feast of Lanterns:

All guests wore Chinese costumes, the ballroom was hung with scarlet, the hall with bright blue; the monsoon mist was pierced with rows of Chinese lanterns along the verandah. A seven-foot dragon with motor-lamp eyes made its appearance, and out of it came a pretty girl who did a Chinese dance. Then Miss Megan Lloyd George in Burmese garb entered in a rickshaw, pulled by Miss Fitzroy [Lady Reading's secretary] and another young lady.[10]

After returning to New Delhi, Megan prolonged her stay again to accompany Lord and Lady Reading on a leisurely visit to Kashmir, so that she spent a whole year in India. Ursula Thorpe (herself married by now) thought that she was having a romance with a young man on the Viceroy's staff, but there is nothing in Megan's letters to Thelma to bear this out. If she flirted with anyone, it may have been with the Viceroy himself, despite the age gap of forty-two years. We recall his eagerness for her company in Paris, and the schoolgirl was now a young woman of twenty-two. Sylvester, for one, suspected that there was 'something between them'.[11] Lady Reading was in delicate health and in the care of a nurse, while Lord Reading was in good shape. In 1930 she died, and at the age of seventy he married his secretary. However, it is unlikely that he offered Megan anything more than avuncular compliments and goodnight kisses.

She came home to find the Tories back in power and the Liberals at a low ebb. Frances Stevenson wrote of this period: 'Although Lloyd George would willingly have helped the Labour government had the Liberals been given any encouragement to do so, he found that Ramsay MacDonald's vanity made any kind of co-operation difficult.'[12] Lloyd George himself put it more strongly, accusing MacDonald of behaving 'like a jealous, vain, suspicious, ill-tempered actress of the second rank'.[13] In a speech to his constituents, he complained:

Liberals are to be the oxen to drag Labour over the rough roads of Parliament for two or three years, and at the end of the journey, when there is no further use for them, they are to be slaughtered. That is the Labour idea of co-operation.[14]

He had also come to the conclusion that the traditional British electoral system, acceptable so long as there were only two parties, was blatantly unfair now that there were three. In 1923 an article in the Liberal Year Book had stated:

The reform of our method of electing MPs has become a practical necessity. . . . There can be little confidence in a system which places the affairs of the country in the hands of men who are selected by one-third of the voters against the declared wishes of the other two-thirds.[15]

The Labour government fell in October 1924. The Communist paper *Worker's Weekly* had published an appeal to soldiers not to fire on striking and demonstrating workers; the editor was charged under the Incitement to Mutiny Act, but the Attorney-General withdrew the prosecution. Raising a hue and cry over this surrender to Bolshevism, the Tories put down a vote of censure and the Liberals supported it. The ensuing election was held in an atmosphere of hysteria, intensified when the *Daily Mail* published a letter (now known to be a forgery) allegedly written by Grigori Zinoviev, general secretary of the Communist International, instructing British Communists to prepare for an armed insurrection. The scare was effective. The Tories had a landslide victory, winning 415 seats. Labour, losing ground for the first time, went down to 152. The Liberals suffered a disaster, which they could legitimately blame on the electoral system. Polling almost 3 million votes out of 16 million, they won only 39 seats.[16] Among the defeated Liberals was Gwilym Lloyd George. Asquith also lost his seat, and went to the House of Lords as Earl of Oxford. He still refused to retire as party leader, though he was now seventy-two years old, but Lloyd George was the main Liberal spokesman in the Commons.

While the Tories could count on a majority of middle-class voters and Labour had a bedrock of support in the working class, the Liberal forces were an ill-assorted mixture of small businessmen, struggling farmers, intellectuals, professionals and Nonconformist congregations. Eighteen of the Liberal constituencies (almost half) were in Scotland or Wales. To make matters worse, Liberals of progressive outlook were going over to the Labour Party. Well-known Liberals who went Labour in the 1920s included Dr Christopher Addison, Sir Charles Trevelyan, William Wedgwood Benn, Arthur Ponsonby and Josiah Wedgwood.

Both politically and personally, 1925 was an unhappy year for the Lloyd Georges. While Lloyd George was on a visit to Italy, Megan had to undergo an emergency operation for appendicitis. It recalled memories of the death of another beloved daughter, Mair, in 1907. Cancelling an appointment with Mussolini, Lloyd George cut short his trip. Sylvester wrote: 'Lloyd George was terribly upset and worried. He took the next train back to London, impatient to be at his favourite daughter's bedside.'[17] Thus Mussolini – unlike Hitler, as we shall see – never had an opportunity to enlist Lloyd George as a sympathiser.

Sir Thomas Carey Evans had found a good position at Hammersmith Hospital. He rose to be medical superintendent and took a key part in making it a leading research hospital with a postgraduate

medical school. Dick Lloyd George was working for a civil engineering company and also had a small farm in Essex. A few years later, he
decided to concentrate on farming and, with the aid of money from his
wife's family, became the owner of West Hill Farm at Brandeston,
Suffolk. Gwilym was active in trying to rebuild the Liberal Party and
regain his seat in Pembroke. Megan, too, was beginning to make
appearances at party rallies and bazaars, to shake hands and
encourage the faithful – often accompanying her father, but sometimes with her mother if the occasion was in Wales, and sometimes on
her own. The family presented an attractive public face, with husband,
wife, son and daughter fighting to keep the good old cause alive. A
note from Margaret to Megan catches the intimacy: 'Don't let Tada
speak without a hat. If he takes if off put it on. I have done it often and
the crowd enjoy it so much.'[18]

The fragile alliance between Lloyd George and Asquith broke down
in 1926. In the unprecedented crisis of the General Strike, Asquith
whole-heartedly supported the government and even wrote a contribution to the British Gazette, the emergency official paper edited by
Churchill, to encourage volunteer strike-breakers in 'their splendid
struggle against the coercion of a new dictatorship'.[19] Lloyd George,
though he agreed that essential services must be maintained, urged
negotiations to end the strike on compromise terms. Asquith called a
meeting of the Liberal front bench to censure Lloyd George. As
Malcolm Thomson, one of Lloyd George's staff, put it: 'The full
bitterness of the Asquithians was loosed upon L.G. Their hatred of
him was unmasked now that they thought the opportunity had come
to ruin him once and for all.'[20]

But as in 1916, Asquith was overplaying his hand. Almost all active
Liberals were appalled by the prospect of another split, and blamed
him for it. On 14 October he was persuaded to resign from the
leadership. At long last, Lloyd George was the undisputed leader of the
party which he had joined forty years ago.

3

Lloyd George's fluency with the pen had saved him from poverty in the
1890s; in the 1920s it brought him wealth. The Daily Chronicle,
which had been bought by the Lloyd George Fund, was his mouth-
piece, and he accepted £10,000 to write thirty articles a year for it,
although the Daily Mail offered him £15,000.[21] For fortnightly
articles to be syndicated in America by the United Press, he earned

another £30,000 a year. Frances Stevenson, no longer on the Civil Service payroll, acted as his literary agent and took ten per cent of his income from these sources, an arrangement which she found amply satisfactory. Furthermore, Lloyd George had a pension of £2000 as a former Prime Minister, and Andrew Carnegie had settled a £2000 annuity on him as a reward for winning the war. For small change, he had his salary of £400 as an MP. The purchasing power of the pound was about fifteen times what it is today, and the standard rate of income tax was 15 per cent.

He used a considerable part of the money for the development of the 700-acre estate surrounding his house at Churt. One visitor wrote:

He loves to show visitors the productive fields which he has reclaimed from the rough, stony heather-hills of Churt. He is intensely proud of them; wide, well-kept tracts of land that had never been cultivated since the beginning of time until he took them in hand.[22]

His plan was to create a fruit farm, but one essential appeared to be absolutely lacking – water. His nephew recalled:

One consulting engineer after another told him that there was no available supply. . . . He consulted a lady water-diviner and, after walking over the scrubland, she found one spot only where the hazel-twig she held was twisted in her hands by an irresistible, unseen force. . . . He then engaged contractors with the latest boring equipment to search for water, but on more than one occasion as they were boring deeper and deeper, finding no water, the contractors advised him to give up. . . . All of a sudden the water gushed out with such force that he was able to irrigate many acres with it.[23]

According to Lloyd George, they had tapped an underground river coming from Wales. His methods of land reclamation were always ingenious. He bought pigs and let them loose to grub up the roots of bracken and unwanted shrubs. He planted lupins to add nitrogen, then ploughed them in. Another visitor recorded:

He would explain that he managed to grow his extraordinary crop of Cox's Orange Pippins in the sandy soil of Surrey because he had bought so many tons of horse manure from Aldershot. 'The only use I have ever found for cavalry,' he said.[24]

Bringing the farm into existence was expensive, and for several years it was a money-loser, but eventually it was profitable. Employing a labour force of eighty men, Lloyd George had joined the class he had so often denounced: he was a landowner. He produced a first-rate crop of apples and also soft fruit, opened a shop on the road to

Farnham and even marketed the fruit in London. Later, he made a success of beekeeping. With an eye to what we may well call Radical chic, the honey was sold in pots labelled: 'From the apiary of the Rt Hon. David Lloyd George, OM, MP'.

Megan, since her return from India, was living at her father's London residence, a handsome Regency house at 2 Addison Road, Kensington. She also spent a good deal of time at Brynawelon, which she regarded as her real home. Lloyd George, knowing that she was a keen gardener, tried to interest her in the estate at Churt, but she was not often there. It was Frances's territory.

Lloyd George's way of life at this time is best described as that of a bigamist, rather than merely an unfaithful husband. Frances still had a London flat, but she also had a bedroom at Bron-y-de. Since she was his secretary and literary agent, and since other members of his staff, such as Sylvester, also stayed overnight, it is not exactly true to say that Lloyd George 'lived openly with his mistress'.[25] Indeed, the relationship was still known to remarkably few people. Nevertheless, Bron-y-de was emphatically Lloyd George's house, while Brynawelon was Margaret's. Margaret too had a bedroom in the house at Churt – there were occasions when her arrival obliged Frances to make a hasty exit by the back door – but she used it sparingly.

The tense situation reached explosion-point in 1926. As Frances told the story in her memoirs:

His family decided to tackle him on his relations with me. A joint letter was written, signed by his wife and all his children, demanding that I should be removed from his secretariat. . . . [He] wrote a terrible letter to Dame Margaret, upbraiding her and the children for attacking him and offering a divorce, which he said he would welcome.[26]

Lloyd George did indeed write a decidedly terrible letter:

It appears that my children are following the example of the children of Noah by exposing their father's nakedness to the world. But his children have gone down the ages as first class skunks for turning on the old man. . . . I must tell you how deeply pained I am to learn that you and *Megan* [underlined] have turned against me.[27]

However, the letter contains no offer of divorce, and it is hard to believe that Lloyd George – who had several times told Frances that he would not imperil his career for her sake – could have welcomed, or even risked, a divorce just when the leadership of the Liberal Party was within his grasp. Sylvester, speaking in 1974 to Colin Cross, who was editing his diaries, cast doubt on Frances's account. Cross recorded: 'It is Sylvester's firm belief that no such correspondence ever took place, although he allows that Lloyd George might have caused Miss Stevenson to think it had.'[28] The text of the 'terrible' letter was published in the collection of his letters to *Frances*, so the truth may well be that it was shown to her and never actually sent to Margaret. When it came to tactical skill, none of Lloyd George's women was ever a match for him.

4

Photographs of Megan in her twenties show a young woman with an alert expression, a ready smile, gleaming brown hair cut short in the style of the period and a well-proportioned figure. Her eyes were blue, always a striking feature in combination with dark hair, although some accounts described them as grey. She was never considered beautiful: by strict standards, her face was too broad, her nose too small and her mouth too wide. But these irregularities – especially the perky uptilted nose – added to her charm. If she was a *jolie laide*, there was no doubt about the *jolie* part of the phrase. It was the mobility of her features, the reflection of an unquenchable inner vivacity, that everyone remembered. Both men and women found her immensely attractive in the precise sense of possessing the power to attract. Emlyn Williams (who was beginning his stage career, and had come across quite a number of pretty or even beautiful girls) judged her to be 'the most attractive girl I had ever seen'.[29]

Megan's height was about five feet two inches. She made jokes about her modest stature; once, visiting a Welsh town as an MP, she told an audience: 'I came here with my father when I was a tiny mite, and I'm not much bigger now.' But she was also sensitive on the subject, and did not like other people to remark on it. Certainly she would have wished to be taller, and felt that in political life it would have added to her dignity and helped her to be taken seriously. Geoffrey Crawshay, with whom she had an affectionate relationship at this time, was exceptionally tall; so was Osbert Peake, a Tory MP with whom she was friendly in the early 1930s. (She jokingly referred to Peake as 'my young man', but there was no serious attachment.) It may be that proximity to these very tall men, for instance on the tennis court or the dance floor, made her feel diminutive. However, it should also be remembered that average heights were less than they are now, and Megan would have come face to face with men – particularly the

Welsh, and particularly the undernourished poor – who were not much taller than she was.

She liked to dress well, chose her clothes carefully, and had natural good taste. Her father had told her that blue was the best colour for her, and she favoured it on most occasions. Some profiles and gossip paragraphs described her as the best-dressed woman in the House of Commons (there may not have been much competition). When going to the theatre or the ballet, she took considerable care over her appearance. But she never overdressed, and wore little jewellery.

She did not suffer from shyness, assumed that people were going to like her, and was consequently popular. Her friends, especially those who went to Criccieth in the summer, were caught up in a tireless, high-spirited round of party games and charades, practical jokes and hoaxes, picnics, outings by car or bicycle, tennis competitions – always with Megan playing a central part. 'She could always make a party go,' Ursula Thorpe recalled.[30]

The links between the three girls who had known one another since 1919 – Megan, Ursula and Thelma – were as close as ever, but Megan also had a gift for making friendships with men. Some of the young men who belonged to her circle were Geoffrey Crawshay, a keen young Liberal and a member of the family that had started the first ironworks at Merthyr Tydfil; Geoffrey Shakespeare, who had been one of her father's staff at Downing Street and then an MP; David Keir, a journalist on the *Daily Chronicle*; Bill Elverston, of the firm of solicitors which handled the legal affairs of the Lloyd George family; John William Morris ('John Willy' to the group), a young barrister from the Criccieth neighbourhood; and Selwyn Lloyd, another barrister, who lived in Liverpool but was Welsh by family background. He and his parents had been spending holidays at Criccieth for years and had got to know the Lloyd Georges. Belonging to the younger generation, Selwyn was, in the words of his biographer, 'thrown very much into the company of Megan'.[31] She spoke for him when he contested Macclesfield as a Liberal in 1929, and was very disappointed when he subsequently became a Tory.

Inevitably, there was much speculation about whether Megan would marry one of these young men and, if so, which. Selwyn Lloyd was strongly tipped by the press, but it seems that he 'never became emotionally involved with Megan'.[32] Once, the over-enthusiastic chairman of a Liberal rally introduced him as her fiancé. 'She was very amused,' Selwyn wrote to his parents. One wonders whether she was.

John Morris, however, was ardently in love with her and proposed to her persistently, but without success. 'Oh, he's so silly,' Megan said when Olwen asked how he ranked as a suitor.[33] Bill Elverston, members of the family recall, was another hopeful wooer. But Megan, unlike many young women who were her contemporaries, had no need to marry for the sake of being married, nor to accept a man who was merely suitable or likeable. She was hoping for a career in public life, she had a home with which she was content, and she had enough money; dependence on a husband was unnecessary. She could take the line that she would only marry a man whom she genuinely loved.

By her mid-twenties, Megan was no longer the girl who had 'fallen for' (to adopt the phraseology of the period) Stephen McKenna and Terry. She may have decided that she had been rather foolish, that these youthful passions had been superficial, and that her parents had been right, at least about Stephen. A few years older, she no longer fell in love easily.

The one man whom she might have married was Geoffrey Crawshay. Ursula's testimony is that Megan was deeply in love with him,[34] and when Crawshay died in 1954 Philip Noel-Baker wrote to her: 'He was the only one I thought good enough to love you, and the man I think who loved you as you ought to be loved. And I know you loved him, and loved to be with him.'[35] Nevertheless, they did not marry. It seems probable (there is no conclusive evidence) that Megan and Geoffrey discussed their relationship seriously and decided that it would not be advisable to spend their lives together – for one reason or another, it would not work. They remained friends. He became a prominent figure in Welsh affairs, holding various official positions, so they met from time to time and Megan occasionally stayed at his house near Abergavenny.

Remarkably, none of these men married anyone else when it became clear that they were not going to marry her. Bill Elverston-Trickett (he added to his name as the condition of a legacy) was ultimately married to the widow of a friend when he was over seventy. Stephen McKenna, John Morris and Geoffrey Crawshay died as bachelors. Perhaps this was no more than coincidence, but it is a tempting speculation that they found no substitute for Megan.

In later years, various answers were found to the question why Megan remained unmarried. It was often said that she was 'married to politics'; yet it is easy to think of women who found political activity perfectly compatible with marriage. Another explanation was that she did not want to lose the Lloyd George name. However, Barbara Castle and Margaret Thatcher did not mind pursuing a political career with a name acquired by marriage, and in any case Megan could have kept her maiden name for political purposes, as Jennie Lee did.

The most widely accepted theory was that Megan could not find a man whom she could love and admire as she loved and admired her father. Naturally, this theory found favour in the Lloyd George family. Her uncle said: 'Lovely girl Megan, but she'll never marry. Whoever gets her down the aisle has got to be as tip-top as her Tada, and where is *he* to come from?'[36] Lloyd George himself stated that 'she had made up her mind to celibacy when she took up a political career.'[37] When Megan was almost thirty, he said: 'She would never allow anybody to dominate her now'[38] – an even more revealing remark.

It is true that Megan's relationship with her father was profoundly emotional. Indeed, she was aware of this herself. She once told John Grigg, Lloyd George's biographer, that she had tried to get on to good terms with Violet Bonham Carter but found it impossible because of Violet's devotion to the memory of her father, Asquith. 'If she'd only known,' Megan said to Grigg, 'nobody could sympathise more than I could.'[39] The implication was that both these daughters were incurably fixated on their fathers.

It does not follow, however, that Megan was so hopelessly 'in love with her father' as to be incapable of loving – or marrying – any other man. The judgement is really a projection back from the fact that she did not marry. The real answer to the question is probably the simple one: that Megan, sadly, never found a man whom she felt able to marry – and who was willing to marry her.

## 5

Now that he was in command, Lloyd George gave the Liberal Party a thorough overhaul. An organisation committee came into existence, headed by Colonel Thomas F. Tweed, to revitalise the party in the constituencies; and a campaign department was created to popularise Liberal policies.

The central idea of these policies was the modernisation of Britain. Many anxious people were beginning to diagnose the failure to innovate as the British disease. As Lloyd George saw it, a programme of practical improvements would be compared favourably with the somnolent indifference of Toryism and the doctrinaire theories of Socialism. He recruited a little army of economists, statisticians and experts in various fields, including William Beveridge, Walter Layton and J.M. Keynes. Discussions under his chairmanship in the big library at Bron-y-de led to the production of a series of book-length documents, with an authoritative survey of existing conditions, a long list of recommendations and a precise costing. Nowadays we are accustomed to political parties undertaking (or claiming to undertake) this kind of project, but in the 1920s it was revolutionary.

The first report to be published was entitled *The Land and the Nation* and was known as the Green Book. It proposed that all land should be vested in state ownership, with security of tenure for renting farmers and generous grants or loans for reclamation of land that had gone out of cultivation (two million acres since 1918). Next came the urban companion-piece, *Towns and the Land*, or the Brown Book. It recommended powers for local authorities to acquire land for housing at fixed prices, a modernised town-planning system and leasehold reform. The final volume was *Britain's Industrial Future*, or the Yellow Book, which presented a plan for investment in factories, ports, and road and rail transport. H. N. Brailsford, a Labour left-winger, commented that any Socialist 'would secretly rejoice if the whole of this wide programme could be realised'.[40]

In the run-up to the next election, due in October 1929 at the latest, Lloyd George decided to concentrate on the issue of unemployment. There had been a million unemployed (or 10 per cent of the labour force) throughout the decade, and the numbers had risen by another 250,000 since the General Strike, mainly through pit closures. This level of unemployment, Lloyd George declared was 'a national evil, a national canker, a national peril'. A booklet entitled *We Can Conquer Unemployment* was produced in March 1929 and widely sold at the popular price of sixpence. It set out detailed plans for the provision of thousands of jobs in house-building, telephone extension and rural electrification. There would also be a new network of broad, fast National Roads (equivalent to motorways). Thus unemployment would be brought down within a year to 'normal levels'. Nor would there be any increased taxation to finance the projects. The money would be found by cutting expenditure on armaments (or, in Lloyd George's words, 'the mechanism of human slaughter').

The Baldwin government had taken one step of which Lloyd George approved. A new Franchise Bill, introduced in 1928, gave women the right to vote at the age of twenty-one, instead of thirty as hitherto. About five million young women would benefit, and women voters would outnumber the men by a margin of 1,600,000. This was greeted with mixed feelings on the Left; it was generally believed (though in the absence of modern opinion surveys, this piece of political folk-wisdom was never proved) that women voted Tory more heavily than men. A Moscow commentary denounced 'the introduction of a new group of five million women voters, for the most part reactionary', as a

Tory plot. Indeed, it may be that Baldwin thought he was making an advantageous move.

Be this as it may, the reform was good news for Megan. She had begun to involve herself seriously in politics and to speak on Liberal platforms. In December 1927 she addressed a meeting at Edinburgh and a Scottish Liberal sent her father an enthusiastic telegram:

Megans speech a great success everybody delighted worth thousands of votes if she will continue to speak in public.

It was still possible, however, that she would limit herself to helping her father, speaking in support of Liberal candidates (Olwen also did some of this) and activity with the Young Liberals. Instead, she decided to become a full-time politician. Probably 'decided' is the wrong word; ever since childhood, she had been moving towards this role.

The motives that impel men and women to enter politics are always mixed – intellectual conviction, altruistic zeal, enjoyment of prominence and popularity, ambition. Only the proportions vary from one individual to another. Megan – the natural orator and natural actress – undoubtedly relished the pleasures of politics. There was some truth in an acid comment made by Frances Stevenson after Megan became an MP: 'It satisfied her innate appetite, which she has had ever since she was a small child, for appearing all the time as it were upon a stage, and being the centre of attraction.'[41] Yet we should give at least equal weight to her sincere concern with problems such as unemployment and with the shocking poverty that she began to observe as she travelled to attend meetings in the cities and the countryside of England, Wales and Scotland. She would have said that she was going into politics to represent and help the powerless and the inarticulate; and this was true.

There were still only eight women in the House of Commons; progress had been slow since 1918. But there was nothing like starting young. Commenting on the Franchise Bill, the *Holyhead Mail* judged: 'Undoubtedly it offers a new career to the sex, because a woman can make £400 a year go farther than a man.' The *Holyhead Mail*, a firmly Liberal weekly paper, was published in Anglesey, and this was the constituency on which Megan fixed her hopes. It was one of the safest Liberal seats in the country, with a majority of over 5000 even at the disastrous 1924 election. Sir Robert Thomas, Liberal MP since 1923, had announced that he would not stand again – not because of age or ill-health, but because he had financial problems. He was a Lloyd George Liberal with no taint of Asquithism, so he could be expected to like the idea of leaving the constituency to an heir – or heiress – to the Lloyd George tradition.

The island of Anglesey (Môn in Welsh, Mona in romantic pseudo-Latin) holds a special place in Welsh history and in the Welsh imagination. Although the land is now open and well cultivated, in the past it was covered in dense forest and was a stronghold of the Druids with their mysterious rites. For bards and patriots, the island is Môn Mam Cymru, 'the mother of Wales'. In her campaign speeches, Megan (coached by her father, probably) recalled that the Tudor dynasty originated in Anglesey and evoked the memory of Owen Gwynedd, who is supposed by some to have discovered America three hundred years before Columbus.

Even today, Anglesey makes an unmistakable impression of tranquillity and seclusion – of being a place on its own. As one walks about its countryside, which is flat or gently undulating, there is never a spot from which one cannot gaze at the formidable mountains of the Snowdonia range across the Menai Straits. It is always a striking view, and with the addition of winter snow and a blue sky it is spectacular. These mountains seem to form a protective barrier, shielding the island from the influences of the outer world. In every other direction, Anglesey is guarded by the encircling sea.

In 1929 Anglesey was an island of farmers and farm workers devoid of industry. Other than the land and the sea, the railway and the Holyhead docks offered the only employment. Virtually the whole population was Welsh and Welsh-speaking, except for a small colony of Irish people at Holyhead. Even the anglicised communities and the anglicised landlord class of Caernarvonshire had no counterparts on the island; English settlers and English second homes were still unthought of. After fighting her first election campaign, Megan told a *Sunday Express* interviewer: 'The people are, of course, bilingual but you don't really get at the villages unless you speak in Welsh.'

To the visitor (not that there were many visitors) Anglesey might have appeared idyllic. In reality, it was a place of anxiety and often of sadness. Unemployment was always well above the national average, and would have been higher but for a tradition among the young men of going off as merchant seamen. Living standards were low and real poverty was common; old people today can remember going to school barefoot. Scores of cottages were in bad repair. Doctors had to cope with a heavy incidence of diseases such as tuberculosis and diptheria, and the only general hospital was across the Menai Straits at Bangor.

In these conditions, it is not surprising that Tory prospects in Anglesey were poor. Labour had fairly substantial support and considering how many Liberal strongholds had fallen to Labour since 1918, caused the Liberals some worry. But the Liberal Party was active

and thriving, with branches in almost every village, a youth organisation, a woman's organisation and over a thousand paid-up party
members.

Megan threw her hat into the ring in March 1928, as soon as the
Franchise Bill was tabled and before it became law. She had, of course,
strong backing from both her parents. Lloyd George wrote to
Margaret on 30 March: 'We must do our best for the fascinating little
monkey. She is excelling [*sic*] my highest expectations.'[42] It was
Margaret who was best placed to help Megan, partly because Lloyd
George was busy enough as party leader, but also because of the
popularity she had won in Wales by her work for social welfare and
her impressive network of contacts and friendships. When Megan
spoke at a meeting, Margaret generally accompanied her, said a few
gracious words and chatted over the tea and cakes. In practice, she was
her daughter's campaign manager.

The campaign for the selection was, indeed, something very like an
election campaign, or perhaps it should be compared to an American
primary. As well as addressing crowded meetings, Megan canvassed
hundreds of Liberals in their homes. At the outset, eight contestants
were listed in the *Holyhead Mail*. The more serious contenders were
Ellis W. Roberts, a barrister, and a Colonel Williams. Megan's assets
were her youth and vitality, her charm when the party members met
her face to face, and the expectation that she might go a long way in
politics; most constituencies like the idea of an MP who is a national
figure. On the other hand, she was politically inexperienced and had
not, for instance, held a position in local government; there was some
resistance to a claim apparently based on right of inheritance
(generally exercised by the sons of Tory grandees); and, although her
birthplace was in nearby Caernarvonshire, the inhabitants of literally
insular Anglesey could regard her as an outsider. There was another
problem too. Liberals with old-fashioned ideas were not keen on a
candidate of the female sex, especially 'a chit of a girl'.

Megan's strategy was to capitalise openly on her potential handicaps – her youth and her sex – by basing her campaign on the young
people and the women. She had just been elected to the useful position
of president of the North Wales Federation of Young Liberals, and the
Young Liberals of Anglesey gave her their enthusiastic support. Her
first meeting, on 19 March, was with the Women's Liberal Federation
of Holyhead. She asserted that women 'had earned the right to hold a
greater response in the councils of the nation', and asked why Wales,
unlike England and Scotland, had no women MPs. The Women's
Federation decided unanimously to nominate her. A week later,

speaking at Newborough, she again stood up for the women and told the audience that the wisest politician of all time was Queen Elizabeth: 'She outwitted every statesman and diplomat she encountered, and of all Tudor monarchs she was the most liberal-minded – and don't forget her ancestors came from Anglesey.'[43]

Through April and May, the campaign forged ahead. Megan had two heavyweight supporters: one was Sir Robert Thomas, who stated publicly that he would give her 'all the assistance in my power', and the other was the Reverend H. D. Hughes, Methodist minister in Holyhead, who was the most influential figure among Anglesey's Nonconformists. On the eve of the selection meeting, her father was able to write: 'It seems to be a cert.'

Just at this moment, her chances were almost wrecked. The gossip columnist of the *Daily Mail* reported that Megan had been among the guests at a 'pyjama bottle party'. For the good folk of Anglesey, a pyjama party was shocking and a bottle party was wicked, but a combination of the two was unspeakable. Urgent pressure elicited a denial:

By an unfortunate mistake, for which I apologise, I was informed that Miss Megan Lloyd George was at the pyjama bottle party given by the Hon. David Tennant last week. . . . Few young women of Miss Megan Lloyd George's age lead such a strenuous political life with so little relaxation.[44]

The chairman of the Anglesey Liberals, William Jones, said that he had been deeply grieved by the report but was now sure that it was untrue. The bandwagon was on the road again.

There were fireworks, however, at the selection meeting on 24 May. Colonel Williams (who made the mistake of speaking in English) accused Megan's supporters of 'unfair tactics', alleging that they had created new party branches consisting entirely of people who promised to vote for her. The chairman interrupted to say that the new branches were part of the natural and praiseworthy growth of the party, and when Williams pressed on he met cries of 'Shame!' and 'Withdraw!' Losing his cool completely, the colonel shouted: 'The first farmer in the world had tenure conditionally, and when the condition was violated he was turned out of the Garden of Eden. It was owing to a woman. Let me tell you she was a young woman too.'[45] When the vote was taken, there were 325 votes for Megan, 285 for Ellis Roberts, and only 14 for Williams. He walked out in a huff and threatened to stand as an Independent Liberal, but this threat was never put into effect.

When the good news reached Churt, Lloyd George dashed off a

rapturous note of congratulations: 'You two Megs did it all your-selves. . . . Three weeks ago you would have been beaten. A month ago you had no chance. Hallelujah! Hallelujee!'[46]

Megan's position as parliamentary candidate made her a new star in the Liberal firmament. In the remaining months of 1928, she was invited to speak at Caerphilly (in support of another woman candi-date), Carmarthen, Halifax, Dundee, Hull, Runcorn, Rochdale, Harrow, Letchworth, Mill Hill and Guildford. At the Carmarthen meeting, she made a point which, just ten years after the end of a devastating war, must have earned heartfelt applause:

Suppose that by common consent of all the nations of the world their armed forces should be reduced to police level, and international law was accepted by all the nations, that would surely be the greatest security against war.[47]

A little less than thirty years later, international law would again be Megan's theme at Carmarthen.


6


Returning in February 1929 from a Mediterranean holiday, Megan went to Brynawelon to prepare for a round of meetings in Anglesey. The day of the first meeting, at Beaumaris, brought a blizzard which was ferocious even by North Wales standards, halting all trains and making the roads almost impassable. Megan, or rather her driver,[48] battled on, but was halted by a snowdrift on the outskirts of the town. Determined to reach the hall, she walked the rest of the way. 'Here I am, home again, ready for anybody and everything,' she announced cheerfully. She was ready in spirit, no doubt, but she had a frostbitten hand and appeared at the other meetings with it bandaged, enhancing her reputation for pluckiness.

In the House of Commons, the year began with tributes to famous men who had recently died – the Earl of Oxford and Field-Marshal Haig. Lloyd George could not avoid pronouncing a conventional eulogy of Asquith, but was not obliged to say anything about Haig.

Baldwin set the election day for 30 May. Because of the three-cornered contest, the possibility of a Liberal revival and the unpredict-able effects of the electoral system, it was hard to foresee the outcome but likely that no party would have an overall majority. With negotiations for a possible coalition in mind, Lloyd George had said at his party conference: 'There is a great and fertile territory common to men of progressive minds in all parties which they could agree to cultivate together.'[49] However, once the campaign began he was bound to tell the voters that his target was a Liberal majority.

One special hope was close to his heart: a victory for Megan in Anglesey. The Anglesey Liberals had chosen John Bellis, a cashier at Holyhead docks, to be her agent. Leaving nothing to chance, Lloyd George invited him to spend a week at Churt and cross-examined him on his knowledge of electioneering techniques. Bellis was, in fact, an organiser of outstanding ability. He had taken charge of the National Eisteddfod when it was held in Anglesey in 1927, chartered a ship to bring Welsh emigrants to their homeland from Patagonia and actually ended up with a profit. He and Megan became firm friends, and worked as a team in five elections from 1929 to 1950.

By general agreement, the Liberals deserved top marks in the 1929 campaign both for organisation and for policy. Tweed's organisation committee worked efficiently and, since there was now no distinction between the Lloyd George Fund and the party finances, plenty of money was available. A former advertising manager of *The Times* was enlisted to run the Liberal poster and advertising campaign. According to Gordon West, one of the team at party headquarters, 'it was extraordinarily well done and was admitted to have been the most successful and forcible propaganda of the election.' The campaign department even had the ingenious idea of producing a romantic novelette designed to appeal to those five million young women, with a Liberal heroine who preserved her virtue despite the lures of villainous Tory and Socialist seducers. A delighted (male) candidate declared that it was 'just the stuff for mill-girl voters'. Much to the annoyance of the professionals, the Women's Liberal Federation complained that it 'insulted the intelligence of women voters' and demanded its withdrawal. The campaign department agreed to withdraw it, but took action only after thousands of copies had gone round the country.[50]

In the realm of propaganda, a significant factor was that 1929 was Britain's first radio election. Ownership of wireless sets had spread in the 1920s as television was to spread in the 1950s, and covered all but the poorest homes. The BBC allocated time on an equal basis to the three parties, with provision for special broadcasts by and for women. Dame Caroline Bridgeman spoke for the Tories, Margaret Bondfield for Labour, and Megan for the Liberals; it was her first use of a medium in which she became proficient. Concentrating on the subject of unemployment, she said:

Think what it means! A million out of work. A great proportion of them young men and women who are at the height of their physical power and

strength. Young men condemned through no fault of their own to idleness –
their physique impaired and their morale injured.

She did not forget to add: 'Unemployment hits the women hardest of
all, for theirs is the care and worry of keeping a home together.'

Unemployment indeed, was the central theme of the Liberal
campaign. The promise, stated by Lloyd George in a keynote speech to
candidates, was that a Liberal government would be 'ready with
schemes of work which we can put immediately into operation'.
Neither Baldwin nor MacDonald could claim as much. Baldwin
argued that prosperity depended on exports and cited the sale of
British bicycles in Africa – an achievement dismissed by Lloyd George
as 'a consignment of push-bikes for enterprising niggers'. MacDonald
could do no better than to sneer at Lloyd George as 'the most
magnificent showman in public life'.

As she went round Anglesey, Megan explained how the Liberal
plans would meet the needs of the island: better roads, electricity
supply for isolated farms, new houses to replace crumbling hovels. She
stressed the prediction made by Keynes, the part-author of the Yellow
Book, that job-creation would enlarge purchasing power and thus
pave the way to more job-creation (a new idea in 1929). In a Holyhead
speech she said that it was 'like throwing a stone into pool – the circle
becomes wider and wider all the time.' At her eve-of-poll rally, she
summed up:

The biggest question of the moment is the conquest of unemployment. Only
the Liberal Party has a policy. Is the nation content to allow things to drift
while the unemployed stand idle and wives and little children suffer hopeless
privation, or is it desirous of putting in hand practical and effective measures
to deal with this evil?

With his usual inexhaustible energy, Lloyd George toured Britain
from Newcastle to Plymouth, making detours to speak for Megan in
Anglesey and Gwilym in Pembrokeshire. Megan's own constituency
kept her busy enough. The voters were scattered among four towns –
Holyhead, Beaumaris, Amlwch and Llangefni – a couple of dozen
villages and countless small farms. The experience of 'meeting the
people' was stimulating, but it was also something of a shock. She had
always been aware of poverty and social inequality, but they had been
abstract conceptions. Now she was directly confronted with men and
women lined and worn in middle age, undernourished children, damp
homes and leaking roofs, beds shared by three or four bodies. It was a
far cry from 10 Downing Street, 2 Addison Road, the Hotel Majestic
and the Viceregal Lodge.

There was another jolt: she had always been treated as an equal by the men and women whom she knew. Only in theory was she aware that there were men who regarded women as innately inferior and unfit to represent them in Parliament. Talking to a French woman journalist who visited Anglesey during the campaign, Megan said that she 'had to fight against such active prejudices with regard to a woman's political career'.[51] When she spoke at outdoor meetings in the countryside, some men assumed that she was fair game for taunting and teasing. She faced them – and faced them down – with the Lloyd George courage and the Lloyd George gift of repartee. When she was making a speech about the condition of agriculture, a man interrupted: 'What do you know about farming? You don't know how many ribs a pig has.' Megan's retort was: 'Come up here and I'll count.'

At the close of their well-conducted campaign, the Liberals reached polling day in confident mood. Lloyd George, in his final speech at Caernarvon, spoke of a 'sensational revival of Liberalism'. The champion optimist was Sir Robert Thomas, who told an Anglesey meeting that there would be 250 Liberal MPs and the next Prime Minister would be 'the father of your candidate'.

But the result of the election was a bitter disappointment for Liberals. They won only 59 seats, a small advance on 1924 but an advance without real significance. (One Liberal, Sir William Jowett, immediately defected to take office under Labour as Attorney-General.) They were becoming, in a phrase that soon caught on, a party of the Celtic fringe; they had won all the five Cornish constituencies, eight seats in Welsh-speaking Wales, and seven in the Scottish highlands and islands. In industrial Britain and the big cities, they had made no impact; indeed, they registered a net loss of seats in Yorkshire and London. Sadly, the *Liberal Magazine* concluded in June: 'It is evident that a large section of the electorate did not believe us when we said we could conquer unemployment.'

Labour won 288 seats, the best score to date and tantalisingly close to a majority. The success was due largely to victories in the cities – twenty-six gains in Greater London, six in Birmingham, three in Cardiff and three in Bristol. The Tories, with 255 seats, had suffered a setback that still left them as a formidable opposition.

More dramatically than ever, this election demonstrated the unfairness of the British system. The Tories, this time, had grounds for complaint, since they had polled 260,000 more votes than Labour to win thirty-three fewer seats. While Labour and the Tories had each polled over eight million votes, the Liberals had polled over five million – a substantial total for a meagre reward. As Lloyd George put it, 'We have once more been tripped up by the triangle.'[52] The Liberals had secured a 27.6 per cent share of the poll – interestingly, almost the same as the Alliance share in 1983. It was hard to see how they would ever do better. On the morrow of the election, commentators judged that the Liberal Party had lost its last chance of being a competitor for power. So far as we know at the time when this book is written, the verdict is justified.

At a personal level, Megan had reason to be quite happy. Her father, as usual, had a thumping majority. Her brother Gwilym had regained his seat in Pembrokeshire. Her friend Geoffrey Shakespeare had scored a narrow win at Norwich. Geoffrey Crawshay failed at Pontypool, and John Morris failed at Ilford, but these had never been on the list of possible Liberal victories.

The figures for Anglesey were:

| | |
|---|---:|
| Megan Lloyd George, Liberal | 13,181 |
| William Edwards, Labour | 7,563 |
| Albert Hughes, Conservative | 5,917 |
| Liberal majority | 5,618 |

While all loyal Liberals had been confident of winning, and it was agreed on all sides that Megan had fought an excellent campaign, the size of her majority was greater than had been expected. When the result was declared in the market square at Llangefni, the waiting crowd went wild. Megan was carried shoulder-high along the street, followed by dancing, singing supporters. Next day she led a cavalcade of cars and buses from Menai Bridge to Holyhead, accompanied by her mother. They were greeted by the town band, their car was pulled by manpower from the sea-front, and they found a crowd of eight thousand waiting at the recreation ground. 'I've never in my life met such kind people as in Anglesey,' Megan said. 'I am very proud to be the Member for Anglesey, and I am also proud indeed to be the first woman representative of Wales.'

She was to be the member for Anglesey for twenty-two years. On that triumphant day in 1929, she might well have expected that it would be for the rest of her life.

# CHAPTER FIVE

# Megan, MP

## 1

The House of Commons that assembled in June 1929 provided ample material for parliamentary sketch-writers. One of the new Labour members was Malcolm MacDonald, the Prime Minister's son; another was Oliver Baldwin, who was the son of the Tory leader but nevertheless a strong Socialist. Since Gwilym Lloyd George had regained his seat, all three party leaders had sons in the House – an extraordinary occurrence.

There were now thirteen women MPs – eight Labour, three Tory, one Liberal and one Independent. Megan's counterpart on the Labour benches, in the sense of being young, attractive and on the radical wing of her party, was Jennie Lee, who at twenty-four (three years younger than Megan) was the youngest woman ever elected to Westminster. Another Labour MP was Lady Cynthia Mosley, who joined her husband, Sir Oswald.

As the governing party, Labour looked fairly impressive. Arthur Henderson, the Foreign Secretary, and Philip Snowden, Chancellor of the Exchequer, were political heavyweights who had been in the party's leadership since 1906. Places were found for respected ex-Liberals: Benn as Secretary for India, Trevelyan in charge of Education. Sidney Webb, the party's theorist, became Colonial Secretary. Margaret Bondfield, as Minister of Labour, was the first woman to sit in a British Cabinet. The up-and-coming Labour men included Oswald Mosley, who was given a junior post in the government with responsibility for tackling unemployment, Hugh

Dalton and Philip Noel-Baker.

Philip Baker has been mentioned as Lord Robert Cecil's assistant at the Paris peace conference. Being a Quaker, he had not fought in the war, but he had helped to create the Friends' Ambulance Unit and had been its commander, both in France and on the Italian front. Through his work he met Irene Noel, who was working as a nurse in a war hospital, and they were married. She inherited a 15,000-acre estate in Greece called Achmetaga,[1] and Philip had now hyphenated his name with hers. He was a foundation member of the League of Nations Secretariat and worked with Fridtjof Nansen, the Arctic explorer and humanitarian, on famine relief and the resettlement of refugees. Under the first Labour government, he was private secretary to Lord Parmoor, the minister responsible for League of Nations affairs. Then, without ever having been a university lecturer, he was appointed Professor of International Relations at the London School of Economics – 'a much better fate than you deserve,' the sharp-tongued Irene told him.[2] His book *Disarmament*, published in 1926, established him as a leading authority on the subject and set out detailed proposals for a disarmament agreement. Another achievement safeguarded him from being regarded as a dry-as-dust intellectual: he had twice (in 1912 and 1920) been in the British running team at the Olympic Games, and on the second occasion won a silver medal. By 1929 he was forty years old and his athletic career was over, but he was still an enthusiastic rock-climber, hill-walker and swimmer. In the general election he had been triumphantly elected for Coventry, turning a Tory majority of 5000 into a Labour majority of 11,000.

Strengthening the League of Nations and pursuing a disarmament agreement were the main planks in Labour's foreign policy, and a man with credentials in these spheres had a serious claim to office. Philip saw himself as a future Foreign Secretary, and certainly hoped to be appointed as Under-Secretary (this was then the number two position, as the post of Minister of State did not yet exist). However, the job went to Hugh Dalton, who had been in the Commons longer and was better known in Labour Party circles, and Philip had to be content with the modest position of parliamentary private secretary to Henderson. Henderson assumed that, since Dalton and Noel-Baker had known each other since they were undergraduates at King's College, Cambridge, they would make a harmonious team. Instead, they were rivals from the start and gradually came to loathe each other.

Twenty-five years later, Philip wrote to Megan:

Its been deep in my sub-conscious (& my conscious) ever since we first sat down together on the Bench in the Lobby in 1929. If you will believe it, & understand it, it will help you to interpret the past.

But always, all day, every day, since we first sat down together, I have longed to have you for my own, my perfect, my brilliant, lovely, exciting, famous, sweet & tender wife; & I've believed that if I had the chance, I could adore you, & cherish you, & love you, & help you, & make you happy, better than anyone else in all the world.[3]

When they sat down on that bench in 1929, Philip was married to Irene. When he wrote in these terms in 1954, he was still married to Irene.

2

As an MP, Megan first raised her voice not in the House of Commons but in a BBC studio. In 1929, the BBC was allowed to relax a hitherto total ban on politics at the microphone and gave special attention to the needs of women. The reasoning was that they might be entirely uninformed on current events because the men took the newspaper to work. Hilda Matheson, then Director of Talks, proposed a series of 'very simple and homely talks on the events of the week likely to be of special interest to women'.[4] One of her ideas was *The Week in Parliament*, a Wednesday morning talk by a woman MP. Balance required an alternation between MPs of the three parties, and Megan was invited because she was the only woman Liberal in the House. Beginning in October 1929, she took turns with the Duchess of Atholl (Tory) and Agnes Hamilton (Labour), and then with Lady Astor and Ellen Wilkinson. In October 1930 she was pressed to resume for another session because, as Miss Matheson put it, 'you have such a gift for it that it seems a waste that you should not do it.'

In the House, Megan made her maiden speech on 7 April 1930. Like her father forty years earlier, she had delayed her début for months while she listened to debates and studied parliamentary conventions. When at last she spoke, it was to speak up for Anglesey. The poverty of which she had been aware since she first got to know the island was steadily and, it seemed, hopelessly worsening.

In October 1929 the Stock Exchange in Wall Street plunged into a sudden and devastating crash. Repercussions were swift and world-wide; in Europe as well as in America, industrial enterprises reduced production, laid off workers or went bankrupt. The crisis became a depression or, more tersely, a slump. In Britain, unemployment rose

commented: 'When she speaks of poverty, especially in North Wales, she can be not only impressively serious but emotionally moving.'

The next speaker was the Countess of Iveagh, who offered the customary congratulations on a maiden speech but also slipped in a trenchant point: 'She [Megan] has made her fellow women Members realise the great addition she will be to their number, which is all too small.'

In Anglesey, the speech strengthened Megan's reputation as a champion of her constituents. It was at about this time that the Reverend H. D. Hughes, the influential minister who had backed her for the nomination, requested a personal favour. His thirteen-year-old son Cledwyn had been in hospital for an operation, and it would be a treat for him to have tea at the House of Commons. Megan was happy to be Cledwyn's hostess, and Cledwyn remembered the occasion almost sixty years later.[7]

In 1931 Megan spoke in the Commons three times. On 10 February she spoke in support of a bill which would enable local authorities to buy land to be leased as smallholdings, especially for the unemployed. As a member of the committee considering the bill, she had secured a change making it applicable to farm workers as well as men from the towns. Her comment on the Tories who opposed the scheme makes interesting reading today:

[Members] who see dispossessed kulaks in every corner, and the hand of Stalin in every clause of the bill, can represent it as being nothing less than the beginning of the Russian system of farming in this country, but I think we can rest assured that Stalin would disdain an experiment on this scale.

The main purpose of the bill was to check rural depopulation. Government policies in the later 1920s, Megan charged, had 'decimated many villages in many parts of the country as effectively as any plague could possibly have done'.

On 10 July she spoke in the debate on another housing bill, and urged that it should be implemented in Wales by a separate authority instead of the usual England-and-Wales machinery: 'I believe, fundamentally and on principle, that Wales in this matter as in many others should govern herself.' She pointed out that, although the 1930 bill was now law, progress in authorising house-building had been so slow that the 40,000 homes envisaged for rural areas would not be completed for a hundred and sixty years. 'That looks like pushing the theory of the inevitability of gradualness to an extreme.' One excuse for delay was that, before families could be rehoused, their existing homes had to be inspected by the Medical Officer of Health. But, Megan protested impatiently:

He has already condemned them, he has already passed a closing order on them . . . but there are families still living in them in spite of these closing orders, in these infected and defective houses, simply because you cannot throw them out into the streets and there is nowhere else where they can go.

A few days later, on 14 July, she had a point to make about the joint committees (of local councillors, building employers and trade-union representatives) which were to supervise housing standards: 'The accommodation would have been far more suitable and more adequate if a woman had been advising the architects. I look forward to the day when women will have established themselves on their own merits.'

When Megan made that speech, the government which was sponsoring the bill had only a few more weeks to live. Inexorably following the economic crisis, the political crisis of 1931 was about to break.

3

Through 1930 and into 1931, it became increasingly clear that the MacDonald government was helpless in face of the depression. When the Liberals pressed for a development loan to finance public works and combat unemployment, Snowden turned down the idea. The Chancellor was a model of financial orthodoxy: nothing could move him from the sacrosanct dogmas of a balanced budget and the maintenance of the gold standard. From within the government, only Mosley urged Keynesian policies. When he could make no headway he resigned. Soon he was to start what he called the New Party and set out on the strange political odyssey that led him to overt Fascism and to a cell in Pentonville prison.

George Lansbury, a veteran left-winger,[8] was looking in another direction. On 15 February 1931 he sent a remarkable letter to Lloyd George, with the assurance that 'not a soul has seen this but my wife'. He asked forthrightly:

Why won't you join the Labour Party? . . . Your help would be invaluable, *as one of us.* . . . All your people in the House would not come with you, but those who count, the young in mind, those who have faith in our common stock, they will come and in any case your coming would crown a progressive

life with the knowledge that . . . when the hour came and you were needed,
you flung aside all thought of self and came over to the new groupings of true
Liberalism and progressive thought.[9]

It is fascinating to reflect on the consequences if Lloyd George had
responded to this appeal. The final phase of his career would have been
very different, and broad new perspectives would have opened out for
Megan, who would undoubtedly have gone with her father. Had she
joined Labour in 1931, she might have had a limitless future in a party
that, whatever its ups and downs, was always a competitor for power.
But MacDonald was still the Labour leader, and Lloyd George, after
his long struggle with Asquith, had had quite enough of in-fighting in a
party which he did not dominate. He sent Lansbury a cautious reply,
and the proposal came to nothing.

By the spring, the government was visibly falling apart and the
Tories were hungering for power. Nerves were quivering under the
impact of warnings of total economic collapse from 'industry' and the
City of London. Politicians in every party were trying to guess what
their prospects would be after the next twist of the kaleidoscope.
When Lloyd George addressed the Liberal conference on 15 May, he
compared Britain's situation to that of the *Titanic* as it approached the
fatal iceberg: 'I would advise my friends to put on their life-jackets and
put their deck-chairs near the boats. Unless, of course, any of them
have already made arrangements to be picked up.'[10] That shrewd
thrust was soon justified. A couple of weeks later, twenty right-wing
Liberal MPs, headed by Sir John Simon, relinquished the Liberal whip
and announced their intention of working with the Tories to defeat the
government. Once again, the Liberal Party was split.

Unable to cope with the deepening slump, MacDonald and
Snowden put their trust in a committee of 'experts', headed by Sir
George May of the Prudential Insurance Company and with a
majority of businessmen. Its report, published on 31 July (not
accidentally, the day after Parliament adjourned), was described by
Keynes as 'the most foolish document I ever had the misfortune to
read'.[11] Most Socialists considered it more wicked than foolish. It
proposed rigorous economy measures, cuts in the pay of the armed
forces and the police (this recommendation led to a mutiny of the fleet
at Invergordon), and a cut of 20 per cent in the already miserable level
of unemployment relief. To everyone except the ludicrously vain
MacDonald, it was obvious that this programme was unacceptable to
the rank and file of the Labour Party, to the great majority of Labour
MPs and probably to a majority of the Cabinet.

At this crucial moment, the Liberal leader was out of action. On 26 July, Lloyd George was suddenly taken ill. The doctors ordered an immediate prostate operation, which in 1931 was much more serious and dangerous than it is now. The operation was performed on 29 July at Lloyd George's London home. With his inherently strong constitution, the patient came through the operation well, but it would be weeks or even months before he could resume his normal activity. He was obliged to entrust the leadership of the party to Sir Herbert Samuel, a man whom he did not much like or trust. He could follow the news and write (or dictate) letters, but he was deprived of the chance to discuss the political situation with his closest adviser – Frances Stevenson. A few days after the operation, noticing that Dame Margaret had gone out for a drive, Frances paid a hurried visit to her lover and left flowers in his room. When Margaret returned, she asked who had left the flowers and a nurse innocently replied: 'Miss Stevenson.' Furious, Margaret attacked Tom Carey Evans for suggesting the drive and accused him of connivance.[12] After that, security was strictly enforced.

Ramsay MacDonald returned to London from his Scottish home on 11 August. He was planning the formation of a coalition, under the name 'National Government', which he hoped would be supported by all three parties. If he broached the scheme before completing negotiations with the Tories and Liberals, however, he risked objections from the Left or even the mainstream of the Labour Party. According to an account by a man who was close to events, MacNeill Weir, 'MacDonald had one big secret to hide. No word or hint must be given that the scheme to form a "national government" – a scheme that had been maturing for several weeks – was about to come to fruition.' In the discreet negotiations of that August, the Tories were represented by Neville Chamberlain and Sir Samuel Hoare, the Liberals by Samuel and a former Asquithian, Sir Donald Maclean. Weir explains:

A vital factor in the negotiations was the fact that the chief spokesman for the Liberal Party was Sir Herbert Samuel. . . . It was lucky for MacDonald that Lloyd George was ill at the time. If he had remained leader of the Liberals, the intrigue that set up the 'National' government would have been well-nigh impossible. . . . He would have blown the project sky-high with the battery of his wit and ridicule. At any rate, the personal relations between the two would have made co-operation impracticable.[13]

It is clear that arrangements for the new government were being finalised while the Labour Cabinet was still arguing over the cuts demanded by the May Committee. Deadlock persisted in Downing Street up to the night of 23 August, with Snowden pressing for the cuts, Henderson firmly against them and the Cabinet split down the middle. Next morning, MacDonald went to Buckingham Palace and emerged as Prime Minister of the National Government. Its small Cabinet contained four Labour, four Tory and two Liberal ministers. Baldwin became Lord President of the Council and, in effect, Deputy Prime Minister; Lord Reading was Foreign Secretary. MacDonald and Baldwin were able to leave out the two men whose strong personalities made them awkward customers — David Lloyd George and Winston Churchill.

Lloyd George agreed, though doubtless without much enthusiasm, to endorse what Samuel had done. Reading had visited him on 23 August to brief him, and perhaps to persuade him. Gwilym was invited to join the government as Under-Secretary at the Board of Trade, and Lloyd George may have been reluctant to veto his son's first chance of office.

MacDonald now discovered that he was a Prime Minister without a party. In the Labour ranks, the only supporters of the National Government were MacDonald himself, Snowden (who continued as Chancellor), J. H. Thomas (a former leader of the National Union of Railwaymen who was regarded by the Left as the man who had sold out the General Strike) and eight backbenchers. Henderson took over as leader of a party that, with 260 MPs, constituted a fairly strong opposition.

The presence in parliament of a strong Labour opposition — slightly larger, in fact, than the Conservative Party — was not to Baldwin's liking, and he at once insisted that a general election should be held. It is hard to say definitely whether this was part of the deal agreed in August, but in any case Lloyd George 'was furious and felt that he had been betrayed'.[14] Objectively, there was no need for an election, since the new government commanded an adequate majority so long as it had Liberal support, and Snowden's emergency budget enforcing the cuts was passed on 8 September by a vote of 297 to 242. Indeed, at a time when national unity was professedly the order of the day, an election could well be — as Megan put it in a constituency speech — 'a faction fight at home which will shake confidence in Britain abroad'.[15] It was nakedly obvious that the purpose of the election was to smash the Labour Party and produce a huge Tory majority.

Fuming at Churt, where he had gone to convalesce, Lloyd George was bitterly critical of Samuel and Reading for not resisting Baldwin's demand. Sylvester noted on 30 September:

L.G. is absolutely implacable. He is dead against a general election. He says there is no need for it. He is also very insistent that Liberal members of the government should threaten to resign as a body if Ramsay and the Tories insist on an election.[16]

They made no such threat, and the election was duly announced on 6 October, with polling on 27 October. Gwilym left the government (perhaps to keep peace in the family) and Reading also left it soon afterwards, but Samuel and the bulk of the Liberals maintained the alliance. Lloyd George's fury was intensified when he found that it was to be a 'coupon' election – ironically, the device on which he had relied in 1918. Samuel had instructed Tweed, as head of the Liberal organisation, to meet the Tory organisers and arrange for Liberal and Tory candidates to avoid fighting each other. Still formally the party leader, Lloyd George ordered Tweed to do no such thing. But in the event, out of 160 Liberals who stood when the election came, only ten had Tory opponents. The ten, of course, included Lloyd George and Megan.

There were now three segments, or fragments, of the Liberal Party. Simon and his followers, taking the label of 'Liberal National', were committed to endorsing any policy adopted by the government, even including the imposition of tariffs. (For the last time in British history, protection versus free trade was an issue in this election.) Samuel's Liberals were prepared to support the government so long as it did not bring in tariffs; this appeared to be a safe course, as Snowden was a firm free-trader. The smallest section was the Lloyd George group, now in clear opposition to the government. In a broadcast from Churt (on medical advice, he did not campaign actively or go to his constituency) Lloyd George described the election as 'a tricky attempt to utilise the national emergency to smash the political influence of organised labour'[17], and urged people to vote Labour where they had no Liberal candidate.

Megan entered the election campaign confidently. She was now well known in Anglesey and had built up a stock of goodwill by taking up individual problems. She understood what poverty meant and was firmly against the cuts. The prospective Labour candidate, T. W. Jones (later MP for Merioneth), announced as soon as he was selected that he intented to withdraw and would speak for Megan. On the other hand, Ellis Roberts – who had fought Megan for the Liberal nomination in 1928 – led a faction of right-wing Liberals in supporting the Tory candidate, Albert Hughes; and Anglesey could not be altogether immune to the Tory wave which was, predictably, sweeping across Britain.

'I still adhere to the old principles and the old leader,' Megan told a crowded meeting at Llangefni on 8 October. Her peroration was:

I for one am not ready to give a blank cheque to a government which may be mainly composed of Tories. I am going to stand on my own feet and for purely Liberal principles. I ask you – are you ready to follow me?

Not surprisingly, the *Holyhead Mail* reported 'cries of "Yes!"'.

Thelma Cazalet was standing as Conservative candidate for East Islington, a working-class constituency with a formidable Labour majority. The bitter political antagonisms of 1931 could not break the links between the friends. Megan wrote:

My sweet,
I have been watching the press for news of my dearest enemy in E. Islington with an anxiety which would bring me under suspicion of all good Liberals, if it were known. Darling, you know that outside my family circle there is not an election in the kingdom which is of so much concern to me. . . . Darling my love, if you want to show your love for me, get in with a thumping majority.[18]

When polling day came, Megan was in with a majority of 4227 – a thousand down from the 1929 figure. In the circumstances of 1931, it was an excellent result. Baldwin had achieved his aim. In the new House of Commons there were 551 supporters of the government, of whom 470 were Tories. Labour was down to 52 MPs, representing its irreducible strongholds in the coalfields and a few other places. Thelma won East Islington; Tories also won Rotherhithe and Mile End. Henderson was defeated and had to give up the party leadership. The only member of the former Labour Cabinet to survive the election (other than those who were in the National Government) was George Lansbury, and he was elected to the leadership.

Samuel's Liberal Party had put forward a limited number of candidates, mainly because Lloyd George refused to release money from his fund for their benefit. Thirty-three Samuelites were elected, exactly balancing the thirty-three Simonites, or Liberal Nationals. Four Independent Liberals, as they chose to call themselves, sat on the opposition benches. The four were David Lloyd George, Megan Lloyd George, Gwilym Lloyd George and Goronwy Owen. Since Owen's wife was a sister of Gwilym's wife, jokers were able to describe the Independent Liberals as a family party.

'The Philistines have triumphed,' Megan told the Holyhead crowd on the day after polling, 'but it won't be long before we're free of the bondage of Toryism.' She can scarcely have believed what she said. It would be fourteen long, unhappy years.

4

After the election, Lloyd George wrote to Samuel formally resigning from the party leadership. It is a curious fact that, in his long career as a Liberal statesman, he was the leader for only five years and led the party in only one general election. As some kind of compensation, he was now Father of the House of Commons. Still in medical care – he was able to walk round the garden by mid-October – he would have liked to spend a quiet winter at Bron-y-de with Frances and her daughter Jennifer.

In the later 1920s, Frances had expressed a desire to have a child before it was too late. Lloyd George agreed, and by early 1929 she was eagerly waiting to see whether she was pregnant. In February she wrote to him:

I am not letting myself be unduly excited in case of a disappointment. But I do most passionately hope that the longed-for thing may happen. It would just put the seal upon our love and be a marvellous fulfilment.[19]

The child, a girl, was born in a private clinic in London. There was, of course, no publicity. Lloyd George – always fond of children, especially girls – doted on Jennifer and loved to see her crawling, and then toddling, on the lawn at Bron-y-de.

This was not, however, the whole story. Frances had been carrying on an affair with Colonel Tweed, the Liberal organiser. Lloyd George knew nothing about it until 1932, when Jennifer was three years old, but in that year a maid employed by Frances, called Rowlands, defected to the other side in the family cold war, took service with Olwen and lost no time in revealing the secret. It was soon passed on to Lloyd George, perhaps in the hope that he would be disenchanted with Frances and would break with her at long last. Sylvester was summoned urgently to Bron-y-de. As he crossed the hall to reach Lloyd George's study, Tom Carey Evans warned him: 'Look out.' Sternly, Lloyd George said, 'You owe your first duty to me', and demanded: 'Do you know about Frances and Tweed?' As usual, Sylvester knew everything. He disliked Tweed, whom he regarded as 'an arch-intriguer',[20] so he confirmed Rowlands's story. In his diary, he wrote: 'He [Lloyd George] was terribly upset. I have never seen him so weighed down with grief.'[21]

In 1937 Lloyd George told Sylvester: 'I have a letter from Tweed saying that he is responsible for the child.'[22] No such letter is to be found in the Lloyd George papers; as he grew older, Lloyd George's statements were not always reliable. In any case, Frances had been forgiven. In 1934 she must have written to promise Lloyd George that she would not repeat her lapse, for he wrote to her: 'I was so pleased to read that you meant to be a good girl. I know you will be happier. The double life is full of worry and apprehension which wrecks the nerves.'[23] Even Tweed was forgiven, and was still working on Lloyd George's staff in the 1930s.

Jennifer had a most unusual childhood. Frances bought a house called Avalon, a mile from Bron-y-de, and the child lived there with a nanny; when she was old enough, she went to a boarding school. She was brought up to call Frances 'Mummy' but was told she had been adopted. Indeed, Frances put through a legal adoption in 1938, when questions were asked at the school. There were various stories – one of them was that Jennifer's parents had been missionaries in China. She was in no way disturbed by this situation. 'I thought it was all quite ordinary,' she says.[24] Meanwhile she went over to Bron-y-de almost every day and was cosseted by Lloyd George, who played games with her, told her stories and sang to her in Welsh. She regarded him as a kindly old man, and had no idea that he had been her mother's lover and could be her father until Frances permitted the publication of her diary in 1971. As for the question of whether her father was Lloyd George or Tweed, Jennifer considers that there is no way of knowing and no point in guessing.

To return to the autumn of 1931: with some reluctance, Lloyd George accepted the advice of his doctor, Lord Dawson of Penn, to speed his convalescence by a journey to a better climate. Ceylon was the chosen destination, and the party included Dame Margaret, Megan, Gwilym with his wife Edna, and Sylvester. From the start, it was an unfortunate trip. Leaving London on 20 November, they crossed France by train to avoid bad weather in the Bay of Biscay and joined the ship at Marseille. In the Mediterranean the weather did not improve: 'cold – rough – uncomfortable,' Megan wrote to Thelma. Lloyd George grumbled that he would be better off at home. In an acid mood, he wrote to Frances pouring out his contempt for the Samuelites: 'What mangy rabbits these Liberal Ministers must be.'[25] At Port Said, Sylvester had the chore of dodging the family to post this letter, while Gwilym and Edna decided that they had had enough and caught a ship home. In the Red Sea it was at least warm, and Megan appeared as Queen Victoria at the fancy-dress party which was *de rigueur* in shipboard routine. But no one had told them about the north-east monsoon which strikes Ceylon in December. To Thelma, Megan lamented:

We've travelled thousands of miles to get away from rain & grey skies, then since we landed we've had nothing but leaden skies & torrential downpour! and we see by the wireless that you've had a heat-wave at home. . . . [Margaret] sees snakes in every corner, is continually saying: 'How glad I shall be to see the boat again!'

Sylvester had a harassing time posting letters to Frances, handing on her letters (the envelopes were addressed to him) and buying presents for her and little Jennifer without being observed. 'Megan watched me like a cat watching a mouse,' he confided to his diary.[26] He had to buy an extra trunk to keep the presents apart from the Lloyd George luggage. By 7 January 1932 Lloyd George was back at Churt, doubtless much to his relief.

The year 1932 saw a change in the political situation. On the insistence of the Tories, the government introduced a sweeping range of tariffs, with the result that the Samuelite ministers resigned and their party went into opposition. Snowden also resigned, took a peerage and retired from politics. He had a house near Churt and was, surprisingly, on very friendly terms with Lloyd George. His successor as Chancellor was Neville Chamberlain, whose skinny physique and icy demeanour were well suited to a policy of rigorous economy.

Megan found an opportunity to protest against that policy when the House debated the economic situation on 11 July. There was no sign of recovery from the depression, and unemployment was only slightly below three million. Nowhere was the outlook bleaker than in Anglesey, and Megan began by saying: 'Never in the memory, at any rate, of present inhabitants of the island has unemployment or depression been as great as it is today.' She explained once again, doubtless without making much impact on the Tory ranks:

It is obvious that each time you cut down schemes, whether on roads, housing, telephones or drainage or other forms of public works, you are throwing people out of work, and that means that at each stage the spending power of these people is reduced. They are thrown from a wage on to unemployment insurance, and then a good many of them eventually on to Poor Law relief. . . . If we want to see the need for true economy in the national interest we can see it in the deserted village, in the waterlogged land and in the derelict tracts of land which are fast becoming man-made deserts.

In this period of deflation, prices had fallen, and this furnished Megan with another argument:

Now that prices are down, why not turn our misfortunes and adversities to good purpose? Why not take the opportunity when prices are down of building houses? . . . If we realise that there are something like 220,000 building operatives out of work, that the need for housing is great and the number of insanitary houses is such that no civilised country should tolerate it, we ought not, even in present circumstances, to cut down.

Her father, meanwhile, had turned aside from the political arena in disgust. Frances recalled: 'He had no intention of again becoming harnessed to the disgruntled, divided and rapidly dwindling party to which he nominally belonged.'[27] From Criccieth that September he wrote to her: 'When I come back I'll tell you all about my ideas. They are not in the direction of regaining the Liberal Party with the cranks and hypocrites at the top who all hate me and have always done so.'[28] She replied soothingly: 'Things will begin to come your way soon, my darling. . . . They will just fall into your lap.'[29]

He was directing his energy into a new channel: writing the history of the 1914–18 war from his point of view. Lloyd George's *War Memoirs* fill six fat volumes, with a total of 5000 pages. For a man of his age – he was seventy in January 1933 – it was a tremendous feat of productivity. The source material was collated by Frances and other assistants, but Lloyd George (unlike Churchill) wrote every word himself. According to Sylvester, he turned out 230,000 words in his opening burst of work from August to December 1932. In another spell – while staying at Marrakesh, away from visitors and the telephone – he wrote an average of 4000 words a day and sometimes 10,000.[30] He received £20,000 for the book rights and another £25,000 for the serial rights. The first two volumes were published in the autumn of 1933, a little more than a year after he had started writing, and the remaining four by 1936. Two volumes entitled *The Truth about the Peace Treaties* followed in 1938. Incidentally, this rate of production tells us something not only about Lloyd George's creativity but also about the pace of publishing in the 1930s.

5

No one who knew Lloyd George believed that he could confine himself entirely to fruit-growing and memoir-writing. Despite the huge Tory majority in Parliament, he thought that public opinion could be mobilised to demand positive measures to overcome the depression. In this he was inspired by what was happening in the United States. Franklin D. Roosevelt became President in March 1933, and the ringing phrase in his inaugural address, 'The only thing we have to fear is fear itself', brought a welcome note of reassurance to millions of anxious and disheartened Americans. His eloquence was inspiring, his broad smile was cheering, and his personal triumph over a crippling attack of polio seemed to symbolise the courage and determination that could bring the stricken nation – and even the world – through to recovery.

The wheels began to turn again, pump-priming measures built up purchasing power, and the creation of the Tennessee Valley Authority was only one of the impressive schemes launched under public control. In another phrase that Roosevelt inserted into the language, it was 'a new deal for the American people'. And a new deal, Lloyd George considered, was just what the British people needed. He submitted proposals on Rooseveltian lines to the National Government, only to have them flatly turned down. He decided, therefore, to appeal to ordinary men and women, starting on his home ground. Speaking at Bangor on 17 January 1935 (his seventy-second birthday), he told an audience of six thousand people:

The whole economic system, which was not working well before the war, has broken down, at least temporarily – some will say permanently. . . . There are millions of decent hard-working people and their children in the richest countries in the world, including ours, who are living below the poverty line at this moment. . . . Too much corn in Egypt, and the Egyptians are starving. There is a flood and we are suffering from drought.

His response to the challenge of poverty in the midst of potential wealth was: 'I give exactly the same answer as Roosevelt gave Congress the other day. I would find work for the workless instead of doles, and I am as convinced as he is that it can be done.'

The speech received an immediate and gratifying acclaim. Within a week, Sylvester was noting: 'Correspondence on L.G.'s New Deal proposals is amazing and takes me all my time to read, let alone deal with it.'[31] Lloyd George had made the scope of his appeal clear at the beginning of his speech:

I am not here to launch a party campaign. I am neither a party leader nor have I any desire to become a party leader. I have had enough of that misery. I am here as a British citizen who has had considerable experience in government to make an appeal to the nation for a great effort.

He proceeded to set up the Council of Action for Peace and Reconstruction. Megan was on the committee, and Liberals rallied to their old leader, but support also came from some prominent people in the Labour Party, including Lansbury, and from Tories with a social conscience, such as Harold Macmillan, who was MP for the hard-hit industrial town of Stockton-on-Tees.

Peace was as vital a concern as reconstruction. While millions everywhere were going short of bare necessities, and while governments were preaching the gospel of rigorous economy, the glaring contradiction was that money could be found for guns. Megan had put her finger on this contradiction in a 1931 election speech:

What is the one thing that constitutes the heaviest burden on the budgets of the world? Armaments. At this very moment, the peoples of the world are going in want while vast sums are being spent on paying for past wars and preparing for future wars.[32]

With much solemnity and many high-sounding pledges, an international disarmament conference met in Paris in February 1932, and then moved on to Geneva. Two disarmament enthusiasts, Arthur Henderson and Philip Noel-Baker, were available to take part in this endeavour, having both lost their seats in Parliament. Henderson presided over the conference, while Philip worked as his secretary and assistant. In his 1926 book, Philip had advocated a four-point programme: (1) a ceiling on military budgets in proportion to the total expenditure of each nation; (2) a ceiling on military manpower; (3) a limitation on the period of conscript service; and (4) a total ban on offensive weapons, including bombing aircraft, tanks, and chemical and biological weapons. These and similar proposals were on the agenda at Geneva.

Agreement, however, never seemed likely. The German delegates, under pressure from a rising spirit of nationalism, wanted every nation to disarm down to the level imposed on Germany since Versailles, while the French felt it necessary to retain an edge of superiority. By 1933 Irene Noel-Baker was complaining that Philip's loyalty to Uncle Arthur (as Henderson was called) was preventing him from advancing his own career. 'You persist in sticking to Uncle and in deluding yourself that you will get something done – I shall despair of you!' she wrote to him.[33] He obeyed her, and resigned. The conference lingered on until June 1934, but finally dispersed without achieving anything.

By this time, Germany had a government which, far from contemplating disarmament, was bent on expanding its armed forces and becoming a dominant power in Europe. On 30 January 1933 Adolf Hitler became Chancellor (the German equivalent of Prime Minister). The torchlight parades which celebrated the Nazi triumph were headed, in some German cities, by army officers in uniform. A few days later Hitler told a gathering of generals and admirals that his aim was 'the conquest of new living space [*Lebensraum*] in the East and its uncompromising Germanisation'.[34]

On 5 March the Reichstag building mysteriously burned down and the Nazis created an atmosphere of hysteria by accusing a Bulgarian Communist, Georgi Dimitrov, of responsibility.[35] Barbed wire went up around sites designated as concentration camps and thousands of anti-Nazis were herded inside. Having won an election which was held in an atmosphere of ferocious intimidation (though, even so, they got only 44 per cent of the votes), the Nazis put through an Enabling Act which gave them unlimited powers. Within a couple of years, all other parties were banned. After the death of President Hindenburg in 1935, Hitler took the title of *Führer* (leader).

Politically, Hitler's strength was that he had something for (almost) everybody. To the unemployed, he promised work; to the middle class, a firm enforcement of order and decency; to the capitalists who covertly financed him, industrial discipline and the destruction of the trade unions; to ex-soldiers (he was one himself) a rebuilding of the once mighty German army. To this brew, he added frenetic attacks on the Jews – as usual in anti-Semitic mythology, they were simultaneously wealthy profiteers and subversive conspirators – and strident denunciations of Bolshevism. The anti-Communist rhetoric was for export as well as for internal use. In the House of Commons diningroom, Megan and Thelma were able to hear Tories praising Hitler as the man who would save Europe from Communism. Lloyd George predicted: 'In a very short time, perhaps in a year, perhaps two, the Conservative elements in this country will be looking to Germany as the bulwark against Communism in Europe.'[36]

However, although Hitler's admirers sought to deny it, some people – notably Winston Churchill – were able to see that Nazi Germany had threatening designs on its neighbours: Austria, Czechoslovakia, Poland. In July 1934 Austrian Nazis assassinated the Chancellor, Engelbert Dollfuss, and Austria would have been swallowed by Germany if Mussolini had not shown his disapproval and rushed Italian troops to the frontier. Mussolini, however, was no peace-lover. He was openly preparing to attack Abyssinia (now Ethiopia), the last non-colonised nation in Africa, which Italy had failed to conquer in 1896.

A primary function of the League of Nations was to prevent aggression. The theory of 'collective security' was that any aggressor nation would be checked by all the other League members, either by economic sanctions or, if necessary, by military measures. The difficulty was that the League itself did not possess any armed strength, so it was dependent on the determination of nations such as Britain and France who, whether through reluctance to take risks or actual sympathy with the aggressor, might decline to put the theory into practice. It was significant that Philip Noel-Baker, who had urged the abolition of the bomber in his 1926 book, was in 1934 proposing the creation of an International Air Police Force and envisaging bombing as a 'direct means of military pressure'.[37] Collective security had failed its first test in 1931–2, when a militaristic Japan attacked a weak and disunited China and conquered the large and economically valuable region of Manchuria. The League passed resolutions but took no effective steps. It did not look as though effective steps would be taken to check Mussolini either. In March 1935 MacDonald and Sir John Simon, the Foreign Secretary, had a friendly meeting at Stresa with the Italian dictator and pointedly refrained from giving him any warnings.[38]

This was a disturbing situation for members of the League of Nations Union, which existed to win support for the principles of the League. Its leading policy-makers were Lord Robert Cecil (now Lord Cecil of Chelwood), Philip Noel-Baker and Professor Gilbert Murray. Although Megan was primarily interested in domestic political issues, notably unemployment and poverty, she was also much concerned about peace-keeping, and was a member of the Council of the LNU. She may have been invited to take this position by Cecil or by Noel-Baker. In 1935 the LNU embarked on a remarkable enterprise – the Peace Ballot. It was much more than an opinion poll as we know it today. Unpaid volunteers were to knock on doors systematically over a period of six months, and their task was not merely to put questions but to explain the issues and stimulate thought; usually they left the questionnaire for a week and returned to collect it. Richard Acland, who was staying at Criccieth when the ballot was being planned, found that Megan was 'bursting with enthusiasm'.[39] Her father predicted sceptically that no more than half a million people would vote, but Megan was ready to bet that he would be proved wrong. So he was: 11,600,000 people, or 38 per cent of the electorate, recorded their opinions.

To some extent, the ballot campaign was designed to vindicate the attitudes of League supporters. As Gilbert Murray complained: 'We were ridiculed . . . as unpractical pacifists when advocating general disarmament, and as warmongers when demanding fulfilment of the obligations of the League against aggressors.'[40] The latter line of attack was in favour in 1935, and the Beaverbrook newspapers denounced 'the Ballot of Blood'; but later myth-makers have depicted the ballot as a manifestation of pacifism.

Almost 90 per cent of the voters answered 'yes' to the question whether an aggressor should be restrained by 'economic and non-military measures'. The next question – whether this should be done 'if necessary, by military measures' – was of course the difficult one. The replies added up to 6,784,000 'yes' and 2,351,000 'no' votes, with a sizeable number of abstentions. The LNU, naturally, claimed this result as a popular endorsement of collective security. Most British people probably did wish to slap down the bombastic Italian dictator, but they might not have been so positive if they had interpreted 'military measures' to mean 'war'. LNU speakers generally suggested that the prestigious Royal Navy should bar Italian troopships from the Suez Canal, presumably with few casualties or none at all. The historian James Hinton is probably right in his judgement that 'what Cecil had pulled off in the Peace Ballot was an irresistible fusion of pacifism and patriotism.'[41]

On the extreme Left, there were some – including Sir Stafford Cripps – who refused to support any military measures taken by a capitalist government, whatever the ostensible cause. The prophet of Welsh nationalism, Saunders Lewis, also took this line, accusing the government of seeking an excuse for a war that would only benefit (English) armament-makers and profiteers. Lansbury, as leader of the Labour Party, found himself in an impossible position, since he was an absolute pacifist on Christian grounds. When the party conference met in September 1935, he offered to resign. This was not enough for Ernest Bevin, General Secretary of the Transport and General Workers' Union, who declared forcibly that it was wrong for Lansbury 'to take your conscience round from body to body asking to be told what to do with it'. Megan's friend David Keir, reporting for the *News Chronicle*, was revolted by Bevin's brutality, which reduced Lansbury to tears.[42] A resolution backing the sanctions policy, moved for the executive by Hugh Dalton, was carried by a large majority. Lansbury then resigned, to be succeeded by Clement Attlee.

Meanwhile, the Tories had taken note of the mood revealed by the Peace Ballot. Sir Samuel Hoare had gone to the Foreign Office when, in June, the decrepit MacDonald was eased out and Baldwin became Prime Minister. At Geneva, Hoare committed Britain in deliberate terms to 'steady and collective resistance to unprovoked aggression'. To the public, this policy was now bipartisan. Baldwin called an election, with polling on 14 November. Mussolini, however, marched his troops into Abyssinia.

Megan told her constituents frankly that she was 'pretty sure' that the government would retain power. Her appeal was:

Our duty is to send men and women to Parliament who will see that they get no peace until they tackle unemployment in earnest, and I want you to send me in to be one of that ginger-up group.[43]

In this election she had a Labour opponent – Henry Jones, a county councillor and Methodist lay preacher, and thus a strong candidate. But her position was now impregnable, and her majority of 4182 was almost the same as in 1931.

Nationally, the Tories were home and dry. Labour regained some of the seats that should never have been lost and came out with 154 MPs; but Thelma held East Islington and Philip Noel-Baker failed to win back Coventry. The Samuelite Liberals won only seventeen seats. Samuel himself was defeated and went to the House of Lords. The new leader, Sir Archibald Sinclair, was a more vigorous and outspoken foe of the Tories, so the Lloyd George 'family party' decided to reunite with the main body of Liberals. Megan had a special reason for favouring this step. The BBC had regretfully dropped her from the *Week in Parliament* panel because she was not a member of the official (Samuelite) Liberal Party; from 1935 she was welcomed back.

Less than a month after the election, a press leak told the world that Samuel Hoare and Pierre Laval, the French Prime Minister, had agreed to a deal that would give half of Abyssinia to Italy. Under a storm of criticism, Baldwin cancelled the deal and Hoare resigned (though he was soon back in the Cabinet). However, no British battleships appeared near the Suez Canal. In May 1936 the Italians entered Addis Ababa. The British government provided the Emperor of Abyssinia, Haile Selassie, with a retirement home in Bath and cancelled even the theoretical application of sanctions. As Megan declared:

The housebreaker has got in. . . . He has beaten and tortured members of the family . . . and the police say: 'What can we do? We don't want to make an enemy of him. We want him to join the police force.'[44]

Hoare's successor as Foreign Secretary was Anthony Eden. He was still under forty years old, had the good looks of a matinée idol, and had held the post of Minister for League of Nations Affairs, so that he was associated in the public mind with support for the League and disapproval of aggression. Twenty years later, he was to close his career by launching an aggressive war and defying the United Nations.

6

Megan was now in her thirties, and she never seemed to get much older. Her personality, her qualities and even her appearance are described in similar terms by those who knew her in the 1930s and by those who met her much later. Jo Grimond's comment on her was: 'perpetually young, perpetually unfulfilled'. He went on to say that she was 'never unresponsive, never overbearing, never dull'.[45] Ursula Thorpe, looking back when she herself was in her eighties, said: 'You can't imagine Megan being old.'[46] John Grigg wrote after her death: 'It is hard enough to believe that Megan Lloyd George was in her sixties; infinitely harder to believe that she is dead. She had the gaiety, spontaneity and vitality of a high-spirited child.'[47]

One reason for her perpetual youthfulness was, undoubtedly, that she was always David Lloyd George's daughter. Even after he was dead, friends often heard her say: 'Tada told me . . .' or 'What Tada thought was . . .' She could talk endlessly about Tada at dinner parties, to interviewing journalists and sometimes to audiences at public meetings. She had sometimes argued with him and even quarrelled with him, but he remained her inspiration in political life and she saw it as her duty to safeguard and carry forward the tradition he instilled into her. 'I am a Radical, as my father was,' she said time and again. It probably did not occur to her that she was doing herself an injustice and making it more difficult for her to gain stature as a political figure in her own right. Since she also inherited the most striking of his personal qualities, her resemblance to him was repeatedly cited and became a journalistic cliché. We shall see that there were also significant differences.

From Megan's youth onward, the Lloyd Georges were a sort of royal family, or at least first family, of Wales. 'The old man', Dame Margaret and Megan herself were recognised and welcomed wherever they went, and crowds gathered when they made public appearances. They were, of course, intensely political and 'controversial', but they also held a position in the life of this small, proud nation that rose above everyday politics. They opened new buildings, exhibitions and flower shows; Lloyd George and, after his death, Megan were the star speakers at the National Eisteddfod. In democratic countries there are not many examples of this kind of 'first family', but we have seen a comparable adulation accorded to the Kennedys in the United States and to the Nehru–Gandhi dynasty in India.

Both Lloyd George and Megan were conscious of their unique status in Wales, but neither father nor daughter became smug or pompous. Clem Thomas, who was her constituency agent in later years, noticed that some constituents were nervous of meeting this *grande dame* of Wales, and recorded:

Always, when their interviews were over, these people would say with real affection: 'She's like one of us, so natural.' Of course, the truth was, Lady Megan couldn't help being 'natural'. She was just being herself. And being herself, she genuinely loved people, dogs and gardens. . . . She would relate in detail the doings of her adored corgi, Huwcyn. Well-kept gardens fascinated Lady Megan, and there are quite a few gardens in the county with plants from Criccieth in them.[48]

Megan's most appealing qualities were her informality, her rich enjoyment of the simple things of life and her sense of fun. Yet, despite her open and outgoing character, her friends realised that in some ways she was a very private person. There were questions that she did not like to answer, and subjects she would not discuss. She disliked gossip and was displeased by any conversation that touched on sexual matters. Her religious faith was strictly her own business, and some people who knew her quite well were never aware of it.

Like her father, she was famous for her charm; it was the most obvious part of her inheritance from him. 'She could charm the birds out of the trees, exactly like her father,' Gwynfor Evans said of her.[49] Clem Thomas used the same phrase in his recollections, but he added: 'Aroused and annoyed she could, and did, lash out with a tumbling torrent of words that stung like a whiplash.'[50] This too was part of the inheritance. Lloyd George had been feared for the verbal whiplash he inflicted on his secretaries, Cabinet ministers when he was Prime Minister, and even his beloved daughter. But he was always able to heal the wound with a forgiving smile when the outburst was over, and this again was true of Megan.

With the charm, the Lloyd George eloquence was the gift that was transmitted in full measure to Megan. In 1950 Hubert Morgan, Labour Party organiser in North Wales, heard her speak in Anglesey during the election campaign. 'You could feel the emotion rising,' he recalled. 'I couldn't help feeling the desire to join her, and I had to remember that I was there to help defeat her.' In 1957, when Megan was standing for Carmarthen, Patricia Llewellyn-Davies had an equally powerful impression: 'She started in English, then she switched to Welsh, and everyone leaned forward as though they wanted to touch her physically. It was electrifying.' Nancy Seear, who sat just behind Megan at a Liberal rally in the Albert Hall in 1948, described it as 'chemical communication – she was sucking in their feelings and spraying them back.' Megan had a huge reception, putting all the other speakers in the shade; but, Lady Seear added, 'I don't think she knew what she was going to say before she started.'[51]

Whether or not this was literally true, Megan's speeches were noted more for their brilliance and their emotional force than for their solid content. Listening to her in Carmarthen, Gwilym Prys Davies thought: 'She had no mastery of policy – it was mostly rhetoric.'[52] She was much more effective on the platform (especially in Welsh) than in the House of Commons – unlike her father, who was a master of both techniques. Megan worked hard at her parliamentary speeches, hunting up the necessary facts and statistics and making one draft after another; but, since this methodical work went against the grain, her speeches were somewhat rare events. Lloyd George wrote to her in 1936:

I am disappointed to find that you have not yet taken any part in the debates. You really ought to do so. It is a first-class mistake, because you are neglecting a great opportunity, and no one can do it better, and very few as well, when you choose to do so.[53]

He was writing from Jamaica, and he added a complaint that Megan had not written to him. However, he was used to her aversion to writing letters. More jocularly, he had written to her in 1919:

My darling little Megan,
So you found time in your busy life to send a letter to your indolent old father to stir him up to a little more activity![54]

Megan was quite capable of seeing the joke against herself. Writing to Thelma on 4 January 1922 (and dating the letter, which she seldom did), she told her friend:

Your amazement will be great I know when you realise that I am answering your letter on the very day of its arrival, but my dear I have made good resolutions, & as it is only 4 days since the New Year they are still unbroken!

From India in 1924 she wrote:

Unfaithful as you have proved yourself to be to your one friend, she waives aside your shortcomings & shows once more her undying devotion by setting herself to a task, which above all others she abhors.

What Megan did not inherit from her father was his immense capacity for hard work, which enabled him to vanquish his opponents in debate and earned him the respect of conservative-minded civil servants. Megan was – the word is inevitable – lazy. Testimony from those who knew her, including those who loved her, is unanimous to that effect.[55] Few were ready to assert that she would have been a success in governmental office. Cledwyn Hughes considers that her imaginative flair, with her intuitive ability to speak for the Welsh people, could have made her a good Secretary of State for Wales (a position he has held himself), but he concedes that she would have needed a very efficient staff.[56] Eirene White, who was a political journalist and then an MP, thinks that Megan had 'a bright intelligence but an untrained mind'.[57] Perhaps we can put some blame on her unsystematic early education, and on the fact that she left school at sixteen and never went to university.

Like most people who are both lazy and charming, Megan was able to cajole others to take tedious chores off her shoulders. 'Couldn't you do it? You're so much better at it than me': that became a family joke. She relied particularly on Olwen. The sisters were very close, and Olwen did not mind taking on the role of the capable, reliable one. Megan used to call her 'my Rock of Gibraltar'. As they grew up, Megan's five nephews and three nieces were also called into service – or exploited, if one chooses that word. They loved her too much to object. In return, she was an affectionate as well as glamorous aunt, always keenly interested in their doings. The eldest niece, Valerie, remembers: 'She never wrote letters, but she always came up with a good birthday present.'[58]

It scarcely needs saying that Megan was often late for appointments. On one occasion, she arranged to go shopping with Olwen and to meet her at three o'clock outside Swan and Edgar's in Piccadilly Circus. After waiting until a quarter to four, Olwen went home. 'You might have hung on a bit,' Megan said when they finally got together. Olwen replied: 'Just think, Megan – it was Piccadilly Circus!'[59]

In a debate on hospital conditions in 1938, Megan attacked the rigorous discipline imposed on nurses – 'nineteenth-century conditions deter twentieth-century girls' – and cited the case of a student nurse whose leave was stopped because she was three minutes late for breakfast. 'I wonder how many of us would survive that test,' Megan commented – speaking, no doubt, from the heart. On one occasion she wrote to a BBC producer, 'To be honest, 10 o'clock in the morning for a broadcast is not a time that appeals to me.' However, her late start to the day had one cause which she would never have cited as an excuse: her period of private prayer.

Her forgetfulness was legendary, especially in the family. Her niece Margaret gives an example:

She invited me and my sister Eluned to go to Stratford-on-Avon to see one of the Shakespeare plays. . . . We set off by train. She had forgotten that we had to change at Leamington Spa and, on being told that we had to, could only put on her hat back to front three times, whilst we practically hurled ourselves and the luggage out of the train. On the journey home Aunty Megan remembered she had left one of her dresses in the hotel where we had stayed. At Leamington Spa Eluned and I had to leave the train and put through a phone call to the hotel for her. When we arrived at Euston she went to the Lost Property to report some other article she had left on the train, and left her handbag on the counter.[60]

Being Megan's secretary, therefore, was no sinecure. Megan Ivor Jones, who had the job in 1938–9, recalls that she wrote the MP's replies to letters from constituents, but two or three weeks sometimes passed before Megan scrawled her signature. Working at the House of Commons, Miss Jones seldom saw her employer before lunch.[61] Priscilla Morton, secretary from 1953 to 1958, used to take advantage of Megan's departure for Brynawelon to tidy her London flat and deal with letters, which might be found anywhere, even under the bed.[62] Helena Dightam, secretary from 1962 to Megan's death, has preserved some of the notes that she found when she arrived for work:

Can you find the tickets for the November handicap? Are they in my briefcase, or somewhere in the flat? *Urgent.*

Oh dear! What is to be done with me. Hang the blasted specs round my neck. So sorry to give you the trouble of going to retrieve them.

Can you beat it. I left my gloves!! – navy blue in Covent Garden last Sat. Row S. Can you tel.?

The laziness and the scatterbrain aspect of Megan's character had their serious side. Because she failed to appear regularly at boring committee meetings, Megan was less effective than she might have been in activities that mattered to her: the League of Nations Union in the 1930s, the Liberal Party through a score of years of battles to keep the Radical tradition alive, the campaign for equal pay, the Parliament for Wales campaign. She was valued more as an orator and a public 'draw' than as a strategist and planner. No one, however, questioned her devotion to these causes nor the sincerity of her convictions. Whatever her faults, she was irreplaceable. Often and truly was it said: 'There's no one like her.'

# CHAPTER SIX

# Into the Abyss

1

While Mussolini got away with his aggression in Abyssinia, Hitler got away with successive steps in the rebuilding of German power. In 1935 he introduced military conscription and started the creation of an air force – the Luftwaffe, which, within five years, would rain destruction on Barcelona, Warsaw and London. In the same year an Anglo-German agreement, over French objections, permitted him to expand his navy and build submarines. In March 1936 he moved troops into the demilitarised zone west of the Rhine (the Allied occupation forces had been withdrawn in 1930). Baldwin, with tears in his eyes, told the French Prime Minister, Pierre Flandin, that Britain had no forces ready to help France in action to push the Germans out, nor would British public opinion support such action.[1]

The response of the Left in democratic countries was a united front against the Nazi and Fascist threat. The *Frente Popular* or People's Front, an alliance of Socialist, Communist and Liberal parties, scored an electoral victory in Spain in February 1936. In May the *Front Populaire* in France scored a similar victory and the Socialist leader, Léon Blum, formed a government. An alliance on these lines was urged in Britain by the small (but at that time not insignificant) Communist Party, by left-wingers in the Labour Party and by some Liberals – including two new Liberal MPs, Richard Acland and Wilfrid Roberts, who had both been elected in 1935 without Labour opposition because of their known Radical outlook. Megan, who was friendly with Acland and Roberts, said in June 1936: 'I should like to see a

Popular Front of a kind formed in this country. But if the progressive forces delay too long, they may never get their chance.'[2]

She was speaking on the eve of a crucial by-election. The MacDonaldite minister J. H. Thomas, caught out leaking budget secrets, was obliged to resign his seat at Derby, which he had won with a 12,000 majority. The Derby Labour Party selected Philip Noel-Baker as candidate. Influenced by the 'Popular Front' spirit, the Derby Liberals decided not to put forward a candidate and most of them supported Philip. He was also supported by Lloyd George's Council of Action, which produced a statement signed by a collection of local worthies, seven clergymen and a rabbi.

Professor Noel-Baker (as the local press generally referred to him) had been writing a magisterial book on *The Private Manufacture of Armaments*, which was published and prominently reviewed in June 1936. (Still more impressively, the 570-page book was announced as Part 1, but he never completed Part 2.) He was a member of the Focus for the Defence of Freedom and Peace, formed a few months earlier on the initiative of a German-Jewish refugee, Eugen Spier; other members included Churchill, Sinclair, the Duchess of Atholl and Gilbert Murray.[3] He was also the chief progenitor of the (mainly Anglo-French) International Peace Campaign, and of course he was a stalwart of the League of Nations Union. Much to the annoyance of the Tories, one message of support for Noel-Baker came from Lord Cecil, who was certainly a devoted League of Nations man but was also a lifelong and eminently respectable Conservative.

At this time, as indeed throughout his life, Philip Noel-Baker was dedicated to the cause of peace. He could have told Megan in 1936 what he did tell her in a letter in 1953:

I have only one real concern in public affairs – *peace*. My father made me care for almost nothing else, before I was twenty, & I always felt he left me a legacy & mandate to carry out when he died. . . . There is only one subject on which I have always been accepted in many countries as a recognized authority – disarmament & international institutions. I'm better equipped by knowledge, work & experience than anybody else. . . . I passionately believe – indeed, in politics I hardly believe anything else – that the Tory govt of 1931 could have got Disarmament & stopped the Second War; if your father had agreed to lead the [Labour] Party, we might even have got it in 1936.[4]

Peace was, therefore, the main issue in the by-election. Although there were serious problems about health and housing, and Philip commented in his speeches on the poverty that he saw as he canvassed, Derby had not been particularly hard hit by the slump, and unemployment in 1936 was only 3.9 per cent. The point highlighted in the Labour campaign was that the voters had a chance to give their verdict on the Hoare–Laval deal and the government's refusal to implement effective sanctions. At his adoption meeting on 25 June, Philip accused the government of sabotaging the League as well as the disarmament conference, and warned: 'Unless the world is well led and wisely guided, it will drift into catastrophic war.'[5] Next day, he called the by-election 'an opportunity to tell the government that they are unclean and must go'. A few days later he said: ' This country may be the next Abyssinia. If so, it will be because it failed to do its duty a year ago.'

The Labour campaign was vigorous, spirited and well organised. All the party's best-known leaders – Attlee, Herbert Morrison, Arthur Greenwood, Stafford Cripps, Hugh Dalton and Walter Citrine of the TUC – came to speak. Bob Newton, a local stalwart whose views were well to the left of Philip's, recalled: 'He was a first-rate candidate. Another man wouldn't have won it. He wasn't what I'd call a Socialist, but he was a good man. I'll never forget that by-election.'[6] As well as the activists of Derby, scores of people from outside the constituency – often middle-class members of the LNU – came to canvass, staff the committee rooms and drive voters to the poll in their cars. In Bob Newton's words: 'All the eggheads in the country were there.'

Polling was to be on 9 July. As the campaign warmed up, it was announced that Lloyd George would speak at a Council of Action meeting to support Philip on 6 July. This 'impertinent intrusion', as Philip's opponent, the National Labour candidate Albert Church, called it, immediately became a hot tactical issue. Noting that the Communist MP Willie Gallacher (elected for West Fife in 1935) was also endorsing Philip, Church discerned 'a Popular Front of the one true Liberal, a Communist, and an intellectual pacifist' – presumably Philip. Lloyd George, Church charged, was 'seemingly anxious to throw in his lot with Communists and extreme and revolutionary Socialists rather than play the game by the country.'

These attacks increased the excitement over Lloyd George's visit. Sylvester, who as usual accompanied Lloyd George, noted: 'The Drill Hall was packed with three thousand people, and thousands stood outside in the pouring rain.'[7] Newton's recollection is: 'There were more outside than there were inside. I never got in myself.' Despite the rain, hundreds of people stood outside to hear Lloyd George's fifty-minute speech through amplifiers.

In championship form, Lloyd George went through the story of Manchuria and Abyssinia and demanded: 'Who ratted?' Answering his own question as usual, he went on: 'These are the rats who scuttled the ship – that's the government you are being asked to vote for.' In more solemn mood, he told the audience:

Scan the firmament and you see the clouds gathering, darkening, deepening, lowering. . . . You may give a judgement that will clear the skies. . . . Mr Noel-Baker does not pay lip-service to peace – he has it coursing through his veins. If he is returned on Thursday, it will not merely be a victory for peace in Derby, it will give heart and hope to people who were broken, weary and faint.

There was torrential rain again on polling day, but the Labour campaigners smelt victory. About two thousand people stood in the rain until the result was declared at twenty minutes after midnight. Philip was in with a majority of 2753.

## 2

Only two months after this success for the friends of peace, Megan found herself involved in a strange and (seen from a later perspective) embarrassing episode. For all her political friends, Hitler and Mussolini were embodiments of menace and evil. Now she was to shake hands and sit round the tea-table with the more diabolical of the two, Adolf Hitler himself. The initiative for this visit came from her father.

Although Lloyd George saw himself as essentially a democrat and a man of the Left, and although he called for resistance to aggression, he had a strange blind spot where Hitler was concerned. He deceived himself lamentably about Hitler's character, and was therefore able to deceive himself about Hitler's intentions.

Hitler's aims, as generally seen at this time, were to free Germany from the position of inferiority to which she had been condemned at Versailles; to build her armed forces up to parity with other major nations; and to bring ethnically German populations into the German Reich. These were, primarily, the ten million Austrians and the three million Sudeten Germans who lived in Czechoslovakia.

The issues were not so clear-cut as they appear with hindsight. Liberal-minded people in Britain had a guilty conscience about Versailles. The rearmament of Germany could be seen as a gratification of national pride, not as evidence of warlike purposes. And the principle of ethnic nationality and ethnic unity was – indeed, still is – the conventional wisdom of our century. After the dissolution of the

Austro-Hungarian Empire, a 'little Austria' had no obvious *raison d'être*, and in the 1920s many Austrian liberals or leftists favoured union with Germany. As for the Sudetenland, while it had never been part of Germany, it had not been ruled from Prague since the demise of the Kingdom of Bohemia in 1620. H. N. Brailsford, criticising the Versailles settlement from a Socialist angle, had written: 'The worst offence was the subjection of over three million Germans to Czech rule.'[8]

In his book *Mein Kampf*, written in 1924 and later translated into English, Hitler had made it clear that he wanted to see German rule established over large regions of Eastern Europe. The *Herrenvolk* (master race) would take possession of the agricultural and mineral resources, while the Slavic populations would have the status of subjects without rights. But in the west *Mein Kampf* was either ignored or dismissed as the visionary ramblings of a man now sobered by the responsibilities of government. Neville Chamberlain was quoted as saying in 1938: 'Hitler wants all the Germans he can lay his hands on, but positively no foreigners.'[9]

Lloyd George, at all events, was inclined to keep an open mind, and in 1936 he made arrangements through the German Embassy to visit Germany and meet Hitler. He was accompanied by Megan, Gwilym and the ubiquitous Sylvester. The first stop was Stuttgart, where Megan annoyed her father by being late for dinner. He stalked out of the dining-room, and Sylvester records: 'She flared up and asked: "Can no one have a personality of their own?"'[10] Reaching Munich on 3 September, they were joined by Thomas Jones and Lord Dawson, 'who said he was interested in Germany from the angle of the health of the individual and the sterilisation of the unfit.'[11]

Most of the two-week visit was devoted to a guided tour of projects started by the Nazi regime – land drainage, afforestation, road-building. Greatly impressed, Lloyd George was almost tempted to believe that Hitler had read the Yellow Book, and his plan for National Roads came to mind when he was driven from Munich to Berchtesgaden on the newly opened *Autobahn*. He told Sylvester:

Germany is building up something which we have not got and which is better than ours. . . . . I put similar proposals to those now being carried out in Germany before our Cabinet. But they wouldn't even sniff at them.[12]

What most impressed the visitors (and many other visitors to Nazi Germany) was the achievement of virtually full employment. It was seldom noticed that this owed something to conscription, something to rearmament, and something to pressure on women to give up paid work and retire to the kitchen. Of course, there were no visits to concentration camps. Describing the trip years later, Sylvester said that they did not exist in 1936 – 'or, if they did, nobody told us'.[13] He recalled, however, that Lloyd George showed his annoyance when a tactless guide plunged into an anti-Semitic tirade.

Meeting Hitler was naturally the high-spot. Lloyd George was invited to the Führer's home in the mountains above Berchtesgaden twice, once on his own and once with the whole British party (Sylvester noted uneasily that there were thirteen people for tea). Hitler made a strong impression, which had not faded when Sylvester was interviewed by the author in 1989: 'He had tremendous personality. He was so decisive. If you put a question, the answer came like a shot from a cannon. And, after all, he had done such wonderful things.' Megan, in a letter to her mother, described him as 'a simple man' and said: 'He was quite charming to us all.'[14] Hitler was certainly on his best behaviour, and was quoted by Sylvester (we remember his excellent shorthand) as saying:

The Allies won the war, but that is not due, in the primary case, to the soldiers of the Allies. Rather that great victory is due to one statesman, yourself, Mr Lloyd George. . . . I am convinced that, had I been in power then, I could have prevented Germany's downfall.[15]

There was, however, one lapse from Hitler's calculated good conduct. He gave Lloyd George a signed photograph, and Lloyd George asked whimsically if he could put it next to a photo of Marshal Foch, the Allied Supreme Commander in 1918. Hitler replied that this was quite in order because Foch was a French patriot, and he felt no hatred for former enemies, but he did have (as Thomas Jones noted) 'a great deal of enmity for Germans who betrayed their country'.[16] He went into a furious diatribe on this subject, and Megan, telling the story in the 1950s, recalled: 'I suddenly realised that the man was deranged.'[17]

In the car returning from Berchtesgaden, according to Jones, 'Megan proclaimed that it had been the most thrilling afternoon of her life.'[18] But a few days later, when she wrote to her mother, her tone was sceptical: 'I believe everyone feels he is a very great man, and everyone here *adores* him, and that he is the one who saved the country! Did you ever hear such a thing!'[19]

As soon as he got home, Lloyd George wrote an article giving his impressions. Friends were dismayed to learn that it was to appear in the *Daily Express*, not in the more congenial *News Chronicle*. They were still more dismayed when they read the article. After fulsome praise of the achievements he had been shown ('It is a happier Germany'), Lloyd George wrote:

One man has accomplished this miracle. He is a born leader of men. A magnetic, dynamic personality with a single-minded purpose, a resolute will and a dauntless heart. . . . The old trust him, the young idolise him. . . . He is the George Washington of Germany – the man who won for his country independence from all her oppressors.[20]

British readers were assured that 'the Germans have definitely made up their minds never to quarrel with us again' – a phrase that uncannily presages Chamberlain's claim two years later. The idea of 'a German hegemony in Europe' was 'not even on the horizon of Nazism'. In any case, it would take Germany at least ten years to build up an army capable of anything but defensive fighting. But the most embarrassing part of the article was:

They have a dread of the great army which has been built up in Russia in recent years. . . . Unfortunately, the German leaders set this down to the influence of prominent Russian Jews, and thus anti-Jewish sentiment is once more stirred up just as it was fading into torpitude. . . . [But] the native good humour of the German people soon relapses into tolerance after a display of ill-temper.

The article was written, according to Kingsley Martin, 'in spite of protests from Megan Lloyd George and Tom Jones'.[21] In his diary Jones described the scene:

We knock out or modify a sentence here and there, but not without pressure, in which Megan joins effectively. I urge him to tone down this sentence [ie 'the Germans will never quarrel with us again'] but he held firmly to it and in it went.[22]

Lloyd George never changed his view of Hitler, even after the war began. In July 1940 he disagreed strongly with Juan Negrin, the exiled ex-Premier of Republican Spain, who called Hitler a lunatic. Sylvester noted: 'L.G. immediately developed a terrific defence of Hitler, saying that he was a genius.' This time, Hitler was compared to Oliver Cromwell.[23]

We should not, perhaps, be too censorious. With the cunning observable in psychopaths, Hitler was able to impress foreign visitors not only with his strength of character and decisiveness but also with his reasonableness and good intentions. Lansbury, who visited him six months after Lloyd George, described him as 'one of the greatest men of our time' and was convinced that 'he *will not* go to war unless pushed into it by others.'[24] But Thelma Cazalet, who attended the Nuremberg rally of 1938 with an official invitation and heard Hitler speak, wrote:

The performance was repulsive. . . . The hoarse and bullying screaming of the orator was intolerable. . . . The really fearsome thing was the hypnotic effect of the Führer on German youth. To them he could do no wrong. I had such an impression of impending tragedy that the thought passed through my mind that if only I had a gun and the guts to use it . . .[25]

Thelma dodged a party at which she could have been introduced to Hitler, and 'bolted for home with all possible speed.'

3

Megan's next trip abroad, in January 1937, was to Jamaica. Her father was spending the winter there, and was in an irritable mood. One piece of news that infuriated him was that Saunders Lewis, who had blown up a Royal Air Force installation not far from Criccieth, was to be tried at the Old Bailey, not in Wales. He wrote to Megan:

I think it an unutterable piece of insolence, but very characteristic of this Government. They crumple up when tackled by Mussolini and Hitler, but they take it out of the smallest country in the realm which they are misgoverning. It is the way cowards try to show that they are strong by bullying. . . . This is the first Government that has tried Wales at the Old Bailey. I wish I were there, and I certainly wish I were 40 years younger. I should be prepared to risk a protest which would be a defiance.[26]

Megan and her mother, after the usual Christmas at Brynawelon, went out to join him and returned with him in February. On the ship, there was a classic Lloyd George family row. Ordered to appear for before-dinner drinks at seven o'clock, Megan was twenty-five minutes late. Sylvester described the scene:

Working himself up into a fit of anger, his face red and his blue-grey eyes flashing, he said: 'You have never once been up to have breakfast with me, either in Jamaica or on the boat, still less to walk with me before breakfast, which you know I like to do.' Then he added with real venom: 'But your mother has always been there. That is what I would have expected of her. But then she is a lady and you are not.' Megan's face went white with rage and her eyes filled with tears. . . . [Later] I returned to the sitting-room to find Megan in floods of tears. 'My God,' she said to me, 'it will be a long time before I forgive him for that.'[27]

Of course, she did forgive him. It was one of the intermittent flaming rows that, like summer thunderstorms, punctuated the relationship between these two quick-tempered, emotional people. Fuses were generally short in the Lloyd George family; only Gwilym was noted for his calmness. Once the storm had passed, father and daughter reverted to their normal affectionate closeness. The actual cause of the row was almost always, as in this instance, trivial. When there were serious disagreements between Lloyd George and Megan – for example, over the *Daily Express* article – they were worked out in a discussion which might be called an argument, but not a row.

By this time, international politics was dominated by the supreme conflict of the 1930s: the Spanish civil war. It had begun in July 1936 with what was intended to be a military coup to overthrow the People's Front government. As a coup, it misfired; hastily mobilised workers' militia units won the upper hand in Madrid and Barcelona. General Francisco Franco, the rebel commander, had to begin a regular campaign to advance on Madrid from his base in Spanish Morocco. On 8 November Madrid's people awoke to see three thousand volunteers from abroad marching from the railway station to the front line. This was the vanguard of the International Brigade.

Over the next two years, perhaps as many as 40,000 men from about thirty countries made their way to Spain to fight for the Republic. They had great difficulty in getting there, they had no hope of protection if they were captured or of pensions for their families if they were killed, and they were sent into action in the most critical battles, incurring heavy casualties. It is no wonder that the Brigade evoked feelings of fervent admiration on the political Left, not least in Britain. Over two thousand of the volunteers were British, including scores of Welsh miners. At home, thousands of people were active in raising funds to help the volunteers and their dependants, and in equipping ambulances. A newspaper photograph of Megan shows her standing by the door of the Welsh Ambulance for Spain.

But Franco had his sympathisers too. Although his forces were always referred to by the Republicans as 'the Fascists', Franco was not a Fascist in any accurate sense; he was fighting to restore a Spain dominated by the historic alliance of army and church. One Tory MP, Sir Henry Page-Croft, called him 'a gallant Christian gentleman'. Another, Thelma Cazalet's brother Victor, spoke at a meeting of the Friends of National Spain and asserted that Franco was 'the leader of our cause today'.[28]

Still, Franco was enough of a Fascist to receive vital support from Hitler and Mussolini. The Condor Legion, dispatched from Germany and operating under German command, consisted of forty-eight bombers, sixty fighters, forty-eight tanks and eight batteries of artillery. Mussolini sent regular divisions, amounting to 70,000 men, to make up for Franco's deficiency in manpower.[29]

Under international law, a government faced with a rebellion had a right to buy weapons anywhere. However, the British government persuaded the French to promote a non-intervention agreement which forbade such purchases, and even to close their frontier on the Pyrenees. The parties to the agreement were Britain, France, Germany, Italy, Portugal and the Soviet Union, all represented on a committee under the chairmanship of Lord Plymouth, a Tory peer. The committee had no teeth, and the shipments from Germany and Italy continued with open cynicism. The Russians, denouncing non-intervention as a farce, withdrew from the committee and sent tanks and aircraft to the Republicans. But their aid was never so extensive, and eventually Stalin recognised that the Republic was not going to win and tapered off his supplies.

In May 1937 Baldwin retired and Chamberlain became Prime Minister. While Baldwin never had much interest in foreign policy, Chamberlain – although his knowledge of the world across the Channel was severely limited – was convinced of his ability to resolve international problems. He saw no reason why it should be impossible to reach sensible and businesslike agreements with Hitler and Mussolini. Archibald Sinclair once commented that, in his experience as Lord Mayor of Birmingham, Chamberlain had settled disagreements between the Water Committee and the Sewage Committee by getting them round the table and he believed that the same methods would work on a larger scale. So he pursued a policy of appeasement – a word which, after the policy was discredited, came to mean shameful surrender, but which Chamberlain always used proudly to represent a desirable procedure.

The Cabinet was now dominated by men who concurred in Chamberlain's way of thinking – Sir John Simon, Sir Samuel Hoare and Lord Halifax. Eden could not match the weight of this formidable and prestigious trio (Simon and Hoare were former Foreign Secretaries, Halifax a former Viceroy of India) added to that of the Prime Minister. Foreign policy was no longer made in the Foreign Office. In November 1937 Halifax went to Germany to hold talks with the Nazi leaders, and Eden was merely informed of what had happened. Lloyd George, who liked Eden, was constantly urging him to assert himself, but in vain. Hitler told his army commander, General von Fritsch: 'Chamberlain was going to get rid of Eden – of that he had full assurance.'[30]

Megan watched the course of events with acute anxiety. The only hope was for a political revolt against Chamberlain's policy, which was opposed not only by Labour and the Liberals but also by Tories such as Winston Churchill, Sir Robert Boothby, the Duchess of Atholl and Thelma Cazalet. Someone who was thinking along the same lines was Irene Noel-Baker, who wrote to Churchill in March 1938:

You, Lord Robert [Cecil], Eden, Archie Sinclair, Attlee, Alexander, my Philip and Lloyd George are a band of warriors in the House & in the country who surely ought to beat that miserable middle class businessman with no scrap of imagination, who to our immense misfortune is now Prime Minister.[31]

Both these women were influenced by Philip, with his passionate concern for peace, his intense convictions and his incorrigible (though, alas, often ill-founded) optimism. They had met on several occasions, since both were active in the LNU. They might have become friends; they were intelligent, strong-minded women whose interests and opinions coincided. But by this time Irene's husband was Megan's lover.

4

By his own account, Philip Noel-Baker fell in love with Megan in 1929 when (as we saw in chapter 5) they 'sat down on the bench in the lobby' together. There is no evidence, however, that she reciprocated his feelings or that they became lovers at that time. They could have seen little of each other in 1931–3, when he was in Geneva. But from 1936, when he won the Derby by-election, they were able to meet every day when the House of Commons was sitting.

It was in 1936, in fact, that they must have become lovers, as we can deduce from later letters in which he takes that year as the starting-point of a new life. He wrote in 1947: 'You see, I've been a much nicer – shall I say much less horrid – person since 1936. In every way – better tempered, more considerate, better ideas, everything you could wish.'[32] A letter written in the summer of 1953 reads:

My little beloved, I long to see your sunburn! You know it is one of my greatest weaknesses, & I remember you saying to me on the telephone in 1936 [the 6 is underlined] or so: 'I'm very brown', & I remember how I wanted to dash up by the next train, to see & kiss you.[33]

Philip's pocket diary for 1937 has been preserved with his papers. He was generally careful not to note appointments with Megan (nor does his name occur in her diaries, of which a couple survive), but this diary contains a lightly pencilled 'Megan' on 28 April. Three days, 27 to 29 September, have KEEP EMPTY written across them in bold capitals. Two more days, 15 and 16 October, had the still more emphatic notation: KEEP AT ALL COSTS EMPTY. Irene, presumably, was in Greece at the time. Until the war, and again after the war, she spent periods of two or three months at Achmetaga.

They both had strong motives for concealing the relationship. Megan was by temperament 'a private person', and certainly did not wish it to be known that she was a married man's mistress; Philip went in fear of Irene. The concealment was successful. The only people of whom we can say definitely that they were aware of the relationship in the 1930s were Megan's close friends, Thelma Cazalet and Ursula Thorpe, and her sister Olwen. To these we can add the Liberal MP Wilfrid Roberts, but his knowledge derived from chance. His London *pied-à-terre* was above Lock's, the hatter, in St James's Street. Gazing out of the window one summer evening, he saw Megan and Philip walking past and jumped to the right conclusion. His reaction was: 'I felt sorry for her. There was no future in it for her.'[34] He was right in this conclusion too.

Philip's marriage was far from being ideally happy. Irene was ten years older than he was, and when they were first married, in war conditions, they must have been comrades rather than lovers. He told the story in a letter to Megan in 1955:

I was 25 when I married; 10 years younger; young for my years, inexperienced & immature in every way, especially socially; under a tremendous nervous strain. . . . After the first year, I took the Second Unit to Italy – more nerve-wracking, & I was just married, & everything was very difficult. The war meant separation for more than 3 years. That didn't help. I was flung straight from 1918 influenza into the Peace Conference, where I worked *desperately* hard, being run down with 'flu & the long aftermath of severe oriental dysentery, which I had in 1917.

That no doubt was the start of processes which have led to the situation of today, where I am often told: 'Of course, you never were a lover in any way; you didn't begin to understand anything about it.' . . . There has always been a total loss of everything that marriage might have meant & ought to have meant.

Philip then admitted that, absorbed in work for the League of Nations, he neglected Irene and their son Francis (the only child, born in 1920). He went on:

Nervous tension meant that I . . . fell down on every duty of my personal life.

And of course that all intensified & *justified* what had always been a tendency to criticize me, see my faults, & make them very plain to me. . . . That all led to quarrels. I was immensely to blame for the quarrels. I was insufferable, & I caused misery. . . . I often thought I sh'd do better to end it. . . . [I was] a poisoned & distorted & frustrated character, unfit for anyone as a companion, unfit for work, unfit for real love. . . . [But] I made great efforts, because otherwise I saw total disaster, by spiritual & mental corrosion of a devastating kind; in a measure, I succeeded.[35]

While allowances should be made for Philip's guilt feelings and self-pity, as well as his desire to arouse Megan's compassion, it does appear that he received little kindness or sympathy from Irene. From Achmetaga (like Margaret Lloyd George from Criccieth) she accused her husband of infidelity while refusing to be with him. In 1922 she suspected him of having an affair with Dame Rachel Crowdy, a woman who had been given the title of Dame for her hospital work in the war and was then head of the Social Affairs division of the League secretariat. 'Your platonic philanderings with people like Dame Rachel supply enough sentiment to keep you going,' Irene wrote acidly.[36]

The words 'platonic' and 'philanderings' are both worth some reflection. Apparently, Irene did not think that Philip and Dame Rachel were having a full sexual relationship. She despised him for his failure to be 'a lover in any way', and evidently it did not occur to her that he might be more successful with another woman.

Philip's letters to Megan show that they made love whenever they had the opportunity, and he at least had no doubt that they achieved mutual pleasure. Sometimes he boasted of his virility and warned her to prepare for a strenuous time. But he also cherished kisses in a parked car or a room in the House of Commons, and one gets the impression that he enjoyed the rituals of courtship, or simply flirting, as much as the culmination. Patricia Llewellyn-Davies, who became his secretary in the 1940s and knew him well for the rest of his life, defines him as 'a romantic puritan'.[37] Although she was aware of his assignations with Megan, she was not certain that they were actually lovers; he had such assignations, Patricia observed, with a number of other women too. An enthusiastic (and very good) dancer, he always wanted to dance with the prettiest girl at the party. Wilfrid Roberts, who also realised that Philip pursued various women, describes him as 'a serious philanderer'.[38] One has the picture of a man who held back from giving the whole of himself to any one woman, and never quite progressed from a delayed adolescence to emotional maturity.

Ursula Thorpe, who strongly disliked Philip and said categorically, 'He was a swine', takes the view that 'he was always just fooling with Megan – amusing himself.'[39] However, if Philip was a flirt, Megan was not. The few people who knew about her relationship with Philip and who can now give their testimony concur that she was the one whose emotions were the more deeply aroused. 'It meant a great deal to her and caused her immense unhappiness,' Ursula remarked. Patricia stated with conviction: 'She was tremendously in love with him.' Asked whether Philip was in love with Megan, she hesitated and said: 'He thought he was.' In fact, Megan was capable of a limitless commitment leading to an experience of supreme importance in her life. We must also take into account a social and moral climate in which a sexual relationship outside marriage was for most people a very serious matter, and remember too that Megan was sincerely religious. It may well be – at least, we have no evidence to the contrary – that she was embarking on her first full love affair at the age of thirty-four, and that it was the only one in her life.

They had been lovers for some time when, in 1938, Philip found himself obliged to answer – or evade – a crucial question: should he seek a divorce from his wife and marry Megan? Unlike Ursula, Thelma Cazalet was warmly sympathetic to Megan and Philip as lovers. She often invited them to her country home, Raspit, near Sevenoaks, so that they could be together without fear of undesired observation. Thelma was also decidedly in favour of marriage as the logical outcome of love; in 1939 she married David Keir. Her advice to Philip was clear and emphatic. He recalled, writing to Megan in 1953:

Thelma told me that I ought to cut all the Gordian knots, & take the risks & the results that came; she told me – this was before the war – everybody did, that everybody accepted it, that it caused a little temporary pain, or even perhaps a lot, but that this pain passed, the new life began, & that the new life for us would have brought us lasting happiness, lasting success, & better work & more achievement than either of us could manage alone. I think that was always in her mind in 1938, 1939, & even 1940. . . . She had no doubts, & she tried . . . to get rid of mine.[40]

Philip reverted repeatedly to this episode in letters written in the 1950s, evidently because Megan reproached him for not taking Thelma's advice. It is surprising, no doubt, that Megan, who was never accused of timidity, did not speak out for herself and thrash the matter out with Philip. She may have felt that to plead with a man to marry her would be undignified and embarrassing. It is equally likely that Thelma said, 'Just leave it to me,' and Megan was glad to be spared the argument. Her conclusion would have been that, if Thelma could not persuade Philip to take the plunge, then she could not do so either.

Evidently, there were two questions that Thelma and Philip did not need to discuss. One was whether Irene would agree to divorce him. The law did not then allow divorce on grounds of breakdown of marriage, so she would have needed to charge him with adultery or desertion. Apparently it was taken for granted that she would be willing to do so. The other question was whether Megan would wish to marry Philip if given the opportunity. Since she was not given that opportunity, we cannot answer this question with certainty, but Thelma was clearly assuming that she would gladly marry Philip if and when he was free. In view of Megan's rejection of her suitors in earlier years and the widespread belief that she was 'married to politics', this was a remarkable assumption, but no one was in a better position to know than the hostess of Raspit.

Another factor of incalculable emotional significance must have been Megan's desire to become a mother. Like many women, she may well have been primarily concerned with launching her career and generally enjoying life in her twenties, and began to think of what she was missing when she reached her thirties. Medical opinion at that time held that it was highly inadvisable for a woman to have a first child after the age of forty, and in 1938 Megan was thirty-six. It is reasonable to suppose that she opened her heart to Thelma on this subject, and this lent force to Thelma's urgings on Philip. She would have told Philip that Megan wished for the fulfilment of motherhood (whether or not Megan told him so herself). It was another theme to which he reverted in letters in the 1950s. In 1953, after a night with Megan – perhaps a night of agonised talk – he wrote to her:

My beloved, ever since last night I've thought of only one thing – you and the angelic babies you should have had. There is nothing you do that you don't do with genius; but there is nothing you do that you would do with such genius as being a mother. I do so ache for you to have your babies – our babies – in your arms, & to see their joy in you, & your joy in them. They would have been such wonderful babies, so lovely, so clever, so amusing, so delicious to see & to hold & to hear & to love.[41]

From the confusion of tenses in this piece of prose, one might suppose that Philip was still hoping for 'our babies' in 1953, when Megan was fifty-one. The realities of past and present were sometimes not very clear in his mind.

At all events, he could not bring himself to cut the Gordian knots;

1939, and then 1940, found him still married to Irene and snatching secretive minutes or hours with Megan. We do not know the reasons for his decision – or lack of decision – but we have no evidence that he was worried about the harm that a divorce would do to his political career. Being named as the 'guilty party' in a divorce suit did not automatically spell political ruin in the 1930s, as it had in David Lloyd George's youth, but the divorce rate was much lower than it is now and Thelma was being unduly sanguine when she declared that 'everybody accepted it'. It might well have created problems for an MP who had a majority of under 3000 in a constituency like Derby, which was scarcely in the van of libertarian thought. For that matter, being disclosed as a married man's mistress could have done Megan no good among the Methodists and Baptists of Anglesey. In later letters, Philip never alluded directly to this aspect of the situation, but he wrote:

Perhaps I had a subconscious feeling, which didn't remain *not* conscious very long, that you were a woman of destiny; that you had a tremendous work to do for the world in the House; that you would do it better if you went on being M. Ll. G.; & that possibly I might bring you a little help & a little happiness without interrupting or breaking up that work.[42]

This, however, can fairly be regarded as one of the rationalisations by which Philip sought to justify his conduct in 1938. He looked back with a mixture of guilt, sentimental regret for 'what might have been', and uneasy self-persuasion that he had not been to blame. He wrote in 1947:

When I search my conscience, its not *there* that my qualms make themselves felt. Its elsewhere, that's the only doubt I ever have; & sometimes *that* hurts a lot. I *hate* selfishness – & perhaps I've been hideously selfish from the very start.[43]

In 1953:

I don't need to tell you how my mind went with hers [Thelma's] along that road. . . . And yet I was quite certain that for you the cutting of the Gordian knots would *never* do. I was absolutely certain you would be deeply, absolutely, unalterably against it, & that you wouldn't easily forgive me if I even tried to make you take that path. I was so certain that I never even talked to you about it, or hinted at it, or tried to lead you round to it in any way. I still believe that on this point I was right. . . .

Was I wrong, my angel? Have I been wrong all this time? I don't believe so, & from first to last, from 1936 until today, I never have. . . . I had to go on loving & trying to help you as best I cd; trying to give what a husband sh'd give, subject only to the limitation that the world should not come to know. . . .

Have I explained everything, my angel? Do you see that I *long* to be everything to you, & always do my best?[44]

In April 1954, after a telephone conversation with her:

You said to me, in tones of reproach:
    (a) that I wd never have broken down the barriers in 1938–40;
    (b) that, in any case, I ought to have tried, & talked to you about it;
    (c) that, in making love to you without being ready to break the barriers, & trying to get you to agree, I had behaved in a most miserably cowardly, cruel, ungentlemanly, heartless & ignoble way. (You didn't use these adjectives; but if your thought were accepted, they wd all of them, & many more, apply.). . .

You won't find it easy to think that always I've had a kind of inferiority complex that has made it difficult for me to believe that people – & especially women – liked me. . . . I never really felt *certain* what *you* thought about me, & never allowed myself to believe what I always *wanted* to believe. . . . *That* became an absolute conviction, not to say an obsession: that you didn't want me to speak, or even to *think*, about breaking the barriers. Was I really wrong? It seemed to me always that, if I got anywhere *near* it, you always made it plain that it was a forbidden thought. . . . As I was sure you wanted me *not* to speak of it, & still more sure that if I did you would say 'No' in such a way that I sh'd be bitterly remorseful that I had brought it up, I never had to face the question. . . . But I always knew, & I know now for an absolute certainty, that if I *had* to face it as a question of immediate decision, I *would* have broken the barriers.[45]

In November 1954:

My beloved, do you know that its only in the last few months that I've *really* believed you wd have married me, if I could have asked you? Even now, I very often don't *really* believe that it is true; I know I could make you happy, but I've never felt nearly good enough or grand enough or rich enough or important enough or handsome enough to make it *right* for you to marry me. What you ought to have had is someone with Anthony Eden's position, Chipps Channon's possessions, Adonis' good looks, Don Juan's power of attraction (without his habits), & the character and disposition of the Archangel Gabriel.[46]

And in 1955:

It wasn't very long before I felt sure that you would be against separation & what Thelma wanted me to do; but it brought conflict into every hour of every day, indeed into every waking thought. . . . Perhaps I did you a great wrong; perhaps I ought never to have looked at you again. Honestly – I've told you a thousand times – I never believed I could do you any harm. For years & years & years I only counted myself one of a large number, & I expected that you wd marry one of them as soon as you felt like it.[47]

There was, in fact, no reason whatever to think that Megan would have married anyone else, nor that Philip was one of a 'large number' of men who interested her. Nor could he rationally have been certain that she would say no to him (especially when Thelma was certain of the contrary); but he could make this credible to himself by not asking her. Although he never admitted it to himself, his real anxiety was that she might say yes and force him into an unwelcome upheaval.

Philip's behaviour inflicted painful unhappiness on Megan, although she was also finding joy in loving and being loved. No doubt she was aware of the irony of being involved in an affair with a married man and thus playing the role for which she had angrily blamed Frances Stevenson. She felt, perhaps, that if she could not have Philip as a husband it was better to keep him as a lover than to force him into a choice that might mean losing him. Or perhaps, as the unresolved situation persisted, in Philip's words, 'through 1938, 1939 and even 1940', she continued to hope against hope that he would come round to acting as she desired.

## 5

In these crucial years, Megan did not take a very vigorous part in efforts to check the aggressors and avert war. Although the cause of the Spanish Republic aroused passionate feelings among anti-Fascists and Radicals, and drove them into intensive campaigning, Richard Acland and Wilfrid Roberts recall that Megan was far from wearing herself out in support of Spain as they did themselves. The vehicle for this sort of activity – and for a People's Front, which in principle Megan favoured – was the Left Book Club. Its meetings and rallies brought together Labour left-wingers such as Stafford Cripps and Harold Laski, Communists, and Liberals like Acland and Roberts. Megan, however, never spoke from a Left Book Club platform, although her father did so on one occasion in April 1939.

Various explanations are possible. Although she had strong views on international issues, Megan was essentially a 'home issues' politician and a champion of her Anglesey constituents. Hitler's successive triumphs, and the increasing evidence that the poorly armed Spanish Republicans were doomed to defeat, made it hard to avoid the feeling that the struggle was hopeless. We must give some weight to Megan's famous laziness and her dislike of committee meetings and planning sessions. Last but not least, this was just the time when she was involved in a personal drama that put a heavy strain on her energies and her emotional strength.

One activity that she did keep up, and greatly enjoyed, was broadcasting. From 1935 onward, speakers in the *Week at Westminster* slot (as *The Week in Parliament* had been renamed) included Megan, her brother Gwilym, her lover Philip Noel-Baker, and her best friend, Thelma Cazalet, as well as R. A. Butler, Robert Boothby and Wilfrid Roberts. Ratings in an internal memo in 1939 were: 'Megan Lloyd George: always good. Richard Acland: promising, needs rehearsal. Wilfrid Roberts: pleasant manner.' Another memo praised Megan's 'easy natural style'.

But *The Week at Westminster* was far from being Megan's only contribution to broadcasting. In 1933 Mosley was invited to talk on Fascism and Megan was commissioned to follow with a ten-minute criticism (sadly, the scripts have not survived). In 1935 she was asked to talk about Emmeline Pankhurst in a series entitled *I Knew a Man* (*sic*); but she was reluctant to do it, probably because of the hostility between the Pankhursts and her father, and passed the job on to Thelma. In 1939 she debated with Florence Horsbrugh (a Tory MP and later Minister of Education) on unemployment, and in 1943 with Kenneth Pickthorn on electoral reform. She was on the panel for two unscripted and enormously popular programmes which were started during the war, *The Brains Trust* and *Any Questions?* These are only the highlights. She was constantly in demand for talks on the European Service, the Overseas Service, and the Welsh Region (in both her languages), so that she became one of the most accomplished and most experienced broadcasters in the country.

When the BBC started the world's first television service in 1937, Megan was immediately invited to face the camera. She was number one in a series called *Personalities*, talking about 'What I Think of the Future of Television'. She appeared on 20 April 1937, after being told, 'If you like to be simply imaginative, let your fancy stray into the future', and assured that the Daimler would get her to Alexandra Palace in thirty-five minutes. She was warned that she could not be seen to look at notes, but she could have them on a blackboard if she wished (the autocue had not been invented). With her experience of extempore platform speaking, she had no problems, and the producer, Mary Adams, wrote to thank her for '(a) the lovely picture you made and (b) the words of wisdom which fell from your lips'.[48]

It was in 1938 that the danger of war became acute and, for a few days in September, seemed imminent. On 12 February the Chancellor of Austria, Kurt von Schuschnigg, was summoned to Berchtesgaden and subjected to a furiously menacing tirade by Hitler. At one point, a German officer entered the room and Hitler said: 'I want to introduce you to General von Reichenau, who will be commander of my armies of occupation in Austria.'[49]

Schuschnigg could not look westward for help. At just this time, Anthony Eden admitted defeat in his unequal battle against Chamberlain. The evidence of intervention in Spain was now so overwhelming that Lord Plymouth's committee was discussing the possibility of troop withdrawals, though without getting anywhere. Chamberlain was bent on holding talks to reach amicable agreements with Mussolini; Eden opposed starting the talks until at least some Italian troops had left Spain. Chamberlain overruled him, and on 20 February he resigned, to be succeeded by Halifax. France, meanwhile, was in the throes of one of its recurrent political crises and was without a government.

Schuschnigg nevertheless announced on 9 March that a plebiscite would be held that Sunday, 12 March, in which Austrians would be asked to vote 'yes' for independence. Diplomats in Vienna forecast a 65 per cent majority. But the plebiscite never took place. On that very Sunday German troops entered Austria and the little country was officially annexed.

Reports from Vienna provided shocking (or, for appeasers, embarrassing) evidence of Nazi brutality. After Hitler's triumphant arrival, mocking crowds surrounded Jews who were forced to scrub the pavements with an acid solution and erase 'Vote yes' slogans. Hundreds, perhaps thousands, of Jews committed suicide;[50] they evaded the journey to the gas chambers which the survivors took a few years later. A Nazi paper published names of suicides under the headline 'Recommended as an example to others'.

Hitler quickly turned his attention to the German minority in Czechoslovakia. The key to the ensuing crisis lies in a sentence written, a few days after its climax, by Keynes: 'The actual course of events has been dictated by the fact that the objectives of Herr Hitler and Mr Chamberlain were not different, but the same.'[51] Hitler wanted to swallow the Sudetenland; Chamberlain thought this was a desirable solution, though he could not say so openly. In May, a German memorandum on a talk with a British diplomat in Berlin read: 'He believed he could assure us that the British government would bring such pressure to bear in Prague that the Czech government would be compelled to accede to German wishes.'[52]

The problem was that the Czechs were ready to fight for their independence and that they had a treaty of alliance with France, which in turn had a treaty with the Soviet Union. France was wobbling, but Stalin told Edvard Beneš, the Czech President, that he would render instant aid if called upon. On 12 September the French Foreign Minister, Georges Bonnet, asked Halifax what the answer would be to the question: 'We are going to march, will you march with us?' Halifax's reply deserves immortality:

The question itself, though plain in form, cannot be dissociated from the circumstances in which it might be posed, which are necessarily at this stage completely hypothetical.[53]

On 15 September Chamberlain flew to Berchtesgaden, conferred with Hitler, and reached agreement that the Sudetenland should be transferred to Germany. Edouard Daladier, the French Prime Minister, came to London a few days later and endorsed this deal, but he remarked that the Sudetenland was not the only point at issue and 'he was convinced in his heart that Germany was aiming at something far greater.'[54] He proposed that Britain and France should guarantee the survival of a truncated Czechoslovakia. Chamberlain saw no need for this, since he was sure that Hitler wanted 'only Germans', but he agreed to give the guarantee.

Then things began to come unstuck. The Czech government accepted the Berchtesgaden decision under protest, but mass demonstrations and a general strike brought about its collapse. A new government was formed under a military chief, General Syrovy, who declared: 'The Army stands and will stand on our frontiers to defend our liberty to the last.' At the same time, Chamberlain met Hitler again at Godesberg and found to his dismay that the German demands had been stiffened. Hitler insisted on a deadline of 1 October and demanded all 'predominantly German' territory, which could mean 51 per cent.[55] No agreement was reached. Chamberlain began to fear that he might be stumbling into a war for which he saw no reason.

France now mobilised its reservists and sent troops to the German frontier. The Royal Navy was also mobilised; the First Lord of the Admiralty, Duff Cooper, was opposed to Chamberlain's concessions. Trenches were dug in London parks and volunteers prepared for air raids. Broadcasting on 27 September, Chamberlain uttered one of the two phrases for which he is remembered: 'How horrible, fantastic, incredible it is that we should be digging trenches and trying on gas-masks here because of a quarrel in a faraway country between people of whom we know nothing.'

The House of Commons met on 28 September in an anxious mood. While Chamberlain was speaking, a telegram was handed to him; it was from Hitler and proposed another meeting next day in Munich. He could not have been astonished, since he had sent an emissary to Berlin to suggest such a meeting, but MPs did not know that. A Liberal, Sir Geoffrey Mander, recalled:

The production of the cable was cleverly staged and took the House by storm. . . . Nearly the whole House rose in enthusiastic acclamation – but not the whole. There were some of us on the Liberal and Labour benches who retained our seats.[56]

The Munich meeting brought together Hitler, Chamberlain, Daladier and Mussolini. Czech representatives came, but were not allowed to take part in the discussions. The agreement reached in the evening satisfied Chamberlain's desire for formal decencies: the annexation would proceed in stages up to 10 October and plebiscites would be held in doubtful areas (actually, they never were). The Czechs were informed of the decisions only after the terms had been signed.[57]

Daladier, returning to Paris, was apprehensive when he saw a crowd at the airport; he thought he would be attacked, or at least booed. Chamberlain, returning to London, had no doubt that he would be greeted with cheers, and he was. He brought home a statement which he and Hitler had signed, hailing the Munich agreement as 'a symbol of the desire of our two peoples never to go to war with one another again'. Flourishing this piece of paper, he declared: 'I believe it is peace for our time.'

More realistically, a German newspaper summed up: 'The will of the Führer is accomplished, as it is written in *Mein Kampf*.'[58]

General Syrovy, announcing that Czechoslovakia had to bow to the Munich terms, told his people:

I am living through the most terrible hour of my life. I am now fulfilling a task so painful that to die would in comparison be easy. . . . We were abandoned. We stand alone. . . . To yield to four great powers and enormous military superiority is not dishonourable.[59]

Duff Cooper resigned from the government, and the Commons debate on 3 October saw weightily critical speeches by Churchill and Eden. Lloyd George gave his verdict a few weeks later:

We handed over a little democratic state in central Europe, the land of John

Huss, wrapped in the Union Jack and the tricolore, to a ruthless dictator. . . . China, Abyssinia, Spain, Czechoslovakia – we have descended during these years a ladder of dishonour, rung by rung. Are we going, can we go, any lower?[60]

Megan, certainly, was under no illusion that Munich had bought peace for her time. In a speech in Anglesey, she said that it meant 'not peace but a postponement of war'. In the House, she spoke on 14 November in an unemployment debate and pointed out that, while Wales was still neglected, over two hundred new factories had been built in London. 'The target is becoming larger,' she remarked caustically.

In the aftermath of Munich, there was undoubtedly a wave of relief and of gratitude to Chamberlain. Nevertheless, when the issues were explained people showed their distrust of appeasement. In by-elections at Oxford and Bridgwater, the Labour and Liberal local organisations agreed to back a single Progressive candidate. The Tory majority in Oxford was halved and at Bridgwater the Progressive, Vernon Bartlett, won the seat. As Archibald Sinclair said: 'The electors seem to be impressed only when the opposition parties can sink their differences in support of beliefs which they hold in common.'[61]

But the largest potential partner in a united front, the Labour Party, refused to have anything to do with it. Stafford Cripps, Aneurin Bevan and others who were guilty of speaking on 'People's Front' platforms were expelled from the party. While Socialists, Communists and Liberals were fighting side by side in Spain, or sharing a hut in Dachau, they could not co-operate in the routine of British politics.

6

In January 1939 the Lloyd George family mustered to travel to Antibes and celebrate the golden wedding of Margaret and David. It was a cheerful occasion, marked by fun and clowning; Gwilym dressed up as his mother and Olwen as her father. We can assume that no one remarked that it was also the 'silver wedding' of Frances and David.

Also in January, Chamberlain and Halifax travelled to Rome for a friendly meeting with Mussolini. The Spanish war was the only irritating piece of unfinished business. The Republican government had disbanded the International Brigade as a despairing gesture of honesty, and to save these Bulgarians, Cubans, Welshmen and the rest from Franco's vengeance. Mussolini promised to withdraw his troops after Franco had won.

Barcelona fell on 26 January, and half a million people – soldiers and civilians – took refuge in France. The Republicans made the melancholy decision to end the struggle if Britain and France secured an undertaking from Franco that there would be no reprisals. The two governments promised to act accordingly, but, as Alvarez del Vayo, the Republican Foreign Minister, wrote with restrained bitterness, 'Unfortunately, this promise remained, like so many others in this unhappy age, only a promise.'[62] On 5 March, Franco's troops entered Madrid and the war was over. According to a reliable estimate, 300,000 Spaniards were executed in ensuing years – three times as many as those who had died in battle.[63]

But Spain was soon off the front pages. On 15 March, German troops marched into Prague, Czechoslovakia ceased to exist, and 'Bohemia' became a German protectorate. It dawned on Chamberlain that Daladier was right and Germany was 'aiming at something far greater'. In a speech in Birmingham on 17 March, he asked: 'Is this the last attack upon a small state or is it to be followed by others? Is this, in fact, a step in the direction of an attempt to dominate the world by force?'

Although the guarantee to the rump of Czechoslovakia had proved useless, Chamberlain began to scatter guarantees like IOUs. A report (quite unfounded) that the Germans were about to invade Romania prompted a British guarantee of that country. Poland too received a guarantee. Here there was a real threat: Hitler was demanding the annexation of Danzig (now Gdansk), which was a 'free city' with a German population, and it was clear that, if the Poles did not agree, they would be attacked.

As Lloyd George and others pointed out, Britain could do nothing effective to defend Poland. Hitler could be compelled to back down only by an alliance of Britain, France and the Soviet Union. The Russians were on record as willing to enter such an alliance; Chamberlain accepted the idea and opened negotiations; but, as the weeks and then the months passed, nothing was clinched. Chamberlain probably believed, as he had been advised by the British ambassador in Moscow in 1938, that the Red Army had been so seriously weakened by Stalin's purges as to be militarily useless. Rebutting this idea, Lloyd George said:

They have the finest air force in the world. They have an extraordinarily powerful tank force. And they are offering to place all this at the disposal of the Allies provided they are treated on equal terms. . . . Why the havering? Why the delays?[64]

The reason for the havering emerged when Chamberlain said in reply that 'the direct participation of the Soviet Union might not be in accordance with the wishes' of the threatened nations. The rulers of Poland, their minds dominated by traditional anti-Communism, preferred to confront Hitler as best they could without any Soviet involvement. Negotiations between Britain and France on the one hand and Russia on the other always foundered on this obstacle. In any case, they proceeded at a dilatory pace.

Not unnaturally, Stalin was considering an alternative policy – a deal with Germany. In May, the Soviet Foreign Minister, Maxim Litvinov, who was Jewish and had a British wife, was replaced by Molotov, a veteran Bolshevik close to Stalin himself. In August, an Anglo-French military mission arrived in Moscow, travelling by ship and train as if the aeroplane had not been invented. The instructions to the British officers warned that agreement 'may take months to achieve' – hardly a stimulus to quick results. On 14 August the Red Army chief, Marshal Voroshilov, asked his visitors whether his forces would be able to move across Poland to make contact with the enemy, and got no firm answer. This was the crunch. On the same day, Ribbentrop, Hitler's Foreign Minister, sent a message that he was ready to come to Moscow. He made the journey (by air, of course) on 23 August, and a treaty of non-aggression between Germany and the Soviet Union was signed without delay.

There was now no reason why Hitler should not attack. On 1 September, German bombers struck at Polish towns and German troops crossed the frontiers. Faced with this conclusive proof of Hitler's unreasonableness, Chamberlain had no way out. Once again the gas-masks were distributed, and three million children left British cities for the countryside. There was still a day of hesitation, which impelled a Tory MP to appeal to the Labour spokesman, Arthur Greenwood, to 'speak for England' – another phrase that has passed into history. But on 3 September (three years after Lloyd George and Megan sat down to tea and cakes with Hitler) Britain and France declared war.

# CHAPTER SEVEN

# 'Never Love Me Less'

## 1

Megan was not in London when the war began. She had gone to Brynawelon as usual when the House rose for the summer recess, and did not return when it was recalled because of the critical situation. She was ill, and in a state of virtual collapse. In a letter written on 25 September 1939 to Margery Wace, a BBC producer, she described her condition as 'severe gastric flu on top of complete exhaustion after a long session'. In an undated letter to Thelma she wrote: 'If only I had the physical strength to do something! But I feel as though I will never be any good again.' Another letter to Thelma, evidently written in late October, reads:

I was glad to have yours this morning; it came at the right moment, when I was just going to have a three hours' test taken by a doctor from Ruthin. It was a godsend. . . . I can't tell you how I feel for you, living in that fearful gloomy atmosphere, although I must admit there have been moments when I could have done with a blackout and deserted streets. . . . I have no news and am not supposed to read the newspapers by doctor's orders.

The war came at the right moment for Megan's brother Dick, who had been going through hard times. His marriage to Roberta McAlpine had ended in divorce in 1931; a second marriage, in 1935, was also unsuccessful. As well as farming, he was a partner in a building firm, but the man who had enticed him into this business turned out to be dishonest. In 1937 the firm crashed, Dick lost all his money, and he had to sell West Hill Farm. Under these blows, he was drinking heavily. But in 1939, at fifty, he was not too old for military service of a sedentary kind. He put on uniform again and was given a staff job in the War Office, where he worked until he contracted tuberculosis in 1944.

Gwilym was also in Whitehall, though not in uniform. He joined the government as parliamentary secretary to the Board of Trade, the post he had held briefly in 1931. On the outbreak of war, Chamberlain broadened the government by bringing in Churchill and Eden, but it was not a real coalition and Gwilym was the only Liberal to join it.

Sir Thomas Carey Evans was now medical superintendent of Hammersmith Hospital. He and Olwen had a house in Du Cane Road, near the hospital.

In the first few weeks of the war, the Germans annihilated Poland with breathtaking speed, adding the word *Blitzkrieg* (lightning war) to the vocabulary. On 17 September the Russians – by an agreement with Germany which was suspected at the time and has been admitted in these days of *glasnost* – occupied the eastern half of Poland, and Molotov announced that 'the Polish state has ceased to exist'.

Meanwhile, it was all quiet on the western front. Instead of the massive air raids for which Londoners had braced themselves, there was only one ridiculous false alarm. By the end of the month, not a shot was being fired nor a bomb dropped anywhere in Europe, and American reporters were coining a new phrase: 'the phoney war'. The tacit truce allowed time for reflection. Since Poland was beyond salvation, was it sensible to continue the war? The question occurred, among others, to Lloyd George.

At the outbreak of war, he had made a suitably patriotic declaration. Recalling the other war, he told the House: 'We had very bad moments, moments when brave men were rather quailing and doubting, but the nation was firm right through. . . . We won a victory for right. We will do it again.' Brooding at Churt after the Polish collapse, he felt less confident. He was himself one of the men who had doubted the possibility of victory in 1916. Now, without Russia as an ally, and with a genius like Hitler directing the enemy war machine, the prospects seemed considerably more dubious.

There were rumours that peace proposals might be put forward, perhaps with the mediation of Russia or Italy; both were neutral nations. If so, Lloyd George advised in a debate on 3 October, 'we should not come to too hurried a conclusion.' Chamberlain agreed to examine any proposals that might appear. He had embarked on the war with extreme reluctance and his happiest days had been in the heyday of appeasement; perhaps he would go down in history as a peacemaker after all. But for anti-Fascists of the Left, this was 'their war' and their commitment to it was absolute. They were shocked by Lloyd George's suggestions. Frances was among those who disapproved, and the comment in the authorised biography of Lloyd George reads: 'It must be admitted that Lloyd George's attitude to the issue at this stage bewildered and pained many of his friends, and seemed very much out of keeping with his known character.'[1]

Challenged by a critic to try out his peace policy on his constituents, Lloyd George spoke in Caernarvon on 21 October. He showed a draft of his speech to Megan, who said: 'There are some passages I don't like – they give a defeatist line.'[2] Probably he toned down these passages. What he proposed was that a peace conference should be held with the participation of neutral nations, if possible including the Soviet Union and the United States. It would not be like Munich, with 'shivering diplomats bullied and hectored by the German dictator'. Should it be impossible to get acceptable terms, which must include the restoration of Czechoslovakia and Poland, the war could always be resumed. But an attempt should be made to 'save the world from the miseries and uncertainties of a prolonged war'.

As usual, six or seven thousand people jammed the hall. Sylvester, who of course came along, had been apprehensive that the reception might be hostile, but this did not worry Lloyd George. 'I haven't forgotten the Boer War,' he told the audience jauntily. The speech went over to 'tumultuous applause' and Sylvester was able to note with relief: 'Not a single heckle or question.'

Megan was not well enough to be present. 'I wish I'd heard his speech the other day and the reception he got,' she wrote to Thelma. 'It must have been thrilling, or it would have been to me anyway.' It was an unhappy autumn for her. She was out of touch with events at a crucial time. Criccieth was dull when she could not go out for walks and picnics; her mother and Sarah Jones were the only company. Worst of all, she was parted from Philip for the first time since they had become lovers. (She and Thelma referred to him as the Greyhound, a name prompted by his athletic record.) She had told Philip not to write because her mother and Sarah would be sure to take note of a flow of letters addressed in the same handwriting; Philip was a compulsive letter-writer and would write almost daily if he wrote at all. But Philip was chafing and Thelma urged Megan to lift the ban, perhaps suggesting a cover address or *poste restante*. Toward Christmas (Megan's letters were undated, as usual, but this one can be dated by the reference to the parliamentary recess) she wrote:

I am writing to Raspit as I expect you will be there when the House rises today. *Not* one word from you today and I am desolate. I know you are busy & worried, but one *tiny* note makes more difference than you can possibly understand, when you're lying in bed and have been looking at the same stretch of sea and mountain for a month. . . . Papa is of course in a great state, poor old pet, about me. He's coming down on Saturday and bringing the Lord Dawson with him who is to make a thorough overhaul and then prescribe I hope. . . . Do you think it wise to allow the Greyhound to write? I should like it. Perhaps a type-written envelope as an alternative might be a good thing. In that case, & suitably disguised, it should be sent direct.

Philip did write, and Megan replied. The letters are lost, but we know from subsequent references that she added a postscript to her letter: 'Never love me less.' This phrase stayed in his mind and became a leitmotiv of their relationship. When he recurred to it, it was to reassure her that her injunction was binding on him:

I will go to sleep, as I always do, remembering the postscript of your Christmas letter, & remembering that you repeated it last week. Of all the sweet things you have ever said, it was by far the sweetest. It left me with a singing heart, & it is singing still. (24 September 1940)

You said again your Christmas message of so long ago: 'Never love me less.' I never shall, be certain; only more & more & more. (14 November 1947)

Always, always I think of the Xmas postscript. Always it is the one thing of which you can be absolutely sure. (10 August 1951)

Megan began to recover after New Year 1940, but now it was Philip who was out of touch. On 30 November 1939, while the war was still 'phoney', another war had begun.

Concerned for security, and particularly concerned because the Soviet frontier with Finland was just beyond the suburbs of Leningrad, Stalin demanded military and naval bases in Finland. When the Finns refused, he launched an attack. The cause of Finland was enthusiastically espoused in Britain, France and the United States, with British Tories manifesting a sympathy for the victim of aggression which they had never managed to muster for Abyssinia, Austria or Czechoslovakia. This sympathy was echoed in the Labour Party (except for its pro-Soviet fringe) and it was decided to send a Labour delegation to Finland. Its three members were Philip Noel-Baker, Sir Walter Citrine of the TUC and John Downie of the co-operative movement. Citrine kept a diary of the trip, quickly published as a paperback.

Travelling by way of neutral Holland, Denmark and Sweden, the three reached Finland on 24 January. They were shown civilian homes which had been destroyed by bombing – this was still regarded as an atrocity – and were escorted to within three kilometres of the front line. Philip was delighted when, because he was the only one who could ski, he left Citrine and Downie behind and scooted off to Kitela, where the Finns had encircled a large Russian force. Russian prisoners, Philip found, were told to walk unguarded to Finnish rear areas, which they happily did although their own lines were closer. He talked to forty or fifty of them and gathered that 'the Russians hated the war and thought it was unnecessary and wrong.' When he offered to take their names so that their relatives could be informed by radio, or to arrange an exchange through the Red Cross, they said: 'For God's sake don't do it. We will be shot as deserters when we get back to Russia.'[3]

Philip's perception of low morale and military incompetence in the Red Army, which had not recovered from the purges, was doubtless accurate enough. However, the veteran President of Finland, Marshal Mannerheim, warned the delegates that his army could not hold out for ever: 'The Russians were concentrating more and more at one spot on the Karelian isthmus, and unless the Finns were able to get the artillery they needed, some day the Russians would break through.'[4] This warning was lost on Philip. When he returned to London with a Red Army steel helmet as a trophy, he told Patricia Llewellyn-Davies that the Finns were winning the war. Her comment was: 'As usual, he was totally unrealistic.'[5]

In Paris, where they stopped for a day on the return journey, and then in London, the Labour delegates strenuously urged that the Allies should send troops, guns and aircraft to Finland. It did not occur to them that these men and weapons might soon be needed elsewhere. But the Russian breakthrough soon came to validate Mannerheim's prediction, and on 9 March the Finns had to agree to peace talks, and then to terms which involved a cession of territory.

Restored to health, Megan returned to London in early March. Ever since 1922, she had been living in the house owned by her father in Addison Road. He was generally at Churt, her mother was generally at Brynawelon, and the London house was Megan's more than anyone else's. In wartime conditions, however, she decided to move in with Tom and Olwen in Du Cane Road. If air raids came, they would at least be together. Later, Megan took a lease of a cottage in the Chilterns, on a ridge overlooking the town of Chesham. It was called Kembledene but she renamed it Halcyon Cottage, presumably because it was calm and quiet when London was a raging inferno.

Megan and Philip met again at the House of Commons. In a twelve-page letter dated '8.20 p.m. Thursday 14.iii.40', he wrote:

I think of you as you were in the dining-room the other night, lovelier than you ever had been, & sweeter, & more difficult not to kiss; & I just think I *can't* live without you; that I must see you & have you all the time. . . . I love you; and I always shall.

This is the earliest of Philip's love-letters that has survived,[6] and it is typical of many in its ardour, its assurances of his devotion to her and its wistful desire to 'have you all the time'. One 1940 letter begins, 'My most beloved Megan', but this was rare and her name is seldom to be found. Most of the letters open with an endearment: 'My sweetest and dearest', 'My little sweetheart', 'My little fairy', 'My little angel', 'My little beloved' and occasionally 'My little Welsh witch'. The possessive 'My' is almost invariable, and the adjective 'little' is very frequent. He hardly ever signed his letters, though he occasionally ended with a 'P'. Each letter came in an envelope marked 'Private' or 'Secret', inside another envelope formally addressed to Miss Megan (or later Lady Megan) Lloyd George. One imagines that any intrusive person who opened the outer envelope would have opened the inner one too, but no doubt this procedure made Philip feel safer.

On 8 April, in another lightning stroke, the Germans seized Oslo and Copenhagen. If an Allied force had been sent to Finland, it would never have returned. But French and British troops were hastily sent to land at small fishing ports along the Norwegian coastline. The real war was beginning.

## 2

The fighting in Norway ended in complete success for Hitler and depressing, humiliating failure for the Allies. Stories filtered back of muddle, indecision and lack of co-operation between army and navy. Since the Germans could use Norwegian airfields, British soldiers had the unhappy experience – soon to be repeated on the Dunkirk beaches – of being divebombed without effective protection. The campaign ended when Allied forces left Norway (except for Narvik in the far north) on 2 May. Five days later, Chamberlain faced the House of Commons for the inquest known in political history as 'the Norway debate'.

Churchill – who, as First Lord of the Admiralty, bore a share of responsibility for the defeat – loyally stood by the Prime Minister in opening the debate. But a Tory, Leopold Amery, attacked Chamberlain with Cromwell's words to the Long Parliament: 'Depart, I say,

and let us have done with you! In the name of God, go!' As the House
of Commons adjourned after the first day of the two-day debate, it was
uncertain whether the Labour opposition would force a division.
Herbert Morrison, who was in favour of it, wrote later:

The shock of the idea continued to bemuse most of my colleagues. . . . I was
asked: 'Suppose we do defeat the government, what are the consequences,
and are we prepared to face up to them?'[7]

It was a difficult decision; Hugh Dalton argued that only a handful of
Tories would desert Chamberlain, and he might then call an election in
which Labour would 'be wiped further out than in 1931'.[8] But the
Labour front bench eventually decided to take the plunge.

In a vote which was difficult to forecast, an intervention by Lloyd
George might make all the difference. On the first day, however, he
would not commit himself to speaking or even to attending the debate.
Morrison recalled:

I sent messages to him through Megan Lloyd George, but for quite a time I
could get no definite reply. Sometimes the answer was that he would think
about it. Sometimes it was that he did not feel like coming to the debate. I
asked Megan to go back again and to impress upon him that this really was a
vital occasion. . . . In the end we got Lloyd George going.[9]

The second day opened with a division in prospect. In the course of a
speech defending himself, Chamberlain said: 'I have friends in the
House.' By reducing the issue to that of personal loyalty, he had made
a fatal blunder. Lloyd George had come to the House, but at that
moment was in his room upstairs. A Liberal MP who was a good
friend of Megan's, Dingle Foot, gave this account of what happened
next:

Megan at once saw the opening for her father. She literally ran out of the
House and found him in his room. Not long after, he came into the Chamber
and delivered the most devastating attack of his career.[10]

The attack was:

It is not a question of who are the Prime Minister's friends. It is a far bigger
issue. . . . He has appealed for sacrifice. . . . I say solemnly that the Prime
Minister should give an example of sacrifice, because there is nothing which
can contribute more to victory than that he should sacrifice the seals of office.

Forty-one Tories voted with the opposition and sixty abstained. The
government still had a majority, thanks to the big Conservative victory
at the last election, but Chamberlain's position was now untenable.

Alarming news two days later intensified the sense of crisis: the Germans were invading Belgium and Holland. A coalition government was imperatively needed. The Labour leaders, who by good luck were able to consult their annual conference that weekend, said that they would serve under anyone but Chamberlain. Hurt and resentful, he resigned. Two names were suggested to head the new government: Churchill and Halifax. The latter would have been the popular choice in the Tory ranks, but – fortunately for his country – he ruled himself out because he was not in the House of Commons.

Adopting the model devised by Lloyd George in 1916, Churchill appointed a small War Cabinet of five: himself, Chamberlain, Halifax, and Attlee and Greenwood from the Labour Party. Ernest Bevin, as Britain's foremost trade-union leader, became Minister of Labour to mobilise manpower (few people spoke of womanpower) for the war effort. Other jobs were shared out according to party strength, with Sinclair getting the Air Ministry. It was not exactly a team that would frighten Hitler. As Lloyd George pointed out to Churchill, 'several of the architects of the catastrophe are still leading members of your government.'[11] To Sylvester, he described the government as a pantomime horse 'with the front legs of a racehorse and the hind legs of a mule'.[12]

Since Chamberlain was still the leader of the Conservative Party, Churchill was less than all-powerful in a political sense, and he felt that his position would be strengthened if he could persuade Lloyd George to join the government. Lloyd George, proud of his successful farm at Churt, was ready to consider becoming a national director of food production, but by the time he made the suggestion Churchill had appointed a Minister of Agriculture. In any case, what Churchill had in mind was that Lloyd George should come in as a counsellor without specific responsibilities. This did not attract him, for two reasons. He was decidedly pessimistic about Britain's prospects in the war; Sir John Colville, a member of Churchill's personal staff, saw him on 13 May and noted: 'He thinks the country is in a hopeless condition, and is generally despondent.'[13] The other reason was that he loathed the idea of sitting in the same Cabinet as Chamberlain. As he saw it, the war was being badly run and so long as Chamberlain had an influence it would continue to be badly run. 'I am not going in merely to cajole and persuade, and certainly not to wrangle,' he said.[14]

It emerged, moreover, that Churchill would be able to make a firm offer only if Chamberlain agreed. After a family discussion, 'Gwilym and Megan agreed that he should not accept under such conditions.'[15] He wrote to Churchill:

This is not a firm offer. Until it is definite I cannot consider it. . . . If you think I can help, I am at your call. But if that call is tentative and qualified, I shall not know what answer to give.[16]

Churchill's reply revealed the weakness of his position:

I cannot complain in any way of what you say in your letter. The government I have formed is founded upon the leaders of the three parties and, like you, I have no party of my own. I have received a great deal of help from Chamberlain. . . . I have joined hands with him and must act with perfect loyalty.

On 6 June Churchill saw Lloyd George and told him that Chamberlain had reluctantly agreed that he (Lloyd George) should join the government, but might require him to be ejected if things did not work out well. Much irritated, Lloyd George said: 'If you cannot stand up to Neville Chamberlain and Margesson [the Tory chief whip, a notorious appeaser] how can you stand up to Hitler?'[17] Sylvester and Frances urged him to accept, as did Beaverbrook, who was now in the government as Minister of Aircraft Production and was keen to get Lloyd George in. But Frances eventually saw it Lloyd George's way:

The offer would be conditional on Lloyd George keeping the peace with Chamberlain, and that if Chamberlain found the arrangement not satisfactory, he could ask Churchill to dispense with Lloyd George's services. . . . It would have been an intolerable situation for him to hold office by grace of Neville Chamberlain, whom he despised, and to be under threat of dismissal if he and Chamberlain fell out.[18]

Megan was not offered a government job. With Gwilym kept on at the Board of Trade, Churchill probably felt that he was doing enough for the Lloyd George family. There was no job for Philip either. Attlee explained to him that the Tory–Labour balance was a limiting factor, and he could not ask for a job in the coalition for everyone who would find a place in a Labour government. This was all the more galling because Philip's contemporary, Hugh Dalton, was made Minister of Economic Warfare.

The events of 1940 are much too famous to need more than the briefest summary here. Driven back to Dunkirk, the British forces in France were brought home between 26 May and 4 June. On 10 June, Italy entered the war on the German side. On 14 June the Germans marched into Paris. Marshal Pétain, once the hero of Verdun, formed a government which sued for peace and signed an armistice on 22 June. Churchill rallied Britain with phrases that have passed into the language – 'finest hour' . . . 'blood, sweat, toil and tears' . . . 'we shall fight on the beaches'.

Inside the War Cabinet, not everyone showed the same resolute spirit. On 28 May, Halifax advanced the view that 'we might get better terms' by making peace at once than by waiting until things got worse. Chamberlain chimed in with the remark that we should be losing nothing if we said 'we were ready to consider decent terms if such were offered to us'. Churchill was able to overrule them with the support of the Labour ministers. Talking to friends later that night, he got to the heart of the matter: the alternative to fighting on was to become 'a slave state', with a puppet government under 'Mosley or some such person'.[19]

It was a time of terrible danger, but not yet of hardship or weariness. Food was rationed but reasonably plentiful. Restaurants made a noble effort to maintain peacetime standards. Philip and Megan often dined at the Dorchester, where Thelma had a room; her brother was a director and, in the absence of tourists, the hotel was almost empty. By an amicable arrangement, the room could be used by the lovers, generally in the afternoon. Philip and Irene had a house at 16 South Eaton Place, a good Belgravia address, which they were renting from Lord Cecil, who had retreated to his Sussex residence. It was only regrettable (from everyone's point of view) that Irene could not make her annual visit to Greece.

Amid the confusion of war, Philip sometimes forgot that he had ruled marriage with Megan out of the realm of possibility. In June, after an enjoyable dinner with Megan and Thelma, he wrote that one of Megan's remarks, to the effect that they would always quarrel, 'really showed that you had no argument worth mentioning against our getting married!'[20] Perhaps it was Thelma who talked him into this mood, or perhaps they all got rather drunk. In resolute Vera Lynn style, Thelma said that 'she was sure that we should be together again at Raspit'. (The skies above Raspit were witnessing the legendary dog-fights between Spitfires and Messerschmitts.) Philip continued:

I don't believe you've ever said a single thing that wasn't both new & right; & I've never forgotten or failed to act on any of them. Soon I shall be perfect, if you persevere! Or I should be, if I had you always with me! That's why, of course, I want to marry you, as I said last night! I want to marry you in spite of the news – & because of it! . . . I want to marry you for a thousand other reasons too – because I want to dance with you & play with you & swim with you, & lie still & talk & talk & talk with you in the sunshine . . .

Before ending the letter, however, Philip realised that he had committed himself too much, and prudently wound up: 'My darling, I want to marry you because I love you. But I will give it all up, because I love you.'

Indeed, this letter shows the man of peace in a distinctly hysterical mood, perhaps comprehensible only to those who remember 1940:

Sometimes I feel quite *devilish* – I *want* the war to spread. . . . I want Indians & Australians to help to kill Italians in Africa, & to kill them quick; I want Americans to kill Japanese & starve their babies. . . . I'm sure now we must have a great & hellish world maelstrom, which will leave every surviving human being with the absolute conviction that there must be a clean sweep of all past follies, & a new start in all regards. I believe you & I will both survive, & will together make that new start.

3

Letters written in July and August 1940 show Philip continuing to oscillate – sometimes offering to vanish from Megan's life, sometimes looking forward to marriage. On 11 July, he wrote:

If you ever find anyone who would look after you as I should, I hope you will marry him very quick. . . . I want you above everything to be absolutely free. You *do* know that, don't you?

On 30 July:

I so bitterly reproach myself if I was selfish on Thursday last. There is nothing in the world I hate so much as the thought that I am a strain; I just can't *bear* it; it makes me want to go out & jump into the river, or anything to get myself finally, completely, & for always eliminated from your life. . . . What can I say about it, except what I've said before: that if you tell me absolutely to disappear, never to come near you again, I will obey? I promise, as I've promised before, & *always* kept my word, whatever its cost me.

On 1 August:

My darling, all day I've been spinning round like a compass in a magnetic storm – right thro' 360°! . . . Part of the time I've felt that I just can't give you up. That if I don't see you, & hear you talk & laugh, & watch you smile, that life will simply be *unbearable*. . . . And part of the time I've remembered you as you were when you told me last night about your difficulties & your fears – & I've felt frightfully happy that I can do something for you by disappearing, by freeing you absolutely & altogether from such fears.

However, by the time he reached page five of this letter and explained what pleasure he derived from a profile view of her nose, he told her: 'When we're married, I'll develop a special technique of lying down & looking up at it, so as to get it exactly as I got it this afternoon.'

On 6 August, 'when we are married' was again an assumption:

I think when we are married we shall have to arrange a private line between two rooms in our house, to which no one can possibly listen, & on which we can have long political & business discussions. It seems that I concentrate on the *talking* rather better when I can't see you!

Megan, it seems, felt that she was having more than enough of his pressing attentions, and let him know it, for he wrote in this letter:

Of course, I will disappear now, as you want me to, & I will stay out of sight as long as ever you desire. . . . Of course, it hurts not to see you, my beloved; & nothing I can do will make me *not* regret the lost opportunities of Thelma's lovely room, just when we've found the perfect chance of safety, solitude & peace.

Marriage, apparently, was being postponed to the end of the war:

I have an absolute resolve to do what you want, to keep you well, to try & find the way that means real & lasting happiness for *you*. Perhaps, when the war is over, I shall see some way to decisive action that will achieve that end.

When the House rose in August, Megan went to Brynawelon and Philip went with his son Francis – now twenty years old and about to join the army – on a walking holiday around Cader Idris, where he was able to gaze across the bay to Criccieth. Before leaving London, however, he experienced the first air raids:

The Raid didn't end until 1.30 a.m., & my maid Barbara was caught out in it & didn't get home till 2.30 & I had to sit up till then to wait for her. . . . Damn – there's another raid sounding! I haven't heard any bombs or seen any fires or searchlights, but I suppose someone is getting it. I think the man must be starting on the plan of trying to keep us all awake. I think he *will* manage that, though its a poor second best to hitting targets, as our brave young men manage to do.[21]

The first really heavy raid was on the night of 7 September, when over four hundred people were killed in the close-packed houses and tenements of the East End. The docks blazed with immense fires – timber fires, rubber fires, paint fires, even a pepper fire. Soon the bombs were falling all over London as the Luftwaffe sought to hit the main railway stations, all of which were put out of action at one time or another. Philip urged Megan to stay in Wales, but she came back to

London the day after the House reassembled and took him by surprise as he was reading. In a note scribbled 'on the Bench', he wrote:

My most beloved, my head is listening to the fearful sufferings of the poor people in the East End; my heart is bursting with happiness & love. . . . I looked up; & there I saw to my delight & amazement & joy that you were here. . . . If I can see you, & you want to let me, I will throw over anything & everything. Six o'clock at the Dorchester wd be best.[22]

For some reason, their rendezvous were generally on Thursdays. At the weekend Megan returned to Criccieth, travelling in a hired car and staying overnight at Broadway in the Cotswolds. Philip wrote, heading his letter: 'Sunday, 22.9.40, 11 p.m. My brother's house in the country':

It seems a lifetime since Thursday. It was so marvellous having you to myself in T.'s room; so much the best & most peaceful & satisfactory time we've ever had, that naturally enough the hours *drag* by until I see you again. And they're all the longer because I've no news of what has happened to you. I imagine it all – your driving away thro' the city before it got dark, & arriving at home [ie Du Cane Road], I hope, well before the Germans started their nightly business; your journey up next day to B'way & your night in the lovely hotel there; your arrival next day at C. . . . I want to know that you got out safely & quickly, that you had no delays or bombs or troubles.

Churchill is said (apocryphally, but the story carries truth) to have muttered after his 'fight on the beaches' speech: 'with broken bottles, I suppose'. The troops rescued from Dunkirk had left their artillery, their tanks and often even their rifles behind. Through the summer, Britain prepared for an invasion. Anyone who walks along the North Downs escarpment in Surrey can still see the concrete defences where a stand was to be made to protect London. It was not an irrational scare; no one had expected the Germans to seize Denmark and Norway in one fell swoop, nor to crush France within five weeks, but they had done it. On 24 September, Philip wrote: 'The invasion hasn't begun. . . . What *can* the Germans be up to? I can't make head or tail of it.'

We now know that Hitler had made no serious preparations for an invasion of Britain. He lacked the shipping, he could not challenge the Royal Navy's command of the sea, and in the dog-fights over Kent the Luftwaffe could not win command of the air. This, indeed, was why its strategy was changed to a bombing assault on London. On 28 September, Hitler made the decision to prepare for the 1941 invasion of Russia.

The autumn of 1940 was the season of the blitz (a popular adaptation of the word *Blitzkrieg*). The sirens sounded on seventy-five nights out of seventy-six. The destruction caused countless simultaneous emergencies:

Every time a bomb pierced a road it tore through the mass of pipes, cables and conduits which lay like a nervous system under the city. Repair went on as the bombs still fell. Where a gas main had been broken, a man from the gas company had to plug its end, working in scorching, poisoned air, or force his way through blazing debris to cut off the supply.... Women would improvise field-kitchens in the gardens or the roads, and burn shattered woodwork or furniture to give their husbands something hot to eat. Water spurted one day from the gas stoves of Pimlico.[23]

After six weeks, a quarter of a million Londoners were homeless. They slept on floors in improvised rest centres, were billeted in undamaged large houses, moved in with cousins or friends, camped in Epping Forest, or dispersed to country towns and villages. Thousands slept every night on the platforms of the tube, thousands more in packed and comfortless shelters. Theatres closed; cinemas mostly stayed open, but sixty were destroyed. Almost every British city had its own blitz – briefer, but just as destructive in proportion to the urban area and the number killed. On 14 November, the centre of Coventry was ravaged and five hundred died; Philip went to see the plight of his former constituents. Then it was the turn of Southampton, Bristol, Swansea, Cardiff, Plymouth, Liverpool, Manchester, Sheffield and even Glasgow and Belfast. In eight months from September 1940 to May 1941, when a ferocious raid on central London rounded off the blitz, 43,000 civilians were killed – well over half of them Londoners.

Philip had to agonise over Greece as well as over London and Coventry. Mussolini, who had annexed Albania in 1939, demanded the submission of Greece. General Metaxas, although he was a dictator of the Fascist stamp, replied on 28 October with a firm 'No' – the anniversary is still celebrated in Greece as 'No Day' – and prepared to fight. Philip commented to Megan:

There is a dictator – & quite a wicked dictator – really converted *by his people*. Everybody says that he cdn't possibly have done anything but resist – he wd have been slung out in a moment by a popular revolt.[24]

The bailiff of the Achmetaga estate, described by Philip as 'a most remarkable young man, handsome, clever, honest, athletic', wrote to say that he was off to the front. Philip voiced his feelings to Megan:

It is really rather awful for those charming, brave, incompetent dears, all of whom I love, even the most rascally. . . . And those charming women in the villages, I keep thinking of what it means to them if their husbands & their sons are killed or crippled – grinding poverty, & *such* hard work for their children & themselves.[25]

4

Neville Chamberlain, attacked by cancer, resigned from the government in October and died in November. This seemed to remove the barrier to Lloyd George taking office, and Sylvester urged him to do so, but in vain. Frances explained: 'He feels that when the crash comes he will have to come in and make peace.'[26] Thomas Jones confirmed this: 'He continued to harbour thoughts of a negotiated peace in which he might be called upon to play a part.'[27]

Another opportunity arose in December. Lord Lothian, British ambassador in Washington (as Philip Kerr, one of Lloyd George's secretaries back in 1919), suddenly died. Remembering Lloyd George's prestige in America, Churchill had the idea of sending him to the embassy, and sent a telegram to Roosevelt asking for his approval. The President replied that Lloyd George was of course acceptable, on the assumption that he would not talk like an appeaser. Churchill's embarrassment was increased when he got a wire from the diplomat in temporary charge at the embassy protesting vigorously against the appointment of the 'appeaser' Lloyd George.

One cannot imagine that Lloyd George would have taken the job. Apart from anything else, Margaret would not have been willing to leave Brynawelon, and if Frances had gone there might have been awkward disclosures in the uninhibited American press. But Lord Horder, when asked for his advice, said emphatically that Lloyd George would be taking grave risks with his health. Churchill then appointed Lord Halifax. Ironically, Lothian and Halifax both had records as appeasers in pre-war days which were much worse than Lloyd George's.

Eden replaced Halifax both as Foreign Secretary and as a member of the War Cabinet, while Bevin and Beaverbrook were also brought into the War Cabinet. Junior posts, too, were involved in the reshuffle. Philip had been thirsting for a job ever since the coalition was formed, and he felt that his chances had been improved by an effective speech he made on 28 November. He overheard Eden remarking to Attlee that it was 'a most awfully good speech', and he wrote to Megan:

Amusing, & possibly useful, because Attlee always regards my remarks & proposals about the war, strategy , air force or what you will, as foolish & tiresome, & he always thinks he finishes me off when he squeaks out: 'It can't be done.'[28]

Then and in later years, Philip's main handicap was the low esteem in which he was held by the two most powerful men in the Labour Party, Attlee and Bevin. Dalton, by his own account, pressed Attlee to find a job for Philip, but in vain. In Dalton's view, 'any No. 2 job other than the Foreign Office' would have been suitable. This seems like a strange proviso, since Philip's expertise was entirely in foreign affairs, but Dalton considered that he had a record of bad judgement. In his diary, Dalton wrote of Philip:

It would do him great good to get his mind, now saddened with lost hopes, frustration over decades, falsified appreciation of every recent war from Abyssinia through Spain to Finland, and personal relationships gone stale, on to some quite remote Department.[29]

The relationship which had 'gone stale' was presumably between Philip and Irene.

Megan was offered the post of parliamentary secretary (or number two) in the Ministry of Pensions. It was an offer that she could not honourably accept. Women MPs were gearing up for a campaign – to be described in the next chapter – for equal treatment between men and women with regard to financial benefits administered by this Ministry. Sir Walter Womersley, the Minister under whom Megan would have had to serve, was adamantly opposed to equality of the sexes. It is possible that the job offer was an attempt to buy Megan off and cripple the campaign. At all events, after she declined the offer she was never given another chance to hold government office.

Philip wrote that he was glad of her refusal 'for many reasons', but had one regret:

It is that I shan't soon hear the cheer when you answer your first question from the Treasury Bench. That would be worth a lot – I'm sure they'll absolutely bring the roof off when it happens, & I sh'd so much like it to be soon, for it wd make me more happy than I can say.[30]

While these decisions were being made in the political world, Megan had another anxiety. Her mother had a fall and cracked a hip-bone; as she was seventy-three years old, any injury was potentially serious. Although Megan herself was unwell at the time (perhaps only with a cold), she went off to Criccieth. As she was leaving she received this letter from Philip:

*Below:* Megan on the beach at Criccieth
*Right:* With her parents and her sister Mair Eluned

*Above:* With 'Puffin' Asquith on a formal occasion
*Right:* Lending a hand in the 1910 election

*Above left:* Frances Stevenson
*Above:* Frances and Megan take a walk in Paris, 1919

*Above:* Megan with a group of Devon Liberals, 1927. The young man in the white shirt is Richard Acland

*Right:* Megan and Cledwyn Hughes handing in their nomination papers as candidates for Anglesey, 1945

*Top:* Megan and her father walking by the
River Dwyfor, where he had walked as a
boy and where he is buried

*Above:* Megan with her father in his study
at Bron-y-de, Churt, on his 80th birthday

*Left:* With her mother

Megan on the platform

*Top:* The women MPs in the 1945–50
House of Commons
*Above:* Megan with (l. to r.) James
Callaghan, Herbert Morrison and
Hugh Gaitskell in Labour's TV
election broadcast, 1955
*Left:* With Aneurin Bevan in
Carmarthen, 1957

*Below:* Megan and her corgi, Huwcyn, in the garden at Brynawelon
*Right:* With Marion Salmon, leaning at Pisa, 1965

*Above:* At Brynawelon with Zosia Starzecka and Huwcyn
*Right:* The last photograph

I do hope you're feeling better, & that you can *rest* a little in the car, & that you aren't *worrying*. . . . Unless your Mother has *really* hurt herself, it is unnecessary & almost wrong for you to let yourself expend your nervous strength to no good purpose. . . . I knew immediately I saw you, & before you said a single word, that you were dreadfully bothered about your Mother, & that you hadn't slept. . . . The last thing in the world which your mother wd want is that you sh'd feel hurt on her account. Especially when, in fact, she's sitting up & the life & soul of the party.[31]

However, Megan and Philip had parted on affectionate terms after a satisfying Thursday. Four days later – realising, perhaps that he had struck the wrong note – he sent her one of his tenderest love-letters:

I am still comforted by last Thursday; I still see your face close, close to mine; I still feel your soft, soft lips, & the lovely, incomparable texture of your arms; I still feel your hand holding mine. My darling, I want you so. I will write again tomorrow – till then, remember that every moment I am thinking of you, remembering you, wanting you, & that I love you with all the power & ardour & devotion of my heart.[32]

Megan returned to London for a week in December, but when the House rose for Christmas she went to Brynawelon again. Olwen went there too, for Dame Margaret was not recovering. In January her condition began to deteriorate seriously. Olwen and Megan decided to tell their father that he was needed.

Margaret had been aware (thanks to Olwen, presumably) of Megan's relationship with Philip. Philip believed that she had reconciled herself to it; he had written in March 1940: 'What I feel for you, my happiness in it, is *not* built on the unhappiness of others; it has not meant *any* unhappiness to anybody except your Mother, & I hope that's all long gone bye.'[33] But Philip was mistaken. Olwen was unhappy about the relationship – according to what she told her son Robin[34] some years later, not so much on moral grounds as because she had a low opinion of Philip and considered that Megan was wasting her time. Margaret's disapproval was much more emphatic. She did have a firm moral view that a love affair which meant marital infidelity was wrong. The fact that, in the opinion of the sensible Olwen, the man in question was in any case unworthy of Megan only made matters worse. When she recognised that she was dying, and that her influence would be removed for ever, Margaret demanded that Megan should promise to break with Philip.

Megan gave the promise. Although she loved Philip as much as ever, to allow her mother to die in this state of deep unhappiness was something she could not do. Moreover, there must have been some serious talking, and Megan – who always had strong opinions, but never claimed that she was right about everything – may well have been persuaded that her mother and her sister, for whom she had real respect as well as affection, were right about this. Finally, the callous letter in which Philip had declined to take Margaret's accident seriously may have tipped the emotional balance against him.

We do not know exactly when, or by what means, Megan told Philip of her decision, but a cheerful note to her written on 18 December was his last letter before the break.

It was a very cold and harsh winter. On 19 January 1941 Sylvester and Lord Dawson travelled by train to Bangor but found that the road to Criccieth was blocked by snow. Dawson enlivened the journey by explaining to Sylvester that Margaret suffered from heart trouble, aggravated by her husband's treatment of her.[35] Meanwhile, Lloyd George set out from Churt to make the journey by car, accompanied by a secretary, Ann Parry. This was, as it turned out, an unwise decision; but the wartime trains were often packed with soldiers, they were slow and unreliable, and the heating tended to break down.

At Bridgnorth the car got stuck in a snowdrift and had to be dug out. Taking the A5 into Wales, they got as far as Cerrig-y-Druidion, where the snow fell so heavily that the car was practically buried. When the news spread that Lloyd George was in trouble, the men of the village, including the Wesleyan minister and the schoolmaster, mobilised to rescue him, and he spent the night at the White Lion. Next morning Dawson reached him on the telephone and told him that Margaret was dead. Sylvester then took the phone. Sobbing, Lloyd George said: 'She was a great old pal.'[36]

'I want your companionship,' Lloyd George told Sylvester. But another blizzard had set in, and Sylvester was immobilised until the next day. Then, with Tom Carey Evans, he was able to go by train via Chester – a long detour – to Corwen. The volunteers of Cerrig had cleared the road so that Lloyd George and Ann Parry could reach Corwen too. Dick and Gwilym, with their wives, came by train from London. After more delay, a train fitted with a snow-plough took them all to Criccieth. Megan met them – 'she just fell into my arms,' Sylvester wrote. On 24 January, Margaret was interred in the family vault which she had commissioned when Mair Eluned died in 1907. Sylvester noted: 'Lloyd George was overcome with grief and in floods of tears.'[37]

Megan was going through the worst time of her life. Her beloved mother was dead. Her grief-stricken father needed, rather than gave, comfort; he now looked like a frail old man, and in fact he had only four more years to live. She had promised to separate herself from the man whom she still loved. She had forfeited political advancement, and the nation was committed to a long war with no sign of victory on the horizon. When she looked out of her window at Brynawelon, over the fields blanketed by snow and the little town invisible in the blackout, her thoughts must indeed have been melancholy.

As we shall see, the break was not permanent, but Megan had given her promise sincerely, and it lasted for five years. Philip's letters testify to the deprivation that it caused him:

When you asked [me] to keep away, I kept away, for five long years, & largely broke my life & nearly broke my heart. . . . That Xmas message, that Xmas postscript, was always in my heart & mind throughout those long, dark, lonely years.[38]

In his long autobiographical letter of 5 October 1955, he wrote: 'Then came the second war; your telling me not to see you, & the blank, empty five years.'

# CHAPTER EIGHT

# Women at War

## 1

At the time of Dunkirk, Britain still had a million unemployed – a glaring indictment of how the country was run in the Chamberlain era. By the end of 1940 the situation had been transformed by the sense of national peril, by Ernest Bevin's energetic mobilisation of manpower and by big call-ups for the armed forces. There was now a shortage of labour in key industries essential to the war effort, and new or enlarged factories were crying out for workers. Where there were not enough men, the sole resource was obviously to meet the shortage with women.

After the Second World War (as, indeed, after the First) a certain mythology was created about women in industry. Women were pictured as venturing out of the home for the first time in their lives, and bravely (if nervously) adjusting themselves to the unfamiliar world of work. Actually the usual pattern in pre-war years had been for girls to work in the period between leaving school and getting married; the change brought about by the war was that they stayed at – or returned to – work. There was also a considerable change in the kind of work that women did. Figures from the 1930s show that 20 per cent of all working women were in domestic service (the largest single category), 15 per cent were in shops and 12 per cent were in clerical jobs. The rest worked mostly in industries where female labour was traditional, such as textiles and pottery. In the war, domestic service practically disappeared, while many shops either closed down or were staffed by old people. There was a sharp reduction in the output of clothing and, of course, pottery. This led to a corresponding increase in the numbers of women working in engineering, and generally in factories involved in war production.

By the height of the war, 7.5 million women were working in industry alongside 10 million men. To these we can add women in uniform in the auxiliary services of the armed forces and in Civil Defence; nurses and hospital staff (increased to meet war needs); women in offices (there was a big change in the balance in the Civil Service); and those who joined the Women's Land Army and worked on farms. If we set aside women who did not work (mostly mothers of young children) and those who were in non-essential jobs, we find that 45 per cent of all women between school-leaving age and sixty were doing war work.

Employers, however, were reluctant to take on women if they could avoid it, and still more reluctant to give them skilled and responsible work. The only people who were likely to make an issue of sex discrimination in the war effort were the women MPs, still only a dozen. They found common ground whether they were Tory, Labour or Liberal. For example, although Lady Astor was an enormously wealthy aristocrat and had been a prominent supporter of appeasement, she was also a strong feminist. Tory women even tended to take the lead, as there were only four women Labour MPs, and one who might have been a vigorous critic, Ellen Wilkinson, had a government job as number two at the Home Office. In March 1940 the women gathered at Lady Astor's London home to set up what they called the Woman Power Committee. At first only a parliamentary group, it was soon broadened to include representatives from women's organisations and women trade-unionists.

The issue that could scarcely be avoided was that of equal pay. Traditionally, it had been taken for granted (by men, that is) that men should be paid more than women for doing the same work because they were maintaining a family. The state sanctioned this inequality by endorsing scales in the Civil Service, local government and the teaching profession which gave women 80 per cent of the men's rate. In 1936 the House of Commons had voted for equal pay in the Civil Service, but Baldwin, then Prime Minister, immediately made it an issue of confidence and forced the House to reverse itself. In private industry the inequality was still more marked; in engineering, women's wages were on average 55 per cent of men's. With the onset of war, women felt that what might have been acceptable in peacetime was intolerable when women were working to help win the war and often incurring real danger. A woman might be living in an industrial town to work in a munitions factory, and perhaps staying at her bench when the siren went, though she could have found safety in a village. Yet even women in Civil Defence, who drove ambulances during the raids and dug injured people out of the rubble of bombed houses, were being paid one-third less than men who did the same job.

Bevin, as Minister of Labour, was adamantly against equal pay and warned in 1942 that, if it were conceded, 'industrial peace might be endangered for the rest of the war.' His contention, which carried weight because of his prestige as a trade-union leader, was that the unions would not accept equal pay because it would be at the cost of necessary improvements in men's rates. In reality, although such attitudes did exist, the unions had a mixed record, and certainly would have been influenced if the Minister had taken a different stand. Bevin's own union, the Transport and General, demanded and won equal pay for bus conductors at just this time. The Amalgamated Engineering Union, which dominated the scene in war industry, had Communist or pro-Communist leaders who could not openly take a position against equality.

In July 1940 employers and unions in the engineering industry signed an agreement 'in principle' to introduce equal pay for equal work. However, there were all sorts of loopholes; for instance, a woman had to serve a probationary period of eight months to get equal pay, and in that time she could easily be moved to a slightly different job and have to start again. In practice, equal pay remained out of reach for all but a lucky few. When the railway companies were asked to pay women booking-clerks the same as men, they replied: 'Since the managers had been unable to find any industry where the principle of equal pay for equal work was applied, they did not see why they should apply it on the railways.'[1]

The House held its first woman-power debate on 20 March 1941. Ralph Assheton, Bevin's (Tory) number two, opened it in a super-cilious tone. 'I am no feminist myself,' he announced unnecessarily, whereupon Dr Edith Summerskill, Labour MP for West Fulham, told him: 'You will be by the end of the war.' Assheton explained that he preferred companionship between the sexes to rivalry. Mavis Tate, Tory MP for Frome, said that this was just why she was a feminist. Assheton went on: 'If men have a fault, it is perhaps that they do not always give the impression of taking women as seriously as they really do.'

Megan then spoke:

Women have been registered for months past and are still without work.

They finally lost heart because they felt there was no part for them in the war machine. . . . It makes one despair a little to think that we have again to go through the dreary process of convincing employers and managers that women are capable of doing skilled work . . . and that they are intelligent human beings.

She gave an example of the state of affairs:

Here you have a man and a woman, both without any knowledge of engineering, starting out from scratch in a training centre. They may have been a waiter and a waitress. From the very first week they arrive at the training centre, the man receives 60 shillings and the woman 38 shillings. . . . What is the Minister's justification for such unequal conditions?

She was followed by Thelma, who had now hyphenated her name with her husband's and was Mrs Cazalet-Keir. Thelma's opening shot was: 'If we had forty or fifty women in the House, this debate would not be necessary.' She pointed out that all the regional commissioners who had been appointed in 1939 to co-ordinate the war effort, all their deputies, and all their chief officers and deputy chief officers were men; so were four special commissioners recently appointed to deal with rehousing of the bombed-out, clearing bomb debris and conditions in shelters; and so were the nine senior officials in the BBC. 'To my mind,' she said, 'a great weakness of public life has been the great difficulty of getting rid of inefficient men.'

The cutting edge of the debate was the question of compensation. On the first day of the war, the government had introduced a Personal Injuries Bill to provide compensation from public funds for people seriously injured in air raids. The scale was 33 shillings for a married man, 20 shillings for a single man and 18 shillings for any woman. The unions at once protested on behalf of the single men, and the scales were raised to 35 shillings for a man and 28 shillings for a woman. This satisfied the unions, but robbed the government of the argument that men needed more money because they were family breadwinners. Indeed, there were no valid arguments against equal compensation, and the government's real reason for not conceding it was that it would be a precedent for equal pay.

Irene Ward, a Tory MP, was the first to raise the issue of what she called 'unequal compensation for equal risk'. Thelma rammed home the point:

Bombs are no respecters of persons. They fall on the just and the unjust, on men and women alike, and in fact, judging by Hitler's well-known dislike for women, it is they who should receive most compensation. . . . One life is worth as much as another, and therefore no difference in rates can be justified.

Edith Summerskill added: 'The cost of living is exactly the same for both; they pay the same taxation.'

Sir Walter Womersley, the Minister of Pensions, tried to argue that the scales were based on the pre-war Workmen's (*sic*) Compensation Act dealing with industrial injuries. This had allowed the injured to claim half of their normal wages up to a stated maximum, and obviously women earned less than men, so compensation at 28 shillings was actually generous. 'One or two women will suffer a little, but I am satisfied that they will be quite willing to suffer this little disability for the sake of their poorer sisters.' But Mavis Tate pointed out that, with the rise in wages in wartime, a woman could often earn 70 shillings, so that even by Womersley's logic she was entitled to 35 shillings compensation. 'You are asking her to go into these factories in time of war, when there is infinitely greater danger than there ever was before, and you are offering her seven shillings less than a man who is doing identical work.'

Womersley's attitude was not shifted by this debate, so on 1 May 1941 Mrs Tate moved that the regulations should be annulled. She quoted a pledge given in 1939 that compensation would depend solely on the extent of injury and 'wages and earnings will not enter into consideration'. She went on:

If we have to face poverty let's face it, but don't let us create injustice, because if we are fighting for freedom, if we are fighting for the things that make life worth living, how piteous it is that we should allow such unjust proposals as these to go forward.

Megan made the point that women were actually going to be worse off than they would have been under the old Workmen's Compensation Act, and appealed: 'Let the Minister meet the readiness of women in a generous spirit and not in a mean and calculating spirit.'

Womersley tried to justify the unequal scales by asserting that someone would always look after a disabled woman, whereas a disabled man might have to employ a paid housekeeper. Obviously rattled, he wound up: 'I don't want to go down in history as a petty-minded, pettifogging mean person, but I am not going to seek cheap popularity by handing out money in every direction.'

The House then divided. Including tellers, twenty-two men and nine women voted for the motion; eighty-one men voted against.

Refusing to back down, the women formed an Equal Compensation

Campaign Committee. By 1942 Mrs Tate was able to claim, after much behind-the-scenes persuasion, that she had two hundred MPs on her side and was ready to move an amendment to the King's Speech. To forestall this, the government set up a select committee to study the problem. However, in the debate on the King's Speech on 25 November 1942, Megan returned to the charge:

The Minister of Pensions has told us that the rates are not based upon sex discrimination. He said that it is not a question of wages, it is a flat rate, and you get the same compensation whether you earn three pounds or eight pounds, unless you are a woman. That is what the right honourable gentleman calls no sex discrimination. . . . I have never heard that there are special rents for women or that fuel costs them less or that there are special prices for food for women. . . . The percentage of women in Royal Ordnance factories is now sixty. . . . These women are working long hours, far too long in many cases. When their work is over they go back to their houses and often have to do their housework. Now on top of that they have to do fire-watching while somehow or other they have to fit in their shopping. These are the women to whom we are to say: 'We are very grateful for what you are doing, but we must have a Select Committee to find out if your life is worth as much as a man's.'

But Thelma was a member of the select committee, and in April 1943 it reported in favour of equal compensation. The Ministry gave in and introduced a single scale – the only solid feminist victory in the war.

Meanwhile, the labour shortage had grown more acute and in mid-1941 the government decided to make registration for work compulsory for women. The plan was that women (to begin with, women under thirty) would be directed to jobs in industry unless they made their own choice first. Problems immediately arose. For instance, was it right that soldier's wives, who naturally wanted to live near their husbands, should be sent to work scores of miles away? Since pregnant women would obviously have to be exempted, anxious moralists foresaw a rush of women to get themselves pregnant, by a speedy marriage or otherwise. But the strongest objection was that the government had no right to compel women to work and be unfairly paid. Edith Summerskill declared that she would not support conscription unless it meant equal pay, and the Woman Power Committee decided to take this line. However, Bevin gave no ground and conscription went into effect. The only concession was a promise that women would be interviewed by women.

In the Ministry of Labour, civil servants were shaking their heads over their minister's obstinacy. One of them, a Mr Tribe, minuted:

'We do not want to court the antagonism of women's interests, political or industrial.'[2] Their solution, reluctantly accepted by Bevin, was to set up a Women's Consultative Committee with official status. It had nine members, including Irene Ward and Edith Summerskill, trade-unionists, and other women with reputations in public life. The official historian of Britain's industrial war effort, in a book entitled *Manpower*,[3] wrote: 'The committee was taken fully into confidence on all questions. . . . The informality of the proceedings made for a free and honest exchange of opinion.'

On the whole, this strategy worked. An independent historian summed up thus: 'The wartime feminists experienced more defeats than successes. Their efforts to influence government policy on the mobilisation of woman-power were largely deflected by Bevin.'[4]

## 2

In the spring of 1941 it was clear that Britain would not surrender to Hitler, and increasingly unlikely that Britain would be invaded and conquered, but it was very difficult to see how Britain would ever win the war. In April the Germans attacked Yugoslavia and smashed its army in another lightning war. Resistance under Tito's Partisans would make this a costly victory, but not yet. The Germans then came to the aid of the Italians, who had been held at bay by the Greeks since the autumn, and Greece went the way of Yugoslavia. British troops were sent to Greece as a Byronic gesture; the result was another Dunkirk, with the loss of some of the men and practically all the weapons. The question now was whether Egypt could be held if the Germans pressed on there. Actually, Churchill knew through intelligence sources that Hitler's intention was an attack on Russia and that this would be the next great drama of the war. But since Stalin refused to believe that this was coming – despite being warned by the British and by his own spies – the outcome might be yet another German triumph.

Lloyd George was as pessimistic as ever. Kingsley Martin made a record of a talk with him in February 1941, even before the Greek débâcle:

He judged that we could not win. How was victory possible? . . . We could not land troops; Germany would far outnumber us. Bombing would not be decisive and Germany was in a far better position to blockade us than we to blockade Germany. . . . At best, he said, he saw stalemate.

In a year's time, Lloyd George declared:

We shall be weaker and Germany will be stronger. Peace will be more difficult to get, the war will have spread everywhere in the world, causing suffering and destruction beyond imagination and it will not be a whit nearer solution.[5]

This pessimism was openly voiced in the House on 7 May, when Lloyd George observed that the war was 'passing through one of its most difficult and discouraging phases'. It was much worse than in the First World War, when France, Russia and Italy were Britain's allies. He concluded: 'I can see no real triumph until the work of diplomacy has been exhausted.'

Another speech in the debate came from Philip Noel-Baker. With his usual lack of realism (as Hugh Dalton or Patricia Llewellyn-Davies would have put it), he explained how Greece could be saved if the right defence line was selected. Replying to the debate, Churchill said that if he were to single out any speech for praise it would be Philip's; but if there was a speech which must be singled out as 'not particularly exhilarating' it was Lloyd George's.

It was not the sort of speech which one would have expected from the great war leader of former days, who was accustomed to brush aside despondency and alarm.... [It was] the sort of speech with which, I imagine, the illustrious and venerable Marshal Pétain might well have enlivened the closing days of Monsieur Reynaud's Cabinet.

Churchill demanded a vote of confidence, and was given it by the huge margin of 447 votes to 3. Megan voted with the majority; her father abstained.

Despite this barbed exchange between the two old friends, Beaverbrook was still trying to get Lloyd George into the government. He sent one of his young journalists, Michael Foot, to Churt in an effort to persuade him. Lloyd George's reaction was: 'Who? Me? Old Papa Pétain?' But, Foot remembers, he said it with a laugh, not with anger or bitterness.[6]

On 22 June 1941 the Germans invaded the Soviet Union. They achieved complete surprise, destroyed scores of Russian aircraft on the ground and advanced fifty miles on the first day. Churchill made a broadcast the same evening declaring that Russia was Britain's ally. His longstanding aversion to Communism was irrelevant: 'if Hitler invaded hell I would make at least a favourable reference to the devil,' he remarked to friends.[7]

Although Lloyd George had been saying for years that the Red

Army was a formidable fighting force, the new alliance did not mitigate his pessimism. When Megan asked him what he thought of the outlook, he answered in one word: 'Despair'. In a talk with the American journalist John Gunther, he said: 'Quite frankly, I think Hitler will win.'[8] But, although the Russians suffered heavy blows and the Germans advanced to the outskirts of Moscow and Leningrad, Hitler could not achieve the victory on which he had reckoned. Moscow and Leningrad held out. In an exceptionally cold winter, the onslaught ground to a halt.

The mood in Britain was of warm sympathy for Russia and an eager desire to help. 'Tanks for Russia Week', when all production was earmarked to be sent to Russia by the Arctic convoy route, saw a big spurt in output.[9] Mrs Churchill launched a successful Aid to Russia Fund. Moreover, political lessons were drawn: many people reasoned that if the Soviet Union, long depicted as a hopelessly inefficient tyranny, could muster such resistance, there must be something to be said for its system. Megan, more in touch with popular feeling than her father, realised that these attitudes might well be significant when the war ended and political life was resumed.

One man who was gratified by this atmosphere was Guy Burgess, the future Soviet mole, who was then a BBC producer in charge of the *Week at Westminster* programme, on which Megan was still a regular. Despite his eccentric personality and his heavy drinking, his superiors regarded him as an outstanding producer and protested when he was transferred to the Foreign Office. Megan was his favourite contributor, and he noted in an office memo: 'Miss Lloyd George is clearly not a fanatical supporter of the Government as at present constituted and this fact does, I think, emerge.'[10]

Although Burgess employed a large panel of MPs and sometimes invited lobby correspondents to give the talk, he was not entirely successful in livening it up. *The Daily Mirror* asked:

Can nothing be done to improve 'The Week at Westminster'? This ought to be one of the most interesting broadcasts of the week. In point of fact it is, except when Megan Lloyd George does it, one of the dullest.[11]

Indeed, Megan had established herself as a star broadcaster. When Mavis Tate was suggested as a member of the panel, she was described as 'not in Megan's class as a broadcaster by any means, but on the other hand she is not displeasing'.[12]

In December 1941 Britain acquired another ally – and another enemy. Japanese bombers made a devastating surprise attack on the American fleet at its base at Pearl Harbor. Within four months, the

Japanese conquered Malaya and Burma from the British, the Philippines from the United States and Indonesia from the Dutch. When Singapore surrendered, 60,000 British and Australian soldiers were shepherded into captivity – many to die of their privations. Cinema-goers in Britain, watching the newsreel of a general walking under a white flag to meet the Japanese, contrasted this tame surrender with the Red Army's inch-by-inch defence of Sevastopol. Nevertheless, ultimate victory was a rational calculation, as it had not been when Britain stood alone in 1940. The potential strength of the great alliance stretching from San Francisco to Vladivostok exceeded that of its enemies.

The turn of the tide came in the closing months of 1942. Unable to take Moscow, the Germans pushed across the Ukraine to reach Stalingrad on the Volga. It was the city that Stalin had named after himself, and he ordered that it must not be lost. Battling for every house and every room, his soldiers held on. Then fresh Soviet troops advanced and surrounded the Germans. The struggle ended with the surrender of 400,000 Germans, headed by a field-marshal. In Egypt, the British won the decisive battle of Alamein and advanced across Libya. To coincide with this action, British and American forces landed in Morocco and Algeria. From the beginning of 1943, the German armies that had swept triumphantly across Europe were doomed to fight on the defensive.

3

Another war was being fought during these years – between Megan Lloyd George and Frances Stevenson. It was fought without guns and bombs, but with intense tenacity and bitterness.

Long ago, Lloyd George had promised Frances that he would marry her if it ever became possible, and after Margaret's death she understandably felt that he should keep this promise. She recognised that a quick marriage would look improper, but considered that a year's delay would be quite enough. Meanwhile, she wished to establish that Bron-y-de was her home. It had been customary for her to retreat to Avalon at weekends when any of the Lloyd George family might appear at Bron-y-de. With Margaret's death, she felt that this rule had no further purpose. Sylvester wrote in April 1941:

There is a terrific row in progress between L.G. and Megan. Since Dame Margaret's death, Frances remains at Bron-y-de during the weekend. Megan saw her there the other day and, as a consequence, just ignored her father and refused to speak to him. Megan was very bitter in talking to me.[13]

There was another problem. As he grew older, Lloyd George yearned to go back to his homeland to live. Saunders Lewis had written an article criticising him for having 'deserted Wales', and it rankled. So long as Margaret was alive, he could not take Frances to Brynawelon, and indeed Margaret would have regarded it as an insult if her husband and his mistress had settled in the neighbourhood. After her death, it was still impossible for them to move into Brynawelon, because Margaret had left it to Megan. But it seemed feasible for them to start a new home in Wales, and Lloyd George therefore bought an old farmhouse called Ty Newydd, a mile down the road from Brynawelon and with the same magnificent view.[14] His plan was to create a fruit farm and achieve for his native district what he had done for the Surrey heathland. The house was in disrepair, so the architect Clough Williams-Ellis was commissioned to carry out an extensive reconstruction. The hope was that Lloyd George and Frances would be married by the time the house was ready for them.

The obstacle was Megan's implacable opposition to the marriage. Writing later when the whole story was public knowledge, Frances recorded that she and Lloyd George discussed the problem with Lord Dawson, who agreed to talk to Gwilym, Olwen and Megan about it. (Dick, still suffering from paternal disapproval, was not consulted.) According to Frances:

Gwilym was sympathetic to his father and to me. . . . Olwen said she would support anything her father wished – but Megan! Dawson said that he could not influence her, that she blew up completely when discussing the matter and threatened all kinds of tragedies.[15]

Thelma was brought into the drama. Lloyd George invited her to lunch, but then said that he was unwell and arranged for Frances to give her lunch instead. Frances asked her to tackle Megan about the marriage. Thelma said that she would do so only if accompanied by a member of the family: 'Olwen nobly agreed to go with me though she did not like Frances any more than did the rest of the family. . . . The interview was as unpleasant as I feared.'[16] According to Sylvester, Megan flared up and said: 'When my father has something to tell me, he can tell me himself.'[17] Evidently, she resented Thelma's intervention, interpreting it as a plea for Frances rather than simple message-carrying. Thereafter, although Megan and Thelma remained friends (and allies in the fight for equal pay), they were never so close as they had been before.

By spring 1942, Frances was asking Sylvester to find out about the procedure of a Baptist marriage, and Lloyd George was planning to go to Ty Newydd for Easter. Megan, as usual during a Commons recess, would be at Brynawelon. Sylvester wrote:

If L.G. takes Frances and Jennifer to Ty Newydd, there will be an unholy row. Megan will regard it as an insult to the memory of her mother. . . . But happily the place is not ready, so he cannot go.[18]

In May, while Megan was at Brynawelon, a lorry-load of furniture arrived at Ty Newydd, and Williams-Ellis showed her the plans for the reconstruction. Frances told Sylvester that she felt justified in going ahead with the marriage. But Lloyd George was now stalling, saying that January 1943 – two years from Margaret's death – would be a good time. This would coincide with his eightieth birthday.

Plans were made, not indeed for the marriage, but for a birthday lunch at Churt. Megan declared that she would not sit down at the table with Frances. Two days before the big day, Dawson wrote to her:

The birthday would seem to offer an opportunity for a gesture because other members of the family will be going down [and] there will be the occasion to carry off any difficulties. And if the gesture were made it cannot be doubted it would make a great difference to your father's comfort and happiness. If you make the gesture, as I hope you will, it must be warm and really friendly in its quality. It need not last long, but you could make the short time Miss S. was there an occasion and then as it would be a family party she would probably go from the room on her own.

Now I want you to listen to me. I both understand and sympathise with your feelings and especially those which surround your mother's memory, but I am sure she would wish nothing but that the evening of your father's life should be made as smooth as possible. He is in need today of physical care and is likely in this respect to become more dependent in the future. Miss S. fills this role and there is no one else at once fitted available and acceptable for this duty.

If it be a fact that what you feared is off, as it appears to be, it must in justice be said she has now made a great sacrifice and from what she said to me I think she has made things easy and put aside the bitterness of her disappointment. . . . You are not called upon to be a friend but only to be kindly, in the way you understand so well, when you meet her in the capacity as a necessary helpmate for your father today.

Knowing that you were brought up as a Christian there can be no question that you should make this gesture. . . . For it is a matter of Christian charity for your father's sake. He has changed his intention mainly for you. From my deep attachment to you I do urge you on the next suitable occasion to make that gesture and make it generously and you will never regret it.[19]

This letter was prompted, no doubt, by a fact of which Dawson had become aware: Lloyd George was suffering from cancer. In January 1941 the family doctor at Criccieth had told Sylvester that he had received a letter from Dawson about Lloyd George's irregular bowel movements: 'He suspected that these stoppages in L.G.'s bowel movements were due to a growth which would not be apparent for some time. . . . He might go off at any time or he might live a number of years.' In November 1942 Sylvester raised the matter with Dawson: 'I told him something I have told no one except Carey Evans: that L.G.'s bowels are peculiar. . . . Lord Dawson was immensely interested in this and thought there might be a growth.' Sylvester also noticed that Lloyd George's energy was greatly diminished. One day in January 1942, after a visitor had stayed all afternoon, 'L.G. was completely exhausted and stayed in bed most of the following day.'[20]

From the standpoint of today's medical practice, it is strange that nothing was done about Lloyd George's condition. But Professor Sir Richard Doll, the distinguished oncologist, comments:

The question arises whether Lord Dawson would have advised doing nothing for a man of 78 suspected of having an abdominal growth. Operations in people over 70 were much more serious in the early 1940s than they soon became with the improvements in anaesthesia and intravenous nutrition and it is quite likely that a consultant would not press an operation on a man of Lloyd George's age, if he did not want to have one. Lloyd George was a strong-minded and independent man and it might well have been in character for him to have refused an exploratory operation. On that assumption the question arises whether an intra-abdominal growth could last 4 years, eventually causing principally exhaustive and progressive weakness, and the answer to that must be yes.[21]

Professor Doll expressed surprise that Lloyd George did not experience severe pain. Whatever the reason, there is happily no record of this; he simply became weaker and needed more and more rest during the remainder of his life. This may well have been ascribed to his age and the demands he had made on himself for so many years. Cancer, we must bear in mind, was a dark secret in those days.

Megan responded to Dawson's appeal and went to the birthday lunch – along with Tom and Olwen, Gwilym and Edna, and two of the old man's grandsons – although Frances was present. She may have thought, as Dawson evidently believed, that Frances had renounced the idea of marriage. Either this was never the case, or there was another change in the course of 1943. Sylvester was instructed to make the practical arrangements for a registry office marriage at Guildford (the plan for a marriage at a Baptist chapel was dropped because it might draw a crowd). The date was fixed for 23 October 1943. But there was a final drama on the evening before.

Megan rang up and insisted that, if her father did not come to the phone, she would appear at Churt next morning. He went to the phone, which was in an anteroom, and was there so long that Frances went to see whether he was all right. 'She returned', Sylvester narrates, 'to say she was certain Megan would make her father ill.' Sylvester went out and heard Lloyd George saying: 'But Gwilym and Edna agree and Olwen agrees. . . . Well, my dear, that shows you are thoroughly selfish.' As he was exhausted, Sylvester took the phone. He quotes Megan thus:

People will laugh at him. I couldn't bear people to laugh at him. . . . He says he'll see me next week, but he doesn't realise he won't. . . . It will absolutely break my heart if he does. He says Gwilym and Edna and Olwen are for it. They are not.[22]

Frances then rang Gwilym, who reassured her about his attitude and promised to come to the ceremony. But Megan made a phone call to him later that night, and in the morning he rang to say that he would have to skip the ceremony, but would come to Churt after it. The happy (or by this time not altogether serene) pair then set off for Guildford with Sylvester and Frances's sister, Muriel. When they returned to Bron-y-de as man and wife, the champagne was ready but the only guest was Jennifer. Gwilym and Edna arrived at tea time, and Sylvester noted that Gwilym shook hands with his father but did not congratulate him. He said to Sylvester 'that Megan was much upset and he'd had a very bad time with her'.[23]

No hint of all these conflicts leaked out publicly until letters and diaries were published in the 1970s. The official biography published in 1948 contained a bland paragraph, presumably composed by Frances:

After the best part of three years of widowerhood his friends were very glad when he married Miss Frances Stevenson, his personal secretary, who had worked with him since 1913 and given him constant and devoted service.[24]

Two weeks after the marriage, Frances wrote to Megan:

My dear Megan, I hope you will read this letter through, as it is written in all sincerity, to ask you if you will not reconsider your attitude towards your Father's marriage with me. I am so anxious that you shall not commit yourself to a permanent and irrevocable estrangement from him, both for the sake of his happiness and your own, and that is why I am sure you would not forgive yourself if you were to be the cause of any sadness in his last years. . . . I am depriving you of nothing in becoming his wife – neither of his affection, nor of any material benefits now or in the future.[25]

There was evidently no reply (Frances always kept letters). In May 1944, Megan, her father and Churchill were talking in the part of the House of Commons known as 'behind the Speaker's chair' when Megan saw Frances approaching and, as Sylvester puts it, 'suddenly flounced off'.[26]

4

After their victory over equal compensation, the women MPs and their allies outside Parliament decided to follow it up with pressure for equal pay. Mavis Tate published a pamphlet in which she used the persuasive argument: 'Where there is real equality of opportunity and of status, you will have real partnership.'[27] What put the issue on the front pages, however, was a strike at the Rolls-Royce factory at Hillington, near Glasgow, which had come into existence to meet war needs and employed 16,000 workers, of whom the majority were women. When the women demanded equal pay and met with a refusal, the entire workforce – women and men – walked out. Bevin sent a message making it clear that there would be no concessions, and the workers ended the strike under protest after ten days.

The Equal Pay Campaign Committee was formed in January 1944, with Mrs Tate in the chair. They found an opportunity in the new Education Bill, which R. A. Butler was steering through the Commons, and which was designed to shape British education for a generation or more. If equal pay could be made the rule for teachers, it would set a precedent for all public employment and in time for private employment too. On 28 March 1944 Thelma Cazalet-Keir moved to amend a clause on remuneration and include the words: 'The remuneration of teachers shall not differentiate between men and women solely on grounds of sex.' She said:

Men and women take the same training and the same certificates, and apply for the same jobs. When they get into the schools they are confronted with the same problems, responsibilities, and conditions of work. In a mixed school they are entirely interchangeable.

Expressing her hope that the Minister would accept the amendment, she wound up: 'I am certain that public opinion is ready, anxious, and waiting to accept the principle which it embodies.'

Edith Summerskill pointed out that 70 per cent of teachers were women, and that the doctors who gave children medical examinations in schools got equal pay. Mavis Tate said that, if a woman were to be paid at a lower rate, 'she must inevitably have worries and pre-occupations which her male colleagues have not got.' Lady Astor declared fervently: 'If this were the last vote I ever gave in my life I would give it in favour of this amendment.' Megan, though she was in the House, did not speak on this occasion.

Butler, replying to the debate, assured the House: 'I am as much desirous of reform as anybody else.' Probably this was not absolute hypocrisy; as a relatively junior member of the Cabinet, he had to conform to Bevin's rigid opposition to equal pay. His argument was that as Minister for Education he himself did not employ the teachers, and a legislative clause affecting pay would cut across the negotiating machinery.

The amendment was carried by 117 votes to 116. The Churchill government had been defeated for the first and only time.

Arthur Greenwood, who had been dropped from the government and was the senior non-official Labour MP, advised Butler to accept the defeat with good grace. Aneurin Bevan said: 'It would be very bad if the House could not express an opinion without involving national unity and the fate of the government.' The House then adjourned, and Churchill called an emergency Cabinet meeting to consider the situation. Bevin took his usual line: 'Any sign of weakness would have the worst possible effect on industrial relations.'[28]

Next day, Churchill told the House: 'At this very serious time in the progress of the war, there must be no doubt or question of the support which the government enjoy in this House.' He was alluding to the cross-Channel invasion which was due to be launched at any time. The idea that the vote on equal pay would fortify the spirits of the German garrisons on the coast of France was of course nonsensical, but Churchill was able to exploit the tense atmosphere of the moment. He announced that the government would ask for the deletion of Thelma's amendment and treat the issue as a vote of confidence. If they lost, the government would resign.

Mavis Tate protested that the position was now 'really farcical', and suggested a royal commission on equal pay as a way out of the tangle. Churchill was adamant. The vote of confidence, as it had now become, was put off for another day so that the whips could round up MPs who had not heard the original debate. The government obtained a majority of 394 to 28. This was scarcely a triumph, since the 'No' votes in a wartime vote of confidence were normally fewer than ten. Bevan, Richard Acland and two Labour women were among the minority. The Tory women, and also Megan, decided that they had been put in an impossible position and abstained.

The teachers continued to get unequal pay. The government did set up a royal commission, but on condition that it confined itself to fact-finding and made no recommendations – a most unusual stipulation. It did not report until October 1946. Equal pay was ultimately granted to teachers in 1956 and became the law of the land in 1970.

5

George Orwell remarked in a wartime essay that it would be possible to know what sort of Britain emerged after the war by seeing whether the railings round private squares in London, which had been removed to be sent to steelworks as scrap, were reinstated or not. (They were.) Wartime experiences and wartime hardships generated a feeling of 'we're all in it together' and an impatience with divisive barriers of wealth, social class and traditional privilege. Peter Townsend, a teenage boy in the war, recalled when he looked back in 1958:

There was an attitude of trust, tolerance, generosity, goodwill – call it what you like – towards others; a pervasive faith in human nature. Then there was a prevailing mood of self-denial, a readiness to share the good things in life and to see that others got the same privileges as oneself; an urge to give everyone, including the poor, the sick, the old and the handicapped, the chance of having certain elementary rights or freedoms so that they could achieve individual self-respect.[29]

Concretely, these attitudes were translated into a demand that society, through state action, should take responsibility for ensuring that poverty and humiliating dependence on charity, so characteristic of the Britain of the 1930s, should never return. Taking note of this demand, the government (which was, after all, a national coalition) appointed a committee under the chairmanship of Sir William Beveridge to chart an all-embracing scheme of social security.

The Beveridge Report was published in December 1942 – by happy coincidence, at the turning-point in the war marked by Stalingrad and Alamein. It made the front pages of the newspapers, was a talking-point in hundreds of factory canteens and barrack rooms, and (in full or in a shortened version) sold 635,000 copies in the bookshops. For the time, it was the Bible of everyone who claimed to be progressive or radical. No one, however, was more enthusiastic about it than Megan Lloyd George. The great question of social welfare – of liberating men and women from the fears and anxieties that derived from insecurity – was, for her, the central issue of politics and the main reason why she was in politics at all. Her earliest memories were of her father's battles to establish social insurance and medical treatment unregulated by the purse for the first time in British history, and she welcomed the Beveridge scheme as an advance from that historic base. Beveridge himself was a Liberal and had served Lloyd George in working out the Yellow Book plans of 1928 which, Megan was sure, could have saved Britain from much of the misery of the depression. She knew him, trusted him and was ready to take her place among his champions.

Megan's memories told her something else: that progress in this sphere always had to be fought for. It would inevitably be resisted by those who were so comfortably circumstanced that they saw no pressing need for it, those who would have to pay for it through increased taxation and those who objected to a greater approach to social equality. She remembered well how her father had been obstructed, and indeed vilified, by the Tories, the House of Lords and the traditional inheritors of power and privilege. Under the coalition, Tories were greeting the report with bland benevolence and fostering an impression that it was uncontroversial, but she had a shrewd suspicion that any post-war Tory government would try to bury it. In fact, that shrewd suspicion was widespread in the factory canteens and barrack rooms too, and was a cogent reason for the excitement about the report. Beveridge, who was no mean publicist and enjoyed his popularity, was ready to exaggerate the revolutionary nature of his proposals, which did no more than extend and systemise the structure created by Lloyd George in 1911. As Townsend saw, he 'tidied up numerous anomalies and extended social insurance to the whole population (largely, it must be said, to the benefit of the self-employed and the middle classes).'[30] But it was precisely the universality of the Beveridge scheme, its disregard of the traditional distinction between those who were in need and those who were not, that strengthened its appeal.

There were two other main planks in the progressive platform. Those who had suffered from pre-war unemployment and MPs who, like Megan, had seen what it meant to their constituencies were determined that it should never be tolerated again. The soldier's question to Bevin when he visited the troops poised for D-Day – 'Are we going back to the dole after this lot, Ernie?' – became rightly famous.[31] Beveridge spelled out that full employment was 'a condition in which there are at all times more paid jobs than men and women looking for jobs'.[32] Finally, it was assumed that everything desirable – a decent standard of living, full employment, social security – depended on co-ordinated planning. Liberals, or at least Liberals who thought on the same lines as Megan, subscribed to this belief as much as Socialists. No one dissented when Wilfrid Roberts told a Liberal conference in 1943: 'We must plan our economic system to make the very best use of all our resources.'

Indeed, the whole political landscape was undergoing a seismic shift to the Left. Even the Conservative Party was not immune; Churchill had dismissed some of the most discredited Chamberlainites, such as Margesson, and promoted men like Butler and Macmillan who placed themselves in the Disraelian 'one nation' tradition. In March 1943 the Prime Minister, in the words of Angus Calder, 'groped his way to the head of the consensus'[33] and made a broadcast about the shape of post-war Britain which even envisaged 'a broadening field for state ownership and enterprise'.

The Labour Party had quietly readmitted the left-wingers expelled in the 1930s; Cripps, after a stint as ambassador in Moscow, entered the War Cabinet. The fact that senior leaders, such as Attlee, Morrison and Bevin, had key government jobs, which kept them silent on divisive issues, gave a new prominence to the men of the Left, notably Aneurin Bevan and Emanuel Shinwell. The constituencies were adopting candidates – Michael Foot and Barbara Castle, among others – who really seemed to believe that the wartime ferment could be the harbinger of social revolution. Philip Noel-Baker, with his passionate belief that the Second World War must be the last and the 1919 relapse into selfishness and power politics must not be repeated, might have benefited from the changing mood. But he had tried too hard to get into the government, and in 1942 he was given the number two job at the Ministry of War Transport, with responsibility for the allocation of shipping. Although it was an uninspiring job with no political implications, he did it capably and staked a claim to promotion in a future Labour government.

Nothing conveys the character of a historical period better than its rhetoric. Beveridge, in launching his report, declared: 'A revolutionary moment in the world's history is a time for revolutions, not for patching.'[34] Yet more sweepingly, Richard Acland promised:

The structural changes in the shape of society which we propose . . . will lead to the emergence of a new kind of man, with a new kind of mind, new values, a new outlook on life and, perhaps most important of all, new motives.[35]

This language struck a chord with an audience which was becoming a new political constituency: the volunteers of Civil Defence and the wartime welfare services, local officials grappling with unprecedented tasks, teachers faced with challenging questions from their pupils, thousands of women taking on jobs they had never envisaged. The war had given them self-confidence and also the spirit of criticism. It had turned people who might have been insurance sellers or hotel receptionists into bomber pilots, firemen, nurses in army hospitals; it had made them travel, talk and read more widely than ever before in their lives. Historians have called this constituency middle-class, but in reality its social origins were diverse. What it represented can best be called radical classlessness.

As a Radical with no very firm anchor in the class structure, Megan was well placed to understand this new constituency and to see opportunities in it. The question was how best to mobilise it. In 1941 Lancelot Spicer, a Liberal businessman belonging to the well-known paper-manufacturing family, took the lead in forming a group called Radical Action, and Megan joined. Other members included Beveridge, Wilfrid Roberts, Tom Horabin, Vernon Bartlett and Clement Davies. Horabin was a left-wing Liberal elected at a by-election just before the war; Bartlett was the Independent Progressive who had won Bridgwater in 1938; Davies – here was a straw in the wind – had been a Liberal National but was now a Liberal. Two similar groups formed at the time were Forward March, headed by Richard Acland, and the 1941 Committee, headed by J. B. Priestley, who had been banned from BBC microphones on Churchill's orders.

In July 1942, Forward March and the 1941 Committee merged to create a movement named Common Wealth. The name, while recalling Cromwellian values, also expressed the idea (deliberately, the two words were separated and given capital letters) that the nation's wealth should be held in common by its people. Megan was sympathetic, but decided not to join. Acland made it clear that Common Wealth would contest by-elections, so that it was in effect a new political party. Megan's perspective was to rebuild the Liberal Party and steer it in a Radical direction.

The three established parties had agreed in 1939 to an electoral truce, which meant that vacancies in the Commons would be filled by the unopposed return of a candidate from the party holding the seat. It was impossible, however, to prevent independents or outsiders from standing. As the popular mood shifted to the Left, the rank and file of Labour and the Liberals became restive under the inhibitions of the truce and could not be restrained from supporting anti-Tory candidates. Between 1942 and 1945, the Tories lost eight by-elections in seats which they had won in the pre-war general election; three were captured by Common Wealth candidates, five by independents. Here was a significant pointer, though not everyone appreciated it, to what would happen in the post-war general election.

How would the Liberal Party fare when the normal political conflict was resumed? Perhaps very well indeed, some optimists thought. Beveridge, whose name was as well known as Churchill's and who incarnated the hopes of millions, entered the political arena when he became Liberal MP for Berwick-on-Tweed in October 1944. The voters in the 'new constituency' were certainly not Conservatives, but they were not convinced Socialists; surely the Liberal outlook would suit them best. Surely the Second Coming was at hand.

The first thing to do, apparently, was to detach the Liberal Nationals from their links with the Tories and re-create the party as it had been before 1931. They would not be obliged to give up their jobs in the government, since some 'real' Liberals were in it too. But a merger would double the Liberal strength in the House and secure the adherence of some MPs who had useful local popularity. Talks were arranged in August 1943 to explore the possibilities. The Liberals were represented, among others, by Violet Bonham Carter, Geoffrey Mander and Wilfrid Roberts. Dingle Foot, who was not present but obtained a report, wrote to tell Megan about the two hours of 'extremely rambling discussion'.

Clearly there was no basis for reunification. The Vichy Liberals, as Dingle called them, took the position that the coalition government should continue after the war; that there would have to be a 'coupon election'; and that Liberals must never support a Labour government, though they might support or join a Tory government on 'an agreed policy'. In his letter Dingle summed up:

The Simonites were quite willing to accept a general declaration that the Party should be free and independent. But, immediately after the merger with ourselves, they would wish to state at once that we intend to remain in the coalition after the war. . . . As far as I can gather nothing remotely resembling a basis of agreement ever looked like emerging from the discussion.[36]

Rank-and-file Liberals, if they were ever told about these negotiations at all (Dingle's letter is headed 'Confidential'), would not have dreamed of accepting the Simonite terms. They may have suspected that something was in the wind, for the 1943 Liberal Assembly passed this resolution:

Continuance of a so-called National Government after the war, predominantly Tory in character, would be fraught with grave danger to national and international reconstruction . . . [and would] shatter the faith of millions of our people who are naturally looking to the post-war Parliament for realisation of their hopes of social security.

Megan heartily approved of this stand. No one could guarantee that, when the time came, the Tories would be beaten, but she was looking forward to fighting them. In Anglesey, she was confident of taking on all comers.

It looked as though 1944 would be the year of victory. British and Americans troops landed on the Normandy beaches on 6 June, and by August they had smashed the German armies in France. Paris, Brussels and Rome were liberated cities. On the eastern front, the Red Army advanced into Poland and Hungary, the Germans withdrew from Greece, and Tito's Partisans marched into Belgrade.

But unlike the First World War, the Second dragged on beyond expectations. The British airborne landing at Arnhem was 'a bridge too far' and ended in disaster. In December the Germans were even able to stage an alarming counter-offensive in the Ardennes. Flying bombs and rockets – precursors of the missile technology of the future – tried the nerves of Londoners who had survived the blitz. Celebrations were unavoidably postponed to 1945.

6

On 19 September 1944, Lloyd George and Frances made the journey from Churt to Criccieth – from Bron-y-de to Ty Newydd. Megan was at Brynawelon, just along the road. When she was told by Sylvester that her father was longing to see her, she replied: 'I'll be delighted to see him, but he must come alone.'[37] Accordingly, he was driven to Brynawelon, without Frances but with the indispensable Sylvester, who wrote: 'She leapt into his arms with a cry of "Tada!" and in a few minutes they were strolling round the garden and everything was once more happy.'[38]

Lloyd George was still planning to clear the hillside around Ty

Newydd and start his fruit farm, but everyone else knew that this was a pipe-dream. Sir Thomas Carey Evans said to Sylvester that 'he would not be surprised if L.G.'s instinct had not led him to his old home to die, like an old dog returns to its lair.'[39]

At the end of the year, David Lloyd George – Father of the House of Commons, MP for Caernarvon Boroughs since 1890 – became Earl Lloyd George of Dwyfor. Thousands of his admirers were shocked by his acceptance of the title, and many still look back with bewilderment and regret. In his great days he had denounced and derided the aristocracy, and had spoken of politicians who took peerages with pity or contempt. His acceptance of the earldom cannot be explained with complete certainty, but there are two theories.

The Lloyd George family believed, and still believe today, that the old man was talked into taking the title by Frances, who wanted to be a countess. This cannot be disproved, but it is not supported by any contemporary account; Sylvester, always on the alert, noted no such wish on Frances's part. She wrote in her autobiography: 'I know it has been suggested that I influenced him in his decision to take it, but indeed I did not.'[40]

The other explanation is that Lloyd George would have been heartbroken if he had been defeated in the post-war general election. It is surprising that a man of eighty-two, well beyond the customary age of retirement for MPs, should have considered standing again; but he did not realise that he was terminally ill, and he was anxious to have a forum for his views on the peace-making. The prospect of defeat was real, since about 10,000 civil servants, without local links and probably with Tory opinions, had settled in the Caernarvon towns through wartime dispersal.[41] Indeed, the Tory candidate did win the seat in 1945 by a margin of 336 votes – although whether Lloyd George would have done better or worse than the actual Liberal candidate is anybody's guess. At all events, if he took a peerage he would be able to make speeches about the peace settlement in the House of Lords.

Sylvester went to both Tory and Labour headquarters in London to enquire about the possibility of an unopposed return for Lloyd George. The idea met with sympathy, but he was told that the decision must be made by the local party organisations, and neither of them would agree. On 17 November 1944 Sylvester got an appointment with Churchill through Sinclair and asked whether Lloyd George could be offered an earldom (though at this stage he was not sure whether Lloyd George would accept). Churchill replied that he would be glad to make the offer. But when the prospect was aired in the Lloyd

George family it met with a highly negative reception. Olwen's account was:

We learnt the truth when Father came to see Megan and myself and said: 'I want to tell you two that the King has offered me an earldom.' Megan's reaction was characteristic. 'You won't accept,' she said. . . . Trying to win her round, Father told her: 'You will be Lady Megan.' . . . The more we thought about it, the less Megan and myself liked the idea. We knew very well that if Mother had been alive, she wouldn't have liked it either.[42]

On 28 November, Frances told Sylvester that Lloyd George had decided to accept the earldom, but it would be advisable not to let Megan know. On 18 December, a Royal Marines courier arrived at Ty Newydd with the formal offer (this was presumably a Churchillian touch). Lloyd George accepted by telegram, and the title was made public in the New Year's honours list. Megan showed her feelings by forbidding BBC announcers to introduce her as 'Lady Megan'.

The old man never took his seat in the Lords, nor did he ever leave Ty Newydd again. Growing progressively weaker, he was easily tired and dozed off at any time. Frances records that, up to the last, he had no pain and did not know that he had cancer. He looked forward to visits, especially from his daughters. Now that the end was in sight, Megan did not keep up her refusal to be in the same room with Frances. Acording to Frances, 'Megan came every day, with a show of friendliness to me. . . . Lloyd George was pleased that she and I – to all appearances – were friends.'[43]

On 9 February 1945 Lloyd George had a bad attack, and Dr Robert Prytherch, who was in constant attendance, thought that the end had come, but he survived. On 26 February Prytherch wrote to Dawson:

I have escorted Megan there twice this week (this still requires patience, diplomacy and time). Each time he has rallied. . . . I think he knows the truth, but so far he is unaware or refuses to recognise his condition. . . . It may be a week, a month or more.[44]

By now, it was publicly known that Lloyd George was gravely ill, and about twenty journalists waited at the gate of Ty Newydd. Of these last days, Thomson wrote:

The farmers round would send in presents of eggs and poultry, the fishermen sent him fish, and the cottagers would bring posies from their cottage gardens. An unceasing pilgrimage wandered up between the fern-covered stone walls of the country lane that led from the village to Ty Newydd, bringing their offerings and their affectionate inquiries.[45]

Lloyd George died on 26 March 1945. His nephew, W.R.P. George, wrote this account five days later:

He had been dying for the last two weeks, and his vitality had been amazing against the erosion of cancer on the liver. I saw him last on the Sunday afternoon in the Ty Newydd library, which had been converted into his bedroom. He was beyond articulation and barely conscious – shrunken, pallid and frail, with his skeleton-like right hand limp on his bosom moving up and down to the rhythm of his laboured breathing. . . . He died Monday night at 8.30. . . . We didn't go up to the death bed scene, but were notified of the end through hearing Megan and Olwen come sobbing out of the bedroom; poor Megan was distraught for some minutes.[46]

Sylvester recorded that those present at Lloyd George's death were Frances, Jennifer, Megan, Olwen, Sarah Jones, Dr Prytherch, Ann Parry and Sylvester himself. According to both Sylvester and Thomson, he died with Frances holding one of his hands and Megan the other.

In accordance with his wishes, he was buried by the bank of the rushing Dwyfor river. The large stone on which he had often sat in his boyhood was placed over his grave. The crowd was enormous; as at so many Lloyd George meetings, the attendance exceeded the available space. His nephew wrote:

The crowd was of the calibre that made Uncle David and gave him sustenance and support all through. . . . Uncle David had wanted them to sing hymns at his funeral, but there was not much singing, and still less sign of emotion, for today it was not a human being known to the majority of mourners who was being buried, but a legend.

Later, Clough Williams-Ellis designed a surround for the grave in local stone. When it was completed, there was a short family ceremony of dedication. Frances was not invited, but she went to the grave afterwards and left a bouquet of red roses. Walking there on the following day with Ursula Thorpe, Megan picked up the bouquet and silently threw it over the hedge into the road.[47]

Frances tried to launch a memorial fund to start an agricultural college, with a base in the house in Llanystumdwy which had been Lloyd George's boyhood home. The Lloyd Georges declined to give her any support. She wrote bitterly in her autobiography: 'It seems that nothing can eradicate my original offence against the family.'[48] The money raised was just enough to make the house into a Lloyd George museum, with Ann Parry as curator. On a visit to Wales, Jo Grimond once walked past it with Megan, who said to him in her best dramatic style: 'Olwen and I will never cross that threshold.'[49]

By his will, Lloyd George left Bron-y-de to Gwilym, who sold it. It was later destroyed by fire, with some suspicion of arson. The Churt farmland and a bungalow on the estate were left to Megan, but she seldom went there. Ty Newydd was left to Frances and she also had Avalon, her own house at Churt.

She was undecided whether to stay on at Ty Newydd. The family presence was weighty; Brynawelon was Megan's home, and the Carey Evanses, since Sir Thomas had now retired, had a house called Eisteddfa, not far away. Frances was made to feel an atmosphere of hostility, and some shopkeepers refused to serve her or did so with ill grace. The most wounding incident occurred when the sixteen-year-old Jennifer went to a film show in Criccieth and tried to greet Megan, who arrived at the same time. Megan had been dutifully polite to Jennifer as well as Frances before the old man's death, but now she ignored the girl.[50]

In April 1946, a year after Lloyd George died, Frances moved to Avalon and put Ty Newydd on the market. From her hilltop home at Brynawelon, Megan was in undisputed command of the Lloyd George territory.

# CHAPTER NINE

# 'Like It Used To Be'

## 1

Within a matter of weeks in the spring of 1945, the world mourned or rejoiced over the deaths of four men who had left ineradicable traces on their epoch: David Lloyd George, Franklin Roosevelt, Benito Mussolini, Adolf Hitler. As Hitler's body dissolved into unrecognisable ashes in his bunker and a Red Army soldier fixed the hammer-and-sickle flag over the ruins of the Reichstag, the Third Reich, vaunted to last a thousand years, ceased to exist after a mere twelve. With the German armies crumbling into fragments, it was not even easy to find commanders to sign a surrender, but on 8 May a suitable delegation did the necessary at General Eisenhower's headquarters near Reims. A great British scientist, Sir Henry Tizard, expressed what many must have felt: 'I feel rather like a patient coming round after a severe but successful operation. Deep down there is a feeling that all is well and that a great oppression has been lifted.'[1]

Churchill would have liked a quick coupon election, with the wartime coalition sweeping the board as in 1918, but Labour and the Liberals had no intention of going along with such a plan. So he offered alternatives: an election fought by opposing parties or a continuance of the coalition until the defeat of Japan. This presented the Labour leaders with a dilemma. Churchill knew — and Attlee, as Deputy Prime Minister, must have known — that the development of an atomic bomb was nearing completion, but it was not due to be tested until July, and no one was sure whether it would be a decisive weapon or even whether it would work. Thus the Japanese war might well last until 1946 or perhaps longer, and Churchill might be firmly in the saddle as a peacetime Prime Minister. But Attlee and his colleagues rated their chances of winning a 1945 election as distinctly poor. Shinwell, then a member of the Labour Party National Executive, related that Bevin, Dalton and most of the leaders favoured staying in the coalition, but the Chief Whip warned that there would be a party revolt – 'the lads will never agree'.[2] So the coalition was dissolved and Churchill formed a Tory 'caretaker' government. The election followed, with polling on 5 July.

With hindsight, it seems strange that Labour's landslide victory was so unexpected, especially after the signals given by the wartime by-elections. But political correspondents differed only as to whether the Tories would win a big or a narrow majority and, says a history of the election, 'the only point on which all were agreed was that there would not be a Labour majority.'[3] True, the Gallup poll yielded figures which were proved by the result to be accurate to within one per cent, but in 1945 few people gave credence to that new-fangled American device.

Although the causes of the Labour triumph were rooted in the changes in popular feeling described in the last chapter, it was also assisted by Churchill's tactics in the campaign. Advised by Beaver-brook and by a protégé named Brendan Bracken, who had developed a taste for black propaganda as wartime Minister of Information, he declared in his opening broadcast: 'No Socialist system can be established without a political police. They would have to fall back on some sort of Gestapo.' Cartoons of the eminently respectable Attlee in SS uniform made readers (including readers of the Beaverbrook press) laugh, and the history quoted above records: 'No one took these warnings seriously.'[4]

Observers who underestimated Labour's prospects were inclined to overestimate Liberal strength. Beveridge, obviously the Liberals' main asset, addressed meetings everywhere from Scotland to Cornwall; it did not occur to him that his own seat at Berwick needed attention. But the Liberal campaign somehow failed to take off. After hearing Beveridge at Edinburgh, Alison Readman wrote: 'One could not but feel that the old fire of Liberalism . . . was now almost extinct.'[5]

In Anglesey, Megan had a straight fight against the Labour candidate. His name was Cledwyn Hughes; we last met him as a schoolboy being taken by his father to have tea with Megan at the House of Commons. He had qualified as a solicitor, started a practice in Holyhead and served in the RAF. Inheriting the family allegiance, he was an active Liberal as a student but was converted to Labour by Henry Jones, who had been Labour candidate in 1935. While home on

began with the admission: 'We have been forced to realise that the world is faced with the possible eclipse of British Liberalism.'[10] This was undeniable, although whether it caused as much distress in Brazil or Burma was another question.

When the little band of Liberals assembled at Westminster, their first task was to elect a leader to fill Sinclair's place. A historian describes the procedure thus:

The remaining MPs knew little of each other's capabilities, and several of them had not even met before the election. They adopted the remarkable expedient of asking each member to withdraw in turn, while the others discussed his suitability.[11]

One notes that the question to be discussed was 'his', not 'his or her', suitability. There seems to have been no suggestion that Megan might be chosen as leader. Thirty years were to pass before a British political party was led by a woman.

The man chosen was Clement Davies. Gradually it was realised that he was an amiable man who tended to agree with the last person who had put a strong argument to him. For example, before the war he had been a member of the Anglo-German Fellowship, a Nazi front organisation – which did not prove that he had real Fascist sympathies, but that someone had twisted his arm.[12] Whatever his qualities were, they were decidedly not those of leadership.

2

On the morning of 27 July 1945, Attlee's first day as Prime Minister, he decided to appoint Dalton as Foreign Secretary and Bevin as Chancellor. After lunch (and there was much speculation about whom he lunched with) he switched them round. It is still uncertain why he did so, but there are grounds for believing that senior civil servants in the Foreign Office intimated that they would find it difficult to work with Dalton.[13]

Attlee and Bevin, replacing Churchill and Eden, went to Potsdam for the final stages of a conference with Stalin and President Truman. The atomic bomb had now been tested, and Truman told Stalin rather vaguely that the United States had a new and powerful weapon. Stalin therefore hastened to declare war upon Japan, and Soviet forces invaded Manchuria. On 6 and 8 August, atomic bombs devastated Hiroshima and Nagasaki. Japan surrendered, and the world was officially at peace.

Bevin may not have wanted the Foreign Office, but he had definite views on foreign policy. Idealistic aspirations such as disarmament, reliance on the United Nations (which was to replace the League of Nations) and enduring friendship between the wartime allies held no appeal for him. Sharp disagreements between the western powers and the Soviet Union, notably on the make-up of a government for Poland, had erupted even before the end of the war, and Bevin applied himself with relish to resisting Russian ambitions.

In completing his list of appointments, Attlee decided to make use of Philip Noel-Baker's international experience by making him Minister of State (as the number two job was now called) at the Foreign Office. Bevin did not want him there, for several reasons. He regarded Philip with contempt and soon coined a nickname for him – 'Fly-by-night'. He had a favourite of his own, a young Scottish MP called Hector McNeil. Nor did he share Attlee's view that Philip or anyone else should be given a government job because he was esteemed in the Labour Party. Reluctantly, he accepted Philip as Minister of State on condition that he could have McNeil as Under-Secretary. Not much more than a year passed before he succeeded in easing Philip out. His biographer sums up the episode briefly but accurately:

Bevin's only concession to party feeling was his agreement to Attlee's choice of the high-minded and respected Philip Noel-Baker as Minister of State at the Foreign Office, where he had little, if any, influence on policy and in October 1946 was replaced by the more congenial Hector McNeil.[14]

Fortunately there was a job to be done which did not impinge on immediate policy decisions and which was right up Philip's street. The United Nations had been brought into existence at a conference in San Francisco in May, but its constitution and rules still had to be drawn up. These would be submitted to the first Assembly, to be held in London in January 1946. Philip became the British member of the Preparatory Commission, and then led the British delegation to the Assembly. In the Commission, he was regarded by the US representative, Edward Stettinius, as 'limited by his preoccupation with the defunct League of Nations'.[15] In fact, the UN Charter emerged as a faithful imitation of the League Covenant, with an Assembly for annual debates and a Security Council in which a few nations (the USA, the USSR, Britain, France and China) had permanent seats and a right of veto.

A question that aroused heated arguments was that of the UN's headquarters. Philip, supported by the French representative, pressed for a return to Geneva, or at least somewhere in Europe, 'the natural and inevitable communications centre of the world'. His fear was: 'If we go to the United States it means that Russia will have a free hand in Europe.'[16] For others, however, the main danger was that the USA might lose interest in the UN and revert to isolationism, as in 1920. Since the Americans and the Russians agreed that the UN should be centred in New York, Philip had to yield. He felt that he had received insufficient support from Bevin and from the Cabinet (of which he was not – though he yearned to be – a member).

Still, he derived satisfaction from his role as leader of the host delegation at the London Assembly, and then in April 1946 in Geneva at the final Assembly of the League, which had to be formally wound up. Speaking in the city where he had dedicated himself as a young man to peace through collective security and multilateral disarmament, he declared:

We know now that we who stood for collective security were right, and that our opponents who ridiculed us were always catastrophically wrong. We know now that the world war began in Manchuria fifteen years ago. . . . Our work has not ended, it has only just begun. This time, both the governments and the peoples are resolved to win.[17]

Megan, meanwhile, had to reconsider her political position. In a speech at Llangefni in October 1945, she congratulated Anglesey on standing firm amid the 'Socialist avalanche' and declared: 'My faith in Liberalism and its future remains unchanged.' But the realistic question was: what should be a Liberal's atttitude to a Labour government which was firmly entrenched in power and determined to carry out its own programme? Foremost in this programme were bills for the nationalisation of the coal industry, the railways, gas and electricity. With a certain amount of hesitation, all the Liberals voted for these measures except one rigorous believer in free enterprise – Rhys Hopkin Morris, MP for Carmarthen. Some Liberals outside the House, however, were unhappy over the prospect of their party becoming an appendage to a Socialist government, and intermittent rumblings presaged future conflicts.

Megan was now living at 13 Cromwell Place, South Kensington. Her flat – living-room, study, bedroom, housekeeper's room – was the top floor of a large nineteenth-century house. (A BBC memo warned a recording team: '70 steps and no lift.') She decided in 1945 that she needed a housekeeper, and a Liberal activist in Anglesey introduced her to a woman named Ellen Roberts who was looking for a job. Thirty-four years old at this time, Ellen had started work as a housemaid at Penrhyn Castle at the age of fourteen, but had spent some years at her Llangefni home looking after an invalid mother. Since Megan was devoid of social snobbery and never insisted on a traditional mistress-servant relationship, the two women became close friends and often spent a morning chatting in Welsh. Ellen also had a cousin called Bessie, who sometimes came to stay (fitting into the flat somehow) and typed letters in Welsh for Megan. Megan's secretary from this time until 1954 was Eileen Brady, who proved efficient and valuable. A later secretary, Priscilla Morton, describes Ellen as 'a plump, bouncy, ebullient Welshwoman'.[18] But Megan's nephew, Robin Carey Evans, thought that she was 'a formidable, difficult type, often very impertinent' and that she bossed Megan in a manner which he found undesirable.[19]

Megan still had her cottage at Chesham but did not make much use of it. Her pocket diary for 1947 notes only two weekends at Chesham, compared with eight at 'home' (Brynawelon), three at Churt, two with Thelma at Raspit and one with Ursula at Stonewalls, her house at Limpsfield, Surrey. A few years later, Megan gave up the Chesham cottage.

Her diary was filled with lunch, tea and dinner appointments, but she preferred to spend her time with a few close friends. The closest personal and political friend was Dingle Foot, who had lost his seat in the House in 1945 but was an influential figure in the Liberal Party. He was a witty, amusing man and she always enjoyed his company; they shared a taste for the theatre and the ballet. He was also a good-natured man, always willing to fetch and carry for Megan, look up the facts and statistics that she needed for a speech, or take some tedious chore off her shoulders. They spent so much time together, including long evenings at her flat, that some political gossips believed that they were lovers. But Ellen Roberts and Megan's nephew Robin Carey Evans – he was in London reading for the Bar and was often at the flat too – were certain that Megan and Dingle were no more than friends, and two surviving Foot brothers, Michael and John, are also sure that this was the case.

Now that Megan's parents were dead, the family was less central to her life. Her brother Dick, after two years in hospital with tuberculosis, found himself hard up and unemployed. In 1947 he went to America on a lecture tour; he liked it enough to stay, found a job working for *Reader's Digest* and did not return to Britain until 1958. Gwilym was still a Liberal MP, but he was steadily moving closer to the Tories and Megan could not see eye to eye with him. Olwen did not often leave Eisteddfa, where Tom died in 1947.

The Tory women MPs who had fought courageously for equal pay and incurred Churchill's wrath – Thelma Cazalet-Keir, Irene Ward, Mavis Tate – had all lost their seats. There was now only one woman in the Tory ranks (two after a 1946 by-election). On the other hand, there were twenty-one Labour women in the House. As a Radical and a feminist, Megan naturally formed close links with them. The battle for equal pay was still being waged, and the obvious way to win was to put pressure on Labour ministers, though they proved less sympathetic than the women had hoped. One of the Labour women, Jean Mann, wrote later: 'Megan was a great favourite in the Labour women's Parliament of 1945; we looked on her as one of us, although at that time she was deputy leader of the Liberal Party.'[20] (Actually, Megan did not hold that position until January 1949.)

Labour men as well as women were also inclined to regard Megan as more or less 'one of us', since they knew that Liberal support for their policies was due to her as much as to anyone. She was on good terms with Attlee and with other senior ministers, particularly Herbert Morrison, who was in charge of the government's parliamentary strategy. She could hardly refuse, moreover, to be friendly with Philip. They were both on the Council of the United Nations Association, which was set up, on the model of the pre-war LNU, to mobilise support for the UN. They had begun to draw closer again at the end of 1944, when he was still a junior minister in the coalition government and she complimented him on a speech in the House. Next day, he wrote to her for the first time (or she kept his letter for the first time) since 1940:

Megan, you were so sweet to me yesterday that I *must* write and say Thank you. I have no one to help me now; I had such a difficult time with Leathers [Lord Leathers, Minister of War Transport] over my speech . . . and I was feeling so wretched afterwards, that I just had to ask you if you thought I'd been a credit to you or not. And you were so sweet to me. . . . But, of course, if you understand me, the rest of what you said was what really mattered.[21]

In 1945 there was only a letter of condolence on the death of Megan's father, and a short letter of good wishes for Christmas which ended: 'I did so love our talks.' Then, while the UN Assembly was meeting in London in January 1946, Megan spoke at a public meeting to mark the occasion and Philip wrote the next night:

I can't tell you how excited and happy I was; it was so exactly like it used to be, when you came and sat beside me. And it was so wonderful to hear you making such a brilliant and lovely speech, and to see how the people *adored* you, & to have you giving me good advice. . . . And it was such *fun* while we were sitting together, and afterwards on the platform at the end – I felt really, singingly, stingingly, magically alive.

Lovely, but less fun, in the little room. . . . I know what I want; but I don't want anything that would mean pain or unhappiness to you. Must it mean that? Must it mean strain? I thought, perhaps, we could be happy together without any of the worry and doubts and conflicts that hit us both so hard before Xmas, 1940. . . .

I won't thrust myself in, if it will upset your happiness in the tiniest degree. If you like, this shall be my last word. You can believe me – I have given you proofs – especially in 1941, when I seemed for months to die by inches. If it *is* my last word, Megan, it brings you my love.[22]

In May, addressing her as 'my beloved Megan' for the first time since 1940, he wrote: 'I think we could be anything, & do anything, and it wd all be right in the eyes of God. But I will be and do what you want.'[23] Megan may, one guesses, have said that some things would not be right 'in the eyes of God'. The next letter, six weeks later, seems to indicate that she was resisting his pressure to resume the love affair:

Be honest, my beautiful, and you'll admit that you know, in your heart, with absolute certainty, with certainty that nothing can shake or alter – you *know* that I've loved you since we first met. I've loved you in *all* the ways in which a person can be loved. I've been, for long, long years your slave. I've waited, waited, waited for you, when waiting was very hard. I've kept away, shunned you, turned my back, when it tore my heart out to do it. . . . I've accepted the dictate of fate that one thing was forbidden. I've *understood* you as no one else has ever done, and valued and appreciated every scrap of you, moral, intellectual and physical, with an intensity that all your other admirers put together couldn't touch. . . .

That's why I can't *bear* it when you say my postcard made you angry. If you had thought it right to let me be your lover, there would be nothing wrong in it, nothing that I could feel wasn't natural and beautiful and right and perfect; to think otherwise would be a blasphemy I simply couldn't stand. Fate has made a barrier I can't break down; all right, I accept it. But I accept it, believing that with you the perfect consummation of all life could and *would* be reached, if only, if only the barrier wasn't there. . . .

No word of yours or mine shall ever spoil the beauty, the nobility, the perfection of what we've had. I won't write or talk of it again, since you so desire; but what I've written now you must, my darling, and you *shall* believe.[24]

Another disappointment was in store for Philip. In October 1946 Bevin succeeded in ejecting him from the Foreign Office and promoting McNeil to the position of Minister of State. Years later, he was still bitter; he told Megan in 1953: 'When I got a chance myself in the U.N., after 1945, I *didn't* miss it. . . . If Attlee had left me there another couple of years, everything might have been different for me ever since.'[25] His new job was Secretary for Air. Kenneth Younger, then Philip's parliamentary private secretary, commented: 'He cannot be expected to get enthusiastic over a Service department with his background of Quakerism and the UN.'[26] Indeed, sending the apostle of disarmament to hobnob with air marshals and inspect bomber squadrons was surely an example of Attlee's quietly malicious – or Bevin's brutal – sense of humour. He accepted the uncongenial job because a return to the back benches might have been the end of all his ambitions, but also because, by long tradition, each of the service ministers had a seat in the Cabinet and therefore a voice in major policy decisions. However, once he had accepted the position, he learned that Attlee was ending this tradition and the Secretary for Air would not be in the Cabinet. He had, in fact, been outmanoeuvred. As his biographer says: 'Exclusion from the Cabinet was a source of desperate disappointment for Noel-Baker.'[27]

To soften the blow, Philip was sent at the end of October to represent Britain at the UN's second Assembly (the first to meet in New York). Presumably this measured the importance that Bevin attached to the UN, but other delegates must have found it curious that Britain was represented by a man who was no longer at the Foreign Office. While he was in the midst of discussions about disarmament, Philip was ordered to come home and look after the Air Ministry.

By this time, hard-headed politicians were ranking him as a somewhat pathetic figure. Eden considered him 'a dreamer and not a doer'. Gladwyn Jebb, the career diplomat who represented Britain in the Security Council, dismissed him condescendingly as 'saintly and well-disposed'. Kenneth Younger noted: 'I find my respect for him steadily dwindling. He seems to have very little grip on reality.'[28] (As we have seen, Hugh Dalton and Patricia Llewellyn-Davies also took this view.) Roy Jenkins, who succeeded Younger as Philip's PPS, thought that he was 'vain and weak' and, looking back years later, described him as 'a wispy idealist'.[29] Jenkins conceded, however, that he had considerable charm and could inspire affection, especially from women.

## 3

Early in 1947, Megan was still trying to keep Philip at arm's length. His immediate objective was to take her to the ballet, as he knew that she was fond of it. He wrote on 7 February:

When I hear your voice, I have a constant reminder that you want me to be 'friendly' only, & I do try, tho' you don't believe it, to do what you want. . . . But when I'm writing to you, then the years simply roll away, and I'm just back where I was in December 1940. . . .

But because I adore you, I *will* do what you want. I've really behaved *extremely* well these last few weeks. I'll go on doing so, and I'll improve, if you tell me I must. But, please, let us have our Ballet party rather soon!. . . . Don't put it off too long, my fairy! And remember we're both lonely people; we don't have too much rest & relaxation and deep heart-warming happiness, do we? Lets get what we can. If the Ballet party was a success, we might repeat it! Which is all to say – lets go tonight, Saturday! Ring me up at the Air Ministry before 12 o'clock.

The breakthrough came, apparently, some time that spring. It is marked by a letter which, very unusually for Philip, was not dated. Megan was about to leave for Brynawelon, probably for the Easter recess.

When I think that you're going away, and that tomorrow night you'll be buried in Welsh cloud for several eternities, I *have* to say it. I *do* love you, altho' I try so desperately not to. I love you to *my* distraction, and perhaps, I'm afraid, to *yours*. I do love you so much that I want you *now*, this minute, tonight, tomorrow, all the time. . . . I love you so much that my thoughts are *now* making your cheeks pinker, & your eyes bluer, & your hair lovelier, & are smoothing away every care and trouble from your forehead and your face. . . .

I want you *now*. HURRY UP! If I'd known you wd be so long, I'd have gone and listened to Douglas Jay.[30] It wd have made the time go. I can't stand any more waiting now – I can't . . . COME, MY BEAUTIFUL AND MY BELOVED! Come now!

Whether or not Megan responded immediately to this appeal, they were soon lovers again. He wrote on 30 April:

My sweetheart, its been *lovely* these days seeing you; its felt quite like it used to be. And you know that you come before everything. . . . I wanted to talk to you about I [Irene] too. I can't write it – we will talk about it at a very early date.

According to Patricia, a reliable witness, Irene never knew that Philip and Megan were lovers. However, she did not imagine that Philip was a faithful husband. She watched his comings and goings with suspicious vigilance, but she could not decide who, among several possible candidates, might be his mistress. Philip, who went in constant fear of discovery, took elaborate precautions to keep the secret. It was one of the most successfully concealed love affairs ever conducted by a politician – in this case, two politicians – and even in the hothouse atmosphere of the House of Commons it never became anything like common knowledge. Among others who were in the House between 1945 and 1955 and were friendly with both Megan and Philip, Michael Foot and Elwyn Jones did not guess at the affair. At most, it was thought that Megan was one of various women whom Philip – who had the reputation, as Roy Jenkins says, of being a *coureur de femmes* – was seeking to attract.

The Labour government had exhausted its first impetus and was running into difficulties. Bitter weather in February 1947 led to a breakdown in the supply of coal, power cuts, shivering homes, factories halted for lack of supplies, and a suddenly zooming (though temporary) total of two million unemployed. British production was still not adequate to reduce dependence on American aid, let alone to bring an end to rationing and satisfy the pent-up demands of consumers. On top of this, Dalton had to resign as Chancellor because of a foolish indiscretion on budget day. His successor was Stafford Cripps, whose ascetic features seemed to symbolise an era of austerity (he had introduced this word into the national vocabulary), patient endurance, and meticulous regulation of social and economic life.

Yet a Liberal report on the economic situation, *Action Now*, found that production was often satisfactory and, if anything was wrong, it was that 'welfare conditions need to be improved in many firms and industries.' As in wartime, the document used the language of planning; it criticised 'the absence of any concerted government policy for using our national resources' and asserted that 'proper planning will get more houses'. It also urged cuts in defence expenditure, arguing that Britain's status depended on 'economic solvency more than excessive forces'.[31] These opinions would have been endorsed by Labour MPs on the Left of their party.

It was Philip's turn to be chairman of the Labour Party and to preside over the annual conference in May 1947. His opening address was vintage Noel-Baker. 'Must we and our children live for ever with the gathering fear of war?' he asked, and concluded: 'We offer Britain something to believe in: the goodness, the generosity, the equality of men; their love of mutual service; their power to control the forces that will shape their world.'

In the car that was taking him to lunch, he wrote to tell Megan that Irene had rated the speech as 'admirable'. Patricia reported: '*All* opinions overwhelmingly favourable.' Elated, he wrote to Megan again while he was presiding over the afternoon session. Evidently she had given him a pen as a present.

All the time I was speaking, I was thinking of you, & feeling as if you were here. Now, all the time, I'm either using your pen, & feeling as tho' I were holding your lovely little hand; or else your pen is in my pen [presumably a slip for 'pocket'] & I can feel my heart beating against it. I have never felt so very close to you, you have never been so much in my heart. . . .

The P.M., Herbert & Hugh all went out of their way to say at considerable length how good my speech was, how well delivered, how well the delegates listened – so its done me no harm, I hope, so far as the powers that be are concerned![32]

When Philip spoke of 'the gathering fear of war', it was not mere rhetoric. The antagonism between east and west was now open and acute. A new phrase, 'the cold war', signified that the western allies and the Soviet Union were actually at war and were merely abstaining from a hot, shooting war. Bevin, aligning Britain firmly with the United States, was the target of criticism from the Labour Left. He took it badly, and complained of being 'stabbed in the back'. Treating the conference to a stern lecture, he declared: 'Ministers have the right to expect loyalty. I grew up in the trade unions and I have never been used to this kind of thing.'

On 5 June, Philip wrote to Megan:

Last night was so *perfect*; you were so beautiful, so *angelic*, that I simply long to tell you how happy it made me then, & how happy it has left me all day today. When I don't see you, the long hours seem wasted; but even that sense of frustration is swamped by remembering what you were like when we were sitting in the car, & on the terrace, & when I said goodbye.

But not all their evenings ended in happiness and tranquillity. On 10 July he was writing:

If you tell me that I am being an unmitigated cad, I am quite prepared to believe it. . . . I really know very little about my conduct or how it may seem to anyone but myself. But when I suddenly realized that you weren't joking, I just couldn't bear it. After the Herriot party,[33] & Thursday night, & my long and fruitless hunt for you on Monday afternoon, something suddenly snapped, & I just had to run & stay away. Forgive me, if I need forgiveness, as I expect I do; but it really hurt a lot.

By 24 July, all was well again:

My most beloved Megan, I have been so happy – so wonderfully happy tonight. I have wanted you so much all day, & had you so satisfyingly in the end; you have been so sweet and so gentle; and so *enchantingly* pretty! There never was anyone like you, & there never will be.

On 4 August:

My most beloved, my most enchanting Megan, never has your spell been on me as it is today. All the morning I was longing to tell you why I love you; all the afternoon I was loving you – as never before; all tonight I've been thinking of present, past & future all at once . . . how wonderful it is to have you now, how wonderful these last few weeks have been. . . . We've had such marvellous times this summer; the night on the terrace, when I took you home at 3 a.m., or nearly; the visit to your flat, when Ellen was 'rummaging', & 'didn't hear us'; the Dorchester dancing party, & our journey afterwards; our walk, and our halt, on the Embankment. . . . The Terrace & the Embankment were so exciting; the Dorchester was so magically romantic; today has been so much the culmination, the complete, necessary, unblemished culmination of such wondrous happiness.

Megan went to Switzerland for a summer holiday, travelling by air for the first time. Philip telephoned Ellen to get the name of the hotel, and they had 'a long talk'. He wrote to Megan:

When I told her that you had told me what she said about coming to me, if she was in trouble about you, she said: 'Well, it would be best, sir, wdnt it? There's no one else would be as good as you.' A sentiment with which I warmly & emphatically concurred![34]

On an earlier occasion, Ellen had offered to ensure that Philip's letters were sent on to Megan when she was at Brynawelon, and he had commented cheerfully: 'So *someone* approves of me.' But Ellen, as she later told her daughter Zosia, did not like Philip, nor did she approve of the relationship. Presumably she felt it wise to flatter him, since he held a privileged place in Megan's life. The visitor to the flat whom she really liked was Dingle Foot.

Philip now had to endure another unpleasant experience in the political sphere. He was asked to go to the UN again – not, however, as leader of the British delegation, but as assistant to Hector McNeil, who was thirty years younger than Philip and had, only a year earlier, been junior to him in the Foreign Office pecking order. Kenneth Younger was shocked: 'It was altogether too much to ask Philip to serve under Hector NcNeil. . . . It would have caused comment and embarrassment in a milieu where Philip is so very well known.'[35] Writing to Megan, Philip relieved his feelings:

It wasn't intended to be insulting, but it *was*; I was absolutely *livid*. . . . I found out that Clem had said it was utterly wrong, but feebly let himself be overborne. . . . I wd have accepted a kind of compromise, but, after last year, to go as No. 3 to H., who is 30 years junior in experience, and who will never learn a half of what I know on *all* the big questions, wasn't easy.[36]

Philip did not go to the UN, but by this time he was finding his job at the Air Ministry more and more intolerable. He told Megan:

I've been most seriously reflecting on the advantages of leaving politics altogether! . . . If I stay in my present job I can do *nothing* to help the country or the world thro' the present crisis; if I leave it, I may make it impossible to do any good later on. . . . I *know* that if I were in the Cabinet I cd have done a *lot* of good in many ways; outside it, I do *none*. And I'm so utterly *sick* of it; its so boring, and stupid. Defence? There's no such thing for the U.K. now except the U.N., & I dislike the signs there a good deal.[37]

Two days later, he told her:

Today I've had a better day – a successful fight with Clem agst Laski & Shinwell in the Natl Executive. . . . At present I'm feeling that they can do what they like about the something Government; if they don't want me in the Cabinet, they can do without me – but I shall feel free to resign at any moment, without consulting *their* feelings in any way.[38]

Francis had just got married and was off to Greece with his wife, Ann. Irene was also going to Greece to direct the restoration of the Achmetaga estate and the rebuilding of the house, which had been accidentally burned down by soldiers of the Italian occupation force during the war. Left alone in London, Philip found it easier to spend time with Megan, but this did not check the flow of letters. A government reshuffle was clearly imminent. It was expected that Arthur Creech Jones, the Colonial Secretary, would be moved, and Philip was keen to get the job; but what he really wanted was to get back into the Foreign Office, with a view to succeeding Bevin as Foreign Secretary at a later stage. He wrote to Megan on 1 October, 'long after midnight':

I went to see C. [Clement Attlee] y'day, & for once wasn't feeble at all. I told

him I *must* have A.'s job (which I believe *is* going); that no one else had so
good a claim; that I must have the F.O. next, that to get it I must now get
inside [presumably inside the Cabinet]. . . . He took it awfully well, approved
of my saying it all, said he'd made no decisions, & almost in words assented
about the F.O.! He says he's made no decisions, but I think I shook him very
powerfully.

Attlee was not in fact intending to move Creech Jones, but he
needed a successor to Lord Addison at the Commonwealth Relations
Office. Addison, who had held office in Lloyd George's coalition
government many years ago, was an old man and due for retirement.
On 2 October Philip reported to Megan:

You know that, on your advice, I went to A. to find out what was happening &
having verified that Christopher [Addison]'s job *was* probably in the market,
I went to C. & put my case very strongly. . . . He was very friendly. . . . I saw
A. again on other business just now; A. said he'd been doing business with C.,
who had himself raised the subject, & asked if he, A., thought I sh'd do it well.
A. replied very strongly that I should. . . . So adding 1 & 10 together, it looks
as tho' the answer may be all right. In any case, you gave me wonderfully
good advice, & A. was very helpful.

The answer was all right; Philip emerged from the reshuffle as
Secretary for Commonwealth Relations. The episode seems to prove
the truth of the adage that the best way to get a job is to ask for it. At
last he was a member of the Cabinet.

Inevitably for Philip, within a month he was immersed in multiple
anxieties. He was responsible for relations with India and Pakistan,
the two new nations which had gained their independence in August.
A million people had been slaughtered in the chaotic partition of the
Punjab, and now armed irregulars from Pakistan were invading
Kashmir to prevent its accession to India. While Philip was grappling
with this Commonwealth crisis, Megan was accusing him of flirting
(or more than flirting) with another woman, referred to in one letter as
Peggy, but impossible to identify positively. Beset by these problems,
he wrote on 29 October:

My darling, I've had a desperate two days – a major crisis over Kashmir; India
& Pakistan as near as nothing at war last night; our telegrams always twelve
hours behind the news. . . . So this note is not what I intended or desire. Its
only to tell you that I love you more than ever, & that nothing & nobody can
ever make the slightest difference to that. I've told you already that there's
*never* been a hint of anything but friendship with P. . . . My darling, you must

not believe what isn't true; you must know that my devotion to you is undying, eternal, infinite.

4

While Megan did not hesitate to vote for the Labour government's nationalisation measures, she was never greatly interested in economic theory and had no fixed views on how extensive the scope of public ownership ought to be. Questions of social reform, affecting the lives of individual men and women, meant far more to her. When the government liquidated the last vestiges of the old Poor Law and established a comprehensive scheme of social security on the lines of the Beveridge Report, she saw this as the completion of the work to which her father had set his hand in 1909. The same could be said of the creation of the National Health Service. Aneurin Bevan, the Minister of Health, got his bill through Parliament by November 1946, but another year passed before he could overcome the hostility of the hierarchy of the British Medical Association and ensure that doctors would work in the NHS. For Megan, it was unthinkable that any real Liberal should wish to undermine the government that was responsible for these achievements, or to promote a Tory comeback.

Her special duty as an MP was to speak up for Wales, in particular for North Wales, and specifically for Anglesey. She had demanded in the 1930s, and she continued to demand after the war, that North Wales as well as South Wales should be a development area, a status enjoyed only by the mining district around Wrexham. She welcomed the industrial initiatives that were bringing new jobs to Anglesey: a clock factory at Holyhead, a Milk Marketing Board dairy at Llangefni, a Saunders-Rowe engineering works at Beaumaris. Doubtless she realised that these schemes brought in workers and technicians from outside who were likely to vote Labour rather than Liberal, but that consideration had to be ignored. However, she looked forward with some anxiety to the next election and took Cledwyn Hughes seriously as an opponent. He recalls: 'We were on polite terms, but I knew she didn't like me standing against her. Once she said to me: "Do you really want to go into politics? It's a hard life."'[39] But, characteristically, she remembered to give him a wedding present.

During these years, there was no sign of a brighter future for the Liberal Party. In seven by-elections the Liberal candidate forfeited his deposit.[40] Liberals were drifting away from their old party in both directions, but more often towards Labour. Tom Horabin, the MP for

North Cornwall, joined Labour in 1947. Sir Geoffrey Mander – no longer an MP, but a man of great prestige among Liberals – did the same. Richard Acland's Common Wealth movement was absorbed by the Labour Party, and he returned to the House as a Labour MP after winning a by-election at Gravesend in November 1947. The idea of joining this trend inevitably crossed Megan's mind, but she would not reconcile herself to hauling down the flag of Radical Liberalism. In December 1947 Liberal headquarters issued a statement denying rumours that Megan was joining the Labour Party. But the rumours persisted, and a year later Cledwyn Hughes was saying to a *Western Mail* reporter: 'I'm sure she is tired of these constant prophecies.'

On 17 November 1947 Lady Violet Bonham-Carter penned a gloomy letter:

Megan dear – I feel I must write you a personal line about the Party and my present feelings about its present and prospects – because I *know* that you and I, though we may occasionally differ on isolated issues (like the H. of Lords!) are fundamentally at one. . . .

Even the election didn't really dishearten me – I still believed we could stage a come-back – a great revival. Well, now quite frankly I no longer believe that can happen (certainly not by 1950). . . . I think Archie Sinclair ought to get back, and it is just possible my son-in-law Jo Grimond *might* win Orkney and Shetland, but these are the only 2 'near-wins' I can find after scouring the figures. . . . You have I believe a Tory against you? and your majority was 2000? One must face the *possibility* of Parliamentary extinction. . . .

What can a Party of 10 do? containing at most 4 'effectives' (and even these not always agreed on major issues). These are my reasons for pessimism. If you can dissipate it by refuting them I shall be *really* grateful. . . .

Lest there should be any misunderstanding, I should be strongly opposed to any sort of 'alliance' on policy – or coalition – or agreement to put or keep anyone in. My one desire is that there should be *a* Liberal Party (an independent one of course) in being in this country. *If* we are swept out of Parliament at the next election there will be none.[41]

The last paragraph was necessary because Churchill was trying to recruit the Liberals into an anti-Socialist alliance. He had made an offer which envisaged the 'complete independence' of the Conservative and Liberal parties but 'broadly similar policies'. If agreement could be reached, the Tories would stand down in a number of constituencies.[42] Evidently Violet thought that Megan might suspect her of being tempted by this overture. But in 1947 it was distinctly premature, and no Liberals favoured acceptance.

Although Violet never succeeded in becoming an MP, Asquith's daughter and Lloyd George's daughter were the two *grandes dames* of the Liberal Party. The contrast in personality and appearance provided irresistible material for cartoonists. Violet was a tall, commanding, aristocratic figure, didactic in her manner – Roy Jenkins calls her 'one of nature's governesses' – and always conscious of her dignity. Unlike Megan, she would never have skipped a committee meeting, been late for an appointment or made a speech off the cuff; nor would she ever have been involved in a secretive love affair. A writer in the *Western Mail* in 1951, after describing Megan as 'still pretty in an inimitable way, petite, vivacious' and 'a feminine Peter Pan', went on to say tactfully that Violet was 'in no need of prettiness'.[43]

The contrast, and of course the inheritance of the feud between their fathers, led many observers to conclude that the two ladies were bitter enemies. They were, indeed, incompatible to a degree that prevented them from ever being good friends, but Lady Violet's son, Lord Bonham-Carter, denies that the relationship between them was, as has been alleged, acutely hostile:

It was not close but it was certainly not 'acutely hostile'. They did not agree on a number of political issues, both past and present, but my mother always enjoyed her company despite this fact. She thought that Megan was uneasy if she thought there was anyone politically to the left of her. She also thought she was lazy, though full of charm.[44]

Megan was still in regular demand as a broadcaster, although she sometimes earned the disapproval of BBC mandarins. In 1952 she appeared on television in a Welsh Region series called *Speaking Personally* which was supposed to be confined to light small-talk. When Cecil McGivern, the television programme director, saw her script, he complained: 'She has turned her "Speaking Personally" into a platform for Welsh Nationalism.' What particularly annoyed him was that she was advocating outside broadcast units taking instructions from Cardiff, instead of always from London as he desired. He grumbled that it was 'most unfortunate', but did not venture to demand that she should change her script.

This was, in fact, one incident in a long-running campaign waged by Megan for freedom and spontaneity on the air. Since pre-war days, she had been a member of the Talks Advisory Committee, which had the function of giving advice on possible topics and possible broadcasters. She argued persistently for unscripted discussions of important political issues. Today, when we take this for granted, it is hard to realise that the idea was once heretical, but in 1938 the Director of Talks, Sir Robert Maconachie, was telling TAC members:

We now have to consider what decision is to be taken with reference to Miss Lloyd George's insistent demand in TAC meetings for live political issues to be discussed at the microphone by MPs. . . . It would give MPs an enormous forum in which they could . . . influence public opinion.[45]

In a subsequent minute, Maconachie produced a classic statement of the BBC philosophy:

One argument . . . is that it would, in any case, be 'entertaining'. This is in my view a very dangerous fallacy. A broadcast talk on any important question must first be 'educative', or at any rate 'informative'.[46]

Evidently he won this round of the battle, for he wrote to Megan on 14 October 1938 (interestingly, in the aftermath of Munich) telling her that it was impossible for her campaign to make progress 'for reasons which I think you will appreciate'. She returned to the charge after the war. The BBC's charter expired in 1946, and the government decided that it should be renewed for only five years, instead of the ten or fifteen which the Corporation desired, pending full consideration of the best structure for radio and for the yet more influential medium of the future – television. The first step was a Commons debate on broadcasting on 16 July 1946. Megan spoke to suggest a committee of inquiry into the BBC's customs and practices and to raise two important issues: governmental authority over broadcasting, which in her opinion had grown in wartime to an extent that should never be allowed in normal conditions, and freedom of controversy.

The Lord President [Herbert Morrison] said today that the BBC is to be independent of the government, but how independent is it to be? . . . Are the privileges extended to Ministers during the war to continue? . . . The mere fact that there is a veto – what the White Paper calls the ultimate sanction – is enough; it is the big stick, and although it has never been formally used, it is there, and it has all the effects of a deterrent. It has a definite unnerving effect on the BBC. . . .

What we want to ensure in this country is that the BBC should become an effective instrument of democracy. But I do not believe it will ever become an effective instrument of democracy while controversy on the air is confined to academic debates and arguments about abstract theories. We should have hard-hitting discussions on issues when they are red-hot. . . . The whole attitude is inhibited, panicky and jittery. From personal experience covering a number of years, I would say that it is not the fault of the staff, or even the executives of the BBC . . . It is the fault, quite definitely, of the system.

In another debate on 19 February 1947 she put her case still more forcefully:

Surely we, who have been born and bred in controversy, and who have a heritage of freedom of speech, can take it if foreigners can. . . . I believe that the hierarchy of the political parties are nervous. They are afraid of this very powerful weapon. . . .

[The BBC should] provide a forum, say half an hour or three-quarters of an hour every week, and leave the time open for improvised discussions on topical subjects as they arise. There should be no difficulty in filling the time – none at all.

The government agreed to set up a committee 'to consider the constitution, control, finance and other general aspects of the sound and television broadcasting services'. The chairman was Beveridge (now a peer), and the members, in addition to three educationalists, were drawn from the political parties: two Tories, of whom one was Selwyn Lloyd, two Labour MPs, and Megan. The committee held sixty-two meetings between June 1949 and July 1950, when Beveridge retired to his rural home to write the report, which was presented in December. By treating the committee with the utmost respect and courtesy, and by putting in a vast amount of written and verbal evidence, the BBC succeeded in convincing its interrogators – including Beveridge, who was at first far from sympathetic – that it was doing an admirable job and should be given the 'Carry on' signal. But, this was not all that emerged from the deliberations.[47]

On the question that most concerned Megan, the report declared itself in favour of 'free use of the microphone for discussion of questions of the day, however controversial the speakers'. The BBC was urged to consider initiating a 'Hyde Park of the air' – 'an opportunity for all minorities . . . to put their messages over, not regularly or at length, but at some time'. However, the report stopped short of saying explicitly that the discussion should be live, unscripted and topical. The word 'discussion' could be interpreted to mean an airing of a subject, even in a formal talk; a subject, after all, can be discussed in a book. Some trenches had still to be attacked.

Megan succeeded in getting Beveridge to recognise that Wales had a 'national identity' and should not be regarded as 'a mere region of the BBC'. The report pointed to 'a compelling need for more staff and more studios' to ensure 'more Welsh broadcasting in both languages'. It proposed national commissions for Wales, Scotland and Northern Ireland, which in due course came into existence. This disappointed people in Wales and Scotland who had been pressing for separate broadcasting corporations.

But the hotly contested issue of the time was whether Britain should have commercial television outside the control of the BBC. This was often seen as a question of whether advertising on the screen (or the radio) was permissible; people who had been to the United States gave horrific accounts of the vulgarity and cynicism of American TV advertising. Probably surprising some of her friends, Megan was one of three committee members – the others were Beveridge and Mary Stocks – who considered that a limited amount of advertising, analogous to press advertising, would do no harm. They were thinking, however, of advertising on the BBC, not of rival channels.[48] What really worried the BBC and its supporters was the possibility that its monopoly of the airwaves might be taken away. Selwyn Lloyd put in a minority report declaring: 'The evil lies in the system, the control by a monopoly of this great medium of expression.'

Beveridge was in a difficult situation. He was a Liberal, free competition was a Liberal dogma, and the Liberal Party's Research Group gave evidence favouring abolition of the monopoly. On the other hand, most of the pressure for commercial television came from Tories, and from interests hungering for 'a licence to print money';[49] and Violet Bonham-Carter, who had until recently been a BBC Governor, threatened to leave the Liberal Party if it came out in favour of commercial television. As it turned out, however, Lloyd was isolated on the committee and was not supported even by his fellow Tory, the Earl of Elgin. The report therefore stated clearly that the committee had no hesitation in recommending a new charter for the BBC as the sole broadcasting organisation. This was endorsed when the government responded to the report with a White Paper in July 1951.

By that time the Labour government had only a few months to live. As soon as the Tories regained power, Ministers and MPs were the targets of an intensive campaign for commercial television. It was successful; Independent Television came into existence in 1954.

In the field of free discussion, especially live discussion, this change of government was bad news. Churchill tried to enforce a rule that no issue likely to come before the House of Commons in the next fourteen days could be discussed on the air. As the timetable of the House was to some extent flexible, this rule was an absurdity, and it was abandoned within a few years, but it was stiflingly restrictive while it lasted. Churchill was also intensely suspicious of unscripted programmes such as *Any Questions?* He seized on an *Any Questions?*

programme broadcast on 14 March 1952, in which Megan took part with Ritchie Calder, Malcolm Muggeridge and the anchor-man of the team, A. G. Street. Having obtained a transcript, toilers at Conservative Central Office made a word-count which proved that Megan had uttered twice as many words as any of the others. Lord Woolton, who had to deal with the matter, calmed Churchill down with the comment: 'This type of programme is particularly difficult to control.' But 'control', one must note, was the operative word.[50]

# CHAPTER TEN

# The Drift to the Right

1

The next few years were dominated by a mounting and at times dangerous intensification of the cold war. For a Radical like Megan, these were difficult years. She had no sympathy with the brutal and cynical version of Communism that we call Stalinism; yet she saw unhappily that anyone with a left-of-centre political philosophy was being labelled as 'soft on Communism', and those who were most loudly insistent that the democracies must 'learn the lessons of appeasement' were often the same people who had applauded the appeasement of Hitler.

In the course of 1947, a Communist monopoly of power was imposed on Poland, Hungary, Yugoslavia, Romania, Bulgaria and the Soviet-occupied zone of Germany. Czechoslovakia still hovered between the rival spheres of influence, and President Beneš – the survivor of the Munich tragedy – headed a liberal regime although the Communists polled well in free elections and held some posts in a coalition government. But in February 1948 the anti-Communist parties rashly provoked a showdown and the Communists won absolute power. Jan Masaryk, the Foreign Minister and the son of the revered founder of the Republic, plunged from a window in Prague Castle to his death; there is still no certainty whether it was suicide or murder. The Prague coup, as it was called in the west, was taken as proof that Stalin's aggressive ambitions were unlimited. American bomber squadrons were brought back – without any formal agreement – to the bases in Oxfordshire and Suffolk which they had used in the war. Ernest Bevin was in the forefront of moves to build a military alliance, the North Atlantic Treaty Organisation (NATO), which came into existence in 1949.

The cold war almost became hot in the summer of 1948. Berlin, a city surrounded by the Soviet zone but with western occupation sectors, was a predictable focus of tension. In the process of reviving the economy of western Germany, a stable currency, the Deutsche Mark, was introduced and was also validated for West Berlin, giving this part of the city a distinct economic status. The Russians responded to this challenge by closing the road, rail and canal links between Berlin and western Germany. Plans were made to break the blockade by sending a convoy down the *Autobahn* escorted by tanks. This might have shown that the Russians were bluffing – or it might not. Luckily, an alternative was adopted. West Berlin's essential needs were met by air transport until, after several months, the blockade was called off. Herbert Morrison's testimony on this episode tells us:

My recollection is that the idea of the airlift originated with Philip Noel-Baker, who was confident that the job could be done. It was a compromise between letting Berlin starve until Russia took over, or risking world war by forcing convoys through on road and rail.[1]

Greatly though Philip had disliked being Secretary for Air, the knowledge he had gained in that position came in useful at a vital moment.

In July 1948 the world was startled by a sudden rupture between the Communist regime in Yugoslavia and the Soviet Union. The Yugoslav leader, Tito, had spent years as a Comintern functionary and lived in Moscow, but the Partisans whom he commanded had made heavy sacrifices for the liberation of their country and he was now determined to be master in his own house. The Partisan record against the Nazis was impressive enough to deter Stalin from attempting to subdue the rebel by force. A side-effect of this clash was to put an end to the civil war in Greece, where Communists had been challenging the British-backed monarchy from strongholds in the northern mountains. With supplies of Soviet weaponry through Yugoslavia blocked, their hopes of ultimate victory vanished. Irene Noel-Baker, who had been devoting herself at Achmetaga to the care of refugees from the war zone, was able to witness the return of normal conditions.

All these confrontations, along with a host of dramas revolving around defections or spy rings, etched sharp lines of demarcation not only across Europe but also within the political arena of every country, including Britain. An anti-Communist consensus covered the bulk of the Labour Party and the trade unions as well as the Tories. The cold war atmosphere inevitably had its effects in the Liberal Party too. Gone, long gone were the days when the 1945 Liberal Assembly could instruct Wilfrid Roberts, off on a trip to Moscow, to convey congratulations and good wishes to Stalin.

At the same time, a desire for closer unity between the nations of western Europe had arisen. This, it was argued, would speed economic recovery, put an end to ancient enmities such as that between France and Germany and create a solid obstacle to the Communist threat. With the impetus given by a Frenchman, Jean Monnet, the European Movement was founded and held a congress in 1948 at The Hague, attended by Lord Layton and other prominent Liberals. Churchill, greatly respected on the Continent, gave his blessing to this movement and made sonorous speeches in favour of unity in European cities (though Monnet and others were disappointed by his failure to translate the speeches into action when he returned to Downing Street in 1951). Looking back today, we can trace the winding course of British attitudes to what is now the European Community, with Michael Foot and Tony Benn upholding British sovereignty and resisting the European embrace in the 1970s and Margaret Thatcher taking up that stance in the 1980s. Only the Liberals can claim that they have consistently urged closer ties with 'Europe'. But in the late 1940s and 1950s 'Europe' was on balance a right-wing rather than a left-wing cause; the Liberals were employing the same rhetoric as Churchill and reproaching Attlee for his negative attitude.

2

'If the State owns everything you will own nothing' – this was the message of a poster much used by the Tories in this period. The nationalisation of private industries, the continuance of wartime controls and reports of what Stalin meant by 'Socialism' were all combined to present the menace of an omnipotent and tyrannical state, making the life of the individual unbearable. George Orwell, repelled by what he saw as the greyness and misery of 1948, changed two digits of the date to get the title for his *1984*; the book, published in 1949, was an immediate bestseller.

No British Socialists really proposed that the state should own every little factory making shoes or socks. Speaking at the Labour Party conference in 1949, Bevan – the standard-bearer of the Left and the chief bogyman of Tory propaganda – made this clear enough:

The kind of society which we envisage, and which we shall have to live in, will be a mixed society, a mixed economy, in which all the essential instruments of planning are in the hands of the State, in which the characteristic forms of employment will be by the community in one form or another, but where we shall have for a very long time the light cavalry of private competitive industry.

Labour policy did, however, require state ownership of what were called, in a phrase of which Bevan was fond, the 'commanding heights' of the economy. The question then arose: exactly what were these commanding heights, and what would be covered by a second wave of nationalisation? The great bone of contention was the steel industry. Steel was certainly vital to the economy, but it was not a raw material like coal or a 'natural monopoly' like gas. Besides, the mines and the railways had been loss-making concerns which private owners were happy to hand over in return for generous compensation, whereas steel was profitable. Here, clearly, was a major battleground.

Because of arguments between Morrison, who did not want a second wave of nationalisation, and Bevan, who pressed for it, the Steel Bill was not introduced until November 1948. It was bound to be rejected by the House of Lords, who still had a delaying power although the government had reduced it from two years to one. Thus public ownership of steel could not be a reality until after the next election, due in 1950; so the Tories could go into that election with a pledge to reverse it if they won.

This postponement had an effect on the Liberal attitude. In 1947, as we have seen, the Liberals were still quite sympathetic to the Labour government, but by 1948 there were manifest signs of that 'drift to the Right' which Megan, in the coming years, was often to perceive and denounce. The 1948 Liberal Assembly called for a 'drastic reduction in government expenditure' and for a committee to be set up with 'wide powers to recommend drastic cuts' – a suggestion which, for Megan, could only revive memories of 1931. Another resolution proposed that council tenants should be given the right to buy their homes. This was the first suggestion of a step which was not taken, even by Tory governments, until after 1979. It ran directly counter to Bevan's plans (his duties as Minister of Health covered the housing programme), which gave priority to an increased provision of housing for rent.

All the Liberals, including Megan, voted against the Steel Bill. Later, after she had joined the Labour Party, she said that she had fought a 'rearguard action' within the Liberal Party against this decision.[2] It does not seem, however, that there was a hard-fought battle. Probably she did not feel strongly enough to treat it as a make-or-break issue, and she certainly did not wish to be responsible for an open split in the division lobbies.

In January 1949 Megan was appointed as deputy leader of the Liberal Party. There had been no such position since Asquith's time, and one might think that if the Liberals could manage without a deputy leader when they had fifty-eight MPs (the strength in the 1929 Parliament) they could do so when they had only eleven. The official announcement stated that she would relieve Davies of some of his 'heavy duties'. He was in fact unwell at the time, and perhaps the need for a deputy was an implicit comment on his lack-lustre style of leadership. But the *Western Mail*'s political correspondent had another comment: 'Her acceptance will dispose of rumours that she is joining Labour.' Having thus proved that she was sticking with the old party, she gave an interview in which she stressed that the Liberals must pursue a Radical policy and added: 'Of course that means shedding our right wing.' This incautious remark cannot have endeared her to those who apparently were in line for being shed.

The problem for the Liberals was to find a policy, and if possible a political philosophy, which did not place them as allies of either Labour or the Tories. In the unkind words of a Labour supporter, Michael Young, they 'teetered between the other two parties like a drunken referee who despite his size is constantly trying to separate the heavyweights and fell each of them with a blow which is neither a left nor a right.'[3] The difficulties of the balancing act are illustrated by a resolution moved by Dingle Foot, and carried, at the party Assembly in March 1949:

This Assembly recognises that the Socialist and the Conservative parties . . . are pursuing policies which can only end in either Marxist or Capitalist collectivism. It holds that the elimination of the Liberal Party would mean . . . the eventual triumph of Socialism, because those who for any reason tire of Conservative Governments would have only the one alternative of Socialism to support. . . . Liberalism provides the Radical progressive alternative both to Conservatism and Socialism. . . . These Liberal principles and the policies by which they are applied can provide the only answer to totalitarian politics as well as the dynamic by which the Free World will successfully withstand the assault of Communist aggression.

In his keynote speech to this Assembly, Davies propounded the theory that Toryism was an anachronism and 'the real fight today is between Liberals and Socialists'. Megan reserved her enthusiasm for the two issues with which she was most at home – women's rights and self-government for Wales. Apart from her strong and sincere feelings on these matters, the Liberal position on both points was more Radical than the Labour Party's. With Bevin a powerful figure in the Cabinet, and Cripps at the Treasury seeking to check inflation by imposing a wage freeze, the government was in no mood to concede the case for equal pay. The Equal Pay Campaign, still vigorous, organised a meeting at the Central Hall at which Thelma Cazalet-Keir took the chair and Megan spoke. It also commissioned a short film, directed by Jill Craigie and with a commentary spoken by Wendy Hiller, in which Megan appeared; the film must have reached a considerable public, as it had 258 bookings.[4] The showpiece of the 1949 Liberal Assembly was a report, produced by a group of women, called 'The Great Partnership', which advocated equal pay, equal training opportunities, better pay and more freedom for nurses, a much greater provision of day nurseries for working mothers, and a reform of the divorce law to give a woman an equal share of the marital home after a break-up. 'It's easier to get a wife out than to get a tenant out,' Doreen Gorsky told the Assembly.

Megan spoke at the Assembly in favour of Home Rule for Wales and Scotland – and for England. 'I don't doubt that the English have real grievances,' she said sweetly. 'They have been governed too long by the Welsh and the Scots.'

Some of the resolutions passed by the assembled Liberals, however, might have been equally acceptable at a Tory conference. They demanded cuts in taxation, a flat rate for all income tax, abolition of the tax on undistributed profits, the progressive reduction of food subsidies, action against restrictive practices in industry and a relaxation of rent control. Later in the year, Megan was alerted to the way the wind was blowing by a letter from Dingle Foot:

Just a week ago I had lunch with Clem [Davies]. . . . Clem produced a document written by Graham Hutton . . . economics for the Very Little Ones. The only two concrete proposals were (a) an all-out attack on restrictive practices of every kind . . . (b) a reduction in the food subsidies. . . .

Clem intends to sound a clarion call next month to blood, toil, tears and sweat. But the quantity of the blood, the nature of the toil, the number of the tears and the precise purpose of the sweat are still undecided. . . . It looks to me as if the Tories, or a section of them, are girding themselves up for an attack on the social services . . . and a rise in unemployment figures. To my mind it would be fatal for us to lend ourselves, even by inference, to this campaign. . . . Even if we have to preach a form of austerity – which is unavoidable – we should do it as *defenders* of the social services and full employment and not as an alternative gang of destroyers.[5]

By now, Britain was in the final year before the next election. In Anglesey, Megan was fortifying her position by working for development and jobs. One project that came to fruition in 1949 was the conversion of the RAF airfield at Valley into a civilian airport, as the base for a service between North and South Wales. Megan travelled on the inaugural flight in the small plane (although she was so nervous that she could eat no breakfast).[6] Regrettably, the service did not prove viable and Valley reverted to the RAF. She also intervened to save three hundred jobs at the Saunders-Rowe plant by persuading London Transport to place an order for fifty buses. For this she was publicly thanked by the trade-union branch, a useful boost for the coming election campaign.

One other event made 1949 a year to remember: Megan celebrated twenty years as an MP. The other women members gave her a party, and in the evening they went to the theatre to see a dramatised version of H. G. Wells's *Ann Veronica*. Perhaps it is significant that this party at the House of Commons was organised by Megan's fellow women, not by her fellow Liberals.

3

In the run-up to the 1950 election, the Tories resorted to a sly manoeuvre to seduce Liberal voters. In various places, the Conservative Association was transformed into a 'Conservative and Liberal Association', set up at a meeting which was packed with Tories and from which Liberals were excluded. As a result, fifty-three candidates were nominated as Conservative and Liberal, Liberal and Conservative, National Liberal, Conservative and National Liberal, or National Liberal and Conservative. Some were National Liberals from the old Simonite stable, but others had never been anything but Tories.[7] One 'Liberal and Conservative' was Gwilym Lloyd George, standing for re-election in Pembroke. Back in 1938, his father had predicted: 'Gwilym will go to the Right and Megan to the Left, eventually.'[8] The old man knew his children.

Another device was to arrange a deal whereby a Liberal and a Tory would carry the anti-Socialist banner in adjacent constituencies. The Liberal candidate for Huddersfield West, Donald Wade, promised that he would not give a vote of confidence to a Labour government, and the Tories did not contest the seat; in return, the Liberals stood down in Huddersfield East. (As it turned out, Wade won the West division and Labour won the East, so the Tories did badly out of the deal.) There were attempts to make similar arrangements in other places, but they did not come to fruition.

The Liberals put forward 475 candidates, the largest number since the days when they could realistically be seen as fighting for power. The justification for this gamble was to be able to say that they could form a government, but this possibility was purely theoretical. The organisation in many of the contested constituencies was amateur in the worst sense and the financial strain was painful, although Lloyd's of London agreed to provide insurance against lost deposits. Further-more, as a historian of Liberalism puts it, 'some of the last-minute candidates were obviously unsuitable people with little political knowledge, who had only accepted candidature after great pressure had been exerted upon them.'[9]

The Liberal manifesto, entitled *No Easy Way*, contained promises to cut the food subsidies, abolish the tax on profits, repeal the nationalisation of steel, and oppose any further nationalisation. On the other hand, it stated: 'The Liberal Party believes passionately in full employment and in maintaining welfare services.' Perhaps tacitly, perhaps through an explicit bargain, the right-wingers had got their way in the economic sphere and the Radicals in the social sphere.

When Attlee fixed the polling date for 23 February 1950, it was clear that there would be a keen fight and a close result. Labour was bound to suffer from a drastic redistribution which had swept away small inner-city constituencies such as Limehouse (Attlee's seat), though the university seats and the business vote had been abolished. Churchill produced a campaign surprise which was more effective than his Gestapo scare of 1945. Nine days before the poll, he called for 'a parley at the summit' between the western nations and Russia, thus introducing 'summit talks' into the political vocabulary. He called for 'a supreme effort to bridge the gulf between the two worlds, so that each can live their life, if not in friendship, at least without the hatreds and manoeuvres of the cold war.'[10] Since he had virtually inaugurated the cold war with his speech at Fulton, Missouri, in 1946, this volte-face caught the Labour leaders on the hop.

As deputy leader, Megan made one of the three broadcasts allocated to the Liberals; the other speakers were Davies and Lord Samuel, now in his eightieth year. The content of Megan's script must have been discussed with Davies and the strategists of the campaign, for it contained demands for reduced taxation and for cost-cutting in the nationalised industries. However, she went on to a passage on the nature of freedom which was surely all her own:

We know that the men and women who tramped the streets of our great cities and the valleys of my country in dull, hopeless despair searching for work were not free men and women. Freedom must be the solid rock on which we must build, but full employment must be the first pillar of our new society; social justice for all must be the other.[11]

Instead of the customary 'Goodnight', she wound up in Welsh with: '*Nos da. Hunan llywodraeth i Gymru.*' English listeners had no idea that this meant 'Goodnight – self-government for Wales'. But they understood in Anglesey.

Megan's Labour opponent was again Cledwyn Hughes, and this time the Tories contested Anglesey. Their candidate, J.O. Jones, was one of those rare birds, a working-class Tory. The atmosphere of 1950 can be gauged by the fact that a speaker at Megan's inaugural meeting at Holyhead made a point of denying that she was a closet Socialist, and assured the audience – rather equivocally, perhaps – that she was 'as much a Liberal as she has ever been'. A thundering editorial in the *Holyhead Mail* denounced the government for subjecting the people to the State, that 'soulless monster', and called on British voters to follow the lead of other European countries, Australia and New Zealand by casting off the thrall of Socialism. Three-quarters of the column might have been written in support of the Tory candidate, but it wound up by endorsing Megan because of her good constituency record. She was fighting a rather low-key campaign, putting the emphasis on local needs such as a new hospital and a better water supply for the farms. She was given a boost by an article in a mass-circulation Sunday paper, the *People*, which described her as 'far and away the ablest woman in politics'.

She won with a majority of 1929, an improvement on 1945. At a figure of 13,688, her vote was up by a thousand, while the Labour vote was virtually static. The big surprise at the count, as the *Mail* commented, was the poor Tory vote. Polling only 3919, Jones barely saved his deposit. Clearly there had been a swing against Labour, but the beneficiary had been Megan, not the Tory.

This general election produced a House of Commons with 315 Labour members, 298 Tories or crypto-Tories and nine Liberals. The narrowness of the Labour majority would obviously create difficulties for the government, and would make the question of whether the Liberals voted with the Tories a vital matter. Attlee carried on with an unchanged team: Bevin at the Foreign Office, Cripps at the Treasury, Morrison in charge of the home front, Bevan still at the Ministry of Health. But Philip Noel-Baker was replaced at the Commonwealth

Relations Office by Patrick Gordon-Walker, who had been his Under-Secretary; once again, it was Philip's fate to be elbowed aside by a junior man. His new job was Minister of Fuel and Power. His predecessor in this post, Hugh Gaitskell, became Minister of State for Economic Affairs. An energetic and opinionated man of forty-four, Gaitskell could expect to exert considerable influence on economic policy, for Cripps was exhausted by his labours and in declining health. The move was bad news for Philip not only because he had been happy at Commonwealth Relations, a partial substitute for the Foreign Office, but also – and much more – because no Cabinet seat went with Fuel and Power. Attlee had reverted to his dismissive view of Philip, remarking: 'He has not advanced his reputation. He was talkative but not illuminating in Cabinet.' Kenneth Younger noted in his diary: 'Poor Philip N.B. has got pushed out of the Cabinet. It was only after much coming and going that he was offered Fuel and Power where he has now gone. He is of course much upset.'[12]

The Liberals had suffered another disaster. No fewer than 315 of the candidates lost their deposits; Lloyd's was unlikely to offer insurance cover again. The Liberal share of the poll was just over 9 per cent, an unimpressive figure for a party contesting every possible constituency. The little band of MPs was reduced to only nine. Frank Byers lost North Dorset to a Tory by 97 votes. Gwilym Lloyd George – scarcely a Liberal by this time – lost Pembroke by 129 votes to the Labour candidate, Desmond Donnelly; this new MP soon became one of Megan's best friends. Wilfrid Roberts lost his seat in Cumberland to a Tory. The only Liberal gains (setting aside the deal in Huddersfield) were both in Scotland: Roxburgh and Selkirk, and Orkney and Shetland. The victor in these remote islands was Jo Grimond, Lady Violet's son-in-law. As he was only thirty-six years old, he seemed to embody the last flickering hope of a Liberal future, and was at once made Chief Whip.

Following the hallowed British tradition, the press zestfully kicked the Liberal Party when it was down. The *Daily Mail* judged that 'their effort chiefly served a wrecking purpose' and advised them to recognise that 'the game is up'. The *Daily Telegraph* predicted the 'final and total eclipse of the Liberal Party'. For *The Times*, the 'irresponsible spattering of the electoral map with hundreds of candidatures' was 'a national disservice'. What enraged these Tory papers, of course, was that the Conservatives might have won the election if only the Liberals had bowed out. But even the *Manchester Guardian*, the traditional oracle of Liberalism, pronounced that it was 'a matter for deep discussion whether a thinly scattered vote of this kind can become the basis for a political party on national lines'.[13]

4

The Tories now adopted a deliberate policy of harassing the government, exploiting parliamentary procedure to cause difficulties and forcing snap divisions. Ministers, obliged to spend the whole day and sometimes the whole night at the House, could scarcely attend to necessary work in their departments. The object, clearly, was to wear down the government so that Attlee would have to call another election. However, if the situation was painful for Labour, it also created a dilemma for the Liberals. They did not want another election, in which they might be in danger of 'final and total eclipse'. Yet most of them were averse to being seen as the saviours of the Labour government. Grimond found that Hopkin Morris, in particular, was 'absolutely rigid in principle'[14] – the principle being that Socialism was the enemy. Recalling 1950 in his memoirs, Grimond wrote: 'The fissure which caused the most trouble was between Hopkin and Megan. Megan was already in love with Labour.'[15] This was an over-simplified view of her outlook, but she certainly had no intention of falling in love with the Tories. Three Liberal MPs – Megan Lloyd George, Emrys Roberts and Edgar Granville – formed a group determined to save the Radical soul of the party.

Right-wingers and Radicals agreed on one point: since it had now been demonstrated that there was no prospect of a Liberal government, it was necessary to decide whether a Churchill or an Attlee government was better for the country. Lady Violet, for one, made her choice. She was no Tory, but she was a fervent admirer and close personal friend of Churchill and (so Grimond remembers) wanted to see him back in Downing Street as soon as possible.

The Radicals, however, were convinced that they represented a majority of the rank and file. A letter to *The Times* signed by Lancelot Spicer and others asserted: 'Radicals are a majority of those still remaining loyal to Liberalism, and are strangely unrepresented in the councils of the party. . . .We believe with passionate faith in the welfare state.'[16] Therefore, the proper course was 'co-operation with Labour on honourable terms to make an effective majority for reform'. Emrys Roberts followed this up by saying that a pact with the Tories would 'split the Liberal Party right through'. He argued that it would be wrong for the Liberals to be absorbed by Labour because there were differences of principle – for example, Liberals were against peacetime conscription – but co-operation was possible and right.[17]

It was increasingly difficult to be sure of what the Liberals stood for. Megan was quoted as saying, 'The party has accepted the permanent necessity of certain controls and a planned economy'; but a member of the party's Council, Sir Alfred Suenson-Taylor, asserted: 'Only the Liberal Party believes in a free market economy.'[18] Right-wing, or at least anti-Labour, Liberals were in the ascendant at the head office which put out propaganda in leaflet form. A leaflet headed 'Did the People Expect This?' was a scathing condemnation of the record of the nationalised industries. Another leaflet, 'Tell the People the Truth', said that welfare policies were right in principle but 'have been allowed to run riot'. This leaflet continued rather petulantly: 'It is idiotic to trumpet: "The standard of living of the people must not be touched." That is an aspiration, not a principle.'

Despite the cross-currents, the trend was fairly clear. With some restraint, Megan said: 'There is no doubt that there has been, consciously or unconsciously, a drift to the Right in the Liberal Party – a drift away from the old Radical tradition.'[19] If this could not be denied, it could perhaps be justified or excused. Lord Layton said in a broadcast:

If it appears that in 1950 the Liberals are leaning more to the Right than is their custom, it is because we feel that the danger of the moment is . . . the scales have been weighted too heavily against initiative and private enterprise.[20]

At the Assembly which met in September 1950 the rhetoric was still, on balance, radical. Philip Fothergill declared in his presidential address: 'We are not a hangover from Victorianism but a party with an urgent contemporary task – to lead the fight for liberty, social justice and radical progress.' Delegates were sharply critical of the Huddersfield deal, and passed a resolution that they were 'very strongly opposed to agreements or pacts to limit or in any way reduce the number of Liberal candidates'. Davies assured the Assembly that he was against any surrender of Liberal principles, and even added: 'There is much that Labour and Liberals can do together for better administration and for carrying through radical reforms.' Roberts, however, believed that he wanted to see the Tories back in power. He remembers that Megan remarked with a shrug that there was no telling what Davies would say or do next.[21]

When the new session of the House began in November, there was an undisguised clash at a meeting of Liberal MPs over the line to be taken in the debate on the King's Speech. Davies said unhappily that the party was badly split, whereupon Roberts interrupted: 'Badly led.' He demanded that policy should be made by consultation between the leader and the deputy leader – Megan – not between the leader and the

Chief Whip. There was plain speaking, too, at a meeting of the Party Committee (selected by the leader and consisting of MPs and other important Liberals). Megan declared: 'The Liberal ship is listing to the right and almost sunk beneath the waves.' Violet replied with a speech blaming Megan for the party's troubles.

A big problem at the time was rapidly increasing inflation, and the Liberals moved an amendment to the King's Speech censuring the government for rising prices. The Tories decided to support the amendment, and it was on the cards that the government would be defeated. The three Radicals abstained, which led to another row, or 'spirited discussion', at the next party meeting. Violet declared: 'They have dealt a blow to Liberal fortunes everywhere. . . . This new-style Radicalism involves for Liberals complete party paralysis.' The three defended their action in a statement:

This procedure makes the division lobby merely an instrument of Conservative Party tactics to which the Liberal Party should not lend itself. We believe that by our action we have reasserted the Radical position which we intend to uphold on every occasion that presents itself.

In Anglesey, Megan explained to her constituents:

Emrys Roberts and myself are like rugged, independent mountain sheep, compared with the Liberal Nationals who like meek lowland sheep entered the Tory fold without protest years ago and have remained there ever since.[22]

Cledwyn Hughes commented:

Lady Megan and Mr Roberts have shown in deed and thought that they are very close to Labour. . . . Lady Megan has described herself as a rugged mountain sheep, but she is unfortunately a lost sheep.

Shortly afterwards, Spicer hosted a dinner at his house in Pelham Crescent (a few minutes from Megan's flat) at which Megan, Roberts and Herbert Morrison discussed how the Liberals could help to stop the Tories from winning power. The guests were careful not to inform Clement Davies, let alone Hopkin Morris, of this private encounter. Morrison said that he would like to see a Liberal-Labour agreement, but he would not be able to carry a majority of Labour MPs.[23]

Meanwhile, Cripps had failed to recover from a stroke which he suffered during the summer recess, and in October he resigned. Attlee appointed Gaitskell as the new Chancellor – a meteoric promotion for a man who had entered Parliament in 1945 and who had, at least in Bevan's opinion, no standing in the Labour movement. Bevan wrote to Attlee to express his 'consternation and astonishment' and to request an interview. The interview, Bevan later told his friend Michael Foot, developed into 'a tremendous row'.[24]

In June, war had broken out between North and South Korea. American forces were fighting to save the South, and Attlee agreed to send a British contingent. The North Koreans were thrown back when General MacArthur launched a counter-offensive and reached the Yalu river, the frontier with China; but the Chinese intervened and pushed the Americans back to the start line. There were fears that MacArthur would use the ultimate weapon, the atomic bomb. The heightened international tension impelled the NATO command to call on member nations, including Britain, to put in hand an accelerated rearmament programme which would have to be financed by a diversion of resources from civilian needs. This sharpened the disagreements between Labour ministers and the Left in their party. By early 1951, Philip was writing to Megan:

I'm wondering a lot whether the Govt is breaking up or not! Perhaps if we get thro' to Easter, we shall survive till better times; but the team is lamentably weak, & so many of the best people being unused or wrongly used.[25]

In March there was renewed talk of possible co-operation between the Liberals and Labour, and even of giving Davies a position in the government. Philip wrote:

I've been thinking a lot about your Clem. Until now you *cdn't* tell him. But soon it may be essential to do so, & I think you should talk it out with Dingle, & perhaps with Frank [Byers] if you can, about how, when, & on what basis you should put it to him – remembering that *his* ambition is to hold high office! I've not forgotten that at the very start of this Parlmt (March 10th about) he said to me one night: 'Somehow the two progressive parties *must* get together to save the world.' Of course, he has hopeless aberrations, & inherently he's quite useless, too; but I think the main trend of his emotions & thoughts (such as they are) *are* for progress & peace.[26]

On 22 March, Gaitskell presented his budget proposals to the Cabinet. A heavy increase in defence expenditure was to be paid for by economies in other fields, and there would be charges for dental treatment and spectacles. This was unacceptable to Bevan, who was now Minister of Labour but spoke as the architect of the Health Service, and to Harold Wilson, President of the Board of Trade. Attlee and the rest of the Cabinet supported Gaitskell; so, when budget day came, Bevan, Wilson and a junior minister, John Freeman, resigned from the government. In his resignation speech, Bevan said of the budget: 'It united the City, satisfied the Opposition, and disunited the

Labour Party – all this because we have allowed ourselves to be dragged too far behind the wheels of American diplomacy.' Philip sent Megan his reaction:

There it is: not a very good speech; some good arguments & figures; a clear & courageous exposure of the Americans' biggest mistake. . . .I'm feeling, as you felt, very *sad* about it; not angry, like my colleagues; I think Nye very nearly as right as they are on the main points – & they've all been terribly feeble, for five years, over the Americans & raw materials. But I hate ruins. . . .And so much that you & I have longed & worked for, my little sweetheart, may be in ruins very soon. And remembering the 1930s, I must say that a House of Commons with a Tory majority seems very hard to bear! Won't it be absolutely hateful?[27]

In the midst of this crisis, Ernest Bevin died. Philip's letters reveal no hopes that he might be the new Foreign Secretary; presumably he had relinquished that ambition. Attlee appointed Morrison, who had always been concerned with domestic affairs and had no aptitude for conducting foreign policy. Truly, the government was on the way to collapse. Through the summer, the Tories waged their war of attrition with repeated all-night sittings. The seventy-six-year-old Churchill played his part robustly, though he was sowing the seeds of the coronary that struck him in 1953; the sixty-eight-year-old Attlee felt the strain. Writing from his room at the House at six in the morning, Philip told Megan:

Clem A. has been on the Bench or in the tea-room all night – which I regard as infantile & idiotic; Edith S. [Summerskill] said in a loud voice just behind him: 'The medical profession say it takes a fortnight to recover from a night like this.' . . . Winston, Anthony & co. are all still here – Winston led a party of them out after this last division; they looked as if they were going to discuss calling it off. But the present forecasts are that we shall sit right thro' till 4 o'cl, & have another all-night sitting on Monday![28]

Megan was in bed at her flat; Philip was proposing to bring his letter to her, dashing between divisions, so that she got it before breakfast. As a Liberal, she was not subject to the stringent discipline imposed by the whips of the big parties. Besides, she preferred to be absent when the majority of the Liberals decided to vote with the Tories. Jean Mann noticed: 'Sometimes she sadly put on her coat and went home before a division because the Liberals had decided on a line she could not support.'[29]

After the August recess, Attlee decided that the government could not face another session like this. He announced on the radio that

Parliament was to be dissolved and that there would be a general election on 25 October.

5

Philip's letters form an oscillating record – something like the temperature graph in an illness – of the course of the love affair: its joys and miseries, its tensions and its conflicts. We should doubtless be able to view this long-running drama in a different light if we could see it through Megan's eyes, but the regrettable fact is that Philip's are the only letters that have survived. Our consolation must be that he wrote often, intimately (if not always sincerely) and at length. In the month of October 1951 he wrote to Megan twenty-one times. He quite often wrote twice in a day, heading the letters 'Letter I' and 'Letter II' or giving the precise time. It is evident that on 5 December 1951 he wrote to her three times and saw her twice. One letter, headed '3.14 p.m. 7.6.51', begins: 'I left you ninety seconds ago . . .' He sent letters by House of Commons messenger when they were both at the House, posted them at the last possible moment, or took them to her flat in a taxi and slipped them through the letter-box. He wrote in his office when he was a minister, on his knee sitting on the front bench, in planes and in trains. On a long train journey, he dashed to post a letter at an intermediate station and on at least one occasion handed it to an engine-driver (it arrived safely). Three letters written during a flight to New York are headed 'Over Birmingham or thereabouts', 'Over the sea before Scotland' and 'Halfway across the Atlantic'.[30] Surely, one thinks, even Philip could not have transferred a letter to an eastbound plane.

Some people are compulsive letter-writers and some are compulsive telephoners, but Philip was both. One letter ends: 'My best & most lovely, I must go and ring you up.'[31] Making a call to Criccieth from London was a slow business in the days before direct dialling, so the impatient lover used the time to write a letter while waiting for the connection. On the snowy morning of New Year's Day 1953 he wrote: 'I'm trying to ring you up, & am writing in a draughty call-box – the glass of the door is broken.'

The need for secrecy complicated the procedure but did not check the compulsion. Since his favourite time for writing was late at night, he had to experience a sudden desire for a walk if Irene was at home. Phoning Brynawelon from the House of Commons was risky, because the switchboard operator would know whose number Criccieth 4 was. He had a network of callboxes in the vicinity, but other MPs might wonder why he was slipping out, and it was a nuisance to save up a pocketful of sixpences and shillings. He was a member of the Royal Automobile Club in Pall Mall, but it was not always easy to phone from there :

I'm doubtful, too, about going to the Club! The evening operator there greeted me with the loudly spoken welcome: 'Same number as usual, sir?' And then he goes thro' the formula I first wrote out for him – C4 thro' L & P [ie Criccieth 4 through Liverpool and Portmadoc]. Its all right when the spectators are few & strangers, as they have been so far – but if a collection of M.P.s turned the corner suddenly it wd be *less* good.[32]

In the spring of 1950 the graph was serenely level:

My most beautiful & dearest & best, I was wanting you so frightfully while I was on the Bench. I felt as I felt last night, but much more so. I thought how wonderfully perfect your hair was, & how perfect what the painters call the bone construction of your face & head, & how fascinating it is when you wrinkle up your forehead, & how I adored every least little bit of you.

And I felt, too, so much more peaceful & *certain* than I've ever felt before. You've been so angelic to me all this last week that you've given me the feeling that I really belong, that you *do* think of me as your possession; that I *am* not only *yours*, but that you deeply & firmly & always *want* me to be yours. Indeed, I felt as tho' I was beginning to understand what it would be like to be married.[33]

And a few days later:

Last night was more perfect, more strangely, totally satisfying than any time we've had since first we met. So short, but so charged with everything that makes life worth living. . . . I had to go for *your* sake, so that you should sleep soon & well. . . . I slept, knowing that you had never been so gentle, so understanding, so generous in all your life before.[34]

In February 1951 all was still going well and he informed her, probably not altogether to her gratification:

Today, I've found it very hard to think of you as a politician at all, because I've been thinking of you as an enchanting little fairy, an utterly delectable femininity, a little adorata whose every movement fills me with happiness, admiration, & most tenderly loving desire.[35]

By the end of the month, the graph was violently plunging. Megan had shown favour to Osbert Peake, of whom Philip had been jealous since the 1930s:

I sat at a long table, where it was easy, natural, for you to come & sit beside me – much more noticeable for you *not* to do it than to do it. But you walk by as if I didn't exist; you welcome O. with ecstasy; & you'll let him keep you till 5.15 or later, I'll bet my last dilapidated shirt. And I have to be at the Office for a meeting at 5.30. . . . And I can't bear it. It knocks me to pieces. Its unnatural, false, wicked, ostentatious for me not to see you when you're so easily to be seen. I can't bear people not knowing that I belong to you. . . .

Its almost 5 o'cl now. I can't work. . . . I shall resign. Its the only way. At least, I shan't any longer be a nuisance, & I shall like to think of you free & unharassed, as you used to be.[36]

It would have been hard for Megan not to feel – and sometimes tell him – that he was indeed being a nuisance. The word recurs in a letter written on 10 April 1951:

I don't want to be a nuisance to you, & I do try *desperately* to exercise restraint; but I can't help longing for you every hour of every day. I want to wake up with you, have breakfast with you, see you in your bath, help to dress you, drive you to your meetings, pick you up again, discuss the news, share your fun & your depressions, see your triumphs. . . . I want to feel that I'm your possession, for you to do with me precisely what you like; & I want to feel that you like to do all sorts of things! . . . When I'm alone [ie without Irene] & you come back to me, & I'm free to see you, & there are no time-limits or other drags on me, I feel that I really *am* married to you – & its such a wonderful, wonderful feeling.

Yet, only two weeks later, the tension was at fever-pitch again. This time it was Megan who was suspicious and jealous. She must have been aware that in political circles Philip had a reputation as a philanderer. She could easily have heard remarks to that effect, perhaps from one of the score of Labour women MPs with whom she was friendly. This would inevitably suggest the painful thought that his devotion to her was neither as exclusive nor as serious as he claimed. Perhaps, as Ursula Thorpe believed, he was only 'fooling' with Megan. Evidently she was driven to voice her suspicions in a scene which drew from him this outraged reaction:

Are you really surprised that you put a knife into me? Try & remember, quite fairly, what you said.

First, that I carried on with all my secretaries. This on the evidence of R.M., whose total acquaintance, on which this really charming &, you thought, *justifiable* comment was made, cannot have amounted to two hours over ten years. It is a really monstrous thing for her to have said, & she can have just no evidence for it *at all*, for my secretaries have always been warm friends of the family.

Second, that R.M.'s general charge was supported by two men. You won't say *what* men, or what they said. . . . But you don't mind them making trouble between you & me; you don't hesitate to accept what they say without giving me a chance to answer; you don't mind leaving a lasting suspicion & a lasting wound, providing *their* confidence is respected & their anonymity maintained.

Third, Peggy. Have I ever refused to tell you about Peggy? Haven't I wanted you to meet her? . . . Does that look as if I had something to be ashamed of or to hide? Peggy is one of my best friends, & I wish I could see her often; so would you if you knew her. . . .

The idea of going to Raspit is utterly *repellent*. So, if you're still of that way of thinking about me, perhaps you will let Thelma know that I can't come. Tear this up, please. *Please.* I shan't write again, or telephone, until you've told me you've torn it up & wiped the memory of it from your mind. It will take a long time to wipe away from mine. I'm utterly miserable, & shall go on being miserable longer than I like to think of.[37]

Megan did not tear up this letter, and he wrote again two days later, anxious to make peace: 'If I was to blame, I apologize & withdraw & express my heartfelt sorrow in any way you wish.' Perhaps fortunately, they saw less of each other during the summer. Megan went to Brynawelon when the House rose, and then for a holiday in Italy with Ursula. When she returned, Philip had to tell her: 'Alas, I'm not alone, & so its terribly difficult for me to fix things about seeing you.'[38] Then came the election.

6

Battered by the catastrophe of 1950, and in bad financial trouble, the Liberals were unequal to another major effort. They mustered only 109 candidates, and even these were badly distributed. Edward Martell, then a prominent Liberal, reckoned that the party fought twenty-nine hopeless seats – that is, seats where the deposit had been lost in 1950 – and failed to fight thirty-four good ones.[39]

The election brought fresh alliances between Liberals and Tories. In Bolton, another town with an East and a West division, there was a share-out on Huddersfield lines. Gwilym stood for Newcastle upon Tyne North, a safe Tory seat, as a Liberal and Conservative. Lady Violet stood for Colne Valley and accepted Tory support, with

Churchill speaking at one of her meetings. If the Tory and Liberal votes cast in 1950 were added together she would have a majority of 500, so journalists homed in on this contest. Who would be the Liberal deputy leader, the *Western Mail* asked, if both Lady Megan and Lady Violet were MPs in the next Parliament?

Clement Davies was veering heavily to the Right, and the Tories did not oppose him in Montgomery. David Butler, then making his name as a political analyst, wrote:

Mr Davies' broadcast, it was widely noted, attacked only the Labour Party and, on points of policy, said little that would have caused surprise if it had come from a Conservative. . . . In an election in which a large number of Liberals had no candidate of their own, this emphasis was regarded by many as particularly significant.[40]

Three days before the poll, the *Guardian* came out with a leader headed 'Time for a Change?' The question-mark may have been added by a nervous Liberal, for the article recommended a full term of power for Churchill as the best choice for the voters. Most Liberal candidates were following Davies's lead and aiming their fire against Labour. Yet there is evidence that Liberal activists around the country were distressed by this tendency, and especially by open acceptance of Tory support. Megan demanded: 'Is this keep-Right policy the line which Liberals in the constituencies want the party to take? I am convinced it is not.'[41] And Martell, after the election, said of Violet: 'Her blatant pro-Tory attitude dismayed many in the party who had hitherto held her in the highest respect, and destroyed the public belief in our independence.'[42]

Cledwyn Hughes was standing for Anglesey again. He had thought of giving up after his disappointing result in 1950, but the Labour agent had persuaded him to follow the motto of 'three tries for a Welshman'. The Tory candidate, Meurig Roberts, was a Health Service administrator and a county councillor in Caernarvon.

Megan had to make a clear choice in her campaign strategy. Now that the sharp differences in her party were public knowledge, fighting on local issues and on her record would not suffice. It was open to her to bid for Tory votes by coming forward as the candidate best equipped to uphold the values of individualism and combat the Socialist menace. Had she made this choice – in the opinion of good judges, including Cledwyn – she might well have won, but she never considered it. Indeed, when the Tories put out a leaflet quoting a denunciation of Socialism uttered by her father in 1925, she protested.

The alternative was to appeal to the Radical tradition, inspire her followers who had always known her for what she was, and maximise the progressive vote. Launching her campaign, she said:

I have always supported and will always support every measure brought before the House by the Labour government to raise the standard of living of ordinary people. I would not be faithful to the traditions of my father had I not done so. . . . Any frontal attack on the social services must be defeated. I am a Radical, I was born a Radical, and I'll be a Radical as long as I live.[43]

As ever, she canvassed vigorously and spoke at three or four meetings every night. She had to make more tactical decisions herself because her trusted agent, John Bellis, had retired. Yet, characteristically, she interrupted her campaign to help a family whose house had been burned down. Luckily, she found a teacher who was about to leave the island and got the homeless family moved into the schoolhouse.

Labour's strategy was to deprive Churchill of the appeal to international détente which had served him well in 1950. A dominant note in the Labour campaign was the charge that the Tories were warmongers, or at least that peace was not safe in their hands. 'If the country wants peace it had better vote for the people who can most surely be relied upon to preserve peace,' Morrison advised. Philip weighed in with an article headed 'Cast Your Vote for Peace' in the *Daily Herald*, then a mass-circulation paper.

The outcome of the election showed, once again, the unpredictability of the British system. The Labour Party polled almost 14 million votes, a record in its history. They were ahead of the Tories by 224,000 votes, or 0.69 per cent of the poll. Yet Labour had a net loss of twenty seats and the Tories had a net gain of twenty-three, to emerge with a modest but adequate majority in the Commons.

Megan, after twenty-two years as MP for Anglesey, was out; Cledwyn was elected with a majority of 595. The Labour vote was virtually the same as in 1950, or indeed 1945. Megan's vote was down from 13,688 to 11,219, and it was obvious that these lost votes had gone to the Tories. Meurig Roberts, Cledwyn recalls, was a much stronger candidate than the unfortunate J. O. Jones and he was rewarded with the reputable poll of 6366. However, the verdict of the *Holyhead Mail* identified the most significant factor: 'She fell because of her independence.'

The local paper had another comment. English people were by now an increasing element in the island's population, and jobs were being given without regard to its Welsh character. During the campaign, Megan had attacked the appointment of a food officer (a necessary post, since rationing was still in force) who could not speak Welsh. The *Mail* had this to say:

It would be interesting to know how many English families have in recent years come to live in Anglesey. . . . The number is sufficient to alter the whole tenor of life. . . .We venture to say that these newcomers to Anglesey tipped the scales against Lady Megan.

There was no comfort anywhere for the Liberals. Violet, even with Churchill's help, had failed to win Colne Valley. A 1950 gain, Roxburgh, reverted to the Tories. Bolton West was, on paper, a Liberal gain, but it clearly depended on Tory votes. The Liberals were now down to six MPs; of these, only Grimond had defeated a Tory. The overall total of Liberal votes, given the small number of candidates, was of course derisory. The two-party system was at its zenith, with over 96 per cent of the votes going either to Labour or to the Tories.

For Megan, there was another depressing fact: her fellow Radicals, Emrys Roberts and Edgar Granville, were among the defeated. There was no longer a Left in what remained of the parliamentary Liberal Party. To a waverer like Clement Davies, this would seem to prove that the Radical appeal was a losing strategy.

The sad truth was that, of the three million people who voted Liberal when they had a candidate, only a minority shared Megan's political outlook. Attlee commented after the election: 'Our loss of seats has been due to the fact that, when it came to the point, more Liberals were Conservative than Labour.' This may sound like a loser's excuse, but David Butler, after examining the figures, found that when Liberals had no candidate of their own about 60 per cent of them voted Tory. Robert Pitman looked at the twenty-two seats lost by Labour and concluded that in seventeen cases the crucial factor was that the Liberals stood in 1950 and not in 1951.[44] Megan would be obliged to ponder on such findings when she considered her future. Had she, perhaps, spent her political life in a party in which her ideas did not and could not prevail?

She met defeat bravely. After the count, she made a tour of the towns and villages, as she had after every election since 1929. The autumn day was sunny; the crowds were more enthusiastic than ever. It was hard, said the *Holyhead Mail* reporter, to believe that she had lost. The links between Anglesey and Anglesey's MP, now severed, had been profoundly emotional. In her final speech she had told her people: 'You have become flesh of my flesh, body of my body.' (It sounds even better in Welsh.)

Cledwyn saw that it was a bad blow to her, although 'she took it with great dash'. For himself, he had a sense of triumph but 'with an element of sadness'.[45] He was not the only one. When he arrived at Westminster, Morrison congratulated him on his victory but added: 'Mind you, Megan is a great loss.'

If Megan was grieved, Philip was shattered. With his usual lack of realism, he had forecast that she would get a bigger majority than ever before. 'I wd double my bets that you get 5000 – I'm *sure* of it,' he wrote five days before the poll. When he heard of the result, his reaction was hysterical. It took the form of anger with the Labour leaders for putting up a candidate against Megan. A few hours after the Anglesey result was declared, he wrote to her:

I just can't believe it; I can't get my mind to grip the fact at all; it doesn't make sense in itself; it proves democracy & Welsh patriotism & pride to be a nonsense; it hurts & hurts & hurts, & I don't get an inch beyond that in my mind; the future is a horror, insofar as it isn't a blank. . . . Above all it makes me *hate* those miserable, little men, C. & H. [Clement and Herbert]. If it were bigotry, that wd be one thing; but its just plain, disgusting cowardice – they're afraid of the bigots.

A couple of days later, he repeated that he felt '*shame* that the party for which I've given my life should have been so caddish, so short-sighted, so cowardly'. This attitude did more credit to his feelings than to his logic. It might have been reasonable for Labour to stand down had there been a risk of the Tories winning the seat, but it made no political sense to forgo a Labour gain.

However, he found some consolations:

For Violet, it is the final & devastating end; for Clem D., the last step but one down the Gadarene slope. For you, it is a rest; a short one, probably most beneficent in every way.[46]

He also offered this reflection:

If *you*'ve not won, in the place where you've been for 22 years, & where every man, woman & child really loves you, then it means that the thing just can't be done. The M.G. [*Manchester Guardian*] is right; Liberalism is a spent force, as a party. Liberals must work in other ways – you must work with us.[47]

Another Labour politician whom Megan counted as a friend, James Callaghan, wrote to her:

I am genuinely sorry you are not in the House & I very much hope you will come back. We cannot sacrifice grace, charm, wit, passion as easily as that.

But you must come back as a Member of our Party. First, because we are right about the malaise & the remedies for the 20th century. Secondly, because there is no other way back.[48]

Was he right? That was what Megan would have to think hard about.

PINTAIL: DUCK AND DRAKE      Peter Scott.

# EX LIBRIS

## MEGAN LLOYD GEORGE.

# CHAPTER ELEVEN

# Crossing the Line

1

At the end of 1951, Megan set out on an extensive journey to the western hemisphere – Canada, the United States and Jamaica. She was in need of a rest, or a change, and a chance to think carefully about her political future. On 10 November the Liberal Council rejected a resolution moved by Megan and Dingle Foot calling on Liberals to resist attacks on the social services, and this was disheartening evidence that the shift to the Right was more than a drift. Churchill, on his return to Downing Street, had offered Clement Davies a place in the Cabinet as Minister of Education.[1] After consulting the other five Liberal MPs, who (even if they were happy to see a Tory government) did not want the party to be submerged in the Simonite manner, Davies declined the offer, but it was widely believed that he would have liked to accept it. The outcome of his talks with Churchill was a statement that Liberals would 'give to the government support for measures clearly conceived in the interest of the country as a whole'. The first business at Westminster was the denationalisation of steel, on which Tories and Liberals were agreed.

Philip, writing from the House, told Megan: 'I'm so immensely happy that you are *not* here, & faced with the hopeless conflict you would have had in your party.'[2] He was appalled, however, by the prospect of her American journey; he anticipated 'months of barren emptiness' and 'utter desolation' in a 'Meganless miasma'. In one letter he said that it would be '1940 all over again' – not a happy comparison. To make matters worse, Megan would be the other side of the Atlantic just when Irene would be in Greece.

In the days before her departure, the relationship was distinctly edgy. She was at Brynawelon and was to sail, with Olwen, on the cruise ship *Medea* on 8 December. Philip wrote on 7 December:

I was left last night after our talk with the unsatisfactory feeling that I hadn't made you understand what I meant about telephoning today – you said: 'Of course, talk to your international lawyer – *far* more important.' *Not* very clever of you. . . . I can't *bear* it that, on the last day of the time you're here, you should think, even for a moment, that I'm 'casual'. I *had* to see this blessed man, & I must still see him; its about my book on intl. law, & that is *money*; & my financial position . . . simply doesn't bear thinking about. . . .[3]

My beloved, if I were your husband, if I had the right to be with you, if I could be present at your triumphs, if I wasn't continually kept outside so much that is most important to you, & that I care so deeply about, you wouldn't suffer from green-eye at all!

Unable to leave it at that, he wrote three hours later:

I hope you don't *still* feel that I'm very cheerful & not missing you at all. . . . You clearly hadn't read my letters – only the first paragraphs. . . . You, on the other hand, were uniformly explosive with pleasure & satisfaction with everything that was happening to you! You never wrote to me, or suggested it; you never hinted by a word that I was being missed; so little did you understand my feelings that you taunted me with the greater ardour of your other telephone correspondents.

The sisters made their way to Toronto, where they stayed with Olwen's daughter Eluned and her husband, Dr Robert Macmillan. Megan did not write from Toronto any more than she had from Brynawelon. Philip complained in February: 'You don't tell me whether you got my telegrams at Bermuda, New York, or Toronto; or any of my innumerable letters, under manifold disguises, to 350 Englewood Drive [Toronto].'[4]

Megan, now without Olwen, was in Jamaica, where she stayed first with Sir Hugh Foot, the Governor, and then with Thelma Cazalet, who had a house called Out of the Blue. Philip was jealous of Megan's friendship (or more than friendship, he suspected) with Dingle, and was therefore prejudiced against the Foot family, or 'the Feet' as he called them. He told her:

Its terribly frustrating writing to a SILENCE. . . . I can't somehow give you my news; it is so remote from you that it can't really interest you, & perhaps by now – it always haunts me – you don't even *want* it.[5]

A letter eventually came, but it did not tell him what he wanted to know:

I don't feel as if I knew at all when you will be with Thelma; owing to your lamentable predilection for Feet, I imagine that it may be some time. But you give me no Footish address, & therefore I can't hope to reach you there. . . . My goodness, you don't remember that correspondence is a two-way traffic, & that its *impossible* to go on *despatching* unless you know whether there is some *receiving* at the other end.[6]

He had been in Greece, but had spent most of the time in bed with flu. When he returned to London, the King died and Parliament was adjourned for a fortnight. He could have spent the free time with Megan if only she had not been in Jamaica. He went to Windsor for the royal funeral – a journey that he did not enjoy, as he had to travel with Hugh Dalton. At last, Ellen rang him up to read a telegram which she had received from Megan: 'I suppose it means that you've only just extricated yourself from the Feet, & arrived with Thelma – if so, you ought by this time to have a large pile of letters waiting for you.'[7]

His troubles were not over. Alone in his big Belgravia house, he fell downstairs in the middle of the night and injured his leg and hip; he walked with difficulty and needed massage treatment for some time. Megan, meanwhile, went by air to Miami and then by train to New York. She wrote to him from the Wentworth Hotel; the letter has survived because she forgot to post it.

Thank you for your letter of welcome to N.Y. but how maddening for you to have such an accident! How *could* you fall downstairs in the middle of the night. If you weren't almost aged 62 (except when I'm about) I should suspect the worst. It's quite evident that you can't look after yourself for a moment. I am so sorry. . . . I shall expect to find you at Southampton sound in wind & fetlock, so no more crawling about at my flat, *please*.

I had a wonderful flight from Montego Bay to Miami. We came down for 20 minutes in Cuba – but I *loathe* flying & it's no good pretending I don't. I think it's the most exhausting form of travel going & yesterday I was quite knocked out. . . .

I had a wonderful experience in Miami. As we touched down almost, a man put his head in at the door, shouted my name, rushed me out of the plane, shouting 'We're holding the train for you.' I was through the doctor's examination (You all right? Fine, thank you, & that was all) the immigration, & the customs in less time than it took us to run round the place. I was bundled into a waiting police car, rushed through Miami with sirens blaring & all traffic giving way right & left, & into the train I fell. . . . So you see how I travel when I'm left on my own, unorganised & unchaperoned! I get there just the same.[8]

The letter opened with 'D.P.' (for 'Dear Philip') and ended with 'Love, M.' – a contrast with the elaborate endearments in which Philip indulged. One is naturally struck by the cool, even distant tone. Except for the joking allusion in the third sentence, Megan might have been writing to any friend or acquaintance. Perhaps, after the quarrels before she left home, and then his nagging letters, she was less than affectionately disposed towards Philip. However, in the absence of other letters from her hand, we do not know how much this one varied from her usual style.

Her stay in the USA was the working part of her trip; she had arranged to lecture in New York, Philadelphia and Washington in order to earn money to supplement the small allowance which, under the tight exchange control of the 1950s, she was able to take abroad. Billed as Lloyd George's daughter, she treated her audiences to reminiscences. She was also interviewed on television and went to Bangor, Pennsylvania, to join the Welsh community in the St David's Day celebrations, postponed from the correct date for her benefit. Then she sailed for home on the *Queen Mary*, which was to reach Southampton on 12 March 1952. Philip made careful plans to meet her without their being seen together; Ellen would go to the ship and take care of Megan's luggage, while Philip waited for her in a Southampton hotel. But his bad luck persisted, for the liner was delayed by storms and arrived a day late. The time they could spend together was dwindling; Irene was due back from Greece on 16 March.

In April Megan had speaking engagements in Wales and Philip went to Scandinavia, attending a dinner in Oslo given by the King of Norway and going on to Helsinki for the Olympic Games. Forty years had passed since he ran in the Olympics at Stockholm. He was in Oslo on 22 April, Megan's fiftieth birthday. He wrote before he left, addressing her as 'my most adored little Centenarian':

Every week, every year you grow *younger*; you *are* much younger in every important way than you were fifteen years ago; you are more beautiful – yes, waistline & all – than you were then; physically, this day means less than nothing at all. Spiritually, it means that, from now on, I shall love you 50 times more than I have done before.[9]

2

It was in 1952 that Megan was involved in an incident which forcibly reminded her that women had to live in a man's world. Her friend Richard Acland launched a campaign against world hunger, and Christian Action, whose chairman was Canon John Collins of St Paul's Cathedral, sponsored a series of lectures to be given in the cathedral. The lectures were not to be part of a religious service, but the other canons were suspicious of anything favoured by Collins. The speakers were to be Acland, Walter Elliott, Ritchie Calder, Professor J. de Castro and Megan Lloyd George; she was to speak on 17 July on: 'Am I my brother's keeper?'

When the plans were made known, the Chapter of Canons refused to allow a woman to occupy the pulpit. Collins told a reporter: 'Inviting a woman will start a controversy. Everything I organise does.' Megan described the objection as 'curious'. After delicate negotiations, a special rostrum was constructed for her below the pulpit. The *Western Mail* assured its readers that 'the rostrum will suit her slim figure and robust style', and that she would be more audible than from the pulpit.

She began with reflections on a familiar text:

'Give to the poor' – no one can take exception to that. But 'sell all thou hast and give to the poor' – then you are being controversial. . . . I really don't think we need fear a little controversy in the House of God. It is of the essence of a living faith.

Then she came to her main theme:

Fifteen hundred million men, women and children are suffering from actual hunger and the problem is becoming more insistent, more urgent, every year. . . . What are we doing about it? . . . The brutal truth is that, in present circumstances, we cannot spare the immense resources that are necessary to tackle this problem on anything like an adequate scale. Why? Because we are too busy turning ploughshares into swords. . . . We need scientists, technicians. They cannot be made available. They are busy perfecting the weapons of destruction to make them more swift, more deadly, more devilish. There is not enough room today in the laboratories of the world for the research workers of peace. . . . In the days before the war, a great Russian spoke with the voice of peace. If only the spirit of Litvinov could inspire the policy of his country today, what a transformation there would be. No people in the world is suffering more cruelly from the crippling burden of armaments than the peasants of Russia.

Her peroration was a pointed thrust at the canons:

We must each make our own confession of faith. We have a duty and a right
to be witnesses to truth, men and women, and in a like degree. After all, it was
. . . to a woman that Our Lord first gave testimony of the Resurrection.[10]

The first woman who was eventually allowed to occupy the pulpit of
St Paul's – speaking during a service, though technically not preaching
– was Coretta King. The invitation came, once again, from John
Collins, and his colleagues did not venture to ban the widow of Martin
Luther King.

3

As MP for Anglesey, Megan had often spoken up for her native
country and attacked English indifference to Welsh interests. To most
English people, it seemed reasonable that decisions should be made in
London for an entity called 'England and Wales', but to Megan it did
not. Scotland had at least some distinctive institutions: there were
Scottish laws which differed from England-and-Wales laws, there was
a Secretary of State for Scotland with a seat in the Cabinet, there was a
Scottish Office in Edinburgh, and from time to time there was a
'Scottish day' in the House of Commons. In 1944 pressure by Megan
and other Welsh MPs had secured one concession – a 'Welsh day'. It
was set for 17 October 1944, and Megan opened the debate. She
began by remarking that, as there had been MPs from Wales for four
hundred years, the occasion was 'somewhat overdue'. Then she
repeated the demands for which she had been pressing ever since
1929: better housing, assistance to modernise farms, cheap electricity,
a better water supply, new roads and investment in industry. Pointing
out that 400,000 workers had migrated from Wales to England
between the wars, she said: 'There is no more effective way of sapping
the vitality and virility of a nation than by taking away its young men.'
But the heart of her message was:

Wales is not an area, not a part of England, but a nation with a living language
of its own, hundreds of years of history behind it, and with its own
culture. . . . It is the Welsh way of life that we are determined to see
maintained. . . . No Englishman can understand the Welsh. However much
he may try, however sympathetic he may feel, he cannot get inside the skin
and bones of a Welshman unless he be born again.

She wound up by reminding the House that the Atlantic Charter – the declaration of war aims adopted by Churchill and Roosevelt – laid down that all countries should be governed according to their own desires:

That provision does not apply only to Poland, Czechoslovakia, Romania – countries far distant. It applies also to Wales. . . . We have fought with you; we have also, many a time and for long centuries, fought against you, but we would now like to be in partnership with you in this greatest endeavour in our long history.

The thin attendance on this 'Welsh day' and the meagre response to most of her demands must have strengthened her belief that Wales needed a different kind of House of Commons – what she defined ten years later as 'a Parliament sitting on Welsh soil and answerable to the Welsh people'.[11] In the post-war years, Welsh aspirations crystallised around the demand for a Welsh Parliament. Early in 1950 a number of men and women belonging to different political parties came together to form the *Undeb* (League) *Cymru Fydd* – a name which deliberately recalled the *Cymru Fydd* movement in which Megan's father had been active in the 1890s. A conference was called in June 1950 at Llandrindod Wells, in the middle of Wales. It decided to launch a Parliament for Wales Campaign and invited Megan to be president of it; she gladly accepted. One of the members of the committee was her cousin, William George.

Megan's attendance at committee meetings was rather spasmodic, and she did not concentrate her energies on the campaign until after she lost Anglesey. In any case, it got off to a slow start. According to Glyn Tegai Hughes, a Liberal who was closely involved, 'it went off at half-cock from the beginning'. There was no money and no effective drive for raising money, and Hughes has observed: 'I've never seen anything so abysmally organised.'[12] Two years after the campaign was launched, it acquired an organising secretary, Elwyn Roberts, who was very efficient; but by that time some of the momentum had been lost and some supporters had drifted away.

The strategy chosen was a petition for mass signature, with a target of one million signatures. As we know from the original model of a petition campaign, the Charter of 1848, the advantage is that it arouses popular opinion and places the issue directly before a large number of individual people, while the disadvantage is that there is no obvious way forward when the petition is rejected. The Welsh petition was signed by 250,000 people. Gwynfor Evans, the Plaid Cymru leader, estimates that 80 per cent of those presented with it agreed to sign – a convincing demonstration of national feeling. The limitation, he says, was a shortage of volunteers to do the legwork (most of them came from the Plaid). Evans stresses particularly that, contrary to some expectations, the response was just as good in South Wales as in the North; 30,000 signatures were collected in the Rhondda valley.[13]

Glyn Tegai Hughes, on the other hand, regards the campaign as a 'relative failure'. He sensed that people were signing the petition out of vague goodwill. No one in Wales argued strongly against it, as Neil Kinnock and Leo Abse argued against devolution in 1979. Had there been a referendum in the 1950s, he doubts whether there would have been a majority for a Parliament for Wales.[14]

One of the handicaps of the campaign was that, although it drew support from individual members of every political party (even a few Tories), the only parties explicitly endorsing it were Plaid Cymru and the Communist Party. Although there is no doubt that Plaid Cymru people – notably the high-principled Gwynfor Evans – worked for the petition out of conviction and not for political advantage, the campaign must have helped to put the Plaid on the map, attract members and pave the way for later electoral victories. The Liberals, too, might have improved their fortunes if they had come out solidly for a Parliament for Wales, but, as usual, they were split. Of the five Liberal MPs representing Welsh constituencies when the campaign started, only Megan and Emrys Roberts were active in it. This aroused suspicions, as they were also the two most outspoken Radicals. By the time the campaign got into top gear, they had lost their seats.

In the Labour Party, the dominant tradition, especially in the South Wales mining valleys which were the party's bedrock, was of comradely alliance with the whole British working class. Assertions of Welshness were a sectarian diversion, to be condemned as Stalin condemned the 'petty-bourgeois nationalism' of non-Russian people in the Soviet Union. Cledwyn Hughes gives an example of this attitude:

I recall a conversation I had with Aneurin Bevan at the historic Blackpool conference of 1945. He was having coffee with his friend, Krishna Menon, the fervent Indian nationalist who was then a prospective Labour candidate. Aneurin welcomed me and I suggested that it was time we had a policy for Wales. He exploded at once and said impatiently that it was all 'chauvinism', and advised me to concentrate on more important problems, and all this in Krishna Menon's presence![15]

Cledwyn was one of the five Labour MPs from Wales who supported the Parliament for Wales campaign. After the 1951 election when he became an MP, his emphatic support built a bridge between him and Megan, and they became good friends. The others were Goronwy Roberts of Caernarvon, T. W. Jones of Merioneth, Tudor Watkins of Brecon and Radnor, and S. O. Davies of Merthyr Tydfil. Only one of these, Davies, represented a classical South Wales industrial constituency, and he was always something of a maverick. This left a solid phalanx of twenty Labour MPs from South Wales who refused to back the campaign. Since most of them were local men and trade-union nominees, the weight of their influence needs no stressing.

The argument most often deployed was that any measure of political separatism must lead to the creation of a separate economy, which would be short of investment resources and therefore incapable of development. There were ways of rebutting this argument, but the greatest admirers of Megan Lloyd George and Gwynfor Evans could scarcely point to their economic expertise. Wrexham, a place where Megan spoke twice on the *Undeb Cymru Fydd* platform, was visited by Herbert Morrison, who predicted that a self-governing Wales would be poorer, and James Griffiths, who declared that it would 'bring disaster'.[16]

There was some danger, indeed, that the Parliament for Wales campaign would become a heresy, to be crushed by the disciplinary methods so congenial to Labour chieftains. Cledwyn recalls: 'There was talk of expelling those who were campaigning and addressing meetings with members of other parties.'[17] Luckily, the fissure cut across the usual divide between Left and Right. Bevan, while emphatically opposed to the Parliament for Wales, had his own reasons for not wishing to see its advocates expelled.

Gwynfor Evans regarded Megan as undoubtedly the main figure in the campaign and the main attraction at public meetings. According to him, she spoke at twenty meetings or more in the course of the campaign. Press reports give the flavour of her oratory. At Chester: 'If not born to rule, we are at least born to govern ourselves.' At Brecon: 'I am not ashamed to be called a nationalist. I am first and foremost a Welshwoman.' At Ystradgynlais: 'Some people support self-government for every other country except their own.' At the Rhyl Eisteddfod in 1953: 'If we, south and north, city and country, shepherd and collier, churches and chapels unite in one faith we shall make Wales as a nation safe for ever.'[18]

The meetings were always good and often remarkable. Cliff Bere, who was the organiser in south-east Wales in the later phase of the campaign, arranged five meetings within a week at Maesteg, Pontypridd, Treorchy, Ebbw Vale and Abertillery. In Maesteg he hired the town hall, and in the other places the biggest chapel. All the meetings were packed, despite pouring rain when Megan spoke at Ebbw Vale and Abertillery, and people had to be turned away. Himself from a working-class background in the valleys, Bere got on well with Megan – 'I liked her Radical attitude.'[19] At Maesteg she objected to the vote of thanks being seconded by Victor Hampson-Jones, who was a 'cultural nationalist' in the Saunders Lewis tradition and a Catholic. Bere substituted a Communist, with Megan's approval.

In 1955, after the close of the petition campaign, S. O. Davies moved a bill to give Wales a Parliament. Supported by very few MPs and neither of the major parties, it inevitably failed to get a second reading. Yet most people who were active in the campaign feel today that it was worth while. For the first time since the 1890s, there was an organised effort to mobilise Welsh national consciousness and voice Welsh demands. However, the results were meagre. In 1954 the Tory government set up a nominated Council for Wales, but Megan commented that it was 'a bone without a marrow – no self-respecting corgi would sniff at it'. (Her own dogs were always corgis.) It was only in 1964 that a Labour government appointed a Secretary of State for Wales, and a Parliament for Wales is still beyond the horizon.

4

Megan hated being out of the Commons after her defeat in 1951, and longed to get into the thick of the political battle again. When a reporter asked her whether she might retire from politics, she flashed back: 'I'm not of a retiring age nor of a retiring disposition.'[20] It could be said, however, that she was not missing much. The Tories did not seem minded to validate the warnings of Labour campaign oratory and make a vengeful restoration of the bad old days. There was no return to mass unemployment, no wholesale assault on the welfare state. Food prices went up when rationing was abolished, but most people were glad to throw away their coupons. There were new cars, new fashion styles now that 'austerity' was a forgotten word, and the novelty of television; with the spur of the Coronation in June 1953, only the really poor and the intellectually refined did not acquire sets. Contentment at home was matched by relaxation of tension abroad. The Korean war ended in a truce, Stalin died in March 1953, and his successors presented a more amicable appearance.

The Radical wing of the Liberal Party, now that it had no MPs, could mount no effective challenge even to Clement Davies's uninspiring leadership. The Radical Action Group, founded in 1941, was still in existence, but it was little more than an informal discussion forum. Generally, the Radicals stayed away from party meetings at which they would be obliged either to accept uncongenial decisions or to engage in pointless wrangles. Megan did not attend the annual Assembly in May 1952, and she declined nomination for vice-president, an honorary post which she had held for several years.

In June 1952 Morgan Phillips, general secretary of the Labour Party, received a letter from an American trade-unionist, Mark Starr, who had been a dinner guest with Clement Davies and was ready to divulge the table-talk. It was hardly sensational; Davies wished that everyone, including Churchill and the union leaders, would subscribe to the principles of Liberalism. Phillips commented in thanking Starr:

Of course he is extremely ineffective and few people take him seriously. . . . The internal position of the Liberal Party appears to be getting worse than ever. Megan Lloyd George and the staff of the Radical Action Group have been refraining from attending recent conferences and Council meetings, and the councils of the party appear to be dominated . . . by those people who wish to work in association with the Conservative Party.[21]

After the 1951 election and the Davies-Churchill concordat, it was widely expected that the Radicals would give up their hopeless battle to reclaim the Liberal Party and join the Labour Party. The names that counted – all former MPs – were Megan Lloyd George, Dingle Foot, Edgar Granville, Wilfrid Roberts and Emrys Roberts. A joint declaration by these five would have been an event of considerable significance. Perhaps it was not in the nature of Liberals to act in such a cohesive manner. 'We debated the matter together for the next three years,' Dingle wrote later.[22] Granville, on his own, joined Labour in January 1952. He contested his old seat, the Eye division of Suffolk, as Labour candidate in 1955 and 1959, but failed to wrest it back from the Tory who had beaten him in 1951. Megan, as we shall see, joined Labour in 1955. Dingle Foot and Wilfrid Roberts followed her in 1956. Emrys Roberts gave up politics and devoted himself to a business career. Megan urged him to resume political activity in the Labour Party, but he felt that he could not honestly do so while making money as a capitalist – a scruple that did not always trouble the consciences of Labour MPs.[23]

Writing to Megan in New York after Edgar Granville had joined Labour, Philip gave this advice:

I've been thinking, too, so much about your big political plunge, & how you'll handle it, when you get home. I'm so very glad that the Caribbean specimens of FEET approved of what you plan to do. I think, so far as I can judge, Edgar's has gone very well – I've not seen him, but that's the comment. Archie [Sinclair, now Lord Thurso] has been seeing Hugh Gaitskell, & is still asking for *pacts*; Herbert is still stalling as hard as ever. I think they may try to get you to take Anglesey for *us* – they're so sure you could have won it; if its really finally & absolutely out (& I should fully approve if you so decided), I think you ought to see Clem at once & say so right away, before you see anyone else at all. Dear me, how exciting to think of your coming back to the House – I can't wait for the day.[24]

There is no evidence that the Labour Party actually thought of putting Megan forward as Labour candidate for Anglesey, since that would have meant ditching Cledwyn Hughes, a young politician who had scored a good win – although the idea might have occurred to such a cynical manipulator as Herbert Morrison. Megan would certainly not have been attracted; it would have led to painful encounters with former supporters. She must have told Philip firmly that it was 'absolutely out'.

When she returned from New York in March 1952 she did not commit herself to the 'plunge'. Philip tried to encourage her by telling her how greatly she would be welcomed in the Labour ranks. He wrote during a Commons debate in May:

While Ralph Glyn was slashing the Govt, one of our Whips leant over to me, & said 'How long have we got to wait for Megan?' And a Trade Unionist (Frank Tomney) said: 'Ah, if only we could get *her*!' in tones I might have used myself![25]

Through that summer, however, Megan was still not ready to make the final break with the Liberals. Attlee wrote in a letter to his brother: 'We lunched this week with Megan Lloyd George. . . . I wish that she would join us, but she thinks it her duty to try to keep the Liberal remnant away from the Tories.'[26]

In her home country, one man with whom Megan was friendly was Goronwy Roberts, a native of Bethesda, who had been Labour MP for Caernarvon since 1945. Philip wrote to her in July:

Last night Goronwy R., to whom I don't often speak, collared me in the Lobby, said he'd been talking to you, that you'd asked after me etc! (which I didn't believe). Then *I* asked after you; & he replied: 'She's *very* well, putting on weight, & thinking of joining the Party!' And he then proceeded at length to ask me to get Herbert to make things easy for you.[27]

In November, Megan made at least a partial decision. She wrote to the Liberal Association of Anglesey stating that she did not wish to be adopted as candidate again. 'I first came to Anglesey', she recalled, 'as the Radical daughter of a Radical leader.' She went on: 'I have latterly been disturbed by the pronounced tendency of the official Liberal Party to drift toward the Right.' Her conclusion was that for her to continue as prospective candidate would be 'neither fair to you nor right for me'. The Anglesey Liberals received this communication with great regret, though perhaps without much surprise. They sent a deputation to Brynawelon to persuade her to change her mind, but in vain.

Megan doubtless took this step for reasons of principle, but she may also have reckoned that it would be very difficult to beat Cledwyn after he had been the sitting member for a number of years. An Anglesey man by birth, he kept up a home in Holyhead and was there almost every weekend; he was proving himself to be as conscientious a constituency MP as Megan (and a more diligent letter-answerer). Besides, she did not want to fight him again. There had never been any animosity between them and they were now friends, as well as allies in the Parliament for Wales campaign. Sometimes, after he had spent the weekend at his home and she at hers, they met at Bangor station on Sunday evening to take the late train to Euston, and she invited him to share her thermos of soup.[28]

When her Anglesey letter was made public, it naturally led to speculation about whether – or when – she would be joining the Labour Party and emerging as a Labour candidate. The *Guardian* told its readers: 'She has broken with the Liberal Party but will make no comments on statements that she is joining Labour. This can surely only be tactful – or tactical coyness.' The press had become rather irritable over what the *Western Mail*, a few months earlier, had called her 'sphinx-like silence'. But the truth was that Megan had still not made up her mind.

One factor that deterred her was that, despite her attractive qualities and her popularity at Westminster, it might not be easy for her to secure a Labour seat. She saw herself emphatically as a Welsh MP and would have been very reluctant to settle for a seat in England or Scotland. Of the twenty-seven constituencies then held by Labour in Wales, some were in the gift of trade unions, including several which invariably sent a miner to Westminster; some, of course, were held by MPs who were younger than Megan or about the same age, and were unlikely to retire or die; some would regard her championship of Welsh self-government as an undesirable aberration; some had never been known to consider selecting a woman.

Another – and more important – deterrent factor was that the Labour Party between 1951 and 1955 presented a far from appealing picture. In the wake of the battle over the 1951 budget and the Health Service charges, Bevanites and Gaitskellites were fighting each other over a wide range of issues, and with a fury and venom seldom directed against the Tories. Megan, when in the House, had been on good personal terms with both Bevan and Gaitskell. She regarded Gaitskell as the right man to handle the economy, while admiring Bevan as the defender of the social services. She could not look forward to being obliged to label herself as either a Bevanite or a Gaitskellite, nor to making a judgement in doctrinal terms as to which man was a true Socialist. Yet her letters from (and presumably conversations with) Philip showed her that the factions were irreconcilably divided. By March 1952, if not sooner, he was committed to the Gaitskell side. With his last letter to Megan before she left New York, he enclosed a cutting to let her know that Cledwyn was being courted by the Bevanites, and wrote:

I wanted to send you the enclosed to show what the Member (the not very Honourable Member) for Anglesey is up to. I thought Nye wasn't dining him for nothing. Actually in the meeting the vote against them was 112 to 41 – the evening papers are calling it a smashing blow to the Bevanites, & a dramatic reassertion of Party leadership. It shows how unreal their talk has been; in fact, 41 was far too many for them, & 112 far too few for us, & I was thoroughly disgusted.[29]

In October, Labour had a particularly acrimonious conference at Morecambe – the conference at which Will Lawther, the Northumberland miners' leader and a stalwart of the Right, retorted to opponents with the elegant expression: 'Shut your gob!' The constituency delegates elected six Bevanites to the National Executive, ejecting Morrison and Dalton and rejecting Gaitskell. Gaitskell then made a speech declaring, 'It is time to end the attempt at mob rule by a group of frustrated journalists', and retailing an estimate that one-sixth of the delegates were Communists or Communist-inspired. An onlooker like Megan might well feel that if the allegation was true it was a sad state of affairs in a major party, and if it was not true Gaitskell was behaving irresponsibly by giving it currency. Philip's account was:

Morecambe has been foul. All the *real* members of the party are very harsh in their condemnation of Nye's tactics. . . . The organisers of the Party are aghast – they say there were anything up to 100 straight Communists in the hall. . . . Hinley Atkinson, the best, cleverest & gentlest of all Labour Party organisers, says Nye now deliberately stirs up dissent in every constituency party, & then talks about unity. Altogether, if you join now, you'll have to make a very careful statement. If you'd heard the pro-Nye speeches, you wd have been *horrified* – pernicious & disingenuous drip, including Harold Wilson.[30]

In February 1953 he wrote:

I think I've won the battle on Defence agst Mannie [Shinwell] – I say 'I' because I made the principal speech against him. . . . Jim G. [Griffiths] told me that they had a fantastically bad Natl Executive this morning . . . he had never seen such bad feeling or heard such bitter talk in the Party before. Its bad. And I'm afraid we haven't finished with it yet.[31]

Inevitably, all this brawling cost Labour a heavy price in public esteem. In May 1953 the Tories won the Labour seat of Sunderland South at a by-election; for the government to win a seat from the opposition was a man-bites-dog event. In another by-election next month at Abingdon, the Tory held the seat with an increased majority. This result was not unwelcome to the Gaitskellites, as the Labour candidate was the Bevanite Ted Castle, Barbara's husband. Philip commented:

George Deer [Labour MP for Newark], who is a sensible old thing, said, when I asked him what he thought of Abingdon: 'I'm glad of it; it will save us from another Morecambe!' I really agree with that. It wd have been disastrous if Ted C. had won. But what a situation when that is true![32]

Bevan and Gaitskell were not the only Labour leaders who detested each other; the whole party was pervaded by malice, calumny and intrigue. Morrison was scheming to depose Attlee from the leadership and secure it before Gaitskell could inherit it. Attlee, seventy in 1953, was staying on in order to dish Morrison. Megan had never been the sort of politician who derives zestful pleasure from personal in-fighting. In the Liberal Party she remained on amicable terms with a man like Hopkin Morris whose political outlook was far from her own. It was no wonder that she hesitated to join a party which, as described in Philip's letters and indeed in what she read in the newspapers, offered such unpleasant experiences.

Punitive intolerance was another unattractive feature of the Labour Party. Threats, warnings, demands for apologies and pledges of good behaviour and, in the last resort, expulsions were the traditional Labour methods of dealing with the dissenter or the rebel. In 1939

Megan had seen Cripps and Bevan expelled for their advocacy of the People's Front, which she had supported. Now, Bevan was repeatedly being called to account for disobeying the whips in the House, for inspiring 'a party within a party' and for articles in *Tribune*, the Bevanite weekly. The process culminated in March 1955 when Morrison and Gaitskell, with Philip's emphatic approval, tried to get Bevan expelled again and were only narrowly foiled.

A Radical could scarcely feel at home in a party with an arsenal of punitive sanctions. In 1950 the writer of a profile of Megan in the *Observer* had suggested that, if she ever changed her party, it would be to join Labour, and then added: 'But she would and could not remain inside it for long. Such an independent spirit as hers, reinforced by so powerful a Liberal tradition, could not be managed by Transport House.'[33] In 1952 the *Guardian*, commenting on her Anglesey decision, thought it probable that she was on her way into the Labour Party but doubted whether she would be happy in it – 'the discipline would irk her'.

We can be sure that all these considerations were in her mind during the three years of hesitation. She was, moreover, reluctant to give up all hope of the Liberal Party. In 1953 another effort was made to rally the Left in the party with the formation of the Radical Reform Group. The leading spirits were Dingle Foot, Desmond Banks and Peter Grafton. According to Banks, the party president, Philip Fothergill, thought that Megan could swing the party to the Left if only she exerted herself and made more speeches to local gatherings. Banks and Grafton went to lunch with her to persuade her to become active in the group. She expressed interest but did not commit herself. Banks had the impression that she would probably decide to join the Labour Party, but still had an open mind.[34]

5

During this period, Philip Noel-Baker was cherishing a scheme which, he thought, could ease Megan conveniently into the Labour ranks and back into the House of Commons. His idea was that she should become Labour MP for Wrexham.

Wrexham, in Denbighshire (now Clwyd), was an industrial town and the centre of the North Wales coalfield. The constituency was a safe Labour seat; at the 1951 election the majority was over 14,000. The miners were the backbone of the Labour movement, and the social and political scene would have been familiar to anyone from the

South Wales valleys. A feature more typical of North Wales, however, was that – although Wrexham was only a few miles from the English border – many people spoke Welsh and there was a strong national consciousness. Megan, clearly, could make herself at home in Wrexham. Geographically, too, it was conveniently placed between London and Criccieth.

The MP, Robert Richards, had won the seat in 1922 and, with a couple of breaks, held it ever since. Respected for his learning, he was at work in the 1950s on a history of medieval Wales. He was a friend of Huw T. Edwards, a remarkable man who was secretary of the Transport and General Workers' Union in North Wales, was influential in the Labour movement and was also a poet and a figure in Welsh cultural life. More than anyone else, according to Glyn Tegai Hughes, Edwards bridged the national, Radical and Labour traditions; Hughes adds that he knew everybody and was 'a supreme operator'. Edwards knew Megan well and was eager to get her into the Labour Party.

By 1951 Richards was sixty-seven years old and his health was fragile; he had been obliged to go into hospital during the election campaign. It occurred to Philip that he would be willing to go to the House of Lords and that Megan would be able to step into his shoes. It does not seem, however, that Philip ever asked Richards directly whether he would agree to this plan.

Still more curiously, Philip airily ignored a vital procedural factor. If and when Richards retired, there would of course be a by-election. The Wrexham Labour Party would hold a selection conference, and there would undoubtedly be a number of applicants for such a safe seat. Under the party rules, anyone hoping for selection would have to be a member of the Labour Party. Thus the right course for Megan was to begin by joining the party so that she could be in a position to be selected as the by-election candidate.

Philip had entered politics at a time when procedures were more flexible. Quite possibly, he did not hold a party card when, as a professor with a League of Nations background, he was first invited to stand for Parliament in 1924. It is also understandable if Megan took his word that party membership did not matter, because her own career had been in the Liberal Party whose customs were always rather informal, and also because Philip had been on Labour's National Executive Committee for years and presumably knew how the machinery worked. Nevertheless, there was no ambiguity about the rule. It had been in force since the 1930s and had been explicitly codified when the constitution was overhauled at the 1953 conference (which Philip attended). Clause 9, sub-section 7, laid down: 'No candidate shall be selected who . . . is not an individual member of the Party and, if eligible, of a trade union affiliated to the TUC.'

The first mention of Wrexham in Philip's letters was in November 1951, when Attlee was compiling the list of resignation honours to which a departing Prime Minister was entitled.

Oh, dear, how I want you here! How I want you with me *always*! I shan't survive long in this morgue without you, so *please* arrange things with C. about Wrexham very soon! I must end by saying that the more I think of it, the more certain I am that this is going to be a very big *forward* step in your career.[35]

In June 1952 Megan went to Wrexham to open a bazaar for the Parliament for Wales campaign. Philip wrote to her in a hasty note (he was expecting Irene to come in within ten minutes): 'I'm so glad Wrexham was a smashing success – I'm sure it always *will* be so.'[36] In October, Megan apparently had a talk with someone who encouraged her to pursue Wrexham. Philip wrote:

I'm so very happy about your news tonight. . . . Don't forget (a) that I told you it wd be so, & that the miners wd be crazy to get you; (b) that I first said 'Wrexham' to Jim G. in a very firm & final voice, & told him we sh'd be *mad* not to fix it.[37]

By this time, someone had been talking, and one of the Sunday papers floated the possibility that Megan might be the next MP for Wrexham. The local paper, the *Wrexham Leader*, pursued the story but could get no hard news from anyone concerned. Under the headline 'Elusive Lady', the *Leader* wrote:

With the maddening yet engaging elusiveness of her sex, Lady Megan remains as the Pimpernel of Welsh politics. . . . Will she justify the predictions that she is Leftward bound and ready to toss her bonnet over the Socialist windmill? And what of Robert Richards? Over him too there hangs the shadow of an enigma. Does he mean to retire from active politics?[38]

Four weeks later, the paper elicited a definite statement from Richards: he regarded the constituency as 'a sacred trust' and had no intention of retiring. That, the *Leader* decided, was the end of the Lady Megan story – 'No longer is her name linked with Wrexham.'[39] But speculation continued that she might become the Labour candidate for one or another Welsh seat, and the *Western Mail* made inquiries at Transport House, the Labour headquarters. A spokesman said that he was nonplussed by the rumours, in view of the obvious fact that

Megan could not be a candidate until she joined the party.[40]

In January 1954 Megan made another Parliament for Wales speech in Wrexham – a 'lively and dramatic speech', according to the *Leader* – and it seems that she visited the town again in July. There was no report in the *Leader*, but Philip sent her a note: 'This is only to wish you a very happy & restful journey, & a very successful time in Wrexham which I'm sure is already busily counting its chicken! May it soon be hatched!'[41] In November she had a visit from 'a couple' from Wrexham, and he wrote to her:

It was lovely to hear about your couple from Wrexham. I had a few words with Bob the other day; I must say it seemed to me almost impossible that he should go on after the next Election. Anyway, he has grown *very* much older; he moves about very slowly; & I should be surprised if, with his present level of activity, he would *want* another five years in the treadmill. No one will *want* to turn him out; but if they knew that you were available, I feel quite certain that they would not let him stand in the way. They could certainly find some method of easing him out gently – H.T. [Edwards], for example, could certainly get Clem to give him a peerage. And I should think that a promise of a peerage would be very attractive to Bob, even if it comes from a man who isn't yet firmly in No. 10. I think Bob will regard the prospect as very good, & good enough to accept on. Certainly Clem can be counted on to do *his* part, if there's any hope of *your* coming back here. . . .

But there's an earlier problem which we mustn't neglect – the timing. I still think it would be much wiser to do it before the Election comes in sight, or any question of a seat has arisen. It will be far better in every way if you can say you haven't decided about a seat, but hate the Tories, & if 6 months can intervene before you take the plunge. That sh'd be easy – I don't believe at *all* in a Spring Election.[42]

Philip was proposing, so far as one can get it clear, that Megan should make a general statement that she hated the Tories (a well-known fact since 1929), then wait six months before actually joining the Labour Party, and then decide about a possible seat. Meanwhile, Bob Richards would be announcing his retirement at the next election, on the promise of a peerage. At the end of this stately course of events, Megan would be invited to succeed him.

Actually, Richards had not been asked whether he wanted a peerage, and according to Keith Wolferton, who was party chairman in Wrexham at the time, he had no interest in it and would have declined it.[43] Churchill had just reached his eightieth birthday and was preparing to retire, handing over to Eden; and, although it did not necessarily follow that a new Prime Minister meant a general election, it was a fair guess that Eden would call one, as indeed he did. Thus a spring election in 1955 was a strong possibility. With the Tories still giving the voters cause for satisfaction, Attlee was unlikely to win that election and be in a position to confer peerages. In other words, every step in Philip's calculation was based on a fallacy.

The scheme, in any case, was never put to the test. Richards suffered a heart attack and died on 22 December 1954. Next day, Philip gave Megan his considered advice – that she should, in calm confidence, await an offer from Wrexham:

1. I don't think that you or any intimate associate (e.g. me) should try to do anything to *provoke* an offer; that might come to be known, & might be misinterpreted. . . . In any case, you wdn't dream of doing this, I know. . . .

2. But there are at least 5 people, unless I am much mistaken, who will try to move in the matter, & probably very quickly: Clem A., Herbert, Morgan P., Goronwy (first of all), H.T. You might also add Cliff Protheroe (who will run the Selection Conference) & Ungoed [Sir Lynn Ungoed-Thomas, Labour MP and Solicitor-General in Attlee's government]. I should think they have all already been on the warpath & I should be much surprised if you haven't already heard from Goronwy & H.T. Anyway, I'm very certain you will in the *early* future.

3. They will want to know your general reaction, in order to take early action themselves – & early action may be important. Nothing *formal* can happen for *weeks* – perhaps the middle of February before the Selection Conference happens. . . . So you have time to think.

3. [a mistake in numbering] It is, of course, *possible* that they will say that you ought to have been a member of the party before; I mean, the doctrinaire Labourites. But in fact the *rule* doesn't apply to *adopted* candidates, only to people on the *Panel*.

4. It wd be far nicer if you cd be a member, & have a General Election without being a candidate, & then come in at a By-Election. This wd disarm all criticism. . . . But things don't happen as we want them. Wrexham is the perfect seat for you. . . . Therefore, I don't believe you sh'd miss the chance.

5. And of course, a By-Election gives you the chance of doing the *maximum* amount of harm to the Tories, & getting the maximum message to the Liberals. . . . It will really be the opening shot in the General Election itself. . . .

6. Of course, it's hell for you – but that will be true whenever it comes. And if you can't *bear* the House, you can leave at the General Election, & become a Peeress (!) . . .

My firm conclusion is that you must prepare to say Yes. We'll argue it out, & perhaps you'll convince me – but I doubt it.

Perhaps the most extraordinary paragraph in this letter was no. 6; Megan was eagerly looking forward to getting back into the House of Commons and would never have agreed to go to the House of Lords. But what Philip was telling her in paragraph 3 (the second one) was entirely misleading. The rule requiring party membership was absolutely definite and said nothing about the panel (a list of possible candidates compiled at party headquarters). Philip's last sentence indicates that Megan was dubious about his advice, and well she may have been. The 'offer' that he anticipated was a fantasy. People like Attlee, Morrison and Morgan Phillips knew perfectly well that she could not be selected without being a party member. No one tried to 'move' on her behalf – least of all Cliff Prothero, regional organiser for Wales, whose duty was to be completely impartial in any selection process. In any case, even if she had been a party member and had been among the contestants, her prospects of victory would have been uncertain. Walter Monslow, an MP who was a native of Wrexham and spoke to the *Leader* after Richards's death, expressed a hope that the new MP would be a local man, adding that there were 'a number of men of outstanding ability'.

Still, Megan did have a talk with Huw T. Edwards, and Philip remained convinced that she would, in American parlance, be drafted for Wrexham. He wrote on 13 January 1955:

I'm *very* happy about your talk with H.T. I think everything is as good as possible. If they *force* this on you, well & good, & it will, as you say, be right. If they don't, well, E. Flint stands ready, & will be cast-iron for you.

This letter is completely mystifying. East Flint, the neighbouring constituency to Wrexham, was represented by Eirene White (daughter of Thomas Jones, whom we met as one of Lloyd George's secretaries). She was seven years younger than Megan, had been an MP only since 1950, was on the National Executive of the party and cannot have had the faintest intention of retiring from politics.

At Wrexham there was a comic episode. A man named Collins, who was a fairground owner and a popular local character, made it known that he would like to be the next Labour MP and was prepared to finance the whole by-election campaign. As he was not a party member, his bid was met with dismissive smiles.[44]

Following the normal procedure, the executive committee of the Wrexham Labour Party drew up a shortlist for the selection conference. There were four names, all of local men. One of them, James Idwal Jones, was headmaster of the secondary school at Rhos-llanerchrug (a few miles from Wrexham), had joined the party in 1918 and was a brother of the Labour MP for Merioneth. On 17 February he was duly selected, and at the by-election on 17 March he held the seat with a satisfactory majority.

6

By this time, Megan had made up her mind: she must join the Labour Party without delay. She would be too late to find a seat in the general election expected in 1955, but at least she would be qualified for subsequent by-elections.

Her move was held up for two irritating reasons. All the national newspapers were on strike for five weeks during March and early April, depriving her of the publicity that she naturally sought for her announcement. The other hindrance was that no one in the Labour Party could think of anything but Bevan's defiance of the leadership – on 3 March, the Bevanites abstained in a Commons vote on the issue of the possible use of nuclear weapons – and the consequent attempt to expel him. Megan wrote to Attlee to consult him about her timing, and he replied:

I read your suggestion with very great interest, and had arranged that Frank Soskice should talk with Dingle on the general proposition. You will, I am sure, realise that for the last week or so we have been rather taken up over the activities of your volatile compatriot from Ebbw Vale.

I rather gathered from your note that you considered that a longish time would have to elapse in preparation. We certainly did not mean that your joining should be a hole and corner affair. Obviously, it would receive a very great deal of publicity and we should certainly welcome it. I think there is a great deal in the question of timing.

Frank is to have another talk with Dingle in order to clear up any misunderstandings, but I must say that I thought you have taken an unnecessarily gloomy view. Perhaps that is our mistake. Could I see you some time soon?[45]

On 5 April, Churchill resigned and Eden became Prime Minister. In a broadcast on 15 April he announced that there would be an election, with polling on 26 May.

Megan's statement, in the form of a long and carefully drafted letter to Attlee, was published on 26 April. She reviewed the events of her political life, including the 'betrayal of the League over Manchuria, Abyssinia, Spain and Czechoslovakia', to make a crushing indictment of the Tory record. The salient passages of the letter were:

I have kept out of politics as I felt I had a responsibility to see the petition for a Parliament for Wales through its concluding stages. But now that there is an election and the fight is on, no one can remain neutral. . . . It is only in the Labour Party that I can be true to the Radical tradition. . . . The official Liberal Party seems to me to have lost all touch with the Radical tradition that inspired it. . . . The Labour Party exists to promote social justice and carry further our progress toward a genuine welfare state. The Tories are the party of privilege. . . . There is a great gulf between the thinking of Tories and Radicals; there is a common attitude of mind and thought between Radicals and Labour.

Attlee made a suitable reply, tactfully recalling the Lloyd George reforms of 1909-11 and the Yellow Book. Radical readers were assured: 'Our Socialism has not been something exotic, but the natural evolution of the British desire for freedom.'

Two days after the exchange of letters appeared in the press, Megan's secretary forwarded to Transport House a list of thirty-seven constituencies where she had been asked to speak in the coming election campaign. Within another few days, the Labour headquarters received seventy-one requests (there was some overlap). The Honiton Labour Party could not find Megan's address and wrote through her brother Gwilym, now Home Secretary in the Tory government; he cheerfully forwarded the letter.

The requests came from every part of Britain – from St Ives and from Falmouth and Camborne, from Caithness and Sutherland and from Ross and Cromarty. Among the MPs or candidates who sought Megan's aid were Desmond Donnelly in Pembroke, Barbara Castle in Blackburn, Fenner Brockway in Eton and Slough, Eirene White in East Flint and Edgar Granville in Eye. In most cases, the letter of invitation explained that the constituency had a strong Radical tradition and that the Liberals had polled six or eight thousand votes in 1950, but there were some variations. Melton claimed to have a large Methodist population. The Northfield division of Birmingham was full of Quakers (George Cadbury, the chocolate millionaire and philanthropist, had been a friend of Megan's father). Edinburgh, mysteriously, revealed 'a great affinity with the Welsh'. Wandsworth Central, whose candidate was Patricia Llewellyn-Davies, included the street where Megan had lived before the age of five. Ardwick (Manchester) contained Lloyd George's birthplace. From Rossendale, Tony Greenwood wrote with disarming ingenuity: 'Lloyd George's mother lived in Rossendale and L.G. was *very nearly* born there.'[46]

The Liberals, still in the doldrums, were again running only just over a hundred candidates, and an appeal to the Liberal vote was Labour's only hope of victory. In the absence of any big issues, reporting of the campaign concentrated on this factor. A *Guardian* headline was 'In Search of the Lost Tribe of Liberals'. A *Times* reporter in East Anglia wrote that the result in several marginal seats would depend on 'the Liberal casting vote'.

Megan was ready to take on a nation-wide speaking tour, something she had never done in any previous election. Her programme was drawn up partly to meet her own wishes and partly on the advice of Labour's strategists. Setting out from Brynawelon on 11 May, she spoke for her friend Goronwy Roberts in Caernarvon, in the marginal Conway constituency and in Merioneth. Next day she addressed three meetings for Tudor Watkins in the sprawling Brecon and Radnor constituency. On 13 May she spoke at a big meeting in Cardiff and also in Barry. After a weekend rest, she spoke on 16 May to big meetings in Manchester and Liverpool; on 17 May at Bradford, Halifax and Brighouse; on 18 May at Luton and Biggleswade. Then she took time out to prepare for a television broadcast in which she appeared on a panel with Morrison, Gaitskell and Callaghan on 20 May. On the following day she went to Portsmouth, Eastleigh and Southampton. On 23 May she spoke in Lewisham, Woolwich and – an invitation she could not have turned down – Wandsworth Central. On the last two days before polling, she was at Norwich, Ipswich and six other places in East Anglia. One of her meetings was in the curiously unpredictable constituency of South-West Norfolk, which produced one of the few Labour gains in the election.

Clearly she was in sparkling form. In Penmaenmawr, when a mischievous questioner asked if she would change parties again in the event of a Liberal revival, she answered: 'That kind of exercise can be undertaken only by Sir Winston.' In Liverpool she gave what the *Guardian* called 'an impressive display of old-fashioned and Merlin-like witchery' and told her audience: 'They call me the wild woman of Wales.' She explained her political change easily: 'The Liberal Party left me, not the other way about.' Part of her speech was a defence of the nationalised industries, especially the railways, by reference to their rundown condition in private hands: 'You should come to Wales and see some of the rolling-stock which nationalisation had to take over. Queen Victoria must have been travelling on her honeymoon on it.'

Violet Bonham-Carter was also not a candidate, having chosen not to try again at Colne Valley, and was on a tour of her own. At Kendal on 16 May she attacked the Labour Party for its 'schizophrenic caterwaulings' and remarked: 'The Labour Party is bursting at the seams and, to judge from her speeches, Lady Megan is not going to stitch up the seams but to tear them wider apart.' Then she invaded Anglesey, where she said that the 'common aim' was the defeat of Socialism and the way to achieve it was to vote Liberal. Voters should beware of the Labour appeal – 'the hook is baited with the Radical tradition, dangling between free teeth and spectacles.' Without referring to Megan by name, she declared: 'You won't find me scrambling on to any bandwagon, whether it is painted red or blue. I hold fast to the Liberal faith which is the heritage my father left me.'[47]

This was more or less what might have been expected, but an unexpected intervention in the campaign came from Frances, the Dowager Countess Lloyd George. In a letter to the Tory candidate for Farnham, which included Churt, she explained that she was not a Conservative and was 'less and less interested in party politics', but had decided after much careful thought that Eden was the right person 'to lead the country in the critical decisions that lie ahead in the international field'. Her husband, she said, would have approved, as he had the greatest admiration for Eden's 'ability, integrity and selflessness'.[48]

Megan's contribution to the Labour television broadcast was to rebut the idea that there was 'broad agreement' between the parties, and the voters had only to judge which of them would be more competent in implementing generally accepted policies. However, this was just what a great many voters, encouraged by the commentators, thought. The election of 1955 was the quietest and least contentious that anyone could remember, and only 76 per cent of the voters went to the polls, compared with 82 per cent in 1951.

The result was a clear, if not overwhelming, victory for the Tories. With a net gain of twenty-four seats, they had a fairly comfortable majority in the House. The Liberals still had six seats – the same six.

Five days after the election, Philip wrote to Megan:

I hope you will do absolutely *nothing*, & not even *think* of the Election or of politics, for a long time to come. You have been under a tremendous strain, & you have had a superb success, & you must restore your strength, & I hope enjoy the infinite pleasure of repose after effort.[49]

# CHAPTER TWELVE

# The End of the Affair

## 1

Pursuing the thread of Megan's political dilemmas, we have gone ahead of the course of her personal life. In the manner of a Shakespeare play, the drama of her relationship with Philip was mirrored by a sub-plot. It concerned Ellen Roberts.

While Megan was in America in 1951-2, Ellen fell in love with a man named Miron Starzecki, and he with her. Polish by birth, he had served in a Polish squadron of the RAF; at one time he was an officers' mess steward and acquired an outstanding skill in mixing cocktails.[1] His first name was originally Marion, which is a man's name in Polish, but when he came to England he found that it was a woman's name and the nearest equivalent was Myron, which he spelt Miron. After the war he became a cabinet-maker, and in this line of work his skill was equally outstanding. In this capacity he was employed by Robin Carey Evans, who had a flat in Battersea. Megan decided to have her furniture repaired and renovated while she was away, and Robin recommended Miron as 'a good worker and a decent chap'.[2] Philip, who was keeping an eye on Megan's flat during her absence, found that the furniture-repairer was proposing marriage to the house-keeper, but Ellen had doubts. Writing to New York, he explained to Megan:

I think she is unhappy about her future plans. She says . . . that, since she is to marry Myron (she talked as if it was settled & soon) she would have to leave you. Which she couldn't bear to do. Indeed, if it were a choice between the two Ms, in very sooth, I really don't know whom she would choose. . . . But she will certainly try & think up something else, I believe – She may have defects, but her departure would be a veritable disaster & not least to me.[3]

Back in London, Megan told Ellen that there was no need for her to leave the flat. She liked Miron and approved of him as a husband for Ellen.

Then Ellen became pregnant. The baby was due in April 1953, and once again Ellen feared that she would have to leave Megan. On 10 March (Megan was at Brynawelon) Philip wrote:

I've spoken to Ellen on the telephone, & told her I hope that she will be very, very happy; that she mustn't worry about anything; that she must concentrate on trying to keep strong & well. . . . Ellen wept, & said it was an unbelievable relief when she saw you; she had evidently been under a fearful strain.

Ellen was not the only one who was under a strain, for her approaching motherhood reawakened all Megan's regrets about the experience that she had missed. Philip tried to comfort her with a hasty note: 'This is only to say that the loveliest, most perfect & most sacred vision of my life is of you as mother of our babies. All Heaven is there – & I know the tragedy in *my* heart as well as yours.'[4]

The baby was a girl, and was given the Polish name of Zosia. She was born on 20 April, two days before Megan's fifty-first birthday.[5] A month later, Philip came to the flat and was introduced to Zosia. Carried away by emotion, he donated a bar of chocolate (to the baby, apparently) and had nothing to eat when he had to travel to Derby in a train without a restaurant car. But he wrote: 'It was wonderful being with you this morning . . . & seeing E. & the angelic little baby. It made me, perhaps more than ever, long for what would be the happiness beyond all happiness, which now can never be.'[6]

Miron, Ellen and Zosia went to live with a friend in Southend, but they stayed there for only three months. Megan invited Ellen to return, and the family of three lived in the spare room of the flat. In the next winter, Philip wrote: 'Ellen sounds wonderfully glad to be back in No. 13. . . . She has evidently had a lot of worry, & said to me that the thought of coming back to you had been her only beacon thro' the trials of recent months.'[7] It was in Number 13 that Zosia took her first steps and learned her first words in English and Welsh (she never learned to speak Polish). Megan became intensely attached to her and loved playing with her; in effect, the little girl had two mothers. Taking their cue from Megan, friends treated Zosia as a favourite. Dingle Foot, Zosia still remembers, regularly gave her a new doll.

Philip, meanwhile, had troubles of his own. Always anxious about his health, he was haunted by the fear that he would never complete the big book, *The Arms Race*, on which he was working. After his bad bout of flu in Greece in January 1952, he had another attack while in Paris in September, with a temperature of 103. The French doctor who was called in had attended Léon Blum and told Philip: '*Il est mort dans mes bras*' – scarcely a reassuring remark. He rallied to go to the Morecambe conference, but then had a relapse (the Bevanite successes may have contributed) and had to cancel a walking trip in the Welsh mountains and a visit to Brynawelon. In January 1953 he was still not fully recovered, and went to a small hotel in Devon to convalesce. 'I have to be very careful here,' he warned Megan, 'the place is very small, & everybody knows everything, & the telephone exchange is run by the Post Office.'[8] Back in London, he suffered for going out to phone her on a cold night:

It was horrid getting a sudden attack in the Call Box last night; I think it must, after all, have been a chill, for it recurred several times when I got cold; I spent this morning in bed with a hot water-bottle.[9]

Insomnia was another recurrent problem. He told Megan:

I've been in a bad physical & mental condition. . . . I can't sleep properly; I take drugs to make me, & far too much of them; that reduces my mental alertness, tho' perhaps less than not sleeping; in any case, I'm slow & pretty ineffective, & I get far less done than I used to.[10]

His dilemma was one that any insomniac will recognise. If he tried to manage without the sleeping-pills, he lay awake until early morning. If he took strong pills, he slept heavily – 'but I feel like death; thick in the head, no energy, & finding it difficult to settle to work'.[11]

He was in his sixties now, and had driven himself hard all his life. But he had to keep up with Megan. While in Canada, she had been examined by her niece's husband, Dr Macmillan; he reported with astonishment that her physical condition was that of a young woman. Nevertheless, another of Philip's worries was that she might fall ill. 'I should go gradually but surely mad, & anything might happen to me.'[12]

An anxiety with a real and serious cause was about the health of his grandchildren, Edward (born in 1949) and Martin (born in 1952). Not only were they delicate, and liable to suffer severely whenever they had a cold or any infection, but they were not developing at a normal pace. 'The babies are really very backward, compared to everybody else's,' Philip admitted. In March 1953 he wrote:

After the House, I went to see my Edward – poor man, both he & Martin have bad colds, & pink-eye, a beastly thing which hurts. . . . Its such bad luck for Edward – the *third* time this term he's had to stay away from school. He's *so* backward, & looks so frail & ill – & it makes me love him so much more; so much that it really hurts a lot.[13]

In August, he thought he had found the source of the trouble:

Yesterday was a difficult & rackety day, owing to lots of things, but principally to the dread discovery that Francis, Ann & Edward (& probably Martin too) are all the victims of dread internal parasites that have held them back, & that are reducing them to miserably unhealthy & nervy creatures now. (Poor Ann broke down the other day when E. was coughing all night with his cold, said that she hated the two babies, & wished she might never see them again – nonsense, of course, but her floods of tears showed how far the parasites have sapped her strength.) Personally, I'm delighted at the discovery, & the promise of the young doctor to cure them all permanently within 3 months; I've believed for a long time that E. was so afflicted, but cd get F & A to do nothing about it.[14]

The parasite theory was a fantasy, and it is hard to believe that any doctor would have credited it. The fact was that, by a malign coincidence, both the boys were Down's syndrome children. Again, it is difficult to understand why this condition was not diagnosed and explained to the parents soon after the children were born, but it appears from Philip's account that the first to recognise it was their mother, and probably this was the cause of her floods of tears.

When Philip realised that his grandsons would always be in need of care, their plight brought out the best in his character. He could be self-centred and demanding, but he could also be tenderly compassionate and he never shirked what he felt to be a duty. Ann could not cope with the problem, and Francis, who had lost his seat in the House in 1950, was trying without much success to make a living by journalism and by running a small features agency. The grandparents often had to shoulder the burden of looking after the children, and Philip – despite his own insecure health and the multiple demands on his time – carried more of it than Irene. In August 1953 he took Edward for a holiday at a riverside hotel at Moulsford-on-Thames. Edward got a feverish cold with a touch of tonsillitis, it was difficult to phone Megan, and on top of everything Chuter Ede, ex-Home Secretary and a notorious Labour Party bore, turned up at the hotel. Yet Philip wrote: 'E. is so good & sweet & amusing that I never get tired of being with him.'[15]

2

The story of the long love affair between Megan and Philip, as depicted in his letters, is a story of interludes of intense happiness punctuated by quarrels and resentments. We should not discount or minimise the happiness; it must have been rewarding enough to keep the relationship going despite the cost in pain and frustration. Although the periods that they could spend together were brief – generally a few hours, sometimes a day or a weekend, seldom a week – they left treasured memories. In the aftermath of a meeting a letter sometimes regretted that it had gone sour, but more often expressed delighted gratitude.

Much of the quarrelling was caused when a hoped-for opportunity to meet did not come to fruition – because of an engagement that either he or she could not break, or because the risks were too great, or sometimes because of sheer misunderstanding. When a meeting was possible and Philip did not make himself free, Megan was ready to accuse him of selfishness or cowardice. Some of his commitments (such as the Anglo-Swiss Society) were sentimental rather than really important, and seemed to show that he did not give her the priority she deserved; there was also the suspicion that his unavoidable appointment was with another woman. In any case, their spheres of activity or interest did not always overlap. Philip would no more have missed the Commonwealth Games than Megan would have missed the Eisteddfod. When she was not an MP and was involved in the Parliament for Wales campaign she spent less time in London, so when she was there she was infuriated if she found that he was going to be in Derby, Paris or Geneva.

Had they been married, they could, like other couples with many responsibilities and full diaries, have gone off in opposite directions – she to Swansea, he to Stuttgart – and joined each other to relax at their shared base. It would be rash to claim that a marriage between Philip and Megan would have been serene and free from quarrels, but the quarrels that did occur arose because they were not married – or, rather, because he was married to someone else. As a woman who had earned respect in her public life, Megan could only feel that the role of the mistress, with its requirements of dependence and concealment, was humiliating. He, on the other hand, felt that she failed to allow for a married man's difficulties. He wrote on 24 February 1953:

The idea that you're not the most important thing in the world to me, that you're not *all* the world to me, is so grotesque that I can't really believe that *you really* believe it; but that does not make it less hateful that you should believe it, on the surface, enough to make you hard & resentful & unkind. My angel, on Saturday morning I just *couldn't* ring up before a quarter to twelve. Don't you understand that when you're in the house with other people it may be *impossible*? . . . If there were anything in the world that I could do, to make you understand that you were all wrong, & that I love you & you only, above everything & beyond everything, I wd do it. If you *want* me in sack-cloth and ashes, well, I am – in any degree you desire.

In the summer of this year, the emotional clouds predominated over the sunshine. The birth of Zosia inspired bitter thoughts of what she had been denied; it was at this time that she reproached him for his failure to get a divorce from Irene and marry her before the war, and that he wrote the letters, attempting to excuse his conduct, which were quoted in chapter 6. Evidently there were some painful scenes. He began his long letter of 19 July by saying, 'I have never been so unhappy as I have in the last three days', and admitted on page 6: 'The way I talked on Friday was cruel & wrong & unjust.'

By the autumn, everything that could be said had been said, they were still lovers, and probably there was a sense of having cleared the air. They had a day together which went well: 'Our day yesterday was lovely; I adored our lunch & the Everest film, & finding you at the Dentists', & making tea, & *afterwards*.'[16] In November they spent a weekend at Raspit which must also have been successful, for Philip wrote some weeks later:

Last night as I lay awake, I went over every detail of our last visit to Raspit, & longed for another visit soon. Thinking of the last made me so *very* happy; it was so perfect & complete. I kiss you as I did then.[17]

In December he had to go to Achmetaga again, but his farewell letter shows that the spell of happiness endured to the end of the year:

My most beloved, its 2 o'clock, & I've not begun to pack! . . . This is only a scrap to wish you the loveliest Xmas ever, & to tell you how happy I have been all these weeks with you, & how I hate to leave you now. I have never felt so very close to you as now. . . . I shall be thinking of you & adoring you every minute till I hold you in my arms again. May it be very, very soon.[18]

However, when he returned from Greece in January 1954, Irene came with him. When Megan wanted to see him, he had to tell her that it was impossible. She was furious, and he wrote:

My angel, tonight was really anguish. It isn't always – no, I won't say that, for you would only twist it. It was so agonizing that I think I shan't sleep at all. . . . If you had come up, I c'dn't possibly have had the chance of seeing you on Saturday or Sunday evening; I *never* can when I'm not alone. . . . Do you think it is because I don't want to? . . . I won't write more, because I only want to say loving things. Come soon, & give me a chance. I've spent half an hour reading the news on the tape from Berlin in the hope that it would bring me back to normal, but it hasn't diverted my thoughts by a hair's breadth. They are all of you, & all of them deeply loving, but desperately sad.[19]

Before amity could be restored, Megan injured herself by a fall and was unable to leave Brynawelon. It was a hard winter; the pipes burst inside and outside Philip's house, 'there were floods all over the place', and his only water supply was in the basement, so that he had to carry a bucket up seventy-six steps to his bedroom. Ellen was having similar problems in Megan's flat. In March, Philip was due to speak at meetings at Bangor and Caernarvon, but this was just the time when Megan was planning a holiday at Malaga – 'basking on Franco soil', as he put it accusingly. Another suggestion also led to nothing:

I always think the Midland, Birmingham, very nice & comfortable. . . . There's a Midland Hotel in Manchester, too, equally comfortable & well-run. I have to be there on Saturday & Sunday, March 6th & 7th, & I cd also be there on Friday, Mar 5th, if *you* could be? Haven't you an engagement that will take you there? Can't you make one?[20]

Considering that the bars and dining-rooms of this type of hotel were always crowded, and Megan was so often photographed as to be almost inevitably recognised, this idea was in strange contrast to Philip's usual obsession with secrecy and bears witness to his impatience. In fact, they did not meet between December and late March.

Troubles were coming in battalions. In March, Edward underwent an operation. After fetching him home from the hospital, Philip wrote: 'He's not well yet, & has been thoroughly pulled down by the anaesthetic, the shock & the pain.' Francis was selected for Swindon, a Labour seat, but Ann was refusing to go there with him. A few months earlier, Philip had suspected that Tony Crosland, the Don Juan of the Labour Party, had his eye on Ann. In June the storm broke:

Ann has had lots of anxieties about Edward & Martin, & she can't find a house for them to move to, & she's been working too hard. Anyway, out of the blue on Friday she told F. that she was sick of it all, & of him; that she was absolutely resolved to leave him for good & all; that she wdn't go near Swindon at any price; that she hated politics & hated Greece, & that they had nothing at all in common. To show she meant business, she went away to an unknown destination on Saturday. . . . I shrewdly suspect she's been seeing Tony Crosland.[21]

Just when this happened, Philip had to defend himself against fresh accusations from Megan. On 16 June, the day after the letter quoted above, he wrote:

I feel that I'm living thro' a nightmare. Do what I can, I'm unable to make you understand that my difficulties when I'm not alone are *immense*, & that I *can't* go beyond a certain limit, or I shall run into dangers as well as difficulties. . . . I can't make you believe that I want to give my whole life to you, & that my only happiness is with you, & that I can't *bear* it when you won't believe that. . . . My beloved, can't you believe that I only live for you? Try, try – or it may do such grievous harm.

She came to London and they were able to spend two nights together, but the wrangling continued and caused him to write:

My beloved, why should we have these misunderstandings? Don't you understand that *all* my heart is yours, & always has been? . . . Won't you believe that I dream every night of being married to you, & having your babies all round me all the time? . . . Don't you think that I understand all that you have wanted from the bottom of my soul, & that, as I said to you, I have a deep & frightful sense of guilt, whenever I think that I'm to blame. . . . Is that intelligible? I hope so, because I must now go & telephone you . . .[22]

To make matters worse, Megan – who had been addressing meetings in South Wales – had gone to stay with her old friend from the 1920s, Geoffrey Crawshay, at his house near Abergavenny. In order to reach her, Philip had been obliged to speak to Crawshay, and had pretended to be a reporter from the *Liverpool Post*. This letter continues:

G.C.'s voice sounded very hostile. . . . He gave me the number where you were dining, but I think he didn't dare *not* to, as I was the *Liverpool Post*. What has he got to be hostile about, I should like to know? . . . Of course, I'm absolutely *green* with jealousy; can you really ask me why? . . . It's absolute *rot* for you to say he was before me. I loved you before you were born, before I ever saw you – I knew you wd happen sometime, & I knew the moment you did. I ante-date them all, & don't you damned well ever forget it, or say anything so foolish again.

He demanded that Megan should send him a 'memorandum' – their codeword for a long letter – but she did not. This drove him to further reproaches:

Yesterday in the country, a whole day of leisure . . . nothing to do all day but talk about marriage to aspiring suitors whose hopes grow more vivid as each encouraging year & visit goes by – & yet could you spare five minutes to send *me* a memorandum? . . . Not a line; not even a symbolic but infinitely precious X could you send. If you'd sent an X, I should have known that it meant that thro' long disuse of the practice, you'd simply forgotten how to write, but were quite prepared, in a friendly spirit, to make your mark, like other illiterates. But no. And then you talk about equality of sexes! . . . I'm very near going back over to black fury at once. Don't you realise that you're spending that weekend is straining & testing me to the very limit? [23]

In the same letter he gave the latest bad news about Francis and Ann. Ann had left home and was seeing a lawyer about a divorce. She had taken Martin with her, but now she said that she could not cope and dumped him on Francis. The little boy was indeed in need of skilled care: 'He's gone back to having constant fits, going blue till he terrifies you; its very dangerous.' With both the boys on his hands, Francis had to hire two nurses – an expense that he could not afford.

Megan was going for a holiday to Majorca ('Franco soil' again). Always averse to flying, she travelled by train and ship. She spent a day with Robin at Lloret del Mar, where he was staying with a group of friends, and he escorted her to catch the ship at Barcelona, where she found that there had been a muddle over the reservations and she had to spend the night on deck. Philip sent his sympathy, but added that Thomas Cook's had always been inefficient. He went to Berne for an athletic event. Then they would meet in Paris and stay at the St Petersburg Hotel for what Philip called 'a honeymoon'. This was the longest uninterrupted time that they ever spent together, and yet it was tantalisingly brief. He met her when she arrived at the Gare d'Austerlitz on the morning of 3 September; they travelled back to London (separately, for reasons of discretion); and on 9 September she went to Brynawelon. Fortunately there was no hitch in the plans and their happiness during these days was unclouded. He wrote after seeing her off:

I have never been so happy as in this last week. We've been so perfectly & wonderfully happy from first to last. Our two film parties, our lovely meals in Paris, especially our exciting dinner, our morning & evening in the St. Petersburg, my coming to the flat after I got home on Saturday night, our delicious Ellen dinners, everything till I took you to the station was quite perfect in every way. That was, in part, my angel, because it *was* a honeymoon. I told you we *needed* it, & so we did. [24]

His satisfaction, however, did not overcome his jealousy, and he was soon writing:

How *hideously* jealous you make me! I just can't *bear* other people being able to come & visit you at B., even to have a drink, when I can't come. I miss you so *frightfully all* the time. You really *mustn't* make me jealous. It hurts. And the only way not to is for you to stay in absolute *purdah all* the time.[25]

The tone was jocular, but the emotional tension was perceptible. In October, there was an explosion. Dingle Foot, who had been defending alleged terrorists in the law courts of Kenya, arrived home sooner than expected and made a long phone call to Megan; and she was unwise enough to tell Philip she was excited. To complicate matters, although Philip was himself urging Megan to join the Labour Party, he believed that Dingle was doing so from base personal motives.

A man comes from the Equator. He arrives on Sunday morning. He spends the whole day . . . trying to get you on the phone. Then he does get you, & talks & talks. What does it mean? Are you quite blind? Because if you are, he's *not*. It means that he's desperately in love with you; that he thinks of you all the time when he's away; that its his first & only pleasure to talk to you the moment you get back. [Megan was out when Dingle first phoned.] He can't rest, & can't be happy, till he does.

And *you* take pleasure in that, & take pleasure in flaunting it to me. Is that wicked? Or is it worse? . . .

But if you come into the Labour Party, so will the Attorney for Africa. . . . Don't you see it? He doesn't really agree with the Labour Party; he *hates* it – & who w'dn't, if Michael was his brother! He's joining because of you; because he's determined to be in the House with you, & see you every day; & because he hopes his present successes, & the rapturous reception of his most unconventional attentions, mean that he will then, with constant intimacy, have far greater successes still. Well, don't say I didn't warn you. Don't try to say it isn't true. I *know*. After all, with all my manifold defects & failings, I am a man. Some day you'll be very sorry, if you carry on like this.[26]

Philip was indeed beset by problems in the autumn of 1954. He was working hard on his book, spurred by a grant of £1500 from the Rockefeller Foundation, and hoped – vainly – to finish it by Christmas. But when he sent fifty pages to Megan at Brynawelon, she angered him by failing to find the time to read them and comment on them. Ann had ignored a letter from a doctor asking her to discuss the children's condition. It then emerged that she was living with John Irving, a BBC producer, and wanted to get a divorce and marry him. She met Francis in the presence of the lawyer, and her attitude shocked Philip: 'A. said she wd never never see him or me or Edward or Martin again; that she didn't *want* to see Edward or Martin, she only wanted to forget them. To forget them! Can you imagine it?'[27] Philip had persuaded himself that Ann would return to Francis, but now he had to recognise that she would not. Martin was beginning to forget her, but Edward missed her – 'he has suffered a lot'. Philip wrote in November. Eventually, the boys grew up at Achmetaga, where they were happier than in trying to cope with London life. Francis married again and had two normal children.

There was a new target for Philip's jealousy, referred to as the Coloured Person or the Coloured Races. Identification is impossible; at this period, a number of Africans representing nationalist movements were living in London and had contacts in British left-wing or liberal circles. John Hatch, who worked for the Labour Party as an adviser on colonial policy, recalls that he introduced Megan to some of them. When she was planning a trip to London in November, Philip wrote:

You propose to go to a Coloured Person Party on the evening of your return; to have a big blind on the following night; to go to more Coloured Parties on Friday, & to leave on Saturday – so that for me there remains only Thursday evening. . . . A nice week's programme, I must say. You mustn't be surprised if I'm very much upset & hurt. How can I get on . . . if every kind of native from all the underdeveloped territories of the world have priority on your first night & your last?[28]

After her visit, he was still wounded:

I feel as tho' I'd hardly seen you – & that last thrust from the Coloured Races was hard to bear. . . . Don't you now see that I'm right? It wasn't like this two years ago; its getting more dangerous all the time. I mean *dangerous* – to you, & to the Coloured Races too.[29]

At this juncture, Geoffrey Crawshay died. Megan was much distressed, but she took on the task of paying tribute to him on the BBC's Welsh service. Embarrassed by the memory of his jealous outburst in June, Philip wrote:

I know you loved him, & loved to be with him – I don't grudge that, & I'm not jealous of it at all; why I was jealous is because I *long* to have you to myself for a weekend in lovely country & all alone – I want what he *had* – but I'm very glad that he & you both had it, & had it together. I know your talk will be wonderful; it will give him all the purity & loveliness & sweetness of your loving heart & mind.[30]

Later in November there was another disastrous contretemps, as this letter indicates:

I'm really broken to pieces, I know I've been foul, & I've said beastly things, & I wdn't have had it happen for all the world. Sometimes I can't imagine how it happens; & yet I really know. What makes me lose control is when you think, or profess to think, that I don't come to you because I don't want to, or because I voluntarily put something or someone else first. Don't you really know what that never, never, NEVER happens? . . . It often happens with you – Dingle's Ballet Party – your first night, & scores of other things, apart from your family – I could quote endless numbers of them. I don't complain. . . . I never see my friends, I hardly ever see my only two remaining sisters. . . . I see Edward very little, I never play any game, I never swim, I never dance, I practically never go to the theatre. . . .

My angel, when I get into that condition, & I'm desperate about getting you & all you say is that I treat you as the last priority it makes it almost *impossible* for me to behave normally with other people, & they all know that something very odd is going on – & that, by your standards is dangerous. . . . And then this frightful thing of sending you away unhappy & ill. I felt as tho' I sh'd never forgive myself, or forget how you looked. . . . And that *nightmare* drive to Euston – I can't bear to think of it.[31]

Bad luck persisted to the end of the year. Francis found an excellent cook, but she 'blew herself to glory' by turning the wrong gas tap, and had to be rushed to hospital. A kitten, to which the children were attached, ran away, and Philip strained a muscle trying to catch it. On the other hand, he wrote 4000 words of his book in a day and he looked forward confidently to Megan becoming MP for Wrexham.

## 3

In 1955 Philip's health deteriorated badly. He started to get un-pleasant stomach pains and consulted Sir Daniel Davies, who diagnosed an ulcer. In July he wrote from Strasbourg, where he was at a session of the Council of Europe: 'I had a very bad night on Saturday, after 9 hours in a Commission, I just didn't sleep *at all*, & my inside was in a very queer condition. So I had to spend Sunday morning in bed.'[32] A few weeks later he was preparing for an important speech in the House on disarmament:

I have moments of less, & moments of more, panic; but I shall certainly be glad when tomorrow is over. . . . I sh'dn't mind so much, if I wasn't conscious all the time of its effect on my inside! Nervous tension is what people with gastric ulcers should avoid; & I'm *not* avoiding it, & altho' I've had no real pains, I have had – & have – funny & abnormal feelings which oughtn't to be there. I have to drug myself to sleep – & that isn't so good![33]

Since he was sometimes too unwell and tired to go out for a walk in the evening – and this was visible to Irene – posting letters and making phone calls was more awkward than ever. He wrote on 31 May:

You really were wicked that morning, & that night before, & the night after [on the telephone]. . . . If I could say where I was going, all would be easy, of course; but if I have to invent things, I *must* make them plausible, & even so, its very difficult for me not to give away my feelings. . . . I'd had a tiring day on Friday, & it simply wasn't *possible* for me to come out after dinner & stay up late. Moreover, when it rains, most of inventions go west on the spot – & that night it rained most vilely. All this you *must* make an effort to understand.

This letter is significant for another reason. The question that had plagued their relationship from the start – whether they could ever be married – was becoming more acute. Letters written in 1954 and 1955 revert to it fourteen times, with Philip assuring Megan that there was nothing he would like better or that he already regarded her as his wife. Thus:

Honeymoons begin marriage, don't they? Marriages that are right, as ours is, intensify & multiply love. (12 September 1954)

If only I was married to you, everything wd be perfect. (6 November 1954)

In everything essential you *are* my wife, & I honour you & want to serve you as thro' you were not only my wife, but my Queen. (30 November 1954)

So please believe . . . how I long to have a husband's rights to help you & see you thro' all the tough times ahead. (7 February 1955)

But now a new note was struck, with references to marriage as a practical proposition. He was writing on 31 May:

I've always said that, if you want to change your life, you *shall*, & I will help you. You can absolutely rely on that, & you know it, even if it means tearing my heart from my body with my own hands.

Two days later he repeated: 'If you want to marry, I'll do everything in the world you want. You know that. Even if it kills me.'

A letter like this is not easy to explain. It may mean that Megan was pressing him to get a divorce and marry her and that he was promising to do so, while stressing the emotional pain that he would suffer. It is possible, alternatively, that she was threatening to break with him and marry someone else (although it is not clear what he meant by helping her). On either interpretation, it seems that she was finding their relationship no longer tolerable on the terms that had prevailed for so long.

However, nothing decisive happened. In August, Philip went to the Swiss Alps for a holiday with Professor A. C. Pigou, who had been his teacher and mentor at Cambridge, and two other men. The customary bad luck pursued him. Although he avoided strenuous climbing and attempted only 'a very little mountain', he sprained an ankle; it became swollen and gave him considerable trouble. The next day Pigou suffered what appears to have been a fairly serious stroke. The local midwife was recruited as nurse, but Philip was indispensable because he was the only one of the party who spoke German and the doctor did not speak English. He escorted the Professor back to England and failed to meet Megan in London before going off to Cumberland to resume his holiday. This brought the usual reproaches, and he wrote from a hotel at Loweswater:

I won't explain further about Monday. If I'd known sooner, I wd have taken an extra day in London, & everything wd have been easier. As it was, I tried to get a 'plane from Geneva the night before, as the Prof was better. There wasn't a place! . . . Won't you believe that when *I can't* do something, I simply *can't*, & that's the damnable end of it? You said my explanations made it plain that I didn't *want* to see you! What a cruel, grotesque, *absurd* thing to say! . . . It was utterly different from your cruel telephoning on Tuesday night – you *knew* I wd ring up & kept the coloured races on to scare me off. . . . My beloved, no more misunderstandings or recriminations, *please*.[34]

She was still angry with him a week later, and he pleaded:

*What* can I say to persuade you of the difficulties I face here? Don't you really understand that to go out after dinner for a two-hour walk in the rain is something that I just can't do without giving an explanation that I *can't* give? . . . And its terribly difficult for me to write when I can be walked in on at any moment, & the post goes once a day at lunch-time, & the pillar-box is another long walk away.

Its waste of life, it really is, for you to say that unless I write & telephone to you openly, I'm a mouse not a man, & to use up weeks being cross with me about it. I could do it, if I say why I'm doing it & to whom. Do you want me to?[35]

While he was in Cumberland, trying to work on his book in difficult conditions, Megan went with Olwen for a holiday on the Normandy coast. The lovers arranged to meet in Paris on 14 September for another honeymoon. Philip was worried lest Olwen should decide to come to Paris too, but she did not, and this honeymoon too was a success. He wrote on 23 September: 'I think all the time of Paris. . . . It was an idyllic honeymoon, only much too short.'

Despite his precarious health, he was constantly on the move. He went to another country hotel with Irene, warning Megan: 'I certainly won't be able to send you any proper memos until I'm alone (next Friday) & until then even tiny notes are very difficult, because I've nowhere to hide them till I can go to the post.' Then he had another Strasbourg meeting, and at the end of the month there was the Labour Party conference at Margate. For the first time, Philip and Megan were at the same party conference; they took the risk of staying at the same hotel.

He was trapped between Irene, who was relentlessly vigilant and suspicious, and Megan, who was scathing about his cowardice. Feeling the need to defend himself, he sat down on 5 October to write a nine-page letter, which began:

When I got to my house last night, after leaving you at the flat, I was immediately asked: 'Where *have* you been?' . . . This wasn't easy to answer. Talk of a haircut, when I hadn't had it cut, wasn't very convincing, & it evoked the reply: 'Well, that was a waste of time, especially as you don't need a haircut anyway. From your guilty look, you might have had an assignation.'

This was the introduction to a long account of the tribulations of his marriage (quoted in chapter 6). The later pages of this narrative throw some light on how it was maintained:

I made a great effort, saying nothing, but trying hard. So did other people [ie Irene], saying much & often bitter things like those I've quoted – but also really trying. Trying to help in my work, & in my writing & in other things. I had always from the very start tried to help her over Greece, & I was useful, especially in her very bad times after the two wars. . . . I made great efforts, because otherwise I saw total disaster, by spiritual & mental corrosion of a devastating kind; in a measure, I succeeded.

But that success inevitably carries consequences. You live in the same house; you discuss the people you see, the jobs you have to do; of course, the questions come: 'What have you done this afternoon? Where have you been? With whom did you lunch & dine etc?' . . . It isn't only getting myself out of these horrid & constant difficulties; its also not giving rise to suspicions that I'm hiding something . . . its protecting *you*. When you say you won't agree to be 'fitted in' with all my other pleasures, engagements, & satisfactions, it is just shutting your eyes to what is a constant & sometimes *terrible* complication in my life; the questions are inevitable, unless I smash everything up, which you don't want.

Just as in 1938-9, Philip was assuming that Megan did not want him to 'smash everything up' – that is, to end his marriage. This assumption justified him in carrying on as he had for almost twenty years: meeting Megan when it was feasible and convenient, concealing the affair from Irene, and explaining to Megan that she was being reckless and unreasonable if she found this situation hard to bear. But what did Megan want? We have no firm evidence, and the likelihood is that she herself did not know, or that she wanted different things at different times and in different moods. This would account for her accusations and her explosions of anger – the outward expression of her unhappiness. She was aware that other women – Ellen Roberts, Ursula Thorpe, Olwen – were hostile to Philip and would be relieved if she broke off the relationship. If she could have done so, she would also have been calmed and relieved, but she could not, because she loved him and was unable to cease loving him. When it came to the point, she could not contemplate losing the happiness that they intermittently achieved during their 'honeymoons'. Meanwhile, the quarrels and the reproaches became more and more bitter, the strain became more painful, and she had a growing sense of being in an intolerable situation. Something had to give.

What did give was physical health. Megan began to suffer from unpleasant warts on her arms and neck, which may have been caused by an infection but may also, partly at least, have been psychosomatic. At the same time, Philip's stomach pains grew worse, and in November he went into hospital for a gall-bladder operation. Megan did not venture to visit him; perhaps she remembered the scene in 1931 when Frances Stevenson visited her father after his operation. She sent flowers and a card, which must have been discreetly worded to avoid arousing Irene's suspicions. Irene wrote to her on 2 December:

My dear Megan,

I only just discovered your card in a drawer in Philip's bedroom in the hospital, or I would have written long ago to thank you for your lovely present of flowers.

Philip has had a frightful time and I have been horribly anxious; but it seems today – after another setback – as if he were really through the wood at last.

Love from us both,
Irene

P.S. Philip was very much pleased with your 'fraternal' greetings!

On Christmas Day, Philip wrote in shaky handwriting:

This is to wish you a very happy Xmas, & all the joys that you can wish for or imagine. It grieves me bitterly that I cannot be with you in the flesh – the all too something flesh – but my heart will be with you from the moment you wake until you lay your little head down & close your eyes in sleep.

It was Megan's casual habit to make notes on any piece of paper that she happened to have with her. On the back of this letter we can read: 'Rugby Union Twickenham. The Welsh Rugby Union, Imperial Buildings, St Mary's Street, Cardiff.' We can also read 'integr integrity'. It looks as though she was trying out the spelling. Why integrity was on her mind at that time, we can only guess.

## 4

On 8 February 1956 Irene Noel-Baker died from a sudden and completely unexpected heart attack.[36] Although she was seventy-six years old, Philip's sense of guilt and his continual anxieties about his own health had combined to make him feel that, if anyone was in danger of dying, he was. Unwilling to convict himself of wishing for Irene's death, he had excluded the possibility from his mind. The event therefore struck him as a disorientating shock.

Megan was in London and her friend Ursula Thorpe was visiting her. Philip telephoned and asked her to come to his house immediately. She was reluctant, but he insisted, so she found a taxi and went. He took her by the hand and led her into the room where the dead body of Irene was lying on a bed. There she had to stand with him for some minutes of vigil. As soon as she could, she took another taxi back to her flat.

Ursula vividly remembers that Megan was 'very much distressed and upset'.[37] Robin had the same impression two days later when he drove Megan home from the House, where she had gone to listen to a debate. She told him what had happened, and this in itself surprised him, since she had never talked to him about her relationship with Philip (although he knew about it from his mother). Of her experience at Philip's house she said: 'It was unbelievable.' Robin saw that she was deeply hurt.[38]

Nevertheless she made a brave effort to give Philip moral support, but the strain – aggravated by her own ill-health and the irritating warts – was too much for her, and she retreated to Brynawelon. Things were going from bad to worse. On 18 March Philip was involved in a car accident – surely the last thing he needed at this point. He wrote next day:

My beloved, I have had to write letters about my stupid collision last night, &
now I've only time for a tiny note.

In any case, I couldn't write very much. I told you on Feb 8th that I had had
a smashing blow, & that it would take me *very* long to recover. I did not then
know what it would be like. I do now; it is far harsher than I dreamt.

You have had a *horrible* strain, & you have been as sweet to me as it was
possible for anyone to be. I hope you will now get really well – I have felt your
horrid illness to be so dreadfully my fault. Thank you for everything more
than I can say. My love to you & my blessing.

It was a puzzling letter, and the more so because it was the only one in
six weeks from a man who was normally a compulsive letter-writer.

In April, Philip left England to spend two months at Achmetaga – a
longer period than he had ever spent there in Irene's company. He
passed his days walking round the estate and admiring the improvements she had made: he joined the pilgrims at the Feast of St John, the
peak of the Orthodox religious year; he commissioned an architect to
design a memorial to Irene; he received the condolences of the King
and Queen of Greece, who were personal friends.[39] He did not write
to Megan, but satisfied his need for verbal expression by keeping a
diary, largely devoted to thoughts of Irene. He recalled:

The Customs officials at the frontier, the guards on the trains, all knew her
name, and always passed her through with touching courtesy and respect.
Very many ordinary people knew her work during the war, and very many
officers in the army remembered how she went regularly to Achmetaga all
through the Communist siege of the village.[40]

All this time, Megan heard not a word. Naturally, since she loved
Philip, she would have wished to share his feelings in this time of stress,
and she wanted to know something of his intentions. For all that she
knew, he might have been thinking of staying permanently in Greece
and of retiring from British politics. The House was sitting and he was
a member of the Shadow Cabinet; never before had he neglected his
responsibilities. But, above all, she was given no sign of his intentions
where she was concerned.

Those who knew the story of the long love affair – primarily, Ursula
and Thelma – naturally expected that after a decent interval Philip
would marry Megan; and Megan herself was entitled to expect this.
There was an obvious parallel in the long love affair between her
father and Frances and their marriage following Margaret's death.
Bitterly though Megan had opposed that marriage, it did constitute a
precedent which was bound to come to her mind. Moreover, while

Lloyd George's promise to marry Frances 'if it were ever possible' had been essentially theoretical and had remained dormant since the early days of their relationship, Philip had repeatedly and ardently – and with increasing frequency in 1954 and 1955 – stressed his positive desire to marry Megan. Further, whereas the marriage of Lloyd George and Margaret had been rooted in love and had been a partnership of real emotional significance (this, indeed, was why Megan felt his second marriage to be a sacrilege), Philip had told her that his marriage to Irene had been a mistake from the start, had never been enriched by love and had been kept going only by conscious and strenuous efforts. These factors made it logical to think that there was no reason whatever why he should not marry Megan now that the sole obstacle was removed. After all, he knew that it had been her wish for twenty years and he was on record as assuring her that it was his wish too.

Philip returned to London on 18 June. After a few days of nerving himself for the task, he sat down on 22 June to write this letter:

My beloved, I must so start, tho' I know that it will grate on your ears, & throw you into hostile distrust of all that follows. I must so start, because its true. . . .

I know that you have more to forgive than I can hope to have forgiven. I know I have acted as cruelly & as unforgiveably as you now feel that I have. I know that nothing I can say can excuse or explain the long past, the near past, the present. I know it is too much to ask you to believe that I have constantly thought of you, & suffered horribly in my heart & conscience as I thought. I suffered *for* you, & I suffered a thousand times more because of my tragic consciousness of all the wrongs I had done so [*sic*].

I must now tell the truth, as I've always *meant* to tell it to you, & never succeeded – tho' I've *never* consciously told you what was untrue.

I think you know a lot of it already. I think you know what happened to me on February 8th. I suddenly found, in an instant, that I loved Irene far more & far more deeply than I knew. I suddenly found that a knowledge of her wonderful qualities, & of her true nobility, was deeply embedded in my heart and mind. I suddenly found that our life together; our building a home; our making of friends; Francis, Edward & Martin; our common interests in the U.N. & a thousand other things; above all, our deep love of Achmetaga & the Achmetaga people & the Achmetaga world – I suddenly found that all this was far more important, & far more wonderful in my mind than I had understood. And above all, I found that I had a terrible, overwhelming sense of disaster, because there were so many things I would like to have done that it was too late ever to do; so many opportunities forever missed; so much

happiness I would like to have given, could have given, that I should never now be able to give. I have been tortured – it isn't too strong a word; indeed, there's no other – by remorse about *you*; I was tortured, & still am, by remorse
about her as well. . . .

Achmetaga is wonderfully beautiful; having Edward there was a deep happiness, altho' he started with 10 days' flu, was five weeks handicapped by a broken collar-bone & mild concussion, & was cursed by the horrible, maddening, & horrible difficult affliction of worms, both at the beginning & again (owing to his collar-bone) at the end. The beauty, the sunshine, Edward, the country walks, the swimming, cured me *physically*, & left me very well. But there, of course, every person I saw, every place I went to, everything I used & handled, reminded me of the past.

And when I came home on Monday, I found just the same *stab* thro' my mind & heart as when I went away. I don't quite know what people mean when they talk of 'getting over' a disaster that like [*sic*]; in any case, I haven't got over it, & I don't see when I'm going to, or how I'm going to, in any early future that counts.

I was unconscious of this, or nearly all of it, until Feb 8th; then it swamped my life. It doesn't mean that I love you any less; it doesn't mean that you weren't a comfort to me in those terrible weeks; it doesn't mean that I wasn't deeply touched & moved by all that you did for me then, & by all your tenderness. . . .

It *does* mean that I was conscious every moment that I had treated you in a way for which there are no words, & for which contrition & remorse are of no
avail. It *does* mean that I can't now give you what I would like to give, & would try desperately to give, if it were any good. It *does* mean that when I am with you, or think of you, there is always present another dark, unhappy, very powerful train of thought, sometimes conscious, sometimes sub-conscious, but never absent. It does mean that I understand that I am now confronted by problems, & beset by anxieties & troubles, that I must face & resolve alone – & that until I have faced them, & got in some way onto an even keel, I have no right to seek to see you, or to take from you any of the precious gifts of life & love & companionship & wisdom that you have given me with such prodigal generosity for so very long.

My beloved, this isn't disloyalty to you. I say it out of loyalty, & because I truly love you, as I always have. I say it because I can't go on unless you understand . . .

The letter reached Megan at Brynawelon. As Ellen later told Zosia, she ran down to the end of the garden with the letter in her hand. Ellen followed her; she was weeping uncontrollably.

Despite the assurance that 'I truly love you', it was impossible to read this letter as anything but a rejection. It was a contradiction – a betrayal – of all Philip's promises and pledges. No doubt, his behaviour towards Megan (and indeed his behaviour towards Irene) would have surprised the many people who had paid respectful tribute to his high-mindedness, his integrity, even his saintliness. But we may reflect that other men – such as Tolstoy, Picasso and Bertrand Russell – behaved just as badly to women and nevertheless remain secure on their pedestals.

# CHAPTER THIRTEEN

# The Conquest of Carmarthen

1

In both British and international politics, 1956 was the most eventful year since the end of the war. Those who lived through it would always remember it as the year of Suez and Hungary.

Watching the House of Commons from the gallery, Megan saw new actors in all the leading roles. As Prime Minister, Eden had failed to chalk up any significant achievement and was being criticised for his lack of firmness. Always thin-skinned, he was looking for a chance to prove his political virility. After Attlee's retirement, Gaitskell was elected as Labour leader in January 1956, easily defeating Bevan and Morrison. Clement Davies was heading for retirement too, though he stayed on until the Liberal Assembly in September. The new leader, Jo Grimond, adopted the rhetoric of Radicalism and promised to check the drift to the Right, but co-operation with Labour was not his purpose. His hope was 'to replace the Labour Party as the progressive wing of politics in this country'[1] – an aim that seems no closer to realisation in 1991.

The man whose challenge aroused Eden to buckle on his armour was Gamal Abdel Nasser, the dictator of Egypt. He was planning to build a huge dam across the Nile at Aswan and counted on loans from the United States and, to a lesser extent, from Britain. On 19 July the US Secretary of State, John Foster Dulles, announced abruptly that the American promise of a loan was cancelled. Furious, Nasser retaliated by the only means in his power. Speaking on 26 July at Alexandria – the town that had been bombarded by British warships in 1882 – he announced the nationalisation of the Suez Canal Company.[2]

The company's head office was in Paris and its directors were British and French. Eden's immediate impulse was to send an expeditionary force to occupy the canal zone, from which British troops had been withdrawn only two years before. The French Prime Minister, Guy Mollet, was in full agreement, because Nasser was believed to be arming the rebels fighting for the independence of Algeria. But military experts advised that the operation could not be mounted in less than six weeks.

There were political obstacles too. Although Gaitskell shared Eden's view that Nasser had acted outrageously, he soon made it clear that Labour would oppose the use of force. President Eisenhower told his press conference: 'I can't conceive of military force being a good solution.' So the crisis fizzled like a damp fuse from August to October.

However, just when the world thought that the attack on Egypt had been shelved, a plan was devised for carrying it out under a plausible excuse. The Israelis would invade the Sinai peninsula, Britain and France would declare that the canal was threatened, and their forces would move in with the alleged purpose of separating the combatants. On 16 October, Eden and his Foreign Secretary – Megan's old friend, Selwyn Lloyd – endorsed the plan at an off-the-record meeting in Paris with their French opposite numbers. A week later, in conditions of yet greater secrecy, David Ben Gurion and Moshe Dayan, the Israeli Prime Minister and Chief of Staff, clinched the deal with Mollet and Lloyd in a secluded private house in a Paris suburb.[3]

One reason for the secrecy, obviously, was to spring a surprise on Egypt; another was to cover up the conspiracy (which was never admitted by Eden and Lloyd, even when they wrote their memoirs years later); but a third and equally important reason was to deceive the Americans. When it was all over, Mollet was jovially frank about this in an interview with American journalists: 'We were afraid that if we had let you know, you would have prevented us doing it.'[4] Eden assured Mollet at the 16 October meeting: 'The USA will show displeasure, but won't stop us.'[5]

Meanwhile, another crisis was coming to the boil. Nikita Khrushchev, who had come to the top in the Soviet Union, made a sensational speech in February 1956 revealing the criminal injustices and the catastrophic mismanagement of the Stalin era.[6] While Russians reacted with bewilderment, the lifting of the lid caused explosions in other parts of the Communist empire. In the wake of riots in Poland, Wladyslaw Gomulka – a man who had been reviled as a deviationist and had spent years in prison – emerged as the new leader and announced: 'The road of democratisation is the only road to Socialism.' Hungary too had its Gomulka: Imre Nagy, expelled from the Communist Party in 1955. On 23 October, while crowds surged through the streets of Budapest and demolished a huge statue of Stalin, Nagy was installed as Prime Minister and a former political prisoner, Janos Kádár, was made party leader. But two things happened in Hungary that had not happened in Poland. The hated security police fired on demonstrators and caused a bloodbath; and Russian tanks, belonging to the forces which had occupied Hungary since the end of the war, were deployed to restore order.

Fighting between the Soviet troops and improvised groups of young fighters went on for several days.[7] Khrushchev appeared to be inclined to conciliation, and on the morning of 30 October the Soviet government issued a statement which admitted 'unsolved problems and downright mistakes' in the relations between Socialist countries, conceded that troops should be stationed in another country only by consent, and promised an immediate withdrawal from Budapest. A few hours later, news arrived that the Israelis had invaded Sinai.

Outside the closed circle of the conspiracy, no one knew what this portended. The US ambassador in London went to see Selwyn Lloyd, who gave him no hint of a possible British reaction. But at 4.30 in the afternoon Eden announced in the Commons that an ultimatum had been sent to Egypt and Israel: they were to cease hostilities and withdraw to a distance of ten miles from the Suez Canal. Unless they obeyed, British and French troops would occupy the canal zone. Dulles declared that the ultimatum was 'one of the most brutal ever delivered by any nation' and that the USA had been 'consciously misled'.

If the ultimatum was a surprise for Washington, it was just as much of a shock for Moscow. The Russians may have deduced that the western powers were taking advantage of the confusion in Hungary to eliminate Soviet influence in Egypt – even, perhaps, to launch a worldwide offensive. They decided to cancel the withdrawal and send fresh troops into Hungary.

As the twelve-hour ultimatum expired, British aircraft from Cyprus bombed Port Said. Gaitskell denounced 'an act of disastrous folly whose tragic consequences we shall regret for years', and Labour moved a vote of censure. From the Tory benches, however, Lord Hinchingbrooke predicted: 'If our troops return home victorious, the government might hold a general election in which honourable members opposite, having opposed the policy of the government, will be swept into the dustbin of opposition for half a century.' It was an excitable, but not an illogical, suggestion. Had the operation succeeded, the 'Suez factor' might have achieved what the 'Falklands factor' did achieve in 1983. But the 'if' was crucial. The frankest statement was made by another Tory MP, Lady Tweedsmuir: 'I support government policy in this matter, but it has got to work.'

Next day, Philip Noel-Baker suggested a peace-keeping operation by a UN force. 'If the United Nations asked Sweden and Switzerland to send in forces to police the zone,' he asserted, 'they would do it tomorrow.' Selwyn Lloyd replied: 'The United Nations has not the power to take action and produce practical results.' He was soon to be proved wrong.

The Suez crisis was, in fact, a tonic for Philip. He had written to Megan in August: 'I am still in the lamentable condition I have been in all this year. So many things inside me have been broken in the last nine months, & they're all broken still, & I don't know if they're ever going to mend.'[8] His best chance of recovery was to think of problems broader than his own, and Suez imposed this on him. Central to the argument were the values he had always upheld: international law, the collective restraint of aggression, political honesty. Labour's parliamentary team – Gaitskell, Bevan, Noel-Baker and Griffiths, four men with very different styles and talents – made rings round Eden and Lloyd in the ferocious debates of the Suez days.

The Security Council met to consider an American resolution calling on all UN members 'to refrain from the use of force or threat of force'. It was vetoed by Britain and France – an embarrassing action, since British and French spokesmen had been as emphatic as anyone in deploring the Russian use of the veto. But resolutions of the General Assembly were not subject to the veto. On 1 November the Assembly demanded a cease-fire and a halt to all military movements. On 3 November another resolution asked the Secretary-General to submit a plan for an international force within forty-eight hours. In only thirty-six hours the plan was ready, the commander was appointed, and six nations offered contributions.

Eden himself had made it impossible for his Suez operation to be a *fait accompli* before it could be checked. To preserve secrecy, he had insisted that the invasion force, which had to come by sea from Malta, should not set out until the ultimatum was announced. It was only on 5 November that paratroops seized the first objectives in the canal zone, and the seaborne forces landed the following day. However, while they moved too slowly, the Israelis moved too fast. By 3 November they had reached all their objectives in Sinai[9] and, not wishing to antagonise the Americans too much, accepted the cease-fire. The Egyptians had rejected it – understandably, since they were trying to defend themselves – but on 4 November they accepted it too. Thus, even if the plea of 'separating the combatants' had been honest or justifiable, it was now irrelevant. Once ashore, the Anglo-French force set off down the canal-side road, but it was a hopeless race against time. The American attitude was unrelenting, and the Chancellor of the Exchequer, Harold Macmillan, who had been one of the keenest enthusiasts for the Suez adventure, had to tell the Cabinet that the pound was in danger of imminent collapse and was being refused American support. Bowing to the inevitable, Eden and Mollet ordered a halt. General Stockwell, the commander on the spot, said regretfully: 'There are many who say: why didn't we take Cairo? It would have been bloody good fun and we would have enjoyed it.'[10]

But Hungary's fate was sealed. At dawn on 4 November the Russians moved into Budapest in overwhelming force and by the end of the day they were in control, though sporadic resistance contined for some weeks. About three thousand lives had been lost in the two rounds of the fighting.[11] Kádár, who had gone over to the Russians, formed a new government; Nagy and his associates took refuge in the Yugoslav Embassy. On 23 November they left it with assurances that they were free to go home, but they were deported to Romania, then a docile Soviet satellite. On 16 June 1958, after a secret trial, Nagy was condemned to death and executed. The official version of events under the Kádár regime was that October 1956 had been a Fascist, counter-revolutionary coup, defeated by Soviet fraternal assistance; only in 1989, Europe's year of change, was it redefined as a popular uprising, as Hungarians had known all along. In June 1989, in the presence of an enormous crowd, Imre Nagy was ceremonially reburied in Budapest.

Eden's adventure had ended in shame and disaster. Those who had opposed it from the start were able to claim that they were upholding Britain's better traditions. On 1 November Griffiths had spoken of 'deep humiliation in being present at Britain's worst hour' and Bevan had said: 'When we had almost all the world against us before, we had honour on our side. In this matter, we are dishonoured.' He was aware, however, that not everyone drew the right conclusions. When the House held its inquest on Suez on 5 December, he conceded: 'Of course they have support in the country. They have support among many of the unthinking and the unreflective who still react to traditional values.' His tone turned to solemnity as he warned:

The social furniture of modern society is so complicated and fragile that it cannot support the jackboot. We cannot run the processes of modern society by attempting to impose our will upon nations by armed force. If we have not learned that, we have learned nothing.

In the opinion of connoisseurs, it was the most impressive speech that Nye Bevan ever made. Megan, who was listening from the gallery, called it 'brilliant'. She wrote to Bevan:

You can judge of its revolutionary character and effect by the fact that it brought Violet Bonham-Carter and me together in almost glowing unity in the gallery. A thousand congratulations![12]

Eden did not hear that speech. Part of the blame for his behaviour, contrasting so painfully with his record and reputation, can be traced to his physical condition, an inflamed bile duct. In a state of exhaustion, he went to Jamaica for a three-week rest, but this did not restore him to health, and on 9 January 1957 he resigned. Macmillan, playing his hand astutely and outwitting Butler, made the move from Number 11 to Number 10.

2

The Liberal MP for Carmarthen, Sir Rhys Hopkin Morris (he had been knighted in 1955), was in agreement with the government action at Suez,[13] but made no public statement to that effect. On 21 November 1956 he attended the House, was taken ill when he reached his London home, and died during the night. Political observers were quick to see that the Carmarthen by-election would be a significant test of opinion.

Carmarthen was a large constituency (there were 112 polling stations) of remarkable variety. Its heartland was the Towy valley, regarded as the best farming land in Wales, which supported prosperous dairy farms. The northern part of the constituency, bordering on Cardigan, was rugged hill country, with struggling sheep farms, tracts of forestry and compact, self-contained villages. There were two mining areas: one to the east with Brynamman as its centre, and the other to the south bordering on the Llanelly constituency, whose MP was Jim Griffiths. On the coast there were a few modest holiday resorts (Laugharne already attracted visitors looking for the originals of the characters in Dylan Thomas's *Under Milk Wood*). Carmarthen was the only sizeable town; it was chiefly an administrative centre and market town, but had some light industry. The constituency had an emphatically Welsh character, and Welsh was spoken almost as widely as in Caernarvon and Anglesey.

Morris had held Carmarthen since 1945. (In earlier years he had been MP for Cardigan, and had then dropped out of politics to serve as a London magistrate.) Because of his socially conservative outlook and his strong opposition to nationalisation and state control, he had been unopposed by the Tories. The post-war redistribution had brought the Brynamman mining area into the constituency, and this had made Morris's majority wafer-thin (187 in 1950, 467 in 1951). However, the swing to the Right had enabled him to raise his majority to over 3000 in 1955.

With the prospect of a by-election, the first question was: would the Tories stand? If they did, a Labour victory would be almost a foregone conclusion. If not, other questions would be decisive. How big was the personal vote which Morris had earned by his high-principled character, his courtesy and kindliness? Could the Liberals find a candidate capable of holding their 1955 vote? Could Labour, on the other hand, find a candidate able to win over those Liberal voters who regarded themselves as Radicals? Some questions could be answered only by guesswork: what did the voters think about Suez, and how many would be impelled by Suez to change their normal allegiance one way or the other?

There was yet another imponderable factor. Plaid Cymru had been steadily gaining strength, especially since the Parliament for Wales campaign had made self-government a live issue. The Plaid candidate in 1955, Jennie Eirian Davies – wife of a Free Church minister in Brynamman – was attractive, energetic and eloquent, and had polled nearly 4000 votes. Gwynfor Evans, the Plaid leader who enjoyed considerable respect and popularity, lived in the middle of the constituency and was a member of the county council. Estimates of the probable Plaid vote in the by-election ranged from 5000 upward. Whether most of these votes would be drawn away from the Liberals or from Labour, no one knew.

Even before Hopkin Morris's death, Suez was hotly debated in Carmarthen. On 6 November, the very day when the troops landed in Egypt, the county council passed this resolution: 'We call on the government to retrace its steps and accept the majority decision of the United Nations.' As the council was evenly divided between Labour and independent members, it was significant that the resolution was carried by 40 votes to 23. A pacifist councillor, D. J. Jones, spoke of 'moral degradation', and Gwynfor Evans expressed a 'sense of outrage'. The council then unanimously decided to send a protest to the Soviet Embassy about Russia's action in Hungary. Clearly, there was no disposition in Carmarthen to limit the thinking of councillors to parish-pump matters. The local paper, the *Carmarthen Journal*, devoted its leader on 9 November to praising Eden's policy ('as brave as it was honourable') and attacking Gaitskell for his lack of patriotism. Week after week until Christmas, the *Journal* pressed the case for the government. However, the paper was well known to be the organ of the local Tories.

A few days after Hopkin Morris's death, Plaid Cymru announced that Jennie Davies would again be its candidate. The Labour Party, too, moved quickly. The first to suggest that Megan Lloyd George would be the ideal candidate was Megan Griffiths, an active member of the women's section. Her husband, Trevor Griffiths, was head-master of the school at Carway, a mining village in the south of the constituency. He warmed to the idea of Megan's candidacy as enthusiastically as his wife, and they worked busily to drum up support. Megan had backers in London too; Hugh Gaitskell was eager to get her back into the House, and Morgan Phillips thought that no one else could be better equipped to win a Welsh marginal seat with a Liberal tradition. In a pending by-election (though not in an ordinary selection conference) the National Executive was empowered to suggest – and even, if necessary, to impose – a candidate. On 1 December, it put forward Megan's name.

She had still to win at the selection conference, which was fixed for 8 December. There was a shortlist of four, of whom two had a real chance: Megan and a twenty-eight-year-old barrister, John Morris (no relation to the John William Morris whom Megan had known in her youth, and who was now a judge). Making a survey of the delegates, Griffiths reckoned that they were evenly balanced.[14] This was bad news from Megan's point of view, because the party chairman supported Morris and could use his casting vote in the event of a tie. When Trevor and Megan Griffiths arrived in Carmarthen for the selection conference, they were disturbed to find that a delegate from an outlying village, who was committed to Megan Lloyd George, was not present. To their relief, he turned up before the vote was taken. His motor bike had failed to start, but he had persuaded a friend who was the local bus driver to put on an extra service which was not on the timetable. Thanks to this example of Welsh ingenuity and initiative, Megan was selected by forty-six votes to forty-five.

John Morris was young enough to survive the setback. He set his sights on Aberavon, a steel town with a rock-solid Labour majority. The elderly MP, Will Cove, was contemplating retirement; an allusion in one of Philip's letters indicates that Megan had been interested in Aberavon in 1956. Morris was selected to succeed Cove, won the seat in 1959, and – as this book goes to press – is still MP for Aberavon.

On 12 December the Liberals selected John Morgan Davies as their candidate. He had a farming background and worked for the Fatstock Marketing Corporation, but this asset was not the main reason why he was chosen. His political outlook was typical of those right-wing Liberals who, as Megan had often complained while she was still in the Liberal Party, were indistinguishable from the Tories; and – the vital point at this juncture – he approved of Eden's action at Suez. Stating the obvious, the *Journal* had reported a 'general feeling' that the Liberals must endorse the Tory government's policy if they were to hold Carmarthen, since they could do so only with Tory votes. As soon as he was selected, Davies made his attitude clear: 'Britain and France halted hostilities in the Middle East. . . . The real enemy of mankind is the Soviet Union.'[15] He then attended a private meeting of the Conservative Association to answer questions about his views. On 17 December the Tories decided not to contest the by-election. Their brief statement did not give explicit support to Davies, but the implication was clear enough.

All the candidates were now ready, but polling day would not be until 28 February 1957, after the new register came into force. This was certain to be a notable by-election, of the quality that journalists call 'historic'; and it would be a contest in which the differences of principle were plain and uncompromising. The three candidates agreed on nothing, except that they were all against Sunday opening of pubs.

Both Megan and Morgan Davies had a problem: each diverged from party policy on an issue that evoked strong feelings. In Megan's case this was the issue of a Parliament for Wales. Her stand, which was amply on record, was not supported by the Labour Party's national leadership, nor by most Labour MPs from Wales. Questioned by reporters after the selection conference, she made it clear that she stood by what she had been saying since 1950. At her first big meeting, in Carmarthen on 6 February, she plunged into the question at the outset: 'I shall stick to my point of view. I shall continue to try and persuade my colleagues . . . that Wales must have the direction of her own domestic affairs.'[16] And she pointed out that Labour policy did at least call for a Secretary of State for Wales – 'a great advance on the present position'. But the Plaid, predictably, accused her of relegating the issue to a minor place. Evans said that the question was not why the Plaid was opposing Megan, but: 'Why is Lady Megan fighting us if she is seriously in support of any measure of Welsh self-government?'

However, any embarrassment for Megan on this question was slight in comparison with Liberal embarrassment over Suez. It was impossible to deny that the candidate's attitude was in conflict with that of the party as a whole and especially of the leader, Jo Grimond. There had been some wobbling when Labour first divided the House on the night of 30 October; three of the six Liberal members – Clement Davies, Roderic Bowen and Arthur Holt – voted with the Tories. But Grimond, anxious to avert a split of the kind that had plagued the Liberals ever since the Boer War, pulled them back into line, and the Liberal group in general voted with Labour in subsequent divisions. On 10 November the Liberal Council roundly condemned what Eden had done as 'unlawful, foolish and dangerous'. In the debate of 5 December, Grimond made the same point as Bevan, if less eloquently: 'In the modern world it is simply not possible to march about places with large armies enforcing the British point of view.'

In January, Megan moved into the Ivy Bush Hotel in Carmarthen and prepared to open her campaign. The accepted procedure in by-elections is that candidates should follow the advice of the professionals who know what is, and what is not, in the best interests of the party. Labour's professionals in Carmarthen were Cliff Prothero, the regional organiser, and his assistant, Hubert Morgan. But Megan had never been a by-election candidate before – nor a Labour candidate – and she had her own ideas about strategy and tactics. Picking up the gossip in the bar of the Ivy Bush, the *New Statesman*'s correspondent, John Morgan, wrote: 'There are tales of tempestuous arguments between candidate and agents.'[17]

Prothero's inclination was to stage a low-key campaign, in which Megan would shake as many hands as possible, chat with farmers on market day, and win hearts through her smile and her charm. He was right in thinking that she was accomplished in these skills, but she knew that it was on the platform that she could score real triumphs and carry conviction with the voters. In English towns and cities the public meeting was in decline, and candidates often addressed tiny audiences consisting of supporters and journalists, but in rural Wales the old traditions still flourished. Jennie Davies (peaking too soon, probably) had spoken at sixty-eight meetings by 1 February and predicted that Megan would speak only in the larger centres of population. Megan therefore insisted on the full programme of meetings to which she had been accustomed in Anglesey. During

February each of the three candidates spoke at four or five meetings every evening (except Sunday, of course).

The main argument was over the content of the campaign. Prothero, like Bevan, realised that the Suez adventure had been supported by many of 'the unthinking and the unreflective'; he had a shrewd suspicion that quite a number of working-class people who normally voted Labour were in this category. In his opinion, while the Labour candidate should of course stand by the party's condemnation of Suez, it would be advisable not to dwell on the subject any more than necessary. There was a useful local issue ready to hand: the price paid to dairy farmers by the Milk Marketing Board had just been cut by fivepence a gallon. The safe course would be to put milk, rather than Suez, in the forefront of the campaign.[18]

Megan flatly rejected this advice. As soon as she was selected, she promised that the main issue in the by-election would be the Suez aggression 'and all its disastrous consequences'. When each candidate was given space in the *Journal* for a policy statement, she nailed her colours firmly to the mast:

The most vital issue in this by-election is peace. If that is lost, nothing else matters. . . . Suez showed beyond a shadow of doubt the great gulf between the Labour and Tory parties. Therefore, the first issue is whether we are for Tory lawlessness or against it.[19]

Megan adopted this strategy, in the first place, because she whole-heartedly believed what she was saying. Her thinking was in line with Bevan's in the speech that had impressed her so much; in a world in which a major war could expose humanity to the annihilating power of nuclear weapons, random aggression on the lines of Suez was just as reckless as it was immoral. As she said on 8 February at Whitland: 'The great question is whether we are going to prevent nuclear war from coming on us. Unless we are prepared to stick to the rule of law, there is going to be nothing in the world which can avert a war.'

In Wales this language evoked an echo. She was appealing to beliefs – in moral principle, in political integrity, in the virtues of peace-making – which had been instilled in the audiences at her meetings in the schoolrooms or the chapels where she was speaking. The memory of Henry Richard, a nineteenth-century Radical MP who earned the name of 'Apostle of Peace', was still alive, and she did not forget to bring his name into her peroration.

It was also important, if she wanted to bring the campaign to life, to stress that there was a real contrast between opposing political values. Her talk of the 'great gulf' between the parties was not mere rhetoric.

In recent years, she remarked, the idea had grown up that the parties were in basic agreement as to aims and differed only with regard to methods; but Suez had made clear the 'deep and dangerous cleavage' that divided the nation. All her life, Megan recognised that if one had sincere beliefs and serious purposes in politics one necessarily had enemies. Her enemies were the Tories, and Liberals who allied themselves with Tories.

A subsidiary advantage of the emphasis on Suez was that it prevented the Plaid candidate from being the only one to take a strong stand. Jennie Davies's condemnation of the aggression was forthright; for her, it was 'the criminal continuance of the London imperialist policy in Cyprus and Kenya'. The Labour Party, she added, was making political capital out of the situation, but had no consistent policy of opposition to imperialism and war. If that could credibly be said of some Labour politicians, it was not a charge to which Megan was vulnerable.

But Megan's chief tactical gain from making Suez the dominant issue of the campaign was that it enabled her to keep up a devastating attack on Morgan Davies – 'the Suez candidate', as she called him – and to deprive him of any claim to represent true Liberal values. To defend what Eden had done, she pointed out, was also to subscribe to the fundamentals of Tory policy, since the new Prime Minister, Macmillan, was unrepentant about Suez. This was the note she struck at Carmarthen on 6 February:

Liberals in Carmarthen, as elsewhere, used to be against the imperialism, the jingoism and the militarism of the Tories. I can't believe they have changed. If they have not changed, they can't vote for this strange, unnatural alliance. Have we any reason to believe that the government has turned its back on the policy which culminated in Suez? . . . This is the greatest single issue on which this or any other constituency can give its verdict today. We have been brought to the edge of the precipice by the Tory government.

By putting the Suez issue in the forefront, Megan was highlighting the contradiction between Morgan Davies's views and those of his party leader. 'I agree with Mr Grimond,' she was fond of telling her audiences with a smile. Grimond was faced with a dilemma: should he speak in Carmarthen, concealing his disapproval of Davies as best he could, or should he stay away, incurring the charge that he had failed to support the Liberal candidate in a crucial by-election? He had been leader for only a few months and was vulnerable to criticism; he decided that he could not afford to be blamed for the loss of the seat. In his memoirs, he wrote that having a pro-Suez candidate was 'to say the least of it, awkward' and commented: 'Looking back, I should probably have disowned him. In the end I spoke for him but did not attempt to paper over our disagreements. It was an unhappy affair.'[20] When he did speak in Carmarthen, he certainly demonstrated his unhappiness. He said that there was room for disagreement, that 'there is of course a case to be made for the government', and that: 'I've always said that this country had a duty to take some action when the attack by Israel commenced.' In fact, he edged as close as he could to Davies's position without actually identifying himself with it. At Kidwelly, when he was asked point-blank whether the Liberal candidate had Tory backing, his reply was to enquire whether the absence of a Communist candidate meant that Megan had Communist backing – an effort which evoked shouts of derision. As for Roderic Bowen, the Liberal MP for Cardigan, his method was to dismiss the subject of Suez by saying: 'This is not the time for carping criticism.'

Davies showed signs of being unhappy too. When the candidates wrote their statements for the *Carmarthen Journal*, Megan placed her stand on Suez in her opening paragraph, but Davies put it near the end of his contribution and merely said that the UN should be made an effective weapon for peace. His formula was 'I would like to think that British action in Egypt halted a major war', but at his press conference he declined to say whether he actually did think so and closed the topic with: 'I've been very frank, but the time has come when we should forget Suez and try to promote peace.'[21] But on 11 February at Llanarthney he hazarded: 'It may be a pity we did not complete the job. That would have been realistic and would have restored the prestige of the United Kingdom.'

It became clearer every day that Megan had been wise to insist on holding meetings in every village. Many voters made it a point of honour to listen to all the candidates and there were undoubtedly some who, in classic democratic style, did not make up their minds until they had done so. Megan's natural oratorical powers had been strengthened by almost thirty years in politics and seven election campaigns, while Davies was a poor speaker by any standard. Her personality was as electrifying as ever, and Davies was considered by the *Tribune* reporter to have 'as much personality as a television set with a defective tube'. Above all, she spoke with sincerity and passion on the issue which she had successfully pushed to the forefront of the campaign, while Davies's handling of it was patently defensive and evasive.

3

As the campaign got under way, friends flocked to help Megan. Dingle Foot, who had now joined the Labour Party, moved into the Ivy Bush Hotel to play his part. The MP for Pembroke, Desmond Donnelly, who was another of her best friends, was also at her side from start to finish. Indeed, 'at her side' was more than a metaphor. When Hubert Morgan phoned her room for the first time to ask if she was ready to discuss the day's programme, she invited him to come up, and he found her sitting up in bed in a négligée with Dingle Foot on one side and Donnelly on the other. 'I was a bit embarrassed,' Morgan recalls. 'I'd never seen a lady in bed before, other than my wife.' He was also rather shocked to see these three members of the bourgeoisie eating hard-boiled eggs with their fingers.[22]

Cledwyn Hughes received a phone call from Megan, asking him to speak for her because 'some people are saying I was a rotten MP for Anglesey'. He responded to the call and stayed for several days, speaking in villages and also at the big meeting in Carmarthen Market Hall. He said: 'If it were not for the fact that the people of Anglesey held her in high esteem and she was an effective constituency member, there is no doubt that Anglesey would have been won by Labour in 1945.'

Philip Noel-Baker came to support Megan in her stand on Suez. At a meeting at Llansaint, he stated: 'Britain's action might have been a mortal blow to the United Nations, but for the stand taken by the United States and other countries and by Labour in the House of Commons.' Since the scene at Irene's death-bed, he had seen Megan only at the party conference in October, and he probably did not see her in Carmarthen. Cledwyn was surprised to run into him in the street, together with Patricia Llewellyn-Davies, who had brought a team of Labour prospective candidates to help in the canvassing.

Trevor Griffiths, taking time off from his school, drove Megan to her meetings. She prepared her speeches carefully, enquiring about local problems and finding the right approach for each place – although the message about Suez was never omitted. There was a crisis on the first night when her speech notes could not be found and she had to improvise; they were later discovered in the lid of the typewriter. She preferred speaking in Welsh, but sensed from looking at the audience which language to use. Griffiths would hold up his watch when it was time to move on. After she got back to the hotel, she dropped into an armchair, kicked off her shoes, and relaxed with a gin and French.[23]

John Morgan went with her one evening and wrote in the *New Statesman*:

At this hall – high on a hill, anthracite small-coal on the path, a horse champing the grass in the graveyard – people sat on window-sills and stood on the steps outside in the cold. Scheduled to speak for 15 minutes, Lady Megan spoke for 30 in her best form . . . passionate about the 'criminal folly' of Suez, now ironic and now angry about the Tories, the stabbing finger a revolver-barrel firing off the rhetorical questions. . . .

In the car the driver, very stern, said: 'We're over half an hour late.' 'Oh, but I couldn't leave them. They were so wonderful', the full blaze of charm directed at the driver. . . . Another crowded hall. Dissident notes here . . . 'Tell me, Lady Megan, what party did you belong to when you voted for the nationalisation of coal?' The answer, slow and firm: 'I am a radical, like my father before me. The Liberal Party is no longer the home for radicals. You say I have changed. It is not *I* who have changed.'. . .

The end of the evening's five meetings, the time 10.30. . . . A man runs on to the platform. During her speech he has written a Welsh poem in praise of Lady Megan. 'Read it to me,' she says. He declaims it and is rewarded with a smile so dazzling that he is clearly stunned. 'Isn't that lovely,' says Lady Megan to me, 'he's written me a poem.' Her eyes are wrinkled-up with delight; the whole face clenched in a fist of gaiety.[24]

Hubert Morgan, Labour's assistant organiser, thought that she was a delightful woman with a warm personality, but from his angle 'a rather superior being'. After all, she had grown up in Downing Street and always lived in comfort. 'She didn't understand that this is a cruel world,' he reflected. He accompanied her when she went down a pit for the first time in her life. He guessed that she found the miners uncouth; the quarrymen of the North were more old-fashioned and respectful to a lady. She was surprised to see a miner in the street with his shirt open to the waist. Morgan could see that she was more at home in the rural villages; on her way to a mining community, she asked anxiously: 'Do you think they'll accept me?' But Trevor Griffiths, who lived in a mining community himself, was positive that the miners took to her. Cliff Prothero recalls that, when he was in Brynamman with her at lunchtime and they could find nothing resembling a restaurant, they were invited by the people in a whole row of houses.[25]

All the meetings were crowded and successful. It often seemed to the visiting journalists that there were more people in the hall than there could possibly be inhabitants of the village. The peak of the campaign was on 18 February, when Nye Bevan – who had never spoken in Carmarthen before – was billed to speak in the Market Hall, a large building sometimes used for boxing-matches. Although an entrance fee of a shilling was charged, four thousand people poured into the hall half an hour before the meeting was due to start, and passed the time by singing Welsh hymns and folk-songs. Bevan, in top form, gave a graphic account of how Eden had departed from Downing Street:

The Tory tribe got together and decided that a sacrifice must be made. Only libations of blood upon the altar would suffice. In such circumstances, after so monstrous a crime and so deep a guilt, no old ram would do – only the most precious lamb in the flock. And so the Prime Minister was sacrificed. But don't imagine that the lamb was dragged willingly to the sacrificial stone. He had to be hauled there.[26]

After Bevan and Cledwyn Hughes, Megan – according to Prothero's recollection – made a rousing speech, reminding the crowd of what her father had done for working people. However, no report of this speech survives; the reporters presumably ran for the phones when Bevan sat down.

Repeatedly Megan pressed home the fact that Davies depended on Tory help. 'Don't let us think for a moment that the Conservatives are taking no part in this election,' she warned. Asked by a journalist whether she considered that there was a Tory-Liberal alliance, she replied: 'It's not so respectable as an alliance – it's collusion.'[27]

Towards the end of the campaign, the Tories dropped the pretence that they were leaving their followers free to decide how to vote. Alarmed by the way things were going, the chairman of the Conservative Association issued an appeal to all Tories to vote Liberal. Whatever the differences between Tories and Liberals, he asserted, they were in agreement that 'foreign policy should be in the hands of experienced statesmen'.

The Labour strategists were now confident of victory. Two other by-elections since Suez had registered a sharp fall in the Tory majority, and on 14 February – a fortnight before polling in Carmarthen – Labour captured the marginal seat of North Lewisham. This was an encouraging portent for Labour campaigners, but it would be hard to imagine two constituencies more different than North Lewisham and Carmarthen. Megan had still to win on her own battleground.

Griffiths reckoned that the mining areas were solidly Labour, the town of Carmarthen was evenly divided between Labour and Liberal, and there was a significant Plaid vote in the hill country. He estimated that the Lloyd George name was worth at least a thousand votes from lifelong Liberals, and could not detect any 'turncoat' feeling against Megan. Prothero, although Megan had rejected his advice on how to wage the campaign, was sure that she was winning simply because she was a first-class candidate. But Megan herself refused to make any predictions, even in private; it always brought bad luck, she believed. Following her custom in Anglesey, she arrived at the count with two prepared speeches – one for victory and one for defeat.

Polling day was spring-like and free from rain. On the following day – St David's Day – the count began at nine in the morning and went on until half past one. The reason was that 87.5 per cent of the electorate voted – a figure that would have been high in a general election and was astonishing in a by-election. Thousands of people waited in the square outside the Shire Hall and saw Megan appear with a happy smile on her face. The result was:

| | |
|---|---|
| Megan Lloyd George, Labour | 23,679 |
| J. Morgan Davies, Liberal | 20,610 |
| Jennie Eirian Davies, Plaid Cymru | 5,741 |
| Labour majority | 3,069 |

Megan, relieved and elated, called it 'a wonderful and magnificent victory'. Prothero was pleasantly surprised; the majority was bigger than he had expected. Megan had scored an outright victory over her main opponent, for the Labour vote showed an increase of 2600 on the 1955 figure and the Liberal vote a fall of almost 4000. In numbers large enough to be decisive, Liberal voters had been won over. Whether this showed that they accepted her claim to represent the Radical tradition, or that they agreed with her about Suez, or that they were irresistibly captivated by her personality, the result was equally satisfying.

Megan's victory tour of the constituency took up Friday afternoon and the whole of Saturday. In one village, a man shouted: 'You're as good as your father.' Megan called back: 'If I'm half as good that will do.'[28]

# CHAPTER FOURTEEN

# In the Labour Party

## 1

When Megan took her seat in the House as member for Carmarthen, she was received with rousing cheers from the Labour benches. The cheers were for Megan Lloyd George as well as for the by-election victory. MPs who had known her as member for Anglesey appreciated her distinctive personality, her forthrightness and sincerity, her charm and wit. She was among friends; Jim Griffiths, Nye Bevan, Cledwyn Hughes, Eirene White, Desmond Donnelly, and Goronwy Roberts were among the Labour MPs for Welsh constituencies whom she knew well. Dingle Foot was not in the House, but he arrived there after winning another by-election six months after Megan. Hugh Gaitskell, the party leader, also ranked as a personal friend. He was a guest at Brynawelon at least once, and planted a tree in the garden which is still flourishing.

At a political level too, Gaitskell was glad to welcome Megan. The Tories were on the ropes, and he looked forward confidently to getting into Downing Street when the next election came – which, unfortunately, would not be until 1959 or 1960. However, when he examined the by-election figures in the course of this Parliament, he could not help seeing that the votes lost by the Tories were going to the Liberals more often than to Labour. The Liberals, indeed, were staging something of a recovery from their nadir; Mark Bonham-Carter, Violet's son, won Torrington at a by-election in March 1958. A convert who could bring Liberal votes to Labour was therefore a precious asset, and Megan at Carmarthen had shown her ability to do that.

Yet, although she was welcomed, she was not altogether happy in the Labour Party. Once she started to attend the meetings of Labour MPs, which were generally rambling and unfruitful even when they were not quarrelsome, she found the experience disappointing. Philip, who still wrote occasional letters, tried to cheer her up:

I've felt very keenly your disappointment in the Party since you've been back, & its made me very miserable. Of course, all political Parties are horrible, & the nearer you get to the top, the less attractive they seem. Who knows it as well as you? . . .

Hugh G. is not a very great man . . . . But even now he is by *far* the best leader the Party has ever had! . . . And altho' they aren't yet very grand, the average ability of the Members of the Parlty Party go on improving! I know you will help to bring it something it very badly needs — faith & daring & selflessness.[1]

Like her father, Megan was impatient with men of limited outlook whose mental processes were laborious and plodding, and there were plenty like that in the Labour Party. A more serious problem was that she had to adjust herself to another political vocabulary. She considered herself a Radical and often spoke of Radical traditions; but this was a word not much used in Labour circles, except by men whose inheritance was akin to Megan's, such as the Foot brothers. The significant word was Socialist. Megan was willing to call herself a Socialist, but she would have had difficulty in producing a definition, and she was bored and alienated by abstruse debates on the theme. In the Liberal Party she had always been on the Left; in the Labour Party there was a risk that her indifference to Socialist theory might — against her will — align her with the Right. She felt that, while right-wingers approved of her just because her traditions were those of David Lloyd George rather than Keir Hardie (let alone Marx), left- wingers viewed her with reserve and were sceptical of her credentials. Her position, therefore, was uncomfortable. Looking back, Cledwyn Hughes says: 'I'm not sure she quite settled down in the Labour Party.'[2] Patricia Llewellyn-Davies (who was never an MP but was personally close to many of the party's leading personalities, especially on the Left) puts it more bluntly: 'She was never one of us.'[3]

Since 1951, the disagreements between Left and Right had been personalised and sharpened as a feud between Bevan and Gaitskell. In 1956 the feud was patched up by an uneasy truce. The two men could not like or trust one another, but their hostilities were obviously harmful to the party, so Gaitskell accepted Bevan as Shadow Foreign Secretary and they co-operated effectively in the Suez crisis. In 1957, however, it seemed possible that they might part company again over an issue which aroused deep feelings in the Labour Party: the issue of nuclear weapons or, as people generally said then, the H-bomb.

In recent years, the United States, the Soviet Union and Britain had all manufactured and tested this terrifying weapon. The truth about the noxious effect of the tests had gradually leaked out, despite official denials; scientists predicted an unknown number of cancer and leukemia cases caused by radiation. A campaign to stop the tests was started. But, given that the bomb could not be developed without being tested, those who were opposed to the tests had to face the question of whether they were also opposed to Britain's possession of the bomb. Both for political and for moral reasons, many people decided that they were.

We have seen how seriously Megan took the danger of nuclear war at the time of Suez, and she naturally accepted the logic of outright opposition to the bomb. In her first constituency speech as MP for Carmarthen, at a victory rally on 25 May 1957, she said: 'Wales should give the lead in asking the government not only to stop the H-bomb tests, but also in demanding that the making of the bomb should stop.'

Disarmament negotiations had been proceeding at Geneva for years, but no agreement was in sight. The western nations had tabled a seven-point plan which was assumed to be unacceptable to the Russians; but Khrushchev, embarrassingly, accepted it, so the proposals were withdrawn. Still more embarrassingly, in 1957 Khrushchev announced a six-month suspension of Soviet nuclear tests and invited the USA and Britain to follow suit.

In July the Labour Party demanded a debate on disarmament. It was opened by Philip Noel-Baker in a carefully prepared fifty-minute speech. Drawing on the research which he had been carrying out for his book, he outlined the horrifying new developments in techniques of mass slaughter – nuclear, chemical and bacteriological – and asked: 'What has happened to the moral standards of mankind?' Then he castigated the western governments for their 'indifferent, spineless and defeatist' attitude at Geneva.

Megan spoke in this debate with her usual crispness and clarity:

Disarmament commissions have been sitting for over ten years. . . . All this time, the weapons of destruction have been increasing in number and in power a hundred and a thousand-fold. . . . There is no defence against the hydrogen bomb. In fact, the great deterrent has become – let us be quite honest – the greatest argument in the world for disarmament.[4]

She had some pointed questions for the Minister of Defence (who was to reply to the debate): 'What, in this context, is to be the definition of an expert? Are the experts to be Service men – are they to be chiefs of staff? If they are, their labours are likely to be prolonged and inconclusive.' Then she went on to plead for a response to the Russian suspension of tests:

The suspension of tests will not prevent the Russians, the Americans or ourselves from adding to the stockpile. That is also perfectly true. But the adding to the stockpile is going on anyway, with or without an agreement, so we should be no worse off in that respect than we are now. But it would give the first check to the arms race, because without tests there can be no development of weapons. . . . How many more H-bomb powers will there be in the next few months if there is not a moratorium? Who are we to complain? We are not in a position to blackball any country for joining the H-bomb club. . . . I want to ask the government, in all sincerity and honesty, whether they think that it will be easier than it is now to suspend H-bomb tests when more countries have the bomb. . . . I appeal most earnestly to the government to agree to this very limited Russian proposal to take this first vital step. I believe that, if they do not, the people of this country will call them to account for their neglect. I beg them, in the name of all humanity, to accept at any rate this first, partial step.

That was clear enough. By this time, however, those who wanted to see a Britain without nuclear weapons were being called upon to confront a further question: should Britain retain the bomb until a disarmament agreement had been achieved, or should she, if necessary, give it up unconditionally? Clumsy new words – multilateralist and unilateralist – entered the vocabulary of the argument.

Hugh Gaitskell was a convinced and unyielding multilateralist. So was Philip Noel-Baker; in the debate, he said emphatically, 'We want to get rid of nuclear stocks by a world-wide agreement' and dissociated the Labour front bench from any taint of unilateralism. He had spent the whole of his adult life working for disarmament agreements, and the idea of renouncing a weapon without an agreement was alien to his thinking.

As delegates gathered in Brighton for the party conference in October 1957, it was clear that this would be the big issue. Most of the constituency parties favoured unilateral nuclear disarmament, but Gaitskell had a secure majority in the National Executive and could rely on the block votes of the big trade unions. Bevan's attitude was the subject of fervent speculation. He had been among the first to denounce the recklessness and futility of a reliance on nuclear weapons; he had made speeches which came close to, if they did not fully endorse, the unilateralist view; but he was still, as Shadow Foreign Secretary, a member of Gaitskell's team.

Before the debate began on 3 October, it became known that he had decided to speak on behalf of the Executive and urge the rejection of the unilateralist resolutions. His speech, in which he described unilateralism as 'an emotional spasm', was delivered in an atmosphere of dramatic tension.[5] The voting was predictable; the constituencies were crushed by the block vote. It was not the end but the beginning of an argument that would divide and convulse the Labour Party for the next four years.

Megan did not speak at Brighton, but she aligned herself with the multilateralists. Radical though she was, she had always believed that desirable objectives – such as self-government for Wales – should be achieved by negotiation, not by a unilateral move. In her lecture in St Paul's Cathedral in 1952 she had pleaded eloquently for disarmament but stated firmly that disarmament by Britain alone would achieve nothing. Besides, as a recruit to the Labour Party, she was in no position to join a rebellion. She was naturally reluctant to oppose a policy favoured by both Gaitskell and Bevan; if these two men, so often at loggerheads, were in agreement, there was at least a presumption that they were right. Finally, the Carmarthen Labour Party, unlike most of the constituencies, was 'moderate' in outlook and supported Gaitskell on this as well as other issues.

The unilateralists decided to launch an independent movement, the Campaign for Nuclear Disarmament. Its inaugural meeting on 17 February 1958 was a triumphant success, and the march from Aldermaston to London at Easter put CND dramatically on the map. Membership increased rapidly during the summer, with Wales as a notable strongpoint, and the campaign attracted thousands of people who had never hitherto been involved in any political activity.[6] Nor was it short of 'names': they included Bertrand Russell, Canon Collins, J. B. Priestley, Michael Foot and Megan's old friend from her Liberal days, Richard Acland. If Megan had thrown in her lot with CND, she would have been one of its most valuable assets and a star speaker at its meetings. She would also have created a distinctive episode in her life-story. But there was never a likelihood that she would take that decision.

Philip's book, *The Arms Race*, was published in June 1958. It was a monumental opus, with eight parts – two of them devoted to nuclear weapons – and forty-five chapters. Though specialists received it with respect, it won little public attention, for it was appearing at the wrong moment. Those who cared about disarmament were immersed in intensive argument for or against CND and were not inclined to peruse what *The Times* called 'a dispassionate appraisal of the possibilities of international control of disarmament'. Abroad, however, *The Arms Race* established Philip's reputation beyond challenge, and in 1959 he was awarded the Nobel Peace Prize.

## 2

During this period, there was a slender and never very hopeful possibility of a revival of the love affair. Occasional letters, devoid of passionate endearments but written in wistfully affectionate terms, indicated a tentative *rapprochement*. On 16 May 1957 Philip wrote: 'Perhaps I cd drive you home? Supper afterwards if you like.' On 20 May: 'Will you dine tomorrow or Wednesday evening?'

It seemed that they were drawing together again as they had after the break from 1940 to 1945. This time, however, Philip could not muster the passionate appeal that had once enabled him to overcome Megan's hesitations. In emotional terms he was, as he himself admitted, a burnt-out case. There was an even more significant difference: he had treated her in a way that she could not easily forgive. She told him, it appears, that before there could be any chance of their being lovers again he would have to recognise honestly where he had been at fault and make a serious effort to behave better in the future. She urged him to 'be himself' – to regain the moral stature and the integrity of former days.

She was due to speak in Derby, his constituency, on Saturday 1 June, and he suggested that he might accompany her, although he had no constituency duties himself that weekend and was about to make another trip to Greece. He wrote on 29 May:

I don't need to tell you that I have been miserably unhappy all these days & weeks. You know it.

You want me 'to be myself', you say. But in reality you want me to be what I was two years ago. Ever since the day I went into hospital, I have had smashing blow after smashing blow; & I'm covered with wounds, inside & out, that haven't begun to heal. . . . I have tried to be enough of what you wanted to make our being together a success. I've failed, you judge. I know I'm quite hideously to blame over everything, & that is what makes me unhappiest of all. . . .

Is it any good my proposing that I should try once more? That I should come to Derby with you on the 10.15 on Saturday & back by the 5.47? If you say 'Yes', I'll come. If you say 'No', I'll go to Greece that day.

Evidently they had a talk on the following day, and he wrote again:

I couldn't go on this morning because there was such a horrible gulf, & things that I simply can't make you understand, & can't now bear even to talk about. But it isn't true that I think only of myself, or that I've sunk into a hopeless moral morass without making any efforts. I have made tremendous efforts. . . . Its one long effort all the time. It would have been very easy last year to do what everybody else of my age has done [presumably to leave the House of Commons], altho' they hadn't had an operation. I hung on, & still hang on, & try – & nobody but you knows what it costs. . . . I love you, & I want to cherish you. I don't ask for forgiveness, that would be caddish. I only want you to understand the last sentence but one, & to believe that it is true.

She agreed to his going to Derby with her, and the day went off well. In the plane to Greece on 3 June he wrote:

I thought we had a very happy day on Saturday, & I was very proud of you. You *did* look beautiful, so did the dress & the hat, & you made a beautiful speech, & I thought our journeys were lots of fun, & our dinner party in somewhere nice & new.

But there was no real chance of a reconciliation. After his return from Greece, he had to write: 'I know I'm absolutely *foul* – no one knows it so well as I. When you speak to me as you did last week from Criccieth on the 'phone, it seems to break something inside me, & I can't even try.'[7]

In October they were both in Brighton for the party conference, and apparently they had a tense personal encounter in the midst of that crowded week. Philip wrote on the Saturday after the conference closed:

I'm very glad, too, that we had our talk on Wednesday night, tho' I felt very nearly dead while it was going on. I won't write now all the 'explanations' I will give you in November. There are a lot of things which I think I had better say now, which I didn't say before, because I didn't want to inflict any more wounds on you than I had given you already. Do you know what I mean when I say 'non-conflict'? It is that that I need now more than anything. . . . I can't do more now than say that I wasn't running away from a talk, only from what I feared might make everything incomparably worse – And I'm very very grateful to you for the talk – & much more than that, but I can't find the words –

My love to you – I kiss you. P.[8]

In the long sequence of letters from Philip to Megan, this is the last. There is no trace of the 'explanations' promised for November. Either he did not write again, or she did not keep the letter. So far as we know, the talk on 2 October 1957 was the last they ever had on anything other than a political level.

3

More and more as time passed, Brynawelon was Megan's real home. When the love affair with Philip was over, the London flat no longer served a purpose as a secret meeting-place, and she had no reason to be in London when the House was not sitting. Nor was the spare room suitable as a home for the Starzecki family now that Zosia was growing up. Megan remembered the beach picnics and the rambles in the fields from her own early childhood, and was strongly of the opinion that London was no place for a small child. In 1955 or 1956[9] she asked Ellen to take over as housekeeper at Brynawelon. Sarah Jones was still there, but she was an old woman, and looking after a large house was beyond her strength; she died in 1958. Megan gave occasional dinner-parties in the flat – she was a good cook and could easily manage on her own – but it was essentially a *pied-à-terre* for an MP with a base elsewhere.

Just as in her young days, Megan retained what Emlyn Williams had called a twofold personality. In London she shopped in Bond Street, went to Covent Garden, dined sometimes at the French Embassy. In Criccieth she gossiped with local people in the post office or on the street corner. She kept up a close friendship with Mrs Catherine Johnson, whose home was a small house in the lane that ran alongside the garden of Brynawelon. Often – sometimes even three times a day, Mrs Johnson remembers[10] – Megan clambered over the garden wall and they went for a walk with Huwcyn, Megan's corgi. They always talked in Welsh. Mrs Johnson does not recall that Megan ever discussed whether she should leave the Liberal Party, or why she was disappointed with the Labour Party, or anything of that kind.

Megan was drawn back to Brynawelon through her love of her native territory, but also because of Huwcyn, because of Zosia, and because of the garden. She worked in the garden whenever she had time, but it was the responsibility of a full-time gardener, Harry Prole. Brynawelon won prizes year after year at the North Wales horticultural show, and the garden was open for the benefit of charities. A record kept in 1955 shows that it was open eleven times during the season, and Megan also gave a garden party for friends. Her last secretary, Helena Dightam, recalls that on Mondays Megan returned to London with flowers in an old fishing-basket which had belonged to her father, and arranged them in the flat before she attended to letters and messages.[11]

However, a certain amount of friction developed between Megan and the Starzeckis.[12] Miron felt that when Megan was at home Ellen was too much at her beck and call and that Megan piled work thoughtlessly on her shoulders (there were no maids or other staff). Once, about two hundred people from Carmarthen arrived in coaches to spend the day in the garden, and Ellen had to produce the refreshments single-handed. What Ellen resented more than this was that Megan kept Zosia constantly by her side; people in Criccieth began to say that the child was really being brought up by Megan. It was mortifyingly obvious that Zosia found Megan a glamorous figure and adored her uncritically. She was always asking when Megan would be coming back if she was in London. With later reflection, Zosia says, 'Megan did tend to annex people' – and she was annexed with a passion that, in the light of Megan's frustrated desire for motherhood, can be all too easily understood. Eventually, in 1962, the Starzeckis decided that they must have a home of their own. They moved to a house in Tanygrisan Terrace, Criccieth, and Miron found work with the architect Clough Williams-Ellis in his pseudo-Italian village at Portmeirion. A woman named Emily Thomas became housekeeper at Brynawelon. But there was no final breach or quarrel, and Zosia was able to pay frequent visits to Brynawelon – especially in the birthday week in April, when Megan and Zosia exchanged presents.

In Carmarthen, as in Anglesey, Megan was a good constituency MP. She was there once a fortnight and held a surgery either in the town of Carmarthen or in a smaller place. This involved her in time-consuming and complicated journeys, since she tried hard to go to Brynawelon at the weekend even if she could spend only a day there. It was possible to go from Criccieth to Carmarthen by train, but the trains were wretchedly slow and in 1962 the line from Aberystwyth to Carmarthen was closed. Usually Megan went to Aberystwyth in a friend's car or a taxi, and Trevor Griffiths met her on the promenade and drove her to Carmarthen.[13] More often than not, she stayed with the Griffithses in the schoolhouse at Carway. One summer, they mentioned that they wanted to see the Oberammergau Passion Play but had heard that all the tickets were gone. Megan secured tickets through the West German ambassador.

Dick Lloyd George, the unhappy bearer of the title of Earl, returned from America in 1958 without a home or a job. Megan met the former need by letting him have the cottage at Churt which had been left to her by her father. Desperately short of money, Dick produced a biography of David Lloyd George which catered to demands for titillating sensationalism; Lloyd George was depicted as a satyr from whom no woman was safe. Dick was drinking heavily again, and it appears that most of the book was ghost-written by journalists on the Sunday paper in which it was serialised. Megan and Olwen tried unsuccessfully to prevent publication. Despite this distressing episode, Megan kept up a relationship with her brother. Whatever he did, a Lloyd George still belonged to the family.

Her other brother, Gwilym, was out of politics. On becoming Prime Minister, Macmillan required the Home Office as a consolation prize for Butler and offered Gwilym no other position. In his usual easygoing way, Gwilym took this turn of the wheel philosophically and went to the House of Lords as Lord Tenby.

Olwen and Megan were as close as ever, and met almost daily when Megan was at home. Olwen had disapproved of Megan's leaving the Liberal Party and the sisters had argued about it, but without bitterness. Megan was greatly attached to Olwen's sons and daughters, scattered though they were. Eluned lived in Canada, Margaret in the USA. Robin gave up the law in 1957 and started working for the Lombard Bank. In 1962 he was put in charge of the bank's operations in Australia and spent much of his time there; eventually, after Megan's death, he made his home in Australia. Only Benjy (so called because he was the youngest) stayed at home at Eisteddfa and managed the farm.

4

The date chosen by Macmillan for the next general election was 8 October 1959. In his bid for a third consecutive Tory victory, he relied on a simple material calculation. The slogan on the big posters was 'Life's better with the Conservatives. Don't let Labour ruin it.' For the majority of the population, life really was better. Despite glaring contrasts of wealth and poverty, the outstanding characteristic of the 1950s was that, for the first time in their lives, many working-class families owned cars, refrigerators and washing-machines, bought houses on mortgage, and took holidays on Spanish beaches. The catchword of the time was 'affluence' and the phrase that went the rounds was 'You never had it so good'.[14] The millions who benefited from these improvements were described in popular sociology as 'class hybrids – working-class in terms of occupation, education, speech and cultural norms, while becoming middle-class in terms of income and material comforts'.[15] These (or enough of them) were Macmillan's followers. Beaming his approval with a jovially patronising air, he exuded a warmth with which the donnish Gaitskell could not compete.

Gaitskell nevertheless believed that he could win, and Megan hoped that he was right, for she expected him to give her a position in his government if he became Prime Minister (though there is no evidence that he made her a definite promise). In Carmarthen, at least, she had no worries. For the first time since 1935, the Tories contested the seat. Their candidate, J. B. Evans, was a local man with a knowledge of farming, but he could expect nothing better than third place. The Liberal candidate, Alun T. Davies, was more presentable than the Davies of 1957, but he had no chance of winning without Tory votes. In the result, Megan's vote was slightly down from her by-election score, but her majority – at 6633 – was more than doubled. The Plaid candidate lost his deposit; the Tory saved his by forty votes.

Nationally, however, the Tories were clear winners. They gained twenty-eight seats, of which ten were in the Midlands and nine in London. Labour gained five seats, four of them in Scotland. These gains and losses mirrored with considerable precision the distribution of the new 'affluence'. The Liberals still had only six MPs but got a higher share of the poll than in preceding elections.

One man who had predicted the Labour defeat was Aneurin Bevan. A journalist who accompanied him on his speaking tour observed that he looked 'tired and weary'.[16] After the election he was found to be suffering from cancer. An operation failed to save him, and he died on 6 July 1960. His constituency, Ebbw Vale, passed at the ensuing by-election to his friend and political heir, Michael Foot. By 1989 it had achieved the remarkable record of having only two MPs in sixty years.

The year 1960 was one of fierce and unrestrained conflict in the Labour Party. The cause of unilateral nuclear disarmament, making headway that no one in CND expected, gained majorities at the conferences of the Transport and General Workers' Union and the Amalgamated Engineering Union. With the votes of some smaller unions and most of the constituency parties, it was assured of victory when the party conference met at Scarborough in October.

Philip spoke in the debate and declared: 'If we now let the world believe we have lost hope of general disarmament, we shall deny the very forces on which our hopes for peace and socialism depend.'[17] But no speeches could affect the casting of the mandated block votes. Gaitskell replied to the debate with a defiant pledge: 'There are some of us who will fight and fight again to save the party we love.' That party was soon split wide open, with the conference majority on one side and the leader, backed by most of the MPs, on the other.

Gaitskell's choice of words showed that he saw the issue as not solely one of nuclear disarmament but of the whole ideology – indeed, the whole character – of the Labour Party. His supporters, with George Brown taking the most energetic role, organised themselves into a body which they called the Campaign for Democratic Socialism. A commentator recorded: 'Brown's biggest catch was Philip Noel-Baker, whose record of work for disarmament for over forty years was second to none among Labour MPs.'[18] But as Philip had clearly identified himself with the Right of the party, at least since 1951, he could scarcely be described as a catch.

On October 1960 Gaitskell came to speak in Llanelly, whose MP, Jim Griffiths, was a staunch ally and had until recently been the party's deputy leader. Megan, who shared the platform, expressed the view that 'if there were a Labour conference next week, the Scarborough decision would be reversed'. She added that, if Gaitskell stood firm, he would 'retain his great prestige in the country and help the party to retain its prestige and self-respect'. Feeling that West Wales was good territory for him, Gaitskell came to Carmarthen in April 1961. He thanked the Carmarthen party for sending him a telegram of support after Scarborough, remarking that it 'came at a difficult moment'. He knew by now that the tide was turning. Thanks largely to a change of front by the engineers' union, the party conference of 1961 reversed the policy adopted in 1960. Gaitskell's prestige was indeed high; he had fought and he had won.

During these years, Megan spoke in the House less often than when she was MP for Anglesey. Then, she was one of the small band of Liberals and sometimes had the duty of speaking for the party; now, she had to compete for the Speaker's eye with over two hundred other Labour MPs. But in February 1958 she made a notable speech, which she must have enjoyed, in opposition to life peerages, an innovation which the government was introducing. Butler, in moving the Life Peerages Bill, had explained: 'Many people are reluctant today to accept hereditary peerages.' Megan conceded this point: 'I thoroughly disapprove of the hereditary principle, except occasionally in the House of Commons.' But she derided the claim that life peerages were necessary in order to increase the number of opposition peers.

Nobody could really believe that honourable members opposite could no longer bear to see a small band of Socialist peers carrying such a heavy load. Such attentions, of course, were very touching, but so very sudden. After all, they have been able to bear this sight with fortitude for a long period. . . .

The House of Lords, as constituted today, has become in one sense rather an embarrassment to the Conservative Party. It is too much of a Tory thing. It is composed of over 500 Conservative peers, representing 55 per cent of the membership. . . . Such a majority is not really necessary any more. It is too blatant. It is almost shy-making. . . . Many of them have come to the conclusion that they wish that this too solid majority would melt a little. . . . So the government have decided on this simple, ingenious and disingenuous expedient of giving the House of Lords a new look without altering its character, its power, or its function. . . . Every recruit of distinction will help to make it more respectable and, therefore, more dangerous and less vulnerable to attack. . . . In fact, the party opposite gains everything by this bill and gives practically nothing away. All the substance is retained – the hereditary principle, the permanent majority, and the delaying power: all the features which are so objectionable and which are, indeed, completely indefensible in a democracy. . . .

One other curious argument has been raised. . . . It is said that if the House of Commons gets out of touch with the electorate, and when it exceeds its mandate, members of the House of Lords, representing nobody but themselves, with some infallible sixth sense, with the kind of sensitive antennae which obviously belong only to hereditary peers, are able to judge to a nicety, as members of the House of Commons are not able to do, what is the feeling in the country. The interesting thing is that this remarkable instinct is never called into play when a Conservative government are in office.[19]

Here, of course, Megan was echoing what Lloyd George had said in 1909, and in his characteristic style. She wound up by quoting the words of a 'famous man': 'They are representative of nobody. They are inaccessible to argument. When you hear it said that all the House of Lords wish to do is to ascertain the will of the people, do not be deceived by that.' Doubtless, most of the House assumed that Megan was quoting her father. To the delight of her friends, she revealed that the source of the quotation was Winston Churchill.

Altogether, it was an entertaining as well as an instructive debate. From the far Right, a few Tories opposed the bill – Lord Hinching-brooke because he found it patronising to give anyone a non-hereditary peerage, and Enoch Powell because tampering with the Lords might lead to tampering with the monarchy, which was also not logically defensible. Jennie Lee then reiterated Megan's point that the purpose of 'this dishonest, furtive bill' was to make the Lords more respectable. 'We were quite willing to allow the House of Lords gently to fade away,' she said; but the Tories needed 'a barrage behind which they can defy the will of a majority of the people'. To general amusement, she speculated that Gaitskell 'might even decide to invite me to become a peeress'. She asked: 'Do I go into the second chamber saying that I don't believe in a second chamber?' The idea of Jennie Lee as a peeress was obviously too laughable to contemplate. But the device of the life peerages did indeed make membership of the House of Lords acceptable and blunt all demands for its abolition; and Jennie Lee ended her distinguished career as a peeress.

Most of Megan's speeches were devoted to Welsh concerns, and particularly to unemployment. By 1959 the figures had risen to 8.1 per cent in Carmarthen, 9.4 per cent in Caernarvon and 12 per cent in Anglesey. Her own constituency was hit by pit closures, the closure of branch railway lines, the closure of seven tinplate works whose technology had become outdated, and even the dismissal of sixty-five teachers thanks to the closure of village schools. She found herself repeating the protests and warnings that she had voiced before the war:

Migration is something that Wales won't stand for again. We had enough of it in the past. We simply cannot afford to debilitate the whole of a community. (16 December 1957)

Many of the old signs, all too well known in the valleys, are coming back – the anxious, drawn faces, the queues at the employment exchanges. (4 November 1958)

If these communities which are Welsh in language and Welsh in culture are broken up, it will be impossible to rebuild them. (6 February 1959)

She asked for Welsh and Scottish committees, instead of a single British committee, to decide on grants for new industries: 'How will a committee sitting in London know the difficulties of Cwmllynfell? – let alone the fact that its members can't pronounce it.'[20] She criticised the inadequacy of the National Coal Board's research budget, comparing it to the huge sums lavished on military research – 'a sad commentary on the society which we are seeking to defend'. And she pleaded for a relaxation of the strict rules governing compensation for miners whose health had been ruined in the pits:

I can't say in my heart that we meet their suffering in a generous or open-hearted spirit. It seems to me that we meet it in far too niggling and niggardly a way. We shelter behind restricted and narrow definitions. . . . The onus of proof is weighted heavily against the claimant.[21]

In 1960 she joined in an outcry over the appointment of a new chairman of the Broadcasting Council for Wales. It was an important job, since it also carried the position of Welsh national governor of the BBC. The appointment was made by the Minister for Welsh Affairs, a title created in 1954 as a small Tory concession and tacked on to the other responsibilities of a member of the Cabinet. The first such minister was Megan's brother Gwilym, when he was Home Secretary, but under the Macmillan government Welsh affairs were added to the duties of the Minister of Housing, Henry Brooke, a pompous and insensitive person whom Megan acutely disliked. His choice as chairman (the word 'chairperson' was still unknown) of the Broad-casting Council was Mrs Rachel Jones, wife of the Dean of Brecon. Not only was this lady utterly unknown in Welsh public life – her name did not appear in *Who's Who in Wales* – but she could not speak Welsh. She was therefore unable to hold any opinions about the considerable number of programmes which went out in that language.

Megan made a furious speech, warning that 'this attempt to bring back the old Establishment in Wales will fail.' She called for Brooke's resignation and told him across the floor of the House: 'When he leaves, the bells will ring and the flags will fly in the consciousness of Wales.' And she asserted: 'The key and the only key to the Welsh culture of centuries is the Welsh language. . . . Welsh culture does not begin and end with Dylan Thomas and Gwyn Thomas.'[22] The MPs who tried to defend the appointment used the well-worn argument that the majority of Welsh people could not speak Welsh, but Megan had an answer to this: 'It is not we who are asking for a monoglot chairman. On the contrary, we are asking for a bilingual chairman.' But the whips were on, and the censure motion which Megan was supporting was defeated – as she indignantly predicted – by the votes of English Tory members.

Reviewing this phase of Megan's political career, one is conscious of a slackening in intensity. As one MP among many in a large opposition party, she was no longer in a pivotal position: she had lost a role without finding an empire. She had fought the battle that gave her career its essential meaning – the battle to save the Liberal Party as a significant, progressive and genuinely Radical force – and she had been honourably, but decisively, defeated. Now, she could only fight smaller battles for Wales and for Carmarthen. In 1962 she was sixty. The love affair that had been the grand drama of her personal life was also in the past. Now she felt neither the need nor the capacity to make further demands on her energies. The fires were dying down.

Vicky cartoon of Megan

# CHAPTER FIFTEEN

# Do Not Go Gently

1

In 1962 Megan moved from Cromwell Place to another flat at 202 Kennington Lane, south of the Thames but not far from the House of Commons. Her new secretary, Helena Dightam (who was divorced), shared the flat, and Helena's teenage son Adrian was also there in school holidays. At weekends, when Megan went to Brynawelon, Helena went to her parents' home in Worthing. Hitherto Megan had kept to a purely business relationship with her successive secretaries; but she soon became fond of Helena and Adrian, and Helena found that working for Megan – with the continual flow of random conversation and jokes – was different from her previous experience of being an MP's secretary. 'It was', she recalls, 'a very special time for me.'[1]

One day in the spring of 1962, Olwen and her daughter Margaret had tea with Megan at the House. As they left, Margaret said: 'Auntie Megan looks thinner.' The remark gave Olwen some anxiety; there had been times in the past when loss of weight had been a sign that Megan was wearing herself out and in need of rest, or even starting an illness. However, Megan was proud of her figure and might have been dieting, and in any case she hated talking about her health, so Olwen tried to put the incident out of her mind.[2]

In May, Megan came to a Sunday lunch at Eisteddfa with Olwen, Benjy and Benjy's wife Annwen. After lunch, Megan said to Olwen: 'I'm a bit worried about something – I'd like to show you.' What she had to show was a lump on her breast. Olwen, a surgeon's widow, had enough medical knowledge to see that it was cancerous and already dangerously advanced. 'How long have you had this?' she asked. Megan answered, 'Just a few weeks', but Olwen did not believe her.

She would have been still more alarmed if she had known of an earlier incident at Brynawelon. Ellen walked into the bathroom when Megan was having a bath, and saw something on Megan's body which she recognised as a *dafad gwyllt* – a Welsh name for an external skin cancer. When she asked about it, Megan said casually: 'Oh, I've had that for twenty years.' This cannot possibly have been the truth; Philip, always worrying about Megan's health as well as his own, would undoubtedly have sent her to a doctor. There was an old man at Pwllheli who practised some kind of alternative medicine and who, Ellen believed, knew how to get rid of a *dafad gwyllt*. It was tragic, Ellen said later to Zosia, that Megan had never consulted him.

After seeing the lump, Olwen insisted that Megan should be examined by Dr Robert Prytherch, the family doctor who had cared for their father in his last illness. He advised an immediate operation. Three days after that Sunday lunch, Megan underwent a mastectomy in St Mary's Hospital, Paddington. Olwen, who came to London with her, found that the surgeon who performed the operation was a brusque, unsympathetic man. He said to her: 'It may be all right, but it was very extensive.' Olwen realised that the operation was too late. Prytherch, too, considered that the cancer was practically certain to recur after a period of remission.

The *Western Mail* reported on 1 June 1962 that Megan had been in St Mary's for 'a minor operation' and had said that she would be 'off duty for a fortnight'. It was only on 26 July, however, that the paper described 'a perky, smiling Lady Megan' returning to Westminster. 'I've never felt better,' she told the reporter, assuring him that she had made a complete recovery.

Despite this disinformation effort, the fact that Megan had been under treatment for cancer could not be entirely concealed. Trevor Griffiths thinks that the word spread from the hospital, many of whose nurses were Welsh, and that 'quite a few people' in the constituency knew. Robin remembers that Megan made a will and that it was witnessed by a nurse. Dr Tudor Jones, who was in partnership with Prytherch in Criccieth, believes that the truth was generally known in Megan's home town.[3] Indeed, rumours spread farther afield. Benjy and Annwen had to deal with a number of letters offering miracle cures.

However, life went on. In January 1963 a statue of David Lloyd George was unveiled in the House of Commons to mark the centenary of his birth. For the family, it was the occasion for an enjoyable reunion. They sent no invitation to the Dowager Countess Lloyd George, the still unforgiven Frances, but she was invited by the Speaker of the House and duly appeared. The family ignored her presence.

In the same month, Hugh Gaitskell died. He was the victim of a rare immunological disease – so rare that there were rumours that he had been poisoned by the KGB. Megan's nephew Owen (the present Earl Lloyd George) was visiting her at Brynawelon when she heard of Gaitskell's death on the radio. Her reaction was: 'Oh, my God, I suppose we'll have Harold Wilson now.'[4] She had never been friendly with Wilson, and her friend Marion Salmon (widow of Sir Eric Salmon) recalls that she regarded him with contempt.[5]

In June, legislation was introduced to allow peers to renounce their titles. This was a victory for Tony Benn, who had inherited the title of Lord Stansgate and had fought for the right to return to the House of Commons. Megan welcomed the bill, saying:

It carries the gradual liquidation of the hereditary principle one stage further. I should like . . . to see it done not in easy stages but at one fell swoop. The hereditary principle is an archaic survival, as archaic as rotten boroughs.[6]

The political outlook was changing in the Labour Party's favour. The prosperity that had won the Tories the 1959 election had given way to economic stagnation accompanied by unemployment. Macmillan's popularity was declining and he was seen as a tired old man, incapable of coping with contemporary problems; Wilson, a generation younger, seemed to be bursting with energy and fully in touch with the needs of the time.

In October 1963 Macmillan had to undergo a prostate operation. He was told that he would need a prolonged convalescence. With the government in difficulties and an election due within at most another twelve months, this was a prospect he could not face, and he resigned. Too late, he discovered that his medical advice had been too cautious and President de Gaulle, an older man, had taken the same operation in his stride.

The Prime Minister's resignation came at the worst possible moment for the Tories, in the midst of their conference at Blackpool. They had, at that time, no procedure for the election of a leader, and they presented the public with the unattractive spectacle of a hectic power struggle. Butler, the man with the best credentials, was outmanoeuvred and robbed of the prize for the second time. The contestants included two peers, Lord Hailsham and the Earl of Home, who were eligible because they could renounce their titles under the new rules introduced, ironically, for the benefit of Tony Benn. The victor was the outsider – the fourteenth Earl of Home, a Scottish aristocrat who seemed to be the incarnation of what, decades ago, Lloyd George had called 'an effete oligarchy'. He emerged as Sir Alec Douglas-Home and returned to the House of Commons (he had sat there in earlier years) after a rather farcical by-election in the Highlands.

The election, deferred until the last possible date, was held on 15 October 1964. Most Labour supporters thought that Wilson would make mincemeat of Douglas-Home and victory was a certainty, but Wilson himself reckoned that the result might be close. There was sure to be, at the very least, a swing to Labour, so Carmarthen was absolutely safe for Megan. To all appearances, she was in perfect health. Helena Dightam, who knew about the cancer operation, thought that Megan had made a complete recovery and could be regarded as cured. Gwilym Prys Davies, who did not know about the operation, had no idea that she had ever had any health problems. He was a solicitor from Pontypool, not without political ambitions, gaining experience by helping in the Carmarthen campaign. Seeing Megan walk from the station to the Ivy Bush, he thought she had all the graciousness and the confident supremacy of a queen.[7]

As usual, Megan hit hard. Her audiences might be unaware that Douglas-Home had been Neville Chamberlain's parliamentary private secretary at the time of Munich, so she enlightened them. Her question at her first meeting of the campaign was: 'Are you going to trust the men of Suez and the men of Munich?'

The Liberal candidate, again, was Alun Davies. The Conservative was Hilda Protheroe-Beynon, wife of the Tory chairman in the constituency; Gwynfor Evans stood for Plaid Cymru. Megan's majority was almost exactly the same as in 1959. Evans had a better score than Mrs Protheroe-Beynon but both lost their deposits.

On the morning after the poll, Megan knew that she was an MP but did not know whether there would be a Labour government. The election was so close that the result which gave Labour a majority did not come in until two o'clock on Friday afternoon. When all the results were in, Labour had 317 seats, the Tories 303 and the Liberals nine. Thanks to Grimond's vigorous leadership, the Liberal vote had risen to over three million, or 11 per cent of the poll. It was this Liberal advance, clearly, that deprived the Tories of victory.

When Wilson formed his government, he made some innovations. There was to be a Department of Economic Affairs, headed by George

Brown, to plan and stimulate the revival of the economy which was the government's main priority. In practice, this led to bitter in-fighting between the DEA and the Treasury. Another new creation was the Ministry of Overseas Development, entrusted to Barbara Castle. It lost its impetus when she was moved in a reshuffle, and was eventually absorbed into the Foreign Office. Yet another precedent was the appointment of a Minister of State for Disarmament. If this job had been given to Philip it would have crowned his career, but he was seventy-five years old and there were no more rewards for him. To general bafflement, Wilson gave the job to Alun Gwynne-Jones, defence correspondent of *The Times*. As he was not an MP (nor, so far as anyone knew, a member of the Labour Party), he was given a peerage and became Lord Chalfont.

The most welcome innovation, in Megan's eyes, was that there was at last to be a Secretary of State for Wales, with Cabinet rank and an adequately staffed office in Cardiff. The obvious man for the job was Jim Griffiths. Wilson's statement outlining the powers and responsibilities of the new Welsh Office was greeted with jubilation. T. W. Jones, MP for Merioneth, hailed it as 'a historic event for Wales' and then broke into Welsh to relieve his feelings. Megan congratulated Wilson 'on being the second Prime Minister to recognise the nationhood of Wales'.[8]

She would have been happy to work as number two to Griffiths, her friend and political neighbour, but she was not offered this job, nor any other in the new government. Although she had not counted on a job from Wilson as she had from Gaitskell, she had nevertheless hoped, and Cledwyn Hughes – for one – knew that she was disappointed. He asked Wilson why Megan had been passed over, and Wilson replied that she had not been in the Labour Party long enough.[9] In view of the Gwynne-Jones appointment and the appointment of Dingle Foot as Solicitor-General, this was an unconvincing explanation. The truth, probably, was that Megan was the kind of independent-minded backbencher who is a popular figure in the House but does not usually get a government job.

In Carmarthen, the rumours and anxieties about her health persisted. One man who was worried was Clem Thomas, who had been Labour Party agent for several years and was now a journalist working for the *Carmarthen Times* (a rival to the *Journal*). In the course of a telephone conversation, which his memory places in January or February 1965, he asked her directly: 'Is it Big C?' She replied: 'Yes, it is – but don't let it out.' Thomas assured her, 'It's safe with me', and never mentioned the conversation to anyone. He believed, however, that he was not the only person to guess.[10]

In March 1965, Megan was involved in a row with Carmarthen-shire farmers. The government had announced its annual price review, and she was understood to have called it satisfactory. She was invited to speak at the county dinner of the National Farmers' Union on 25 March, and explained that she had really said that the review was more satisfactory than it had ever been under the Tories. But she did not placate the farmers and, as the *Journal* reported, 'there was some booing'. Despite its Tory allegiance, the *Journal* treated Megan fairly, and its comment was that she 'lived up to the family reputation for political courage'. She ended her speech with: 'Thank you for giving me roast chicken and thank you for not giving me the bird.' The farmers' complaints evidently made an impression on her, for she said in the House when the review was debated on 31 March:

We must ask ourselves whether the dairy farmer is getting a fair share of the money. It is he who takes the risks and works the long hours, and he is entitled to an adequate reward. . . . Out of the fourpence that the housewife pays, the farmer receives only one penny.

If she could not be a member of the government, she was determined to carry on as a good constituency MP and a defender of local interests. Her enemy was the hidden cancer. In 1965 the remission period was coming to an end.


2


In the summer, Megan liked to spend a few nights at Stratford-upon-Avon. Then she usually went for a holiday abroad, either with Olwen or with Ursula Thorpe. In 1965 she wanted to go to Stratford and to Italy. It appears that there was some confusion and uncertainty about these plans, and on 16 July Olwen wrote to Helena Dightam:

I'm so sorry about the Stratford dates. I asked Megan last w'end if she could go; but of course she cannot possibly say now. I could go & would like to. I expect I shall hear from Mrs Thorpe.

What about the trip abroad? . . . I am told that the Riviera beaches are covered in thick oil. . . . I don't fancy going there somehow.

Olwen decided against going to Italy, and Ursula could not manage it, so Megan decided to travel there alone and join Marion Salmon, who was already there with her son Anthony, a clergyman on leave from his parish in South Africa. Robin saw her off at Victoria; as usual, she was in a rush and only just caught the train, but she was her normal 'bright sparkling self'. Lady Salmon had the same impression and had not the least suspicion that Megan was ill. To all appearances, she was in the best of health and in high spirits, and clearly enjoying herself. Yet there can be no doubt that, in this month of September 1965, the cancer was attacking again and Megan must have been in pain. Looking back today, Lady Salmon comments: 'I can only think she didn't want to spoil our holiday (my son's and mine).'[11]

They stayed at Fiascherino, on the coast; there was no oil on the beach, and Megan took pleasure in swimming and walking. Then they went to Florence and Pisa. Anthony took a photograph of the two ladies standing in front of the Leaning Tower and, just for fun, they leaned in the opposite direction to the tower. When she saw the photo, Megan remarked: 'Well, I've never leaned so far to the right in my life.' On 22 September, she sent Adrian Dightam a cheerful postcard from Florence:

We lunched on this terrace today overlooking the Ponte Vecchio – the old bridge with shops right across it! so you can do your shopping on the river without danger of falling in! Hope you had a lovely time in Paris. See you Xmas holidays.

Still travelling alone, she went from Florence to Strasbourg to attend a session of the Assembly of the Council of Europe. This was a forum in which parliamentarians from all European nations (other than the Communist bloc and Franco's Spain) met to discuss matters of common interest. It was not linked to the European Community, to which Britain did not yet belong. Assembly members were not elected, but were appointed by governments in a way that reflected the balance of parties in the national Parliament. Harold Wilson, who had the power of appointment as Prime Minister, had selected Megan as a member of the British Labour delegation. Presumably she qualified because her knowledge of international affairs dated back to the 1919 peace conference, and because of her fluent French. Wilson may also have seen the appointment as a consolation prize when he decided not to give her a government job.

After returning from Strasbourg, she spoke at a Labour Party meeting in Carmarthen on 9 October and was reported as saying:

The Government had honoured its pledge to raise pensions and sickness and unemployment benefits, although faced with the gravest economic crisis in history. She had recently been to the Council of Europe Assembly. Its members felt that Britian was emerging from the economic crisis.

Back in Criccieth, Catherine Johnson remembers that in October Megan was 'very sick'. She was nevertheless optimistic, and one day she told Mrs Johnson that the doctor had given her good news and she was celebrating by buying a new coat. 'But we all knew it was hopeless,' Mrs Johnson says.[12] The good news must have been an invention of Megan's, for Prytherch was well aware that the cancer was terminal. Visible secondary carcinomas appeared; worse still, the cancer had spread to her lungs and caused a leakage of fluid, which made her short of breath.

The *Carmarthen Journal* of 15 October reported on a week which Megan had spent in the constituency. On Monday she accompanied John Mackie, a Scottish farmer who was number two in the Ministry of Agriculture, on a visit to Carmarthenshire farms. On Tuesday she was at a Young Socialists' meeting. On Wednesday she did a walkabout in the market and the shopping centre and made two speeches, one at a Labour meeting in Kidwelly and the other at the Pensioners' Association. On Thursday she went round a new factory in Kidwelly, visited some outlying villages to discuss the unsatisfactory bus services, and spent the evening with the women's section in the upper Gwendraeth valley (which meant a long drive back if she was staying at Carway). On Friday she visited the secondary school at Cefneithin, went to the mining area to look at opencast sites which were causing noise problems, and attended the party executive committee in the evening. For a healthy young MP, it would have been quite a busy week. For a woman of over sixty suffering from cancer and undoubtedly in pain, it was an astonishing effort of determination and courage.

About this time, Megan refused to see Dr Prytherch any more. He told her frankly that the cancer was spreading, and she replied: 'Nonsense!' But she told Annwen Carey Evans afterwards that she had a sleepless night, and she felt that Prytherch should not have spoken to her in this way late in the evening. After she dismissed him, Tudor Jones took over the case.

On 4 November 1965 Megan made her last speech in the House of Commons. It was the annual Welsh day, an occasion she never missed; and her speech was true Megan — serious, forceful and occasionally pugnacious. George Brown was preparing a National Plan, and its Welsh component was in the hands of Jim Griffiths. Megan said:

If ever a country suffered from the results of an unplanned economy, it is Wales. I am therefore very glad that at last we are to have a national plan and the Secretary of State is responsible not only for its preparation but for its implementation.

She went on to speak of the pit closures of recent years, which had caused bitter resentment. 'They were made', she said, 'without any attempt at planning and men were left without a prospect of alternative work.' A particular problem was that of partially disabled miners, who were often young and capable of working if the right kind of jobs were available. Incentives were needed to get new industries started in the valleys: 'It is not easy to get an industrialist to go up one of these slightly inaccessible mining valleys, but nevertheless I hope the government will not forget these little communities.'

While on the subject of coal, she launched an attack on Donald Box, the Tory MP for Cardiff North, who had denounced the miners for laziness and described the coal industry as 'an unmitigated disaster'. Box evidently had a gift for irritating the Labour benches, for Dingle Foot described his statements as 'obscene' and 'callous'. Megan said of him: 'He has consistently pursued a policy of undermining confidence ... [and] rendered a great disservice to Wales, to South Wales and to the mining industry.' She paused, and continued: 'Having got that off my chest, I want to turn from coal to transport.' She pointed out that the only motorway in Wales was the short stretch of the M4 from the Severn Bridge to Newport, and even dual carriageways were 'unknown in Carmarthen and farther west'. Her advice to the planners was: 'They must no longer adhere to this measure only of congestion. They must have a new yardstick – the yardstick of development.'

On 13 November the London Carmarthen Society held a dinner at the House of Commons and Megan proposed the health of 'our guests'. This was the last speech she ever made. On 17 November she was back home and sent a card to Helena:

Must let you know I arrived safely, but the road home over the moors was slippery, & very treacherous. Patient just ticking over. Had 2nd injection. All well. Love from H [Huwcyn] and me.

Olwen and Dr Jones now had a serious discussion and, although they both realised that the outlook was hopeless, agreed that Megan should go into the Hammersmith Hospital, whose specialists might be able to suggest ways of relieving her symptoms, of which the most painful was a large swelling on one arm. The Hammersmith had first-class resources, Sir Thomas Carey Evans was well remembered, and the radiologist, Dr Jane Morrison, was a friend of Olwen and Robin. Olwen wrote to Helena on 25 November:

Megan may have been speaking to you before you receive this; but in case you haven't heard, the arrangements now are to travel to London on Mon. I am going with her. She is having that lady chauffeur to meet her in Euston. She is determined to speak in the Agric. Debate on Tues!!

On Wednesday she goes to the Hammersmith Hospital for treatment to the swollen arm. I have a doctor friend in that very department & she will arrange everything. Robin is getting in touch with her tonight & I'll ask him to let you know. I feel that nothing can be done here; but there they have all the very latest methods for that kind of case.

She is remarkably cheerful & really hardly complains – tho' I know that she is in great pain & these pills don't do much for her. She must not suffer any more.

Megan was unable to speak in the agriculture debate, for her breathing had become more and more laboured. She was in hospital for most of December, came home for Christmas and was admitted again on 4 January 1966. On 10 January she returned to Brynawelon; she never left her home again. The *Western Mail* was still referring to 'a virus infection' and saying that she was in hospital 'for observation'. Outside the family circle, friends and political associates were unaware of the seriousness of her condition. Attlee wrote on 7 January:

My dear Megan,
I was so sorry to hear that you were in hospital. I hope that it is nothing serious but only a check up. All good wishes.

Yours ever, Clem.

Dr Jones was able to remove fluid from the lung by aspiration, an unpleasant and painful procedure but one that brought immediate relief. After he carried out an aspiration, Megan breathed more normally, felt stronger, did some gardening, and assured everybody who saw her that she was getting better. Then the fluid began to build up again; the cycle lasted about three weeks. Dr Jones was not a believer in the inevitability of pain, and he prescribed the most potent analgesics he could lay his hands on. Nevertheless, there were times when Megan was in severe pain. Jones was reluctant to prescribe morphine, knowing that she valued her clarity of mind.[13]

A note from Megan to Helena, undated but evidently written in early spring, reads:

Helena bach,
Haven't got down to the get well cards yet but will do so *tomorrow*. Lovely day here, *warm* sunshine, snowdrops lovely and everything bursting [out] right left & centre. Walk round the garden with *great* circumspection! & get

rather *breathless* if I can get *too* enthusiastic! Still I am improving and eating everything that is put before me.

For Megan, the illness was a nuisance, like the illness which had dragged her down for months in 1939 – and more of a nuisance because it came at a crucial political period. The government had lost a by-election in 1965, and the slenderness of its majority made it impossible to carry on indefinitely; in one close division, a Labour member was brought to Westminster in an ambulance. In January 1966 a by-election at Hull produced a good result for Labour, so Wilson decided to call a general election. Polling would be on 31 March.

On 4 March the *Carmarthen Journal* told its readers:

This week it was made clear that Lady Megan would definitely stand again. She was taken ill with a virus infection before Christmas and spent a fortnight in Hammersmith Hospital. Last week it was announced that the doctors had passed her fit and she intended fulfilling her first public engagement on 24 March.

A week later, however, the *Journal* reported: 'Her active participation in the forthcoming campaign is still in doubt. Her doctors advise her to continue her convalescence.' Jack Evans, the Labour agent, said that Megan would wage a short, intensive campaign 'designed to reduce the strain after her recent illness'. Regretfully, he added that she would not be present at her adoption meeting on 19 March.

Far from passing her fit, the doctors knew that she was dying. Those who knew the full truth about her condition – Olwen, Benjy and Annwen – felt strongly that she should not contest the election. Benjy's account is that Dingle Foot insisted that she must stand, saying that it was too late to find another candidate. Foot may have thought that he was strengthening Megan's morale by assuring her that she was able to fight and win another election. What is certain is that she wanted to carry on as candidate and MP. She was fighting to regain her health, she would fight to hold her seat, and she was determined to win both battles. This being so, although some Labour Party members knew that she was seriously ill and that the 'virus infection' story was a fiction, it was morally – and even practically – impossible for them to compel her to retire against her will.

Dr Jones, when asked whether Megan ever accepted that she was facing death, replies: 'I don't think she ever accepted that she had cancer.' The evidence from her conversation with Clem Thomas is that she had in fact accepted it in February 1965. However, it is not unusual for cancer sufferers to change their attitudes. When the decline is far advanced and death is in prospect, this is just the time when some patients – not all, of course – adopt an attitude of denial. This accords with observations made at St Christopher's Hospice, London. Although 95 per cent of patients entering the hospice die within six months – the majority, indeed, in a matter of weeks – a survey has shown that only 30 per cent of them recognised that they were dying, 45 per cent recognised that they had cancer but thought that they had a chance of recovery, and 25 per cent said that they had no idea why they were ill.[14]

Thus, Megan's behaviour was not so extraordinary as it may perhaps appear. Doctors are familiar with what is sometimes called 'cancer euphoria' – a surge of optimism at a stage when, objectively seen, the outlook is hopeless. If we seek a further explanation, we can readily find it in Megan's courageous, independent character. In the face of disasters, whether political or personal, resignation had never been in her nature. Moreover, in a life that ever since childhood had been distinctly privileged, she had come to take it for granted that she was 'a special person'. She had known disappointments, she had known acute unhappiness; yet she had always survived. Somehow – by good luck, by destiny, perhaps by the God in whom she believed and to whom she loyally prayed – she was protected from the very worst that might happen. And so, in the grip of pain and labouring for breath, she refused to believe that the very worst could happen now.

When the election campaign opened, it had to be recognised that Megan would be unable to come to the constituency at all. She sent a message to the adoption meeting:

I deeply regret being prevented from conducting my own campaign, but it is the cause that counts. . . . I look forward to serving you in future as I have tried to do in the past.

Jim Griffiths, who spoke at the meeting, said: 'Lady Megan is a bonny fighter and has tons of courage.' Cliff Prothero did not feel quite sure that the seat could be held with an absentee candidate, and he asked Gwilym Prys Davies to spend the entire campaigning period in Carmarthen, addressing meetings on Megan's behalf. Benjy also came to shoulder this duty.

The Liberals, confusingly, nominated yet another Davies – an accountant named Hywel Davies. The Tories made the mistake of putting forward an Englishman, Simon Day, who came from Devon. Gwynfor Evans stood for Plaid Cymru again. According to the

*Journal*, the campaign was quiet and the meetings were poorly attended. Its comment after polling day was: 'No doubt the campaign in Carmarthen lacked fire and interest because of the absence of Lady Megan.'[15]

Prys Davies was under the impression that Megan was suffering from pleurisy. He had no idea that she was gravely ill, still less that she was dying. Part of his job was to telephone every day at four o'clock and tell her how things were going. She sounded perfectly coherent, and always asked: 'What questions did you get?' He did not tell her that some of the voters asked: 'Are we going to have an *Emergency Ward Ten*?' (This was a popular television serial, set in a hospital.) Benjy was often asked for news of Megan, and his stock answer was 'She hopes to get better' – which was literally true. Prys Davies gathered that Megan might appear in Carmarthen in the final week of the campaign, but she did not. It was only when they were walking back to their hotel after the eve-of-poll meeting that he was told by Benjy that she had a terminal cancer.

A follow-up election is a political operation that sometimes fails to come off, but in 1966 it succeeded. Labour gained fifty seats to acquire a comfortable majority in the Commons. Roderic Bowen was defeated in Cardigan, which became a Labour seat for the first time; and Megan could not have failed to note that the unlikeable Donald Box was turned out of Cardiff North.

Her own majority, at 9233, was at a record high. She polled 21,221 votes, virtually the same as in 1964; her majority was up because of a drop of 3000 in the Liberal vote. Gwynfor Evans drew over 7000 votes, Plaid Cymru's best result yet.


3


Olwen wrote to Helena on 17 April 1966:

I am afraid I cannot give you v. good news of my sister. She has had a rotten week with some new pills – which had a dramatic effect on the fluid situation & got rid of it from the lung & also the arm swelling; but has left her v. exhausted. Poor darling, she is so brave about it all, but I feel that things are getting on top of her now. . . . Wish I could be more cheerful. Robin knows all this – but no one else.

And a week later:

I am really glad that you are at the flat. Its a comfort to know that there is someone there looking after it so well. . . . Poor darling! goodness knows if she'll ever be able to use it. She's had a wretched week & her arm has been most painful & today she had an injection, so I am hoping she'll have a better night. She is very weak. We had hoped to go to London this week for further treatment, but she had to put it off until May 6th. Actually she will travel on the 5th and go straight to the Hosp. – I wonder? I have offered to help with her Welsh letters this end, but she hasn't had the energy to tackle them so far.[16]

The last celebration in Megan's life was the joint birthday; Zosia was thirteen, Megan was sixty-four. When Zosia went to Brynawelon for the exchange of presents, she was startled to see the change in Megan and tried not to show her dismay. Megan was as kindly and affectionate as ever. She had difficulty moving across the room, but was refusing to stay in bed.

In London it was still not realised that she was in a desperate condition. Harold Wilson wrote her a formal letter on 26 April:

My dear Megan,
We are all very sorry that you are not well enough to attend at the House. I think in the circumstances it would be wise not to call upon you to serve in this year's delegation to the Council of Europe. . . . Please accept my sincere thanks for your past help in this field.

Megan then wrote to the Prime Minister – unfortunately, her letter cannot be found[17] – and he replied on 4 May:

Just a brief note to thank you very much for taking the trouble to write to me. You should not have bothered. But it was good to hear from you and I must say I agree with what you say about 1918/22 and all the problems at the present time.

Since Megan wrote so few letters at any time, it is ironic that the last in her life should have been addressed to a man for whom she felt so little liking as Harold Wilson. But, despite her weakness and despite the recurrent pain, her mind was clear and she was still concerned with political matters. In 1966, the government introduced a new tax, called the Selective Employment Tax, levied on employers according to the number of their employees. This 'payroll' tax was very unpopular – it was abandoned within a few years – and was particularly resented by farmers. After Megan's death, the *Carmarthen Journal* quoted 'a close political friend' on her views:

Right up to her last week she was concerned about the effect of the payroll tax on farmers. She told her friend to tell Carmarthenshire farmers that she intended to fight for them against the tax when she got better.[18]

This friend was probably Trevor or Megan Griffiths, who drove up to Criccieth and had lunch at Brynawelon. The *Western Mail* wrote in retrospect that, up to a fortnight before her death, Megan 'assured friends that she felt much better' and 'believed that she would recover and would soon be back in the House'. When Olwen mentioned that she was going shopping in Bangor, Megan asked her to buy some chocolates of a brand that she particularly liked, and also to look round for a dress that might suit her. Right up to the end, Olwen said in looking back, Megan believed that she would get over her illness. 'Although', Olwen added reflectively, 'you could never tell with Megan.'[19] Dr Jones testifies: 'She never gave up.' Benjy, still amazed, says: 'She fought like mad.'

Yet Megan was growing weaker day by day, and from the beginning of May she was obliged to stay in bed. On 3 May Olwen wrote a short letter whose scrawled handwriting reveals her distress:

I tried to cope with some of her letters this morning; but she just can't cope – poor darling – looked so ill today – & can't eat anything or she feels v. sick. Its too pathetic – & she is struggling so hard. I feel so helpless.

At this time, Megan was offered a decoration – the CH, or Companion of Honour – in the forthcoming honours list. Had she been at full strength she might have attached little importance to it, or even declined it, but now she accepted with touching gratitude.

Another Carmarthen man, Islwyn Thomas, visited Megan on 5 May; he was probably the last visitor outside the family, except for Catherine Johnson, who was with her every day. He said later: 'She was unaware that her condition was serious. She was confident that she would get better, and just a few weeks before, she had supervised the re-planning of her garden, which was her pride and joy.'[20]

Knowing that the end could be only a few days away, Dr Jones prescribed morphine, which had the effect of making her unconscious or semiconscious for a good part of the time. But she rallied when, on 12 May, she received the official letter stating that the Queen had approved the award of the CH. Olwen retained a memory of Megan saying: 'Where's that letter? I must have that letter.' The honours list was, in fact, made public on the day after her funeral.

On the morning of 14 May, Olwen went to Brynawelon with Robin, who had taken time off work and was staying at Eisteddfa. Megan did not seem to be worse than she had been in the previous few days. Robin asked her to sign a cheque for Helena's salary and expenses. She took the pen, but she was too weak to sign. With a laugh, she said: 'I can't sign my name now – whatever next?' However, she made another effort and managed to sign.[21] It would have been in character, one feels, if 'Whatever next?' had been Megan's last words.

Catherine Johnson was at Brynawelon in the afternoon and evening, and realised at about eight o'clock that Megan was sinking into irrevocable weakness. It seems that Megan herself realised at last that she was dying, and her defiance melted into resignation. She made a gesture of reaching out with both arms and said: 'Tada – yes – I am coming.'[22] The doctor was called, but at half past eight on that May evening Megan was dead.

4

On 18 May 1966 Megan was buried together with her mother and her long-dead sister Mair in the family vault. It was a sunny day. There was, first, a short service attended by the family in the garden of Brynawelon. The service in the cemetery was conducted by the minister of the Methodist chapel which Megan had attended, and the singing of her favourite hymn, *Tyddyn Llwyn*, was led by the choir who had gone to Brynawelon every Christmas to sing carols and had always been invited into the house for a warming drink.

The crowd almost filled the little cemetery. All the family was there, including Eluned, who flew from Canada. From Megan's constituency came the Mayor of Carmarthen, a group of farmers and a group of miners, and also her political opponent, Gwynfor Evans. Among the friends who came to say farewell were Ursula Thorpe and her son Jeremy, Cledwyn Hughes, Goronwy Roberts, Dingle Foot and Desmond Donnelly.

Philip Noel-Baker was not there. He knew that his presence would not be welcomed by Megan's family, and perhaps he felt that he would be unable to restrain his grief. But there was someone else who did defy the hostility of the Lloyd George family. An elderly woman stood near the gate of the cemetery and did not mix with the other mourners. It was the Dowager Countess Lloyd George – Megan's teacher, Frances Stevenson.

# Epilogue

The by-election to fill Megan's place as MP for Carmarthen was held on 14 July 1966. The Labour candidate was Gwilym Prys Davies. Although Trevor Griffiths considered that he was 'a marvellous candidate' and likely to be an excellent MP, Davies himself did not expect to hold the seat. Megan's personal vote was lacking; moreover, the voters felt that they had been cheated when the Labour Party presented them with a terminally ill candidate. Gwynfor Evans won the by-election with a majority of 2436, to become the first Plaid Cymru MP in history. Labour regained the seat in 1970; Evans won it again in the October 1974 election; Labour won it in 1979 and holds it today.

Megan's other old constituency, Anglesey, was held by Cledwyn Hughes until he lost it to a Conservative in 1979. It was won by Plaid Cymru in 1987.

Megan's brother Gwilym died in 1967 and her brother Dick in 1968. Her sister Olwen died in 1990 at the age of ninety-seven.

Frances, Countess Lloyd George died in 1973. Her daughter Jennifer is alive and well.

Philip Noel-Baker retired from the House of Commons in 1970 and, after a period away from Westminster, accepted a life peerage and became Lord Noel-Baker. Together with Lord Brockway (Fenner Brockway), he launched the World Disarmament Campaign in 1980, and he continued to travel the world making speeches to plead the cause of disarmament even when he was almost blind, deaf and confined to a wheelchair. He died in 1982 at the age of ninety-three.


Megan's home, Brynawelon, was sold after her death. After a period in private hands, it became a nursing home in 1988. By a pleasing coincidence, the matron is Frances Prole, daughter of the gardener who secured so many horticultural prizes for Megan.

David Lloyd George's last home, Ty Newydd, was also a private residence, but in 1989 it was acquired by a trust and in 1990 it began a new life as the Taliesin Centre, where courses in creative writing are given in English and Welsh. Thus the Welsh language is heard again in the old farmhouse; we can be sure that this would have been a source of gratification to David – and to Megan – Lloyd George.

# Notes

## Chapter 1

1 *Lloyd George: Family Letters*, edited by Kenneth O. Morgan (University of Wales Press and Oxford University Press, 1973). Unless otherwise stated, all Lloyd George family letters are quoted from this edition.
2 Speech at Bangor, 21 May 1891.
3 David Lloyd George's father died young and his maternal uncle, Richard Lloyd, assumed the paternal role. Hence he used 'Lloyd George' as a dual surname, and was always irritated if referred to as 'Mr George'. But his brother was content to be known as William George.
4 For a detailed survey, see John Grigg, *The Young Lloyd George* (Eyre Methuen, 1973), and the same author's *Lloyd George: The People's Champion* (Eyre Methuen, 1978).
5 The full text of this speech and others made in Lloyd George's Radical period, including the Limehouse speech, can be found in *Better Times: Speeches by the Rt. Hon. David Lloyd George* (Hodder & Stoughton, 1910).
6 Unpublished memoirs of D. H. Daniel, quoted in Grigg, *The Young Lloyd George*, pp. 33–4.
7 W. R. P. George, *Lloyd George, Backbencher* (Gomer Press, 1983), p. 24. The author is David Lloyd George's nephew.
8 House of Commons, 24 June 1891.
9 Grigg, *The Young Lloyd George*, p. 270.
10 Speech at Carmarthen, 27 November 1899.
11 Speech at Bristol, 6 January 1902.
12 Don M. Cregier, *Bounder from Wales* (University of Missouri Press, 1976), p. 175.
13 21 August 1897.
14 26 May 1897.
15 24 May 1902.
16 Grigg, *The Young Lloyd George*, p. 73.
17 Olwen Carey Evans, *Lloyd George was my Father* (Gomer Press, 1985), p. 43.

## Chapter 2

1 Emlyn Williams, *George* (Hamish Hamilton, 1962), p. 377.
2 Interview, 1989.
3 Don M. Cregier, *Bounder from Wales* p. 152.
4 *Observer*, 4 June 1950.
5 R. J. Minney, *'Puffin' Asquith* (Leslie Frewin, 1973), p. 20.
6 Those who have read L. P. Hartley's novel *The Go-Between*, or seen the film, will know about the hot summer of 1911.
7 7 August 1911.
8 Olwen Carey Evans, *Lloyd George was my Father*, p. 63.
9 24 July 1924.
10 *Lloyd George: A Diary by Frances Stevenson*, edited by A. J. P. Taylor (Hutchinson, 1971), entry of 20 November 1914.
11 *Stevenson Diary*, 8 February 1916.

12  Lord Riddell, *More Pages from my Diary (Country Life, 1924),* p. 179.
13  *Stevenson Diary,* 8 April 1915.
14  Speech at Caernarvon, 9 December 1909.
15  Radio talk, 'Childhood Days', 18 June 1950.
16  Roy Jenkins, *Asquith* (Collins, 1964), p. 285.
17  John Grigg, *Lloyd George: From Peace to War* (Methuen, 1985), p. 144.
18  Frances Lloyd George, *The Years that are Past* (Hutchinson, 1967), p. 74.
19  Briand may in fact have been quoting someone else; the origin of the phrase is uncertain. But it was new to Lloyd George, who told Frances that evening: 'I wish I'd said that.'
20  *Stevenson Diary,* 4 April 1915.
21  The *Guardian's* editor, C. P. Scott, was a close friend of Lloyd George, so Asquith probably regarded this leader as a move in the plot against him.
22  Radio talk, 18 June 1950.
23  Richard Lloyd George, *Lloyd George* (Muller, 1960), p. 151.
24  Quoted in Paul Guinn, *British Strategy and Politics, 1914 to 1918* (Oxford University Press, 1965), an excellent study of the subject.
25  The news was received with dismay and even incredulity; many people insisted that Kitchener must have survived. Claud Cockburn's version was that he reached Russia and re-emerged under the name of Stalin.
26  Lord Beaverbrook, *Politicians and the War* (Hutchinson, 1926), p. 209.
27  *Stevenson Diary,* 14 November 1916.
28  Thomas Jones, *Lloyd George* (Oxford University Press, 1951), p. 70.
29  Grigg, *Lloyd George: From Peace to War,* p. 438.
30  *Stevenson Diary,* 12 October 1915.
31  Jenkins, op. cit., p. 426.
32  Margot Asquith, *Autobiography* (one-volume edition, Eyre & Spottiswoode, 1962), p. 319.
33  *Stevenson Diary,* 19 April 1917.
34  23 August 1915.
35  *Stevenson Diary,* 11 March 1915.
36  *Stevenson Diary,* 12 March 1916.
37  *Stevenson Diary,* 15 January 1917.
38  Both notes in *My Darling Pussy,* edited by A. J. P. Taylor (Weidenfeld & Nicolson, 1975).
39  *Stevenson Diary,* 4 August 1916.
40  *Stevenson Diary,* 12 February 1920.
41  Interview, 1989.

42  Keith Feiling, *The Life of Neville Chamberlain* (Macmillan, 1970), p. 74.
43  *Stevenson Diary,* 16 March 1917. Soon after Lloyd George became Prime Minister, the King promoted Haig from general to field marshal, a pointed indication of their mutual esteem. In private letters, the King assured Haig that he could rely on royal support in any showdown with Lloyd George.
44  Hankey, *Supreme Command,* vol. 2, p. 701.
45  This document was preserved by Mr James Young of Criccieth, to whom I am indebted.
46  Michael Foot: 'David Lloyd George', in *Loyalists and Loners* (Collins, 1986), p. 143.
47  Frances Lloyd George, op. cit., p. 142. Lloyd George realised, she says, that he would never again hold office with a Liberal majority.

## Chapter 3

1  This pencilled diary is in the National Library of Wales.
2  Frances Lloyd George, *The Years that are Past,* p. 149.
3  Botha and Smuts, former Boer generals, represented South Africa. Hughes was the Prime Minister of Australia. The Chief of the Imperial General Staff was Field Marshal Sir Henry Wilson. The Maharajah was a member of the Indian delegation; India was ranked as a Dominion for international purposes. Lord Sinha was an Indian who had been given a British peerage.
4  Eleutherios Venizelos, Prime Minister of Greece and a good friend of Lloyd George; he had brought Greece into the war on the Allied side.
5  F. E. Smith, a Tory member of the government. In 1919 he became Lord Chancellor and took the title of Lord Birkenhead.
6  The incident was most unfortunate, since Raymond Poincaré was the most anti-British of French politicians. After his term as President, he was Prime Minister in 1922–4 and had bitter disputes with Lloyd George.
7  Thelma Cazalet-Keir, *From the Wings* (Bodley Head, 1967), p. 16.

8    Speech in London, 12 November 1918.
9    *Stevenson Diary*, 17 January 1920.
10   Both Allenswood and Garrett Hall schools have long ceased to exist, and none of Megan's reports survives. Olwen Carey Evans recalled that she did 'reasonably well' (interview, 1989).
11   Interview with Lady Valerie Daniels, 1989.
12   Letter to the author, 1990.
13   Emlyn Williams, *George* (Hamish Hamilton, 1961).
14   24 September 1920.
15   Williams, op. cit., p. 378.
16   Cazalet-Keir, op. cit., p. 59.
17   *Stevenson Diary*, 17 April 1936. Surprisingly, this note was made at a time when Lloyd George had reverted to a Radical stance. Churchill was not in fact a Tory until 1924. Sir Robert Horne was Chancellor of the Exchequer in the coalition government. Sir Eric Geddes was Minister of Transport.
18   Lord Beaverbrook, *The Decline and Fall of Lloyd George* (Collins, 1963), p. 9.
19   Olwen Carey Evans, *Lloyd George was my Father*, p. 68.
20   Interview, 1989.
21   *Stevenson Diary*, 10 May 1921.
22   *Stevenson Diary*, 15 May 1921.
23   *Stevenson Diary*, 4 July 1921.
24   *Stevenson Diary*, 6 July 1921.
25   9 May 1922.
26   30 April 1922.
27   J. Kunitz and D. Haycraft, *Twentieth-Century Writers* (H. W. Wilson, New York, 1942).
28   Oddly enough, Margaret had been unable to marry Lloyd George until she was twenty-one because of parental disapproval.
29   25 January 1923.
30   I am indebted to Mr Justice Edward Cazalet for permission to quote from this and other letters. This letter was undated, but it includes a reference to 'the arrival of Princess Mary's son', ie the present Earl of Harewood, born 7 February 1923. It was written from 26 Onslow Gardens, Lloyd George's temporary home after leaving Downing Street.
31   Quoted in Tom Cullen, *Maundy Gregory* (Bodley Head, 1974), p. 29. Gregory was a shady go-between in the sale of honours, and this is an excellent and entertaining biography.

32   25 October 1922.
33   15 August 1923.
34   Thomas Jones, *Lloyd George*, pp. 280, 282 and 290.
35   Cazalet-Keir, op cit., p. 64.
36   Interview with Trevor Griffiths, 1989.
37   The accusation has been made against all the three outstanding Welsh politicians of this century: David Lloyd George, Aneurin Bevan and Neil Kinnock.
38   Jones, op. cit., p. 90.
39   *Liberal Magazine*, August 1921.
40   Quoted in Jones, op. cit.
41   Quoted in G. R. Searle, *Corruption in British Politics, 1895–1930* (Clarendon Press, 1987), p. 340.
42   Trevor Wilson, *The Downfall of the Liberal Party* (Oxford University Press, 1965), p. 287.
43   Letter to Roger Cary, 9 January 1956; in BBC Written Archives.
44   Cazalet-Keir, op. cit., p. 49.

Chapter 4
1    A. J. Sylvester, *The Real Lloyd George* (Cassell, 1947), p. 112.
2    Sylvester, op. cit., p. 121.
3    Trevor Wilson, *The Downfall of the Liberal Party*, p. 287.
4    Harold Nicolson, *King George the Fifth* (Constable, 1952), p. 384.
5    Originally, this was an acronym for Westernised Oriental Gentleman.
6    Neither Olwen nor Ursula, when interviewed in 1989, could remember a man with this name, but it occurs in a letter from Megan to Thelma.
7    All these letters from India are undated.
8    23 March 1924; in National Library of Wales.
9    3 July 1924; quoted in Olwen Carey Evans, *Lloyd George was my Father*.
10   Mark Bence-Jones, *The Viceroys of India* (Constable, 1982), p. 235.
11   Interview, 1989.
12   Frances Lloyd George, *The Years that are Past*, p. 217.
13   Wilson, op. cit., p. 268.
14   Speech at Caernarvon, 22 April 1924.
15   The article was unsigned, which added to its authority as the Year Book was an official party publication. It may well have been written by Lloyd George and certainly expressed his views.

16 Strictly speaking, there were forty-two Liberal MPs, including two representing university seats and the Speaker who was elected unopposed.
17 Sylvester, op. cit., p. 98.
18 Undated.
19 Quoted in Sylvester, op. cit., p. 151.
20 Malcolm Thomson, *David Lloyd George: The Official Biography* (Hutchinson, 1948), p. 32. The title-page of the book states that it was written with the collaboration of Countess Lloyd George (ie Frances) and it can be assumed to convey her interpretation of events.
21 Thelma Cazalet-Keir, *From the Wings*, p. 81.
22 Gordon West, *Lloyd George's Last Fight* (Alston Rivers, 1930), p. 23.
23 Lecture given by W. R. P. George at Llanystumdwy, 8 June 1989.
24 Kingsley Martin, *Editor* (Hutchinson, 1968), p. 282.
25 The phrase used by A. J. P. Taylor in *English History, 1914–1945* (Clarendon Press, 1965), p. 74.
26 Frances Lloyd George, op. cit., p. 218.
27 In *My Darling Pussy*.
28 *Life with Lloyd George: The Diary of A. J. Sylvester*, edited by Colin Cross (Macmillan, 1975), p. 15 (Introduction).
29 Emlyn Williams, *George*, p. 377.
30 Interview, 1989.
31 D. R. Thorpe, *Selwyn Lloyd* (Cape, 1989), p. 29.
32 Thorpe, op. cit., p. 48.
33 Interview with Olwen, 1989.
34 Interview, 1989.
35 Letter of 9 November 1954.
36 Williams, op. cit., p. 379.
37 *Sylvester Diary*, 30 December 1931.
38 *Sylvester Diary*, 4 April 1932.
39 Interview with John Grigg, 1989.
40 Thomson, op. cit., p. 393.
41 *Stevenson Diary*, 19 October 1934.
42 *Family Letters*.
43 All speeches in this chapter quoted from *Holyhead Mail*.
44 *Daily Mail*, 10 May 1928.
45 *Leeds Mercury*, 25 May 1928.
46 Undated, presumably 25 May 1928; in National Library.
47 Speech at Carmarthen, 7 December 1928.
48 Megan drove a car in her younger days, but when the driving test was introduced in 1934 she either failed it or did not attempt it.
49 Speech at Great Yarmouth, 12 October 1928.
50 West, op. cit., pp. 156, 77–81.
51 Madeleine Vernon in *La Volonté*, 25 May 1929.
52 Interview with *Manchester Guardian*, 3 June 1929.

Chapter 5
1 The estate is on the island of Euboea. It had been bought in 1832 by Edward Noel, a philhellene related to Byron, from a Turkish Bey, Achmet Aga.
2 David J. Whittaker, *Fighter for Peace* (William Sessions, 1989), p. 27.
3 16 November 1954.
4 Memorandum dated 23 July 1929; in BBC Written Archives, Caversham.
5 These figures are from G. D. H. Cole and M. I. Cole, *The Condition of Britain* (Gollancz, 1937).
6 *Observer*, 4 June 1950.
7 Interview, 1989.
8 As a member of the Poplar Borough Council in 1921, Lansbury was sent to prison for refusing to pay the London county precept out of the funds of his poverty-stricken borough. In the 1929–31 government he was Minister of Works and was best known for creating the bathing area in the Serpentine, then called the Lansbury Lido.
9 Malcolm Thomson, *David Lloyd George*, p. 404.
10 *Sylvester Diary*, 15 May 1929.
11 A. J. P. Taylor, *English History*, p. 288.
12 *Sylvester Diary*, 4 August 1931.
13 L. MacNeill Weir, *The Tragedy of Ramsay MacDonald* (Secker & Warburg, 1938), pp. 357, 371.
14 Thomson, op. cit., p. 408.
15 Speech at Llangefni, 8 October 1931.
16 *Sylvester Diary*, 30 September 1931.
17 Broadcast, 15 October 1931.
18 Thelma Cazalet-Keir, *From the Wings*, p. 83.
19 1 February 1929; in *My Darling Pussy*.
20 Interview, 1989.
21 *Sylvester Diary*, 11 December 1932.
22 *Sylvester Diary*, 23 February 1937.
23 14 January 1934; in *My Darling Pussy*.
24 Interview, 1989.
25 29 November 1931; in *My Darling Pussy*.
26 *Sylvester Diary*, 8 December 1931.

27   Frances Lloyd George, *The Years that are Past*, p. 253.
28   28 September 1932.
29   2 October 1932.
30   *Sylvester Diary*, entries in 1933 and 1936.
31   *Sylvester Diary*, 25 January 1935.
32   Speech at Holyhead, 20 October 1931.
33   Whittaker, op. cit., p. 109.
34   J. P. Stern, *Hitler: The Führer and the People* (Fontana/Collins, 1974), p. 157.
35   Brought to trial, Dimitrov defended himself with such courage and skill that the Nazis had to deport him to Moscow instead of imprisoning him. He became general secretary of the Communist International, originating the policy of the united front against Fascism, and eventually the ruler of Bulgaria. It is widely believed that the Nazis set the Reichstag on fire themselves, but the truth has never been definitely established.
36   House of Commons, 18 November 1934.
37   In a symposium published as *Challenge to Death* (Constable, 1934).
38   A contemporary pun quoted Simon at the end of the conference, in reply to Mussolini's '*A rivederci*', as saying: 'Abyssinia!'
39   Interview, 1989.
40   Whittaker, op. cit., p. 123.
41   James Hinton, *Protests and Visions* (Hutchinson, 1989), p. 97.
42   Raymond Postgate, *The Life of George Lansbury* (Longmans, 1951), p. 303.
43   Speech at Brynsiencyn, 24 October 1935.
44   Speech to the Women's Liberal Federation, of which Megan was elected President, 17 June 1936.
45   Jo Grimond, *Memoirs* (Heinemann, 1979), p. 149.
46   Interview, 1989.
47   *Guardian*, 16 May 1966.
48   *Carmarthen Times*, 20 May 1966.
49   Interview, 1989.
50   *Carmarthen Times*, 20 May 1966.
51   Interviews with Hubert Morgan, Lady Llewellyn-Davies and Lady Seear, 1989.
52   Interview, 1989.
53   1 December 1936.
54   10 December 1919.
55   Megan has been described as lazy by Wilfrid Roberts, Gwynfor Evans, Hubert Morgan, Trevor Griffiths, Jeremy Thorpe, Michael Foot and three of her secretaries. Lady Violet Bonham-Carter also considered that she was 'lazy, though full of charm' (letter to the author from Lord Bonham-Carter).
56   Interview, 1989.
57   Interview, 1989.
58   Interview, 1989.
59   Interview, 1989.
60   Letter to the author, 1990.
61   Interview, 1989 (Miss Jones is now Mrs Reeves).
62   Interview, 1989.

**Chapter 6**

1   A. J. P. Taylor, *The Origins of the Second World War* (Hamish Hamilton, 1961), p. 99.
2   Speech to Women's Liberal Federation, 17 June 1936.
3   David J. Whittaker, *Fighter for Peace*, p. 135.
4   19 July 1953.
5   Quotations in this section are from the *Derby Evening Telegraph*.
6   Interview, 1989.
7   *Sylvester Diary*, 6 July 1936.
8   H. N. Brailsford, *After the Peace* (Leonard Parsons, 1920), p. 47.
9   Chamberlain gave a briefing to American and Canadian journalists at Cliveden, Lady Astor's house; his words were thus paraphrased in the *Montreal Star*.
10   A. J. Sylvester, *The Real Lloyd George*, p. 221.
11   *Sylvester Diary*, 3 September 1936.
12   *Sylvester Diary*, 9 September 1936.
13   Interview, 1989. In fact, the first prisoners were taken to Dachau on 20 March 1933, less than two months after Hitler came to power.
14   Megan was writing from a hotel in Stuttgart on 9 September 1936. The letter is in the National Library of Wales.
15   Sylvester, op. cit., p. 213.
16   Quoted in Thomas Jones, *A Diary with Letters* (Oxford University Press, 1954). Sylvester gives a similar account, except that he understood Hitler to be referring to German generals rather than politicians, which is unlikely.
17   Interview (1989) with Jeremy Thorpe, who was present at the dinner party when Megan told the

story. She told it again in a speech of reminiscences in 1959, saying that Hitler 'raved' and that it was 'a very revealing outburst'. *Carmarthen Journal*, 9 January 1959.

18  Jones was persuaded by his daughter, Eirene White, to omit this sentence when preparing his diary for publication in 1954, on the grounds that it might be damaging for Megan. The sentence occurs in the privately printed edition in the National Library of Wales.

19  This part of Megan's letter is in Welsh. I am indebted to Gwyn Jenkins of the National Library for the translation.

20  *Daily Express*, 17 September 1936.
21  Kingsley Martin, *Editor*, p. 286.
22  *Jones Diary*, 16 September 1936.
23  *Sylvester Diary*, 11 July 1940.
24  Raymond Postgate, *The Life of George Lansbury*, p. 314.
25  Thelma Cazalet-Keir, *From the Wings*, p. 134.
26  1 December 1936.
27  *Sylvester Diary*, 16 February 1937.
28  Simon Haxey, *Tory MP* (Gollancz, 1939), p. 215.
29  Italian troops in action at Guadalajara in March 1937 were surprised to find themselves opposed by the Garibaldi Battalion of Italian anti-Fascist exiles and to hear loudspeaker appeals in their own language.
30  G. E. R. Gedye, *Fallen Bastions* (Gollancz, 1939), p. 221.
31  Whittaker, op. cit., p. 163. The Labour politician A. V. Alexander was First Lord of the Admiralty in 1929–31 and again in 1940–5.
32  25 July 1947.
33  1 July 1953.
34  Interview, 1989.
35  5 October 1955.
36  Whittaker, op. cit., p. 26.
37  Interview, 1989.
38  Interview, 1989.
39  Interview, 1989.
40  22 July 1953.
41  18 March 1953.
42  5 October 1955.
43  25 July 1947.
44  22 July 1953.
45  27 April 1954.
46  16 November 1954.
47  5 October 1955.
48  Letter to Megan, 21 April 1937; in BBC Written Archives.
49  Gedye, op. cit., p. 229.

50  On 19 July 1938 *The Times* printed a letter from the Archbishop of York and the Bishop of Chichester citing a 'credible report' which put the number of suicides at 7000.
51  *New Statesman*, 8 October 1938.
52  Andrew Rothstein, *Munich* (Lawrence & Wishart, 1958), p. 82.
53  Taylor, *Origins*, p. 173.
54  Taylor, *Origins*, p. 176.
55  In the event, about one million Czechs found themselves under German rule in October, in addition to Sudeten Germans who were anti-Nazi and Jewish communities.
56  Unpublished memoir in Bristol University Library.
57  One of the Czechs, Hubert Masarik, noted that 'Mr Chamberlain was yawning continuously, without any attempt to conceal his yawns.' They were told by a French official 'that no answer was required from us, that they regarded the plan as accepted.' Gedye, op. cit., p. 483.
58  *Deutsche Allgemeine Zeitung*, 30 September 1938.
59  Gedye, op. cit., p. 486.
60  Speech at City Temple, London, 28 October 1938.
61  Liberal Party papers, Bristol University Library.
62  Julio Alvarez del Vayo, *Freedom's Battle* (Heinemann, 1940), p. 302.
63  This estimate was made by a lawyer who fought for Franco and then took part in court-martial proceedings; quoted in Gabriel Jackson, *The Spanish Republic and the Civil War* (Princeton University Press, 1965), p. 538.
64  House of Commons, 19 May 1939.

### Chapter 7

1  Malcolm Thomson, *David Lloyd George*, p. 448.
2  *Sylvester Diary*, 20 October 1939.
3  Walter Citrine, *My Finnish Diary* (Penguin, 1940), pp. 177, 179.
4  Citrine, op. cit., p. 106.
5  Interview, 1989.
6  Except for one, of no special interest, which (untypically) is undated, and which seems from its content to belong to the 'phoney war' period.
7  Herbert Morrison, *An Autobiography* (Odhams Press, 1960), p. 172.

8   Ben Pimlott, *Hugh Dalton* (Cape, 1985), p. 273.
9   Morrison, op. cit., p. 174.
10  Obituary of Megan Lloyd George by Dingle Foot, *The Times*, 16 May 1966.
11  Letter of 29 May 1940.
12  *Sylvester Diary*, 11 May 1940.
13  Colville's diary; quoted in Martin Gilbert, *Winston Churchill*, vol. 6 (Heinemann, 1983), p. 424.
14  *Sylvester Diary*, 21 May 1940.
15  *Sylvester Diary*, 28 May 1940.
16  Letter of 29 May 1940.
17  A. J. Sylvester, *The Real Lloyd George*, p. 269.
18  Thomson, op. cit., p. 443.
19  Gilbert, op. cit., p. 418.
20  28 June 1940.
21  25 August 1940.
22  18 September 1940.
23  Angus Calder, *The People's War* (Cape, 1969), p. 203. This fascinating book contains eighty pages on the blitz, including many personal reminiscences.
24  28 November 1940.
25  29 October 1940.
26  *Sylvester Diary*, 10 November 1940.
27  Thomas Jones, *Lloyd George*, p. 256.
28  28 November 1940.
29  Dalton's diary; quoted in Whittaker, *Fighter for Peace*, p. 181.
30  16 December 1940.
31  28 November 1940.
32  4 December 1940.
33  14 March 1940.
34  Interview, 1990. Robin is the source of this account.
35  *Sylvester Diary*, 19 January 1941.
36  *Sylvester Diary*, 20 January 1941.
37  *Sylvester Diary*, 24 January 1940.
38  22 July 1953.

**Chapter 8**
1   Angus Calder, *The People's War*, p. 464.
2   Ministry of Labour Year Book, 1941. In the library of the Department of Employment.
3   H. M. D. Parker, *Manpower* (HMSO, 1957), p. 293.
4   Harold L. Smith, *War and Social Change* (Manchester University Press, 1986), p. 223.
5   Kingsley Martin, *Editor*, p. 288.
6   Interview, 1989.
7   A. J. P. Taylor, *English History*, p. 528.

8   *Sylvester Diary*, 9 September and 26 November 1941.
9   One journalist reported: 'If for a single moment a single man seemed to be taking life easily he was urged on by his fellows with "Come on! Old Joe wants that one."' Calder, op. cit., p. 303.
10  BBC Written Archives, January 1942. Burgess also used Willie Gallacher, the Communist MP, as a contributor, noting that he would be 'a popular choice'. This was a dubious claim: politics aside, English people had difficulty with Gallacher's unmodified Clydeside accent. MPs belonging to the Independent Labour Party were ineligible because they did not support the war effort.
11  *Daily Mirror*, 17 November 1942.
12  BBC Written Archives, 6 June 1944. Mrs Tate was also described as 'very energetic, very enthusiastic, very feminine'. Regrettably, she died before she could exhibit these qualities on television.
13  *Sylvester Diary*, 24 April 1941.
14  In a diary entry, Sylvester stated that the house was bought in 1940, but it seems more likely that it was bought after Margaret's death.
15  Frances Lloyd George, *The Years that are Past*, p. 27.
16  Thelma Cazalet-Keir, *From the Wings*, p. 51.
17  Interview with Sylvester, 1989.
18  *Sylvester Diary*, 26 March 1942.
19  15 January 1943; in National Library of Wales.
20  *Sylvester Diary*, 29 January 1941, 19 November 1942, 22 January 1942.
21  Letter to the author, 1989.
22  *Sylvester Diary*, 22 October 1943.
23  *Sylvester Diary*, 23 October 1943.
24  Malcolm Thomson, *David Lloyd George*, p. 456.
25  7 November 1943.
26  *Sylvester Diary*, 24 May 1944.
27  This pamphlet is in the Fawcett Library, London.
28  Article by Harold L. Smith in *Journal of Modern History*, December 1981.
29  Peter Townsend, 'A Society for People', in *Conviction*, edited by Norman MacKenzie (MacGibbon & Kee, 1958), p. 95.
30  Townsend, op. cit., p. 100.
31  There are several versions of this incident, of which one is in Calder, op. cit., p. 657. Calder states that Bevin was moved to tears, which

would be uncharacteristic.
32  Liberal papers, Bristol University Library.
33  Calder, op. cit., p. 616.
34  Calder, op. cit., p. 610.
35  Calder, op. cit., p. 633.
36  7 August 1943; in National Library of Wales.
37  *Sylvester Diary*, 21 September 1944.
38  A. J. Sylvester, *The Real Lloyd George*, p. 295.
39  *Sylvester Diary*, 21 September 1944.
40  Frances Lloyd George, op. cit., p. 274.
41  Sylvester, op. cit., p. 302. The figure of 10,000 seems improbably high.
42  Olwen Carey Evans, *Lloyd George was my Father*, p. 169. But Lloyd George's brother William advised him to accept the earldom, according to an account written by the latter's son on 30 December 1944.
43  Frances Lloyd George, op. cit., p. 277.
44  Sylvester copied the letter in his *Diary*, 26 February 1945.
45  Thomson, op. cit., p. 457.
46  W. R. P. George quoted this account in his lecture given at Llanystumdwy, 8 June 1989.
47  Interview with Ursula Thorpe, 1989.
48  Frances Lloyd George, op. cit., p. 283.
49  Interview, 1989.
50  Interview with Mrs Jennifer Longford (Jennifer Stevenson), 1989.

## Chapter 9

1  Tizard's diary, quoted in Angus Calder, *The People's War*, p. 657.
2  Emanuel Shinwell, *The Labour Story* (MacDonald, 1963), p. 172.
3  R. B. MacCallum and Alison Readman, *The British General Election of 1945* (Oxford University Press, 1947), p. 156.
4  MacCallum and Readman, op. cit., p. 142.
5  MacCallum and Readman, op. cit., p. 166.
6  Interview, 1989.
7  All speeches quoted from the *Holyhead Mail*.
8  In addition, one Common Wealth and three ILP members took the Labour whip, and there were two Communist MPs.
9  Letter dated 22 August (presumably 1945), quoted by courtesy of Mrs

Myra Hughes, John Bellis's daughter.
10  Quoted in Alan Watkins, *The Liberal Dilemma* (MacGibbon & Kee, 1966), p. 43.
11  Roy Douglas, *History of the Liberal Party* (Sidgwick & Jackson, 1971), p. 249.
12  Simon Haxey, *Tory MP*, p. 207.
13  Ben Pimlott, *Hugh Dalton*, p. 413.
14  Alan Bullock, *Ernest Bevin, Foreign Secretary* (Heinemann, 1983), p. 73.
15  David J. Whittaker, *Fighter for Peace*, p. 229.
16  Whittaker, op. cit., p. 230.
17  Whittaker, op. cit., p. 239.
18  Interview, 1989.
19  Interview, 1989.
20  Jean Mann, *Women in Parliament* (Odhams Press, 1962), p. 21.
21  2 November 1944.
22  20 January 1946.
23  22 May 1946.
24  3 July 1946.
25  19 July 1953.
26  Younger's diary; quoted in Whittaker, op. cit., p. 189.
27  Whittaker, op. cit., p. 188.
28  Whittaker, op. cit., pp. 230, 231, 189.
29  Interview, 1990.
30  Jay was then a junior Treasury minister.
31  Liberal papers, Bristol University Library.
32  26 May 1947.
33  A party in London in honour of Edouard Herriot, the veteran French statesman and supporter of the League of Nations.
34  6 August 1947.
35  Whittaker, op. cit., p. 190.
36  26 August 1947.
37  22 September 1947.
38  24 September 1947.
39  Interview, 1989.
40  At that time, the deposit was £150 and was forfeited by candidates who failed to get 12.5 per cent of the votes cast.
41  The letter is in the National Library of Wales.
42  Watkins, op. cit., p. 48.
43  *Western Mail*, 24 October 1951.
44  Letter to the author, 1989.
45  BBC Written Archives, 7 March 1938.
46  BBC Written Archives, 5 April 1938.
47  A full account of the committee's work is in Asa Briggs, *Sound and Vision (The History of Broadcasting in the United Kingdom*, vol. 4)

(Oxford University Press, 1979), pp. 289–420.

48 Megan probably knew about the Canadian Broadcasting Corporation, which was a public-service system modelled on the BBC but nevertheless carried advertising.

49 This phrase was coined by the press tycoon Lord Thomson when he went into television ownership.

50 I am indebted to Mr Leonard Miall for information on this episode.

**Chapter 10**

1 Herbert Morrison, *An Autobiography*, p. 262.

2 She was answering a question at a meeting at Penmaenmawr in the 1955 general election.

3 Michael Young, *The Chipped White Cups of Dover* (Oxford University Press, 1960).

4 It has been transferred to video and can be seen on request at the Fawcett Library, London.

5 15 August 1949, in National Library of Wales.

6 Interview with Myra Hughes, 1989.

7 Davies protested, but received this magisterial reply from Churchill: 'As you were yourself for eleven years a National Liberal, and in that capacity supported the governments of Baldwin and Chamberlain, I should not presume to correct your knowledge of the moral, intellectual and legal aspects of adding a prefix or a suffix to the honoured name of Liberal.' Quoted in Alan Watkins, *The Liberal Dilemma*, p. 49.

8 *Sylvester Diary*, 14 April 1938.

9 Roy Douglas, *History of the Liberal Party*, p. 259.

10 Speech at Edinburgh, 14 February 1950.

11 Broadcast, 10 February 1950.

12 David J. Whittaker, *Fighter for Peace*, p. 204.

13 Quoted in H. G. Nicholas, *The British General Election of 1950* (Macmillan, 1951).

14 Interview, 1989.

15 Jo Grimond, *Memoirs*, p. 147.

16 *The Times*, 9 May 1950.

17 *The Times*, 22 May 1950.

18 Liberal papers, Bristol University Library.

19 Quoted in Robert Pitman, *What Happened to the Liberals?* (*Tribune* pamphlet, 1951).

20 Broadcast, 7 July 1950.

21 Interview, 1989.

22 Speech at Amlwch, 27 November 1950.

23 Interview with Roberts, 1989.

24 Michael Foot, *Aneurin Bevan*, vol. 2 (Davis-Poynter, 1973), p. 301.

25 10 February 1951.

26 20 March 1951.

27 22 April 1951.

28 8 June 1951.

29 Jean Mann, *Women in Parliament*, p. 23.

30 6 May 1954.

31 10 November 1952.

32 3 April 1951.

33 30 March 1950.

34 4 April 1950.

35 5 February 1951.

36 22 February 1951.

37 26 April 1951. I have been unable to identify either R. M. or Peggy.

38 5 September 1951.

39 Watkins, op. cit., p. 60.

40 D. E. Butler, *The British General Election of 1951* (Macmillan, 1952), p. 65. It was in this book that Butler invented the word 'psephology'.

41 Quoted in Pitman, op. cit.

42 Watkins, op. cit., p. 60.

43 Election speeches are from the *Holyhead Mail*.

44 Pitman, op. cit.

45 Interview, 1989.

46 29 October 1951.

47 28 October 1951.

48 31 October 1951; in National Library of Wales.

**Chapter 11**

1 In Churchill's eyes, this was a job of minimal interest or importance. When offering it to R. A. Butler in 1940, he apologised for having nothing better available.

2 12 November 1951.

3 Now that he was no longer a minister, Philip had to live on his salary as an MP and his writing. At that time, MPs did not get an allowance to pay their secretaries.

4 8 February 1952.

5 5 February 1952.

6 8 February 1952.

7 13 February 1952.

8 28 February 1952.

9 18 April 1952.

10 The text of the lecture is in Canon Collins's papers in Lambeth Palace Library.

11  Speech at Wrexham, 15 January 1954.
12  Interview, 1989.
13  Interview, 1989.
14  Interview, 1989.
15  'The Referendum: The End of an Era', lecture given by Lord Cledwyn at the National Eisteddfod, 1980, and published by University of Wales Press, 1981.
16  Reports in *Wrexham Leader*, 1954.
17  Lecture, 'The Referendum'.
18  Reports in *Western Mail*, 1952 and 1953.
19  Interview, 1989.
20  *Holyhead Mail*, 2 November 1951.
21  24 June 1952; in Labour Party archives, Walworth Road, London.
22  Obituary of Megan in *The Times*, 16 May 1966.
23  Interview, 1989.
24  27 February 1952.
25  22 May 1952.
26  Kenneth Harris, *Attlee* (Norton, 1982), p. 502.
27  8 July 1952.
28  Interview, 1989.
29  4 March 1952.
30  3 October 1952. Wilson was in fact beginning to distance himself from Bevan, but was reckoned to be on the Bevanite slate in the constituency voting. The 'frustrated journalists' to whom Gaitskell referred (actually, all successful journalists) were Richard Crossman, Barbara Castle and Tom Driberg.
31  25 February 1953. Shinwell, no longer a left-winger, had been Minister of Defence in the Labour government.
32  1 July 1953.
33  *Observer*, 4 June 1950. Transport House was then the Labour Party headquarters. These profiles were written after an interview with the subject, so the opinion expressed can be taken to reflect Megan's thinking.
34  Interview, 1989.
35  22 November 1951.
36  6 July 1952.
37  16 October 1952.
38  *Wrexham Leader*, 17 October 1952.
39  *Wrexham Leader*, 14 November 1952.
40  *Western Mail*, 10 August 1953.
41  7 July 1954.
42  15 November 1954.
43  Interview, 1989.
44  Interview (1989) with Silas Davies, who at that time was Labour Party

agent in Wrexham.
45  30 March 1955. Megan kept the letter.
46  All the letters are in the Labour Party archives.
47  Speech at Beaumaris, 21 May 1955.
48  *Guardian*, 18 May 1955.
49  31 May 1955.

**Chapter 12**
1  This account was given by Zosia Starzecka (interview, 1990).
2  Interview, 1990.
3  23 February 1952.
4  18 March 1953.
5  Megan used to call this period 'Special Week', and it is indeed remarkable. Hitler was born on 20 April, Queen Elizabeth II on 21 April, Lenin and Megan Lloyd George on 22 April, Shakespeare and Turner on 23 April.
6  20 May 1953.
7  2 February 1954.
8  5 January 1953.
9  21 January 1953.
10  19 July 1953.
11  9 February 1954.
12  10 November 1954.
13  5 March 1953.
14  25 August 1953.
15  14 August 1953.
16  24 October 1953.
17  22 January 1954.
18  18 December 1953.
19  29 January 1954.
20  12 February 1954.
21  15 June 1954.
22  26 June 1954.
23  28 June 1954.
24  10 September 1954.
25  18 September 1954.
26  11 October 1954.
27  15 October 1954.
28  1 November 1954. (This was Philip's sixty-fifth birthday.)
29  6 November 1954.
30  9 November 1954.
31  16 November 1954.
32  3 July 1955.
33  19 July 1955.
34  18 August 1955.
35  24 August 1955.
36  Philip's biographer (David J. Whittaker, *Fighter for Peace*) gives the date as 7 February, but in subsequent letters Philip consistently referred to 8 February.
37  Interview, 1989.

38  Interview, 1990.
39  Whittaker, op. cit., p. 277.
40  Noel-Baker diary, 6 June 1956;
    quoted in Whittaker, op. cit.


**Chapter 13**

1   Speech at Liberal Assembly, 1958.
2   It was doubtful whether this action
    could have been condemned on legal
    grounds. Nasser was taking over the
    company, not the canal which was
    already in Egyptian territory; he
    offered compensation; and he
    promised to abide by the convention
    of 1888, which provided that the
    canal should be open to ships of all
    nations.
3   The plan was recorded in a written
    memorandum. Sir Patrick Dean, the
    Foreign Office man who signed for
    Britain, destroyed his copy on Eden's
    orders, but the Israelis took their copy
    home and Dayan subsequently
    published it. See Moshe Dayan, *The
    Story of my Life* (Weidenfeld &
    Nicolson, 1976), p. 192.
4   Michael Foot and Mervyn Jones,
    *Guilty Men, 1957* (Gollancz, 1957),
    p. 217.
5   Merry and Serge Bromberger, *Les
    Secrets de l'Expédition d'Égypte*
    (Editions des Quatre Fils Aymon,
    1957).
6   Delivered at a secret session of the
    Twentieth Congress of the
    Communist Party, the speech was
    leaked and published in the west.
7   George Mikes, a BBC correspondent
    of Hungarian origin, reported that
    one group had knocked out thirty
    tanks with petrol bombs: *The
    Hungarian Revolution* (Deutsch,
    1957), p. 96.
8   2 August 1956.
9   The Israelis were much more
    interested in the Straits of Tiran,
    which affected the use of their port of
    Eilat, than in Suez.
10  Foot and Jones, op. cit., p. 13.
11  About five hundred lives were lost in
    Egypt, almost entirely through
    bombing.
12  Michael Foot, *Aneurin Bevan*, vol. 2,
    p. 533.
13  Letter to the author from Lord
    Grimond, 1990.
14  Interview, 1989.
15  *Carmarthen Journal*, 14 December
    1956.
16  All speeches in this section are from
    the *Carmarthen Journal*.
17  *New Statesman*, 2 March 1957.
18  Interview with Cliff Prothero, 1989.
19  *Carmarthen Journal*, 15 February
    1957.
20  Jo Grimond, *Memoirs*, p. 197.
21  *Tribune*, 22 February 1957.
22  Interview, 1989.
23  Interview with Trevor Griffiths,
    1989.
24  *New Statesman*, 2 March 1957.
25  Interview, 1989.
26  Foot, op. cit., p. 536.
27  *Tribune*, 22 February 1957.
28  Interview with Trevor Griffiths,
    1989.


**Chapter 14**

1   3 May 1957.
2   Interview, 1989.
3   Interview, 1989.
4   House of Commons, 23 July 1957.
5   A full account is in Michael Foot,
    *Aneurin Bevan*, vol. 2, pp. 567–77.
6   An account of the founding of CND
    and an analysis of its support is in
    Mervyn Jones, *Chances* (Verso,
    1987), pp. 147–61.
7   19 July 1957.
8   5 October 1957.
9   Zosia Starzecka is not sure of the
    exact date. Miron and Ellen both died
    in the 1970s.
10  Interview, 1990.
11  Interview, 1989.
12  The source for this account is Zosia
    Starzecka (interview, 1990).
13  Interview, 1989.
14  'Affluence' was a misapplication of
    the title of J. K. Galbraith's book *The
    Affluent Society*. Galbraith was
    saying that a modern society had
    solved the problem of production, not
    that people were individually affluent.
    'You never had it so good' was coined
    by President Harry S. Truman and
    helped him to win his surprise victory
    in the presidential election of 1948.
15  D. E. Butler and Richard Rose, *The
    British General Election of 1959*
    (Macmillan, 1950), p. 15.
16  Geoffrey Goodman's diary, quoted in
    Foot, op. cit., p. 622.
17  David J. Whittaker, *Fighter for Peace*,
    p. 286.
18  Geoffrey Goodman, *The Awkward
    Warrior: Frank Cousins* (Davis-
    Poynter, 1979), p. 300.

19  House of Commons, 12 February
    1958.
20  House of Commons, 2 February
    1960.
21  House of Commons, 1 August 1961.
22  House of Commons, 19 July 1960.


Chapter 15
1   Interview, 1989.
2   Interview, 1989.
3   Interview, 1990.
4.  Interview, 1989.
5   Interview, 1990.
6   House of Commons, 27 June 1963.
7   Interview, 1989.
8   House of Commons, 19 November
    1964.
9   Interview with Lord Cledwyn, 1989.
10  Interview, 1990.
11  Letter to the author, 1990.
12  Interview, 1990.
13  Interview, 1990.

14  Information from Dame Cicely
    Saunders, founder of St Christopher's
    Hospice.
15  *Carmarthen Journal*, 1 April 1966.
16  24 April 1966.
17  Curiously, 10 Downing Street
    appears to be full of letters that have
    not been sorted. A member of Mrs
    Thatcher's staff kindly tried to find
    Megan's letter, but unsuccessfully.
18  *Carmarthen Journal*, 20 May 1966.
19  Interview, 1989.
20  *Western Mail*, 18 May 1966.
21  Interview with Robin Carey Evans,
    1990.
22  Mrs Johnson remembers the words as
    'Father – yes – I am coming', which
    would raise a doubt whether Megan
    was addressing David Lloyd George
    or God the Father. But Annwen
    Carey Evans, quoting Emily Thomas
    who was also a witness, says that the
    word was 'Tada', Megan's invariable
    word for her father.

# Index